S0-BCT-246

The Presidency of
JAMES K.
POLK

AMERICAN PRESIDENCY SERIES

Donald R. McCoy, Clifford S. Griffin, Homer E. Socolofsky
General Editors

George Washington, Forrest McDonald
John Adams, Ralph Adams Brown
Thomas Jefferson, Forrest McDonald
James Madison, Robert Allen Rutland
John Quincy Adams, Mary W. M. Hargreaves
Andrew Jackson, Donald B. Cole
Martin Van Buren, Major L. Wilson
William Henry Harrison & John Tyler, Norma Lois Peterson
James K. Polk, Paul H. Bergeron
Zachary Taylor & Millard Fillmore, Elbert B. Smith
Franklin Pierce, Larry Gara
James Buchanan, Elbert B. Smith
Abraham Lincoln, Phillip Shaw Paludan
Andrew Johnson, Albert Castel
Rutherford B. Hayes, Ari Hoogenboom
James A. Garfield & Chester A. Arthur, Justus D. Doenecke
Grover Cleveland, Richard E. Welch, Jr.
Benjamin Harrison, Homer B. Socolofsky & Allan B. Spetter
William McKinley, Lewis L. Gould
Theodore Roosevelt, Lewis L. Gould
William Howard Taft, Paolo E. Coletta
Woodrow Wilson, Kendrick A. Clements
Warren G. Harding, Eugene P. Trani & David L. Wilson
Herbert C. Hoover, Martin L. Fausold
Harry S. Truman, Donald R. McCoy
Dwight D. Eisenhower, Chester J. Pach, Jr., & Elmo Richardson
John F. Kennedy, James N. Giglio
Lyndon B. Johnson, Vaughn Davis Bornet
James Earl Carter, Jr., Burton I. Kaufman

The Presidency of

JAMES K.
POLK

Paul H. Bergeron

UNIVERSITY PRESS OF KANSAS

© 1987 by the University Press of Kansas
All rights reserved

Published by the University Press of Kansas (Lawrence,
Kansas 66049), which was organized by the Kansas
Board of Regents and is operated and funded by Emporia
State University, Fort Hays State University,
Kansas State University, Pittsburg State University, the
University of Kansas, and Wichita State University

Library of Congress Cataloging-in-Publication Data

Bergeron, Paul H., 1938–
The presidency of James K. Polk.
(American presidency series)
Bibliography: p.
Includes index.
1. United States—Politics and government—1845–1849.
2. Polk, James K. (James Knox), 1795–1849. I. Title.
II. Series.
E416.B47 1987 973.6'1'0924 87-2174
ISBN 0-7006-0319-0

British Library Cataloguing in Publication Data is available.

Printed in the United States of America

10 9 8 7 6 5 4 3 2

The paper used in this publication meets the minimum requirements of the
American National Standard for Permanence of Paper for Printed
Library Materials Z39.48-1984.

To

Blanche Henry Clark Weaver

and to the memory of

Herbert Weaver

Special mentors and special friends

CONTENTS

FOREWORD

The aim of the American Presidency Series is to present historians and the general reading public with interesting, scholarly assessments of the various presidential administrations. These interpretive surveys are intended to cover the broad ground between biographies, specialized monographs, and journalistic accounts. As such, each will be a comprehensive, synthetic work which will draw upon the best in pertinent secondary literature, yet leave room for the author's own analysis and interpretation.

Volumes in the series will present the data essential to understanding the administration under consideration. Particularly, each book will treat the then current problems facing the United States and its people and how the president and his associates felt about, thought about, and worked to cope with these problems. Attention will be given to how the office developed and operated during the president's tenure. Equally important will be consideration of the vital relationships between the president, his staff, the executive officers, Congress, foreign representatives, the judiciary, state officials, the public, political parties, the press, and influential private citizens. The series will also be concerned with how this unique American institution—the presidency—was viewed by the presidents, and with what results.

All this will be set, insofar as possible, in the context not only of contemporary politics but also of economics, international relations, law, morals, public administration, religion, and thought. Such a broad approach is necessary to understanding, for a presidential administration is more than the elected and appointed officers composing it, since its work so often reflects the major problems, anxieties, and glories of the nation. In short, the authors in this series will strive to recount and evaluate the record of each administration and to identify its distinctiveness and relationships to the past, its own time, and the future.

The General Editors

PREFACE

"Who is James K. Polk?" Whigs raised this taunting question during the 1844 presidential campaign; but they did not grasp its complexity. They merely meant to imply that Polk possessed no genuine qualifications for the presidency, a false suggestion to be sure. The voters answered by choosing Polk as the nation's eleventh president.

Once in office, Polk's actions and decisions certainly caused Whigs and many Democrats to wonder repeatedly about the proper reply to the old campaign question. As the chapters of this book indicate, Polk did not conform to the Whiggish notions about weak or limited presidents who yielded to a vigorous and dominant legislative branch. Imitating the model established by his mentor, Andrew Jackson, Polk set out to dominate the nation's capital in just about every respect possible. He knew, as all effective presidents have known, that the office is more than an enumeration of constitutional duties and prerogatives. Indeed, the presidency is whatever the occupant can make of it (within constitutional bounds, of course). The nation had been accustomed to weak presidents during the nineteenth century; that is, after Thomas Jefferson there had been no strong, activist presidents until Jackson. Jackson's use of powers was such a disturbing break with tradition that the Whig party arose to fight against executive "usurpation." For a variety of reasons, the men who immediately followed Jackson in the presidential office were largely ineffective and unimpressive. When Polk assumed the presidency, he could have easily slipped into the Van Buren–Harrison–Tyler mold; instead, he chose to follow Jackson's concept of the office.[1] Regardless of how one responds to Polk's policies and programs, there is no question that he was a strong executive. The nation would not see such again until the administration of Abraham Lincoln, an old Whig who essentially abandoned Whiggish ideas about the presidency.

The following chapters tell what Polk did as president. In so doing, they reveal a leader who stubbornly insisted that he be in control of the government. After the exasperating process of selecting a cabinet, for example, Polk moved quickly to assert his authority over his official family; along the way he also restored the status of the cabinet. Jackson had played fast and loose with his cabinet and had circumvented it with a special group of advisers (known as the Kitchen Cabinet); but Polk was more circumspect in this regard. As a corollary to his relationship with the cabinet, Polk effectively seized control of the governmental bureaucracy. Upon occasion he boasted, and justifiably so, of his mastery of the details of the functionings of the various executive departments. Because he kept such close scrutiny over them, he was able to control them. This was particularly noteworthy with regard to the Treasury Department, which, since the days of Alexander Hamilton, had been accustomed to functioning more or less independently of the president. But Polk did not permit his secretary of the Treasury to stray from presidential policy or to exhibit independence. One of the chief consequences of Polk's domination was that his administration produced what could truly be called an executive budget, the first such in the nation's experience.

Because the country waged war during the Polk years, the president was compelled to exercise the role of commander in chief. In contrast to James Madison, whose uncertain hand was at the helm during the War of 1812, Polk served impressively as the nation's chief commander. As one historian has recently noted: "Without any military experience or knowledge, Polk organized and controlled the war almost single-handedly, leaving little to his cabinet officers and devoting long hours to the details of military campaigns and supply. Although unfamiliar with military theory, he followed the rules for carrying on limited warfare down to the last detail." There were difficulties and controversies, to be sure, but Polk proved repeatedly that a civilian could handle military matters.[2] Indeed, he dominated the War Department, where a compliant William L. Marcy seemed burdened by the tasks thrust upon him, and also the State Department, where a strong James Buchanan frequently locked horns with the president. Overall, Polk acquitted himself extremely well, and his use of presidential power during wartime set the stage for Lincoln's vigorous (some claimed excessive) employment of the powers of commander in chief.

During Polk's presidency, war was one of the instruments of diplomacy. The successful completion of the Mexican War, for example, resolved longstanding disputes between the United States and Mexico. Concerning the Oregon problem, however, Polk made belligerent noises but no actual warfare. Instead he played a demanding game of diplomacy with Great Britain, and eventually success crowned his policies and procedures. Diplomatic questions were inseparably linked to territorial expansionism; therefore, Polk did not relinquish such matters to the bureaucrats or the diplomats. Exercising firm and direct control over foreign relations, the president accomplished a full agenda—so much so that one historian has declared: "Polk's achievements in diplomacy were among the most remarkable in American history."[3]

If one still wonders about the question "Who is James K. Polk?" let the record be examined further. From Inauguration Day until the day of his departure from the White House, Polk dominated the legislative branch of government. That is, he had a plan—an agenda—that he wanted Congress to implement. Polk consequently had no intention of waiting for Congress to initiate legislation to which he would simply respond by either signing or vetoing the bills. Congress resisted, balked, and fought back at times, but for the most part it acquiesced to the president's legislative program. Polk felt confident in his attitude toward and his relationship with Congress, for he believed that he was the true representative of the people of the United States. Jackson had been the first to express such a startling notion; Polk reiterated it and refined it. In any event, Polk, who had a clear vision of what he wanted from Congress, pushed vigorously to achieve it.[4] No wonder that he was a controversial president both during the 1840s and afterwards. His aggressive and deliberate exercising of power stirred disagreement; this was unavoidable.

Yoked to a consideration of Polk as president should be a discussion and analysis of Polk as a person. While the following chapters do not place great emphasis upon this matter, they do not ignore Polk as an individual. Personal characteristics were often quite influential upon his functioning as chief executive, and on such matters, Polk's detractors have handled him severely. In fact, by now there exists a lengthy list of negative attributes, which have been ascribed to him by historians overly influenced by nineteenth-century criticisms. To be sure, Polk had his faults, both as president and as a person; most of these will become apparent in the chapters that follow. It would be sheer folly to claim perfection for him; after all, he was a mere mortal who, from time to time, committed most of the transgressions that others have done. But despite his flaws, Polk was a highly effective president. Indeed, his successes have ironically generated criticism: Whigs commenced this attack, and scholars have continued it. In modern parlance, Polk has suffered from a bad press. Although my study is not a crusade to promote a new image for Polk, it is an attempt to be fair and even-handed in an assessment of him, as president and as a person.

To assist in this endeavor, I have depended heavily upon the scholars who have already written about Polk and his administration. In addition, I have relied upon the president's own account, found in his remarkable diary. The result of my investigations is not a definitive study of Polk or of his presidency. Instead, much like the portrait artists who visited the White House to capture the president on canvas, I have attempted to portray Polk as I see and understand him. In a manner similar to the variations found in the portraits painted of Polk during his presidential term, my depiction of him differs somewhat from others that are available. How a reader responds to my portrayal of Polk depends in part upon the angle from which he or she views it.

I conclude my prefatory comments with the pleasant assignment of acknowledging my indebtedness. For example, I owe more than I can repay to the excellent scholars who have preceded me in their examination of various aspects of the Polk presidency. Moreover, I appreciate the encouragement given by my colleagues and by our department head, John H. Morrow, Jr. Friends at other universities have likewise been supportive. Secretaries in the History Department, especially Mrs. Dorothy Wilkerson, have been indispensable to me, as they have cheerfully and skillfully typed the versions of this manuscript. The University of Tennessee Library has supported my enterprise in a variety of ways; and its Special Collections Department has gone the second mile by providing a place for me to engage in research and writing. A summer research grant from the university prompted and enabled me to launch the early phases of this project. Professor Wayne Cutler of the Polk Project has been quite helpful on several occasions, for which I am grateful. The three editors of the American Presidency Series have criticized, cajoled, and commended me—all with a view toward assisting me to produce a more worthy study of the Polk administration. Their perceptive efforts and genuine interest are greatly appreciated.

Blanche Henry Clark Weaver and the late Herbert Weaver have influenced me in numerous and formative ways, first when I was a graduate student and then when I worked with them editing Polk's correspondence. My study of the Polk presidency is partial testimony to their confidence in and reliance upon me as a scholar and friend.

Finally, I express my profound gratitude to my wife, Mary Lee, and our children: Pierre, Andre, and Louis Paul. They have believed in me and nurtured me through the rewarding, yet sometimes arduous and tedious, task of producing this book. Moreover, they agreed to the sacrifices often required of them, so that I could have freedom and time to move ahead on this project. Their sustaining love has been a constant reminder to me of my great fortune.

Paul H. Bergeron

Knoxville, Tennessee
September 1986

1

★ ★ ★ ★ ★

THE EMERGENCE OF POLK

The decades preceding the Civil War were dynamic and exhilarating. One historian has referred to this period as "a people in motion."[1] Indeed there seemed to be little that was static during the Jacksonian Era. From such an environment, James K. Polk emerged as a national figure. The churning currents of American life were strikingly evident in the political arena. For example, the dominance of the Jacksonian party and the powerful presidency of Andrew Jackson in the early 1830s galvanized a group to organize a challenge to that hegemony. Calling itself the Whig party, it first entered national contests in the presidential election of 1836 but lost to Jackson's heir apparent, Martin Van Buren.

It could easily be argued that the Whigs' defeat was a blessing in disguise for the new party. The assumption of power by the "Little Magician" promised much for the continuation of Jacksonian power and control. But neither Van Buren nor his party had anticipated the devastating Panic of 1837, which began shortly after the new president had taken office and did not finally abate until after his exodus. Van Buren's remedy for the national economic distress was to seek protection for the money of the federal government. To that end, he proposed the Independent Treasury, whereby federal monies that were on deposit in various banks throughout the nation would be removed and placed in this new federally controlled storehouse. Congress fought Van Buren on this program for three years before finally enacting it in the summer of 1840. By then the nation was only a few short months away from a presidential election day.

1

There was apparently no magic left in the Little Magician by the time the voting day arrived, however. Whigs, having sensed that reality long before, had prepared themselves for the presidential campaign. In fact, as the election year approached, voters across the nation were well aware of the existence of a new two-party system, called by historians the Second American Party System. Free of the taint of a national economic crisis and eager to launch a mass appeal to the electorate, the Whig party staged an elaborate and boisterous "Log Cabin and Hard Cider" canvass in 1840. With an aging and deteriorating folk hero, William Henry Harrison, the Whigs rode into power and turned back Van Buren's bid for reelection.

But no sooner had the Whig party become accustomed to its new status in the national arena than Harrison died—only one month after his inauguration. This sudden turn of events left the Whig party in the lurch, for John Tyler became the president. Not only was Tyler the first vice-president to become president upon the death of an incumbent; but also Tyler was a lifelong Democrat—who had been temporarily on the outs with his party when he was chosen by the Whigs as Harrison's running mate.

Unfortunately, Tyler's desire to assert his authority as president collided with Henry Clay's desire to assert his authority as head of the Whig party. The two men clashed repeatedly in 1841, for example, over the issue closest to Clay's heart—the national bank. They did agree, however, on the repeal of Van Buren's Independent Treasury. More than once, Clay pushed his plan for a new national bank through Congress, only to have Tyler veto it on grounds reminiscent of Andrew Jackson's arguments. Eventually, Tyler proved that he could govern by veto—therefore, no bank bill became law; but Clay had Tyler exorcised from the Whig household. In the next year the president and the Whig-controlled Congress fought over the tariff, another crucial item on the Whig economic agenda. After employing his veto power, Tyler, fearful of the dwindling federal coffers, finally relented and permitted the tariff of 1842 to become law. On the foreign front, Tyler assumed unfinished business, left over from the Van Buren administration, concerning the boundary of Maine and resolved it with the Webster-Ashburton Treaty. Near the end of his term, Tyler turned his attention to the Republic of Texas and attempted to capitalize upon annexation sentiment there and in the United States. But his last effort to ensure a political future for himself failed when the Senate rejected the Texas treaty in the spring of 1844. With that setback, Tyler's days were numbered. Henry Clay, the man who had cast Tyler out of the party, had not only wrested control of

2

the party from him but was now attempting to wrest control of the presidency from the hands of the Democrats.

With a united and harmonious party under his command, Clay reckoned upon little difficulty in leading it to a second presidential victory. His hopes for a fairly easy contest that would place him in the presidential chair were short-circuited, however, by a conspiracy of events that began with his public announcement (in which he was joined by Van Buren) in opposition to Texas annexation, followed by the Senate's rejection of the treaty. As shall be discussed later in this chapter, the Democrats substituted James K. Polk for Van Buren and also endorsed annexation, thus leaving Clay, the Whig standard-bearer, with an entirely different campaign to confront. The result eventually was a defeat for Clay and the Whigs in 1844.

Four years later, however, the Whigs succeeded. The election of Zachary Taylor (who also died in office) constituted the second Whig victory in the decade—incidentally, the only Whig triumphs during twenty years of competing for the presidential sweepstakes. All of this is meant to reinforce the point that during the 1840s the national two-party system was securely established and functioning. Throughout the country the focus was upon the presidential contests and secondarily upon statewide or local elections; moreover, there was an evenly balanced and keen competition between the two parties. That had not been the case during the 1830s and would not continue to be the situation during the 1850s.

While political observers were marveling at the two-party system, they also could not help but notice indications that new challenges were evolving. By the end of the 1840s, for example, the old traditional questions of a national bank, a tariff, and internal improvements—hallmarks of the previous decade—had disappeared, having been overcome by the increasingly important matter of slavery in the newly acquired western regions. This latter concern would dominate the 1850s. Reflective of these transformations was the appearance of the Liberty party in 1840, to give a voice to the inchoate concern about the extension of slavery. Competing once more in 1844, but again with only meager results, the Liberty party yielded finally to the creation of the Free Soil party in 1848 (a topic to be discussed in chapter 9). By that date, cracks in the two-party system had become visible, but it would be left to the decade of the 1850s to complete the process of disintegration.

The enviable system of national politics broke down after the 1840s, partly because of the stresses that territorial expansion placed upon it. Known usually by the popular label Manifest Destiny, this affinity for geographical extension became one of the chief impulses of the decade.

3

It encompassed not only politics but also the nation's economy and ideology. Proponents of aggressive expansionism saw their cause as being endemic in the American experience; moreover, it was, they argued, an undeniable part of the providential plan that this nation should expand to its "natural" borders, wherever they might be. Greatly enhancing this appeal was the reality that the western third of what was to become the United States was waiting to be captured and exploited, without much danger of resistance from the scattered remnants of people. Newspaper editors and politicians derived further conviction from their linkage of territorial expansion with the presumed altruistic notion of extending liberty and freedom (American style, of course).

It is no surprise, therefore, that the Tyler administration moved to bring about territorial acquisition; it almost succeeded. Tyler and John C. Calhoun did in fact devise a treaty with the Republic of Texas that provided for annexation, but the Senate killed it. Its death was attributable to Calhoun's bold venture to link Texas annexation with the preservation of slavery in the West, a move that he thought was important for his political fortunes but a move that was fraught with peril for the fortunes of annexation. Essentially, the nation wanted Texas, and Texas wanted to be a part of the nation. Nevertheless, Calhoun's maladroit handling of the treaty precluded an apparently simple resolution of the matter. In any event, the Texas question subsequently had a direct impact upon the presidential campaign of that year.

Yet the continental vision could not be dimmed by the rejection of the treaty. Instead, the vision gained support, partly because at this moment the nation was successfully emerging from the serious economic depression that had begun in 1837. Americans coveted western lands in order to promote their economic well-being. Several statistics reveal the move toward economic recovery. For example, the total currency in circulation in 1840 was approximately $190 million, but that figure thereafter dropped and continued to do so until 1844; finally, in 1846, the total currency surpassed the 1840 amount; and by 1850 the figure had risen to over $285 million. The number of banks in operation likewise sheds light on the economic situation. At the beginning of the decade, for instance, there were 901 banks, scattered throughout the nation, with total cash of $99 million; but that number declined precipitously in 1841 and continued to decrease until 1843. The number slowly began to rise in 1844 and then expanded gradually to a total of 824 banks by 1850 (a figure that was still below that of 1840), with $115 million in cash. The export-import trade also reflected the positive and negative aspects of the nation's economy in the 1840s. There were trade deficits in several of the years—the most serious of which was in 1850. In 1840 the value of exports had been $132 million, and the value of imports, $107 million—indicating a healthy surplus. In 1850, however, the figures were $152 million in exports and $178 million in imports. The "transportation revolution" that had begun during the 1820s with canals and toll roads continued on into the 1840s, but with a new emphasis upon railroad construction. The miles of railroad that were built reflect something of the mixed economic news during the decade. The period started vigorously, with 491 miles being constructed in 1840, 606 miles in 1841, and 505 miles in 1842. But then a downward trend began, which was not arrested until 1848, when a remarkable 1,056 miles were completed. Thereafter the movement was decidedly upward, as the most significant era of ante-bellum railroad construction got under way.[2] There is reason to believe that had the Mexican War not intervened, the recovery of the nation's economy would have been more impressive during the 1840s. Nevertheless, generally, the latter half of the decade reflected prosperity, despite the unusual demands of a wartime economy.

The expansion of the country's railroads, the invention and utilization of the telegraph, and technological advances in printing that made possible the so-called penny press—all combined to lend additional momentum to the quest for an expanded United States. Statistics about patent applications suggest that the 1840s constituted an invention-oriented period; for example, there were 765 patent applications in 1840, but that number nearly tripled in 1850, to a remarkable 2,193 applications. The people were in motion.

Further evidence of the nation's development is seen in the population data. In 1840 the country boasted a total population of 17,120,000 (almost evenly divided between male and female); but in 1850 it could point to 23,261,000 (again, nearly evenly divided according to sex). Hence, approximately 6,000,000 more were living in the United States at the end of the 1840s than at the beginning. Of the 23,261,000 in 1850, approximately 3,500,000 were urban dwellers; whereas in 1840 about 1,800,000 of the 17,120,000 had been town residents. But there is no question that the nation was still a land of farms and farmers. Of the total labor force of 5,600,000 in 1840, for instance, slightly more than 3,500,000 were in the agricultural sector. By 1850 the total labor force had increased markedly, to 8,200,000, and of that number, 4,500,000 were agricultural workers. Although there had been a gain of about 1,000,000 farm laborers during the decade, the agricultural work force constituted a smaller proportion of the total in 1850 than it had in 1840. Impressive increases in the number of manufacturing workers during the 1840s reveal a nation that was beginning to move in new directions. In 1840, for example, there were 500,000 persons working in manufacturing, but in 1850 that number had more than doubled, to 1,200,000. These statistics were portents of things to come.

The face of America was changing in several respects; equally compelling, however, is that the people of America were changing. Here reference is to the influx of foreign-born population. In 1840 the total immigrant population in the United States was approximately 902,000; but the significant migration of foreigners during the decade raised the total immigrant population to 2,200,000 by 1850 (more than double the 1840 figure). Substantial increases in migration began in 1847 and occurred every year thereafter, with nearly 370,000 arriving in 1850 alone. The ensuing decade experienced the continued influx of the foreign born, so that by 1860 the total immigrant population had nearly doubled again (4,100,000 in that year).

The overwhelming majority of immigrants coming to America's shores during the late 1840s and early 1850s were from Ireland and Germany, and the preponderance of them were Catholic. Not surprisingly, the astonishing increases in foreigners who were living in the United States spawned the nativist movement, first in the cities that were most directly feeling the impact of such a migration, and then spreading throughout the country. This anti-Catholic and antiforeigner crusade reached its climax during the 1850s, but there was abundant evidence of it during the 1840s; it influenced some elections and also stimulated violence and rioting in various places. Again, the people were in motion.

Regardless of how one assesses the nativist movement, it was part of the dramatic reform crusade that enlisted millions of Americans. Most of the reforms had their origins in the late 1820s or early 1830s, but they continued to gain momentum thereafter. The pluralistic nature of antebellum reform was both its strength and its weakness. On the one hand, the cornucopia of causes offered a variety of movements with which to identify; and many Americans belonged to more than one. On the other hand, however, fierce competition among the reform movements deprived them of the numbers of followers that might have made success possible. Another peculiar facet of reform was its commitment to moral suasion. It was widely believed that through example, persuasion, and prayer, American citizens would embrace various reforms, thereby eradicating societal evils. When the desired results did not materialize, however, many reformers and their followers switched from reliance on moral suasion to political action.

The temperance movement is an excellent example. The bulging membership rolls of the American Temperance Society exceeded those of any other reform group. Yet the goals of the society—whether moderation or total abstinence—were not achieved; the drunkard remained on the streets of the cities and villages. Out of frustration and disappointment, therefore, temperance advocates abandoned moral suasion in favor of legislative enactments that might bring about a genuine reform of Americans' drinking habits. A few successes were in fact realized. Similarly, people who were interested in the reform of asylums and prisons eagerly launched campaigns to compel state legislatures to build new facilities and to adopt new practices. The greatest exponent of such reform, Dorothea Dix, was particularly active during the 1840s as she toured many states and demanded legislative appropriations to implement changes. Feminism, however, remained largely an appeal of moral suasion, although some statutory alterations benefited the position of women in American society. One of its milestones occurred at the famous Seneca Falls convention in 1848, at which time feminist leaders enunciated their beliefs—a harbinger of things to come.

Stirred by religious revivals, uplifted by notions of human perfection, and driven by a sense of moral urgency, the antislavery crusade became the most important of all the reform efforts. Its significance lay not in its numbers, for it failed in that regard; rather, its importance lay in the attention that it devoted to the problem of human slavery. With the encouragement of William Lloyd Garrison, the movement was institutionalized in the early 1830s; shortly thereafter, other abolitionist leaders, particularly Theodore Dwight Weld, branched out to the western regions and made their impact. Masters of publicity, the antislavery leadership quickly captured the nation's interest, whether positive or negative. But as the institutionalized movement reaped increasing support, divisions within the crusade likewise grew. Finally, at the annual meeting in 1840, the American Antislavery Society split. This fragmentation was related to controversies over the roles of women and of blacks in the movement, the issue of resistance and nonresistance, and the question of involvement in political action. Although formally divided from that point on, the abolitionist campaign nevertheless pressed forward during the 1840s with its demands for the emancipation of slaves. Because of territorial expansion in the West during Polk's presidency, abolitionists fastened upon a new goal: to stop the spread of slavery. This commitment caused many antislavery leaders to gravitate into the political arena, especially during the 1850s. Gone with the wind was the idea of moral suasion, although Garrison remained committed to his original beliefs. There is no denying that the reform imperative, whether lodged in antislavery or some other cause, remained vigorous and impressive throughout the 1840s. A growing and expanding United States needed the vigilance and devotion of reformers.

But in large measure the reform era belonged mainly to the northern section of the nation. In contrast, the southern region during this same period began to withdraw, or at least to follow a different drummer. Southern sectionalism, which was rooted in earlier times, blossomed; and at some point in the 1840s it produced the fruit of southern nationalism. By the end of the decade, some leaders in the South held up a vision of a new nation carved out of the region below the Mason and Dixon line. Religious denominations seemed to lend support to this dream, as three major Protestant groups split over the question of slavery. The formal establishment of southern churches for the Baptists, the Methodists, and the Presbyterians resulted. Moreover, the culture of the region instantly became sensitive to and reflective of this increased desire for a distinctive southern expression. Audacious political leaders, angered and frightened over the emerging controversy in regard to slavery—a concern that was spurred by the Wilmot Proviso—talked daringly of a southern nation. By 1850 some of these impulses had resulted in the assembling of southern conventions in Nashville. Only the successful completion of the Compromise of 1850 appeared to stall the southern nationalist crusade for a while. As subsequent events would reveal, however, this delay was only temporary, not permanent. At any rate, it is obvious that both the North and the South were experiencing much change during the period when Polk emerged as the nation's leader. Indeed, he was both a representative and an instigator of some of these shifts in events.

As if not enough were happening to create new challenges for the people in motion, gold was discovered in California in 1848, the same year that a peace treaty brought a formal cessation of hostilities with Mexico. By the time that Polk left the presidency, thousands were preparing to move to the Pacific Southwest in hopes of fulfilling the tantalizing dream of finding their own individual El Dorados. Many did, of course, which only encouraged thousands more to answer the alluring call of instant wealth. With reckless abandon and at great peril, thousands of Americans therefore rushed to California. For many, the discovery of gold there confirmed the morality of western expansionism. Manifest Destiny offered tangible and lucrative rewards, or so it seemed.

No summary containing only a few pages can do justice to the 1840s, for books have been written about virtually every aspect of it. Suffice it to say that the setting in which Polk emerged, worked, and died was a challenging one which presented the nation with the great questions of western expansion and the future of slavery. Although dimly perceived at the time, the latter would become the ultimate troubling issue that would absorb, as well as divide, the country during the 1850s. Polk was in the center of its origins, while he presided over the nation.

Who could have predicted that Polk was destined for such greatness and such responsibility? He had been prepared for national leadership by events and influences stretching back to his earliest years. Polk had been born and reared in Mecklenburg County, North Carolina, an environment of fierce independence and self-reliance, bolstered by orthodox Presbyterianism. His father, Samuel, and his grandfather, Ezekiel, were leaders in economic matters, politics, and community influence. Young James imbibed the Jeffersonian views of his family and friends, who extolled the virtues of the agricultural setting and a simple life that was only peripherally touched by a limited government. Moreover, frugality and fairness were almost equal watchwords of the community.[3]

His mother, Jane Knox Polk, instilled in James the Calvinist teachings to which she was so much devoted; her task was complicated, however, by Samuel's reluctance to be regular in attending church. His slightly wayward habits engendered the wrath of the local Presbyterian divine; in fact, the two men engaged in a heated argument at James's baptismal ceremony. On that day, to Jane's dismay, Samuel insisted that they walk out of the church, without the rite of baptism having been administered. This episode at the Presbyterian church doubtless created a sensation around Mecklenburg and doubtless stirred tensions within the family. One readily imagines that young James heard this story repeated many times, the reminders of which must have caused pain and embarrassment to him. In addition, Grandfather Ezekiel gained notoriety in the community when he challenged traditional Calvinist tenets by embracing deism and attempting to persuade others to these controversial beliefs. Little wonder that James, although fairly orthodox Calvinist in his views, never became an official member of any church and did not request or receive baptism until he was on his deathbed.

When he was not quite eleven years of age, James left Mecklenburg County to go with his family to new challenges in Middle Tennessee, south of the Nashville area. Even though he moved, young James never truly departed from the essence of Mecklenburg. To him it was a place

9

"where men lived simply on the fruits of their own labor without expectations of easy wealth and dealt honestly with each other on a basis of rough equality and mutual respect."[4] It was the environment where his republican commitments were fashioned, thanks to the expoundings and examples of his grandfather and his father. Furthermore, it was a place of religious devotion—despite questionable actions by certain members of the family. Figuratively speaking, Old Mecklenburg offered Calvinist instruction and sustenance to James.

Shortly after arriving in Middle Tennessee, the Polk family began to prosper, much as it had done in North Carolina. Young Polk, who seems always to have been of frail physical constitution, begged his parents for a chance to engage in formal studies. They obliged by sending him first to a nearby school that was sponsored by the Zion Church and then, in the following year, to an academy near Murfreesboro, led by Samuel P. Black. In both institutions, Polk grew and developed as a scholar; and there, two staunch and devout Presbyterian teachers inculcated in him the tenets of Calvinism. James's schooling transformed him and added a dimension of refinement that had previously been lacking; moreover, his experiences convinced him that he could excel at studies—a substitute for not achieving physical prowess. Although his health had improved somewhat after he had had an operation the year before he enrolled at the Zion school, he never was robust and frequently became fatigued.[5] Physical limitations, which would plague him all of his life, never dimmed his fierce devotion to hard work, however. Presbyterian praises of personal industry and discipline seemed to stir within James a determination to reach his goals on this earth by working harder than anyone else—a claim that, incidentally, he made more than once during his presidency.

His diligence earned him the privilege of attending the University of North Carolina. After his arrival at Chapel Hill, the twenty-year-old James was examined by the faculty and was admitted to the sophomore class for the term beginning in January 1816. Active in the Dialectic Society, James honed his skills in debate and in leadership. Before long he was widely regarded as one of the top students at the university. The days at Chapel Hill were immensely important to him, for intellectual stimulation, for development of friends, and for general maturation and sophistication. Having thrown himself so devotedly into his work as a scholar and a campus leader, James was too debilitated from these exertions to be able to leave Chapel Hill after his graduation; instead, he had to recuperate for several months before departing for Tennessee.

Returning home in the fall of 1818, James quickly made a decision to study law. That choice led him to Nashville to read in the office of Felix

Grundy, who was regarded as one of the premier attorneys of the region and was already well established as a political leader. Reading through the legal volumes in Grundy's office absorbed the energy and interest of James for the better part of the year 1819, but in the late summer a special opportunity presented itself. When he learned from Grundy, who had been elected to the legislature, that the position of senate clerk might be available, James jumped at the chance. In September he hastened to Murfreesboro, the state capital, and successfully contended for the appointment. After having served during that session, he was chosen again as clerk for the session that commenced in 1821. Polk established a reputation as a diligent, efficient, and effective senate clerk. One imagines that he relished the daily contact with political leaders from across the state and that he desired their approval more than anything else. Meanwhile he managed to complete his studies with Grundy and was admitted to the bar in 1820; shortly thereafter he established a law practice in Columbia, Tennessee.

Busy as he was juggling his careers as attorney and senate clerk, Polk still found time for socializing. As a handsome young man with a promising future, he had little trouble in capturing the attention of females, particularly that of Sarah Childress. She was the daughter of a wealthy and respectable family, with whom she lived in Murfreesboro, a convenient location for the politically ambitious Polk. In 1823 he advanced his political career by being elected to the legislature, and he enhanced his personal life by asking Sarah to marry him. Twenty-year-old Sarah had the potential for being quite an asset for James, for she was well educated, attractive, self-assured, affluent, and prominent. Similarly, she detected in her twenty-eight-year-old fiancé such characteristics as initiative, responsibility, dependability, and devotion. They were married on New Year's Day 1824. It was a dazzling social event, as well as the beginning of a remarkable union that lasted for the remaining twenty-five years of James K. Polk's life and for the remaining sixty-seven years of Sarah Childress Polk's life.

If she had not realized it before their marriage, Sarah was soon to learn that the ruling passion of her husband's life was politics. To be sure, he had a reasonably successful legal practice, but his career as an attorney was a means to an end. While a member of the legislature, Polk identified himself with the democratic reforms being urged by William Carroll, the governor. Recollections of Old Mecklenburg were revivified for Polk; his Jeffersonianism was rekindled. Equally important, however, was Polk's decision to support Andrew Jackson's election to the United States Senate and ultimately to the presidency. Polk never wavered from this early commitment to Jackson. Gaining recognition as a legislator merely fed Polk's desire for further political rewards. Consequently, in 1825 he determined to seek a seat in the United States House of Representatives.

Victorious in that quest, Polk began a congressional career that eventually spanned fourteen years. Elected seven times to the House, he learned campaigning techniques and strategies that put him in good stead with the voters. Polk served during three presidencies, those of John Quincy Adams, Jackson, and Van Buren. Polk's career during the Adams administration was not particularly outstanding, except for his being an avid promoter of Jackson and a consistent backer of low tariffs. But with the arrival of Jackson as the new president, Polk's future brightened in Washington. Characteristics displayed by him earlier were important as he earned endorsement from Jackson, who began to rely more and more upon Polk in the House. Polk's appointment to the Ways and Means committee was the break for which he had been waiting. From that post he was in the center of the controversies over the national bank, the tariff, and internal improvements. In 1833 he assumed the chairmanship of the committee, just in time to be of immense assistance to Jackson in the matter of the removal of federal deposits from the national bank and in regard to an investigation of the bank. Because the president was so pleased with the House report that approved not only his veto of the bank recharter but also his withdrawal of federal monies, he declared that Polk deserved a medal. Although Polk had earlier wavered on the matter of government-financed internal improvements, during the Jackson years he became an ardent opponent and helped to defend the president's famous Maysville Road veto. But irrespective of the critical issues before the Congress, Polk made sure that he tended to the needs and requirements of his constituents in Tennessee; Sarah Childress Polk frequently helped him. His repeated reelection successes are indicative of his careful nurturing of the folks back home.

Enjoyment of the limelight in the House whetted Polk's appetite for even more involvement. Accordingly, he sought the Speakership in 1834, only to lose to his fellow Tennessean John Bell. But Polk bided his time, for he knew that the cleavage between Bell and Jackson would eventually pay off for him. And in the following year, Polk successfully ran as the Jacksonian candidate against the antiadministration or nascent Whig candidate, Bell. Elected first in that year and again in 1837, Polk held the post of Speaker for four consecutive years.

A master of rules and procedures as well as political ramifications, Speaker Polk was effective; he "managed" the House about as well as any Speaker had ever done. But his chief frustration came during the

12

Van Buren presidency as he struggled to push the Independent Treasury bill through the House. Troubled also by antislavery petitions that began to flow into the House, Polk received a foretaste of things that were to come ten years later, when he occupied the presidency. Regardless of the difficulties of the job, however, he enjoyed the prestige and the power. He and Sarah Polk were quite active in the social world of Washington; they entertained frequently (good preparation for the presidential years) and somewhat lavishly, if one notes their wine bills. Having accomplished so much in his years in Washington, Polk paradoxically was beset by a nagging dissatisfaction. The economic panic and the troubles of the Van Buren administration caused him to wonder about his political future; there might be a detour or two for him on the road to the ultimate goal of becoming the nation's chief executive. Doubtless seeking the prudent counsel of Sarah, Polk chose to leave Washington, in the hope of returning some day in a more elevated position. His immediate task would be to seek the gubernatorial chair in Tennessee. Departing from the nation's capital, he could ruminate about fourteen notable years, years in which he had achieved national recognition and had become a force to be reckoned with in the councils of the Jacksonian party. Along the way he had had to bend and yield and compromise—indispensable lessons for an effective politician. But essentially he had remained true to his beliefs in a simple, economical federal government, one limited by the prescriptions of the Constitution and by the rights of the states.

The greatest challenge to Polk's position as a political leader lay ahead of him. He returned to a Tennessee that had been swept up with enthusiasm for Hugh Lawson White, as opposed to Van Buren in 1836, and for other Whig candidates. Polk's assignment was to stem the onslaught of Whigs by unseating the incumbent governor, who was seeking election to a third term in 1839. With the assistance of his wife, the recently retired Speaker mounted a vigorous campaign, his first statewide one. Remarkably enough, Polk was triumphant; the Whig juggernaut had been stalled.[6] As circumstances were to reveal subsequently, this was a temporary setback for Tennessee Whigs; yet there is no denying its significance.

The victory celebrations had barely ended when Polk learned how little power he would have as the state's governor. That did not discourage him, however, for his eyes were fixed upon something else—namely, the vice-presidential nomination in 1840. Polk calculated that his noteworthy victory in the gubernatorial election had impressed enough important Democratic leaders that they would plead for him to run with Van Buren in the forthcoming national contest. As a matter of fact, Andrew Jackson did all that he could to assist Polk, but to no avail. Eventually, the party did not choose anyone as Van Buren's running mate, a bizarre situation to say the least. The national party was in trouble in 1840, thanks to the economic distresses and to Van Buren's ineffectual administration. The Jacksonians were apparently caught off guard when the Whigs ushered in their rollicking "Log Cabin and Hard Cider" campaign. The outcome was predictable: "Tippecanoe and Tyler Too" captured the national imagination and vote; and Tennessee reverted to its Whig loyalties.

Thwarted in his hopes for a vice-presidential nomination and dismayed over the results of the national election, Polk derived some comfort from his decision simply to seek reelection as governor in 1841. Little did he know what was in store for him. Tennessee Whigs decided to continue their mass appeal by nominating a folksy, homespun, comical state legislator. Mastering the art of political image making, they dubbed their candidate "Lean Jimmy" Jones. He was not exactly "Old Tippecanoe," but he was better than "Tyler Too." In any event, Tennesseans were treated to a remarkable spectacle throughout the summer months, as both Jones and Polk crisscrossed the state in a joint canvass. They traded anecdotes, jokes, and barbs but discussed few substantive issues. Polk repeatedly remarked that "the neighing, whinnying and whickering of a regiment of colts, starving for want of a teat," reminded him of the "crying and screaming which is daily heard from Mr. Jones and his party in their greedy scramble for office under the new federal administration." Laughter and applause greeted Polk's jibe at every joint debate. Finally, Jones concocted a telling reply, when he observed that while Whigs were young colts, "the governor himself was an old sucker who had been at it for fifteen years." Jones went on to declare that the farmers in his section "generally let a live, healthy colt be weaned by his dam, but that in the case of the scrubby, unpromising fellow, they generally weaned him about the first Thursday in August," which happened to be election day in Tennessee.[7] Anyone who still believes that Polk was a dull and boring politician has never examined his gubernatorial campaigns, especially those of 1841 and 1843.

Despite his herculean efforts, which caused Sarah to worry about his health, Polk was not able to halt the Whig momentum that had been launched with the presidential victory. For the first time in his life, Polk tasted defeat at the hands of the voters; and it was bitter. Evidently his only consolations were that he had whittled down the Whig margin from its 1840 levels and that he would seek revenge by running again in 1843. Out of a political job for the first time since his selection as clerk of the state senate in 1819, Polk resumed the active practice of law in

Columbia. Sarah's consolation was that she and Polk had much more time together. But it was a short-lived pleasure, because Polk began to map out plans for 1843. His determination was fueled by his ambition for the vice-presidential nomination. If successful in the gubernatorial contest, Polk reasoned, surely the party elders would want him for the vice-presidency.

Unfortunately for him, the 1843 contest in Tennessee was a repeat of the one two years earlier, although there was less joke swapping. Polk lost again to Jones, and with that, his goals for 1844 vanished. This second setback was almost more than Polk could cope with; he went into seclusion for days, during which time his Calvinist tenets were a source both of comfort and of discomfort: discomforting because he could not understand why his disciplined hard work and moral rectitude had not paid off at the voting precincts; comforting because the dogmas had instilled the conviction that he must stoically accept what had happened. Sarah Childress Polk, sensitive to his deep pain, optimistically encouraged him to believe that there would be better days ahead in his political career; and she was right.

As the new year dawned, however, no one would have prophesied that Polk would become the Democratic party's nominee, to say nothing of predicting that the nation would actually choose him as president. Within a few months, however, he had secured his party's nomination and subsequently had emerged as the victorious candidate in November. The first costly mistake that the Van Buren forces made, confidently looking forward to his nomination by the party, was to agree to the postponement of the convention from November 1843 to May 1844. Had the national party assembled at the earlier date, Van Buren would surely have won the nomination with very little difficulty. But in the intervening months, much happened that conspired to thwart Van Buren's selection. The main development was the pursuit of Texas annexation by the Tyler administration in the early months of 1844, a cause that Van Buren felt compelled to disavow. Because he was afraid of losing his base of support in the Northeast, Van Buren declared his opposition to the annexation of Texas by making a public announcement in late April—a costly error for him. In this he was joined by Henry Clay, a move that aroused suspicions among many political observers. Prior to this, it had seemed that Van Buren would easily become the party's nominee, despite his having been defeated in 1840 and his not being a very popular figure within the party. But the anti–Van Buren forces had not been able to focus upon a single leader; moreover, many Democratic leaders were beholden to Van Buren for emoluments and other considerations during his presidency.[8]

Van Buren's antiannexation stance greatly disappointed his mentor, Andrew Jackson, who immediately began to search for an appropriate replacement. Determined to influence the party, Jackson rallied support for a western man who would advocate the annexation of Texas. Two short weeks before the Democratic Convention, Jackson met with Polk to declare his conviction that Polk was the man upon whom the party would have to depend. Always cautious, Polk meanwhile continued the fiction that he was interested only in being Van Buren's vice-presidential running mate. Ironically, many Tennessee delegates to the convention did not favor either man, but instead looked to Lewis Cass. Suffice it to say that when the Democrats convened in late May, the party was in turmoil: a large contingent that was intent upon vindicating Van Buren after his loss in 1840 was offset by an equally large one that was determined to find a new man to lead the party.

Crucial to the eventual outcome was the question of what constituted a majority. Since 1832, when Jackson had forced the party to embrace the two-thirds rule in order to strengthen Van Buren's candidacy for vice-president, the Democrats had held fast to this requirement. Obviously fearing this rule in 1844, however, the Van Buren crowd hoped to persuade the convention to replace it with the simple-majority stipulation. This attempt failed, however, thereby dooming Van Buren's nomination. At the conclave in Baltimore, there was a total of 266 votes; only 134 would be required for a simple majority, but 177 would be needed for a two-thirds majority. On the very first ballot, Van Buren garnered 146 votes, a majority but short of the two-thirds mark. On subsequent ballots his vote steadily decreased, while Cass's surged ahead. After seven ballots, however, the convention had reached a stalemate: the Cass people were unable to mount the big push needed for victory, and the Van Buren people were becoming more and more discouraged with their candidate's dwindling votes. The atmosphere was therefore conducive to the "new man" strategy; whereupon Gideon J. Pillow, George Bancroft, and Benjamin F. Butler swung into action. Lobbying and buttonholing delegates, this trio pointed to a way out of the impasse: They suggested Polk's name, as well as that of Silas Wright. Throughout the late hours of the night, it could not be discerned whether the convention would eventually favor a Polk-Wright ticket or a Wright-Polk ticket. Unbeknownst to many delegates, however, Wright had already penned a letter in which he adamantly refused to be considered for the presidential nomination, should Van Buren fail. Once his stance became generally known the next day in the convention hall, the way was cleared for Polk's nomination, which was secured on the ninth ballot.

In the aftermath of this exhilarating scene, the party quickly moved to designate Wright as the vice-presidential nominee. Dispatching telegraphic messages from Baltimore to Washington, where Wright was serving as senator, the conclave anxiously awaited his reply. But Wright, embittered by Van Buren's defeat, wanted no part of a compromise ticket and so informed the incredulous convention. Many delegates in fact thought that something had happened to the new telegraph machine and therefore refused to believe the messages that were received in Baltimore. Finally, Wright sent his answer by a group of men who traveled from Washington. Compelled to accept Wright's refusal, the convention then, with little thought or debate, turned to George M. Dallas of Pennsylvania as the running mate for Polk. Along the way the party adopted a platform that contained the usual addictions to principle but added a final resolution in support of the reoccupation of Oregon and the reannexation of Texas—thereby providing focus and strength to the party's campaign. This platform, which Polk had no trouble standing upon, clearly reflected the expansionist spirit.

After Polk learned of his nomination (he had not attended the Baltimore convention), he carefully phrased a letter to the convention committee, accepting the honor. In it he committed himself to a one-term pledge, although this had not been a part of the platform. He perceived that such a promise would heal the divisiveness that was evident in the party and would encourage the thwarted candidates to rally to his support, believing that in four years they would have another chance at the nomination. Moreover, Polk had long been an advocate of a one-term presidency, confident that this constituted pure Jacksonian ideology. But the one-term covenant, which was taken quite seriously by Polk throughout his presidency, did not yield the desired effects; rather, it seemed to be disadvantageous to him, because constant jockeying for power and position took place. On balance, it was a mistake; but in the immediate aftermath of the convention, it appeared to be a shrewd move.

Meanwhile the Whig party had convened in early May to engage in the ritual of nominating Henry Clay, who had been waiting for this moment since 1841, when he had forced President Tyler out of the party. Whigs ceased their cheering at Baltimore long enough to adopt a brief platform which mainly praised Clay, Theodore Frelinghuysen, and the traditional views on the currency, the tariff, and the distribution of monies from the sale of public lands. The only astonishing clause in the document was, ironically, the one that pledged the party to the single-term presidency. The great love feast at the Whig Convention stands in marked contrast to the disruptive conclave that was staged by the Democrats later in May.

The only thing that bothered Clay and the Whigs was the problem of annexation, which was scrupulously avoided in the party platform. As the campaign developed, Clay became steadily more cognizant of its importance, especially among his southern brethren. In July he therefore moderated his rigid opposition to the annexation of Texas, a shift that gratified the disheartened southern wing of the party but horrified much of the previously optimistic northern branch. It appears that the more Clay equivocated on this issue, the more damage he inflicted upon his campaign, although in the process he may have saved North Carolina and Tennessee for the Whig party on election day. Any slight improvements in the South, however, were offset by negative reactions in the northern states, as some traditional Whig voters fled from Clay to the Liberty party.

Originating in 1840, the small devoted band of Liberty men again offered James G. Birney to the voters in 1844. Opposed to the extension of slavery, this party was a one-issue party, a rarity in American politics. The Liberty party's position became somewhat clouded, however, when Birney, a former Democrat, embraced traditional Democratic issues. He was even nominated for the legislature by the Democratic party in his home county in Michigan, and he even professed publicly that he preferred Polk over Clay. Such were the vagaries of politics during the summer and fall months of 1844.

As Clay worried about Texas and the Liberty party, Polk had two obstacles to the smooth sailing of his campaign. One was in the person of John Tyler, who had decided to seek the presidency. Utilizing all the persuasion and leverage at his command, including, most importantly, Andrew Jackson himself, Polk endeavored to convince Tyler to withdraw from the contest. Polk eventually succeeded when he and his aides cajoled the *Washington Globe* into putting an end to its criticisms and attacks upon Tyler. With the incumbent president safely removed, Polk faced only one other serious problem: the tariff.

Knowing that this issue was crucial in such states as Pennsylvania, the Democratic nominee endeavored to allay apprehensions about his customary low-tariff views. This effort took the form of a letter to a prominent Philadelphian, John K. Kane, who was advised to show the document to fellow Democratic leaders before making it public. Written scarcely a week after Polk had formally accepted the presidential nomination, the letter avowed his opposition to a tariff for protection only but endorsed the concept of a revenue tariff that might "afford reasonable incidental protection" to American manufacturing. Delighted with this position, Pennsylvania Democrats immediately published the Kane letter and distributed it widely throughout the state. Its similarity to Clay's own statements about the tariff eased the fears of tariff supporters among Pennsylvania Democrats. Although assessed by some as an evasive document, subject to varying interpretations, it actually was a fairly forthright statement—in fact, more so than some of Polk's friends had advised. In any event, the Kane letter played an indispensable role in keeping Pennsylvania in the Democratic column.

Having eased Tyler out of the way and having defused the tariff question, Polk had every reason to be optimistic about his chances for election, particularly as he watched Clay shift his position on the annexation of Texas. Never one to let his positive beliefs override caution, however, Polk worked even more diligently as the campaign progressed, although he refrained from making any new public statements on issues. In his home state of Tennessee he masterminded the canvass, for he was especially anxious to carry it—partly for personal vindication and partly for the necessity of ending the string of Whig victories.

Two nagging questions awaited election day for answers. The first was: How many voters in New York would be siphoned off from the normal Whig vote to go with Birney and the Liberty party? As Clay moderated his opposition to the annexation of Texas, this question became increasingly important. The second question was: How much influence would the nativist movement exert upon local elections in northern cities and states and thereby have an impact upon the presidential contest? Evident Whig sympathies for nativism seemed to augur well for the Democrats, who were assiduously courting foreign-born voters.

These and other questions received answers when the election was over, although one could argue about the exact answers that the voters had provided. One indisputable fact about the 1844 election, however, is its closeness. Polk won a plurality, not a majority, of the nation's popular vote. He failed to carry his home state by about 200 to 300 votes—an exceedingly disappointing loss for Polk. In the end he carried fifteen states, winning majorities in all of them except New York and Michigan, where he secured pluralities. Clay carried eleven states. He won majorities in all of these except Ohio, whose 23 electoral votes made it an important state for Clay. It was the only western state he won. The total national vote was 2,700,000. The Liberty party attracted only 62,000 votes; whereas Polk captured 1,337,000, and Clay won 1,299,000. Nevertheless, the minuscule Birney vote should not obscure its importance, for in New York it spoiled Clay's hopes for victory.

Garnering nearly 16,000 votes in New York, Birney deprived the Whig party of enough votes so as to give the victory to Polk, who pulled only 5,000 more votes than did Clay. New York's 36 electoral votes, the largest number for any state in the Union, were crucial to the eventual national outcome, for Polk won 170 overall, while Clay received 105. Had New York turned out differently, Clay, instead of Polk, would have become the eleventh president.[9]

The two-party system functioned extremely well in 1844, both in turning out tremendous numbers of voters and in maintaining virtual parity between the parties.[10] In such tight elections, various things tip the balance one way or the other. Polk's skillful handling of the tariff issue, for example, enabled him to carry Pennsylvania (26 electoral votes) and, doubtless, to stymie Democratic defections elsewhere. On the other hand, Clay's maladroit handling of the Texas-annexation issue hurt him, particularly in New York, where antislavery men stayed away from the Whig party and went for the Liberty party instead. A third influencing factor, although it is difficult to assess with accuracy, was the burgeoning nativist movement in various cities, which enlisted Whig sympathies, if not support, and therefore forced immigrant voters to the Democratic ranks. Finally, there is no doubt that the annexation question played into the hands of Polk and the Democrats, especially in the South, where it rejuvenated the party and toppled some fence-straddling Whigs into the Polk camp.

Having made these observations, however, one must reiterate that throughout the nation the vote margins were razor thin. Therefore, it is not easy to contend that any one issue swung the election, not even the question of Texas or western expansionism in general. Voter tenacity and constancy, a hallmark of the two-party system, is the most noteworthy thing to observe in the 1844 results. But the retiring president, Tyler, and the incoming president, Polk, believed that the election had been an affirmative referendum on annexation. Although the election returns do not confirm that view, it nevertheless is true that territorial expansionism was attracting increasing numbers of advocates. Polk rightly saw himself as the spokesman for this Manifest Destiny impulse, for in his eyes that had been the central issue separating him from Clay. He would go to Washington determined to enliven and give meaning to the continental vision. The people were in motion.

Before departing from Tennessee for the tremendous new burdens of presidential office, however, weeks of activity and contemplation awaited the newly victorious Polk. Almost immediately, for example, he began to consider the composition of his cabinet, while at the same time he responded to the congratulatory messages that poured into his home at Columbia. Moreover, he gave serious thought to the future of the *Washington Globe,* under Francis P. Blair's editorship. Somewhere in the midst of these concerns and the scattered moments of celebration, Polk devoted some time to ruminating upon his emergence both as the party's nominee and as the eventual winner. Having earlier suffered through the worst parts of his entire political career—two successive defeats for the governorship of Tennessee—Polk had suddenly emerged from these terrible disappointments to become the nation's chief executive.

Emboldened by this dramatic turn of events, Polk vowed to be a vigorous president, one who would exercise control over the party, the Congress, and the nation. He wanted to convince the voters that they had not made a mistake. Having emerged from the ignominy of political defeat, Polk was ready, as the new year of 1845 arrived, to leave the familiar haunts of the Duck River for the more challenging environment of the Potomac. By late January he had departed, not to return until slightly more than four years later. Washington awaited him with tense, excited feelings. Those who anticipated much, who sensed that the people were in motion, were not to be disappointed. Immediately upon arriving in the nation's capital, Polk became the central figure there—a position that he did not relinquish through four exceedingly troublesome years.

First, however, he had to complete the task of identifying and selecting the men who would constitute the official family of his administration.

2

★ ★ ★ ★ ★

THE PRESIDENT'S MEN: THE CABINET

About a month after learning that he had in fact been duly elected president, Polk declared to his close associate Cave Johnson, "In any event I intend to be *myself* President of the U.S."[1] There is no question that Polk entered into this new phase of his political life with a stern determination to be in charge and to control people and events, insofar as humanly possible. The first immediate challenge to this commitment lay in the selection of a cabinet to work with Polk for the next four years.

That the task of designating his "team" would be a difficult one was evident at the outset. The Texas question, which had loomed large in the presidential campaign, now loomed as a threat to the unity and harmony of the Democratic party and thereby as an obstacle to Polk's smooth transition into the leadership of that party. Perhaps unluckily for the president-elect, John Tyler decided to resurrect the Texas-annexation matter during the session of Congress that convened one month after election day. Thus, while Polk was struggling valiantly to secure his cabinet personnel, debates and decisions over Texas were disturbing the political scene in Washington. Inexorably linked to this specific problem was the question of what Polk should do with Tyler's cabinet and, especially, with Secretary of State John C. Calhoun. The president-elect became so vexed by all of these considerations that it took him three and one-half months to tap the six men who would be his executive department heads and his principal advisers.

One of the several ironies of the selection process was that the calculating, methodical Polk found himself, three days before his

Inauguration Day, with four of his six cabinet posts still unfilled. He therefore hurriedly rearranged some of his carefully crafted strategy to dash off letters inviting certain men to join his official family. But even in the sudden pressure and haste that uncharacteristically marked the selection process, the new president had the satisfaction of having remained essentially true to his original intentions about the personnel of his cabinet. For instance, back in the months of November and December, when Polk had sought the guidance of Andrew Jackson and two or three other close political allies, he had arrived at the notion that there should be a symmetrical geographical distribution of the cabinet members. For example, one should be from New York, one from Pennsylvania, one from New England, one from Virginia, one from the Deep South, and one from his home state of Tennessee. At the end of January, when he departed for Washington, that is precisely the composition he had worked out, at least on paper. James Buchanan, from Pennsylvania, was to occupy the most prestigious post of secretary of state, while Azariah C. Flagg of New York would hold the second slot in the cabinet, as secretary of the Treasury. Andrew Stevenson of Virginia would head the War Department, thereby satisfying the demands of that important state; and George Bancroft of Massachusetts would lead the Navy Department, thus placating New England's desire for representation in the new administration. From the Deep South, Polk planned to tap Robert J. Walker of Mississippi to be his attorney general, while the home-state man on the team would be Cave Johnson, to lead the Post Office Department. By Inauguration Day, although both the arrangement of positions and the men to fill them had been altered noticeably, still the geographical placement conformed to the early blueprint.[2]

Implicit perhaps in this commitment to a shrewd distribution of state and regional representation was the notion that Polk should have an entirely new cabinet, with no holdovers from Tyler's. Modern students of the presidency could easily be perplexed about how and why this should have been a problem for Polk. But there was precedent for an incoming president to retain all or some of his predecessor's cabinet; moreover, there were three people in the Tyler group of 1844 who presented special difficulties. One was Tyler's secretary of war, William Wilkins of Pennsylvania, who happened also to be the brother-in-law of the new vice-president, George M. Dallas. Apparently because he was easily lost in the conflict of heated rivalries in Pennsylvania, Wilkins received no serious consideration from the president-elect. John Y. Mason, Tyler's navy secretary, was another matter, however, for Polk felt very attached to him, a bond that dated back to their college days at

Chapel Hill. Yet Polk's closest advisers urged him to jettison Mason along with all the other Tyler appointees. Polk ironically reneged on his pledge to have an entirely new cabinet when at the eleventh hour he plucked Mason out of deserved obscurity to give him the post of attorney general. The man in Tyler's cabinet who presented the most delicate situation to Polk was Secretary of State Calhoun. Fearful of alienating the Calhoun element in the party, Polk agonized over a palatable strategy for easing Calhoun out of the way. One approach was to dangle a foreign post in front of him, but Calhoun professed no genuine interest in such. Actually, the problem more or less solved itself when Calhoun indicated through emissaries that he would willingly step down from the State Department with friendly feelings toward the incoming president.[3]

Although Pennsylvania was to be represented in his administration in the person of Vice-President Dallas, Polk early committed himself to placing someone in his cabinet from that state. In Polk's mind, James Buchanan, whose career he admired, was the man for the State Department slot. Polk had two major worries about this particular appointment, however. First, could he get Buchanan to forswear presidential ambitions? Polk deemed it vital to the smooth functioning of his forthcoming administration to require pledges from all cabinet members that they would not actively seek either the presidency or the vice-presidency while serving under his aegis. Buchanan, whose political aspirations were known and feared, finally gave an answer to Polk that seemed to be in compliance, in that he promised that he would not exert himself for the presidency while in the cabinet without Polk's permission. On the other hand, declared Buchanan, he certainly would not say in 1845 that he would not be a candidate for the presidency in 1848. Apparently Polk wanted Buchanan in the cabinet strongly enough to overlook the secretary's skillful, but obvious, hedge on the vow of political celibacy.[4]

The second concern that was occasioned by Polk's desire to place Buchanan in his administration was intrastate rivalries and interpersonal jealousies. Not surprisingly, Dallas took a very jaundiced view of Polk's proposed elevation of Buchanan and consequently tried to block it by direct intervention. Because Dallas and Buchanan represented opposing factions in the Democratic party in Pennsylvania, more than a cabinet appointment was at stake. Indeed, the control of the state party, as well as personal political dreams, was involved in the Dallas-Buchanan feud. But despite Dallas's almost nuisance-level pleadings with Polk against Buchanan, the president-elect resolutely stuck to his decision to have Buchanan in the most prominent spot in his cabinet.

After all, Polk could not overlook the wide support that Buchanan enjoyed, including the endorsement by Pennsylvania's presidential electors, or the important role that Buchanan might play in helping to get Polk's plans for a lowered tariff through Congress, in spite of expected opposition from the Keystone State.[5]

Although the elevation of Buchanan caused some irritation and unhappiness, it did not stir the antagonisms that Polk's efforts to appoint a New Yorker did. From the vantage point of Tennessee and even at closer range in Washington, Polk, along with many others, had immense difficulty in discerning the right course to take to reward New York. One month after his election, Polk turned to Silas Wright, the newly elected governor of that state, with the offer of the Treasury portfolio. This was in fact the very first move that the president-elect made to staff his proposed cabinet. Doubtless, Polk reckoned in advance that Wright, not wanting to abandon the governorship to which he had recently been chosen, would not accept any position. In any event, in early December the letter went forward to Wright, and shortly thereafter a negative reply returned. Polk felt a sense of relief, for he had not been truly certain that he wanted a dominant leader such as Wright in his official family.[6] Now he could derive comfort from knowing that he had made the appropriate gesture toward New York. But what Polk did not understand at the moment was that Wright's refusal opened a Pandora's box and contributed incalculable woe to the young president-elect, for every move he made thereafter to satisfy New York's demands for a cabinet seat was fraught with hostility and ill will on the part of some prominent state leaders. In retrospect, Polk could have looked back and wondered if Wright's refusal was the blessing in disguise that he had at first assumed it to be.

Well aware that his candidacy had widened the breach in the New York party, Polk hoped that he could heal such a rift through a cabinet appointment. As indicated above, he first sought the wishes of the Wright–Van Buren element of the party, because that group had been the most lukewarm, if not antipathetic, toward his campaign. But in his desire to win back the support of this segment, Polk at the same time could not ignore the Conservative wing, which had enthusiastically supported him in New York. The weeks prior to his actual arrival in Washington were filled with a succession of letters to and from leaders of both factions of the state party. Van Buren was not hesitant to counsel the new president and, especially, to warn him of the pitfalls of mistreating or shunning the Van Buren crowd. Not being reluctant to seek two positions in the administration, he and his cohorts strongly recommended Benjamin F. Butler for the State Department and Azariah

C. Flagg for the Treasury. Polk's initial response was that he would probably appoint either Butler or Flagg, not honestly telling Van Buren and Wright that he had already decided upon Buchanan for the secretary of state post. In any event, when he left Tennessee, Polk was fairly certain that although Butler would not get the appointment that his supporters wanted for him, at least Flagg would be named to the Treasury.[7] Once in Washington, however, Polk, nearly overwhelmed by pressure in behalf of Robert J. Walker (whom the president had wanted as attorney general) for the Treasury post, abandoned Flagg.

What to do with Butler became the next question. The increasingly complex New York political situation added to Polk's uncertainty. Finally, on 25 February, one week before Inauguration Day, he wrote to Butler, offering him the War Department headship. Butler was offended by the proffered job, however, for he had wanted either the State or the Treasury portfolio; therefore he declined. He did not know that at that moment, Van Buren and Wright had written to him in New York City, entreating him to accept the less prestigious War Department slot, so as to checkmate the Conservative wing of the party, particularly William L. Marcy. Ironically, by refusing Polk's offer, Butler believed himself to be doing precisely what his mentors had wanted.[8]

On 1 March, Polk turned to Marcy as the last-minute hope to secure a New Yorker for the cabinet. Readily responding in the affirmative to Polk's letter, Marcy did not disappoint the president. Polk's offer to Marcy and Marcy's acceptance of it mightily disturbed the political waters of the Empire State, but the president had no reason to be surprised at this reaction. Conservative political leaders, such as former Governor William C. Bouck and Senator Daniel S. Dickinson, as well as newspaper editors, had steadily mounted a campaign in favor of Marcy, who, by virtue of his experience in state government, was probably better suited for the Treasury rather than the War Department. Before he left Tennessee for Washington, Polk was mindful of the intense interest in behalf of Marcy—a recognition that became even clearer after Polk arrived in the capital. Aiding Marcy's cause was the important fact that he enjoyed some support, albeit limited, even among some of the Van Buren element. In the meanwhile, Polk had abandoned his interest in Andrew Stevenson of Virginia, the political realities having forced him to do so. It was simply more important to take care of New York's needs; Virginia could be placated with a lesser spot if necessary. At one point in the frantic days of searching for a suitable New Yorker, Polk asked the two new senators, Dickinson and John A. Dix, to make a recommendation for a secretary of war. But their joint suggestion, a little-known judge named Jacob Sutherland, was so far off target that

Polk could not act upon it. Finally, Polk turned to Butler, who declined, and then to a member of the rival faction, Marcy, who accepted.[9] If there had been a wailing wall in Albany, most of the Van Burenites and possibly some Conservatives, who were unhappy over the number three spot rather than a higher one, would have found their way to it, once the dust of the intrigue over the cabinet appointment had settled. And perhaps Polk would have joined them.

Even the attempt to reward Walker for his work at the Democratic Convention and for his vital support of Texas annexation in the Senate created more difficulties than Polk had anticipated. By the time the president-elect left Tennessee for the nation's capital, he was convinced that he wanted Walker in the cabinet, thereby satisfying the expectation of a representative from the Deep South, since Calhoun had already graciously withdrawn. According to Polk's view of things, Walker would fit conveniently into the post of attorney general. But no sooner had Polk reached that conclusion than he began to receive a great deal of advice urging a more lofty station for the Mississippi senator. The chorus of support for Walker increased in tempo and in volume, once Polk had arrived on the scene in Washington. Naturally, after he had decided definitely upon Buchanan for the State Department, Polk had to deal with Dallas's unhappiness. Dallas and Walker had family ties, since Walker had married Dallas's niece. Moreover, Walker, formerly of Pennsylvania, also had political connections in the Keystone State. Spurned in his effort to block Buchanan's appointment, Dallas turned his energies to securing a prominent post for Walker. Others soon joined the fray, especially congressmen and other political leaders from Mississippi, one or two of whom coveted Walker's seat in the Senate. Walker likewise enjoyed solid backing from several influential north-western congressional leaders. Pressured by the rising tide of endorse-ments for Walker, Polk at first resisted and penned a letter in mid February offering the portfolio of attorney general to Walker. No sooner had he done so, however, than he changed his mind and did not send the invitation to the senator. According to Congressman Jacob Thompson of Mississippi, Polk on the day before the inauguration formally tendered the position of attorney general to Walker, but Thompson, later that same day, persuaded the frustrated Polk to switch Walker to the Treasury Department. While Thompson's dramatic story is captivating, it also apparently lacks corroborating evidence. Instead, the fragmentary record seems to indicate that Polk made his decision to name Walker to the Treasury post two days prior to Thompson's visit. In any event, on the eve of the inauguration, Walker accepted the more elevated appointment, to the chagrin of some Van Burenite politicos who knew that he was not one of them.[10]

The chess game that Polk was playing with his cabinet assignments required him to make two or three additional moves. Having success-fully positioned Walker in the Treasury slot, Polk then had a vacancy at the attorney generalship. With seemingly little hesitation or consultation with others, on 3 March, Polk tapped his long-time friend John Y. Mason to head the Attorney General's Office. With similar rapidity and insula-tion from advisers, Mason agreed to join Polk's official family.[11] Also on that same day, Polk at long last offered the headship of the Navy Depart-ment to George Bancroft. Polk had wanted Bancroft all along for this po-sition, for they had enjoyed a mutual-admiration relationship for some time prior to Polk's election; but Polk had stalled in the face of the confu-sion and complications over the New York representative in the cabinet. Bancroft and Polk had been in contact for months, through correspon-dence and in person. Polk had no trouble in thinking of Bancroft as the most suitable New Englander for the cabinet; besides, Van Burenites were favorably disposed toward an appointment for Bancroft. Further-more, Bancroft's defeat in 1844 for the governorship of Massachusetts had perhaps engendered additional sympathy and support from Polk, who had twice failed (in 1841 and 1843) in gubernatorial contests in Ten-nessee. At any rate, Polk indicated early that he wanted Bancroft in his cabinet, but the historian-writer actually preferred a foreign assignment to a cabinet position. Apparently, Polk assured Bancroft that a diplomatic mission might be his later, after devoted service in the cabinet, and Ban-croft was willing to take his chances that leadership of the Navy Depart-ment would serve as a stepping stone to more desirable duties. Accord-ingly, he accepted and promised his "best and most assiduous exertions in the conduct of the department." Some mild displeasure was ex-pressed over Bancroft's appointment by some disappointed New En-glanders; this was followed by a perfunctory attempt to block or stall his confirmation by the Senate.[12]

The final piece on the cabinet chessboard was not a bishop or a king; he was a political knight—-Cave Johnson of Tennessee. Like Mason, Johnson had been a long-time political and personal ally of Polk's. They had been involved together in many of the political struggles in their volatile home state, and they had made "the long march" to the presidency. Very early in the cabinet intrigue, Polk had intimated that he might go with either Johnson or Aaron V. Brown for postmaster general. In reality, Polk's mind seems to have been fixed on Johnson all along, though Brown would continue to be a valuable ad-viser and ally and would, in 1845, win the governorship in Tennessee for the Democratic party after two earlier abortive attempts by Polk. Johnson had many years of service in Congress to his credit, which meant, in effect, that he knew his way around in Washington. In fact, in the delicate weeks prior to the inauguration, Johnson was Polk's valuable eyes and ears in Washington, a role that he continued to play throughout the administration's days. Although some other names had been mentioned to Polk as appropriate persons to head the Post Office Department, he disregarded them. Therefore, on 17 February, the day he invited Buchanan into the cabinet, Polk also extended an invitation to Johnson.[13] Simultaneously, the most prestigious and the least prestigious posts were filled in this manner.

Strange as it may seem, on the day when he was sworn into office, Polk was still uncertain about the final composition of his cabinet, for he had not yet heard from at least two prospective members, Marcy and Bancroft. Had they turned him down, the saga of cabinet woes and intrigue would have continued on into the early days of his new administration. Luckily, on 5 March the president received Bancroft's letter and probably Marcy's at the same time, thus concluding for the time being the prolonged quest for six men to furnish administrative leadership as well as political advice and support. The cabinet-selection process had been undeniably tedious and laden with conflict, leaving ample room for later debate over whether Polk had accomplished his goal of restoring party unity and harmony by his choices. But there is no denying that once in place, the cabinet served well and with notable continuity. A year and a half later, Bancroft left the cabinet, and then, in the spring of 1848, Nathan Clifford departed. Otherwise, Polk's cabinet established an enviable, if not remarkable, record for stability. Five of the original six men stayed for the entire four years; Polk made only three changes, with a total of eight men serving under him. This record stood in marked contrast to Jackson's and Tyler's poor showing in turnovers of cabinet personnel.[14]

It is not surprising that Bancroft resigned in September 1846, for he had been thirsting for a diplomatic post from the beginning. At the propitious moment, when Louis McLane was ready to retire from the rigors of his work on the Oregon negotiations, the English mission became available. The president was more than willing to reward Bancroft, whose work in the cabinet and in the Navy Department he greatly admired. In the summer of 1846, Polk and Bancroft began to confer about the foreign post that would be most agreeable to the secretary, and the president promised the French post to him. But by 1 August, in a conversation with Mason, Polk indicated that he would send Bancroft to England, the assignment that Bancroft preferred. If

Bancroft accepted, Polk noted, he wanted Mason to shift over from the Attorney General's Office to the Navy Department. Three days later, Bancroft accepted Polk's generous offer of the London assignment. A month later, the president, accompanied by Mason, walked over to Bancroft's house, and Polk expressed his praise and gratitude for Bancroft's work. Bancroft resisted Polk's overtures to write a public letter lauding his tenure at the Navy Department but did consent to having a special article prepared by John Appleton, chief clerk in his department, for publication in the *Washington Union*. In mid September, when Bancroft left Washington for Boston and subsequently England, the president commented on "the utmost harmony and good feeling" that prevailed "between Mr. Bancroft and the Cabinet."[15]

With his usual pledges of devotion and servitude, Mason moved over to the Navy Department in the fall of 1846. Prior to this transfer, Polk had been searching for a new attorney general. The top candidate was Franklin Pierce of New Hampshire (obviously, geographical distribution would continue to be observed), but Pierce declined the honor. Meanwhile, Mason presided over both the Navy Department and the Attorney General's Office. Near the end of September, Polk informed the cabinet that he was considering Nathan Clifford of Maine for appointment but that he wanted more information about him. Finally, on the thirtieth of the month, Polk wrote to Clifford, inviting him to accept the attorney generalship. Clifford responded affirmatively in a letter of 12 October. Three days later, an apparently eager Clifford arrived in Washington, ready to confer with the president and to receive his official commission; on 17 October he attended his first cabinet meeting. Presumably, Clifford fitted in immediately and went about his chores at the Attorney General's Office.[16] There was no hint of any trouble until mid December, when Clifford suddenly informed a startled president that he wanted to resign. The attorney general read aloud his letter of resignation, which expressed approval of the administration and his relationship with the cabinet but gave no reasons for his decision to leave. Exhibiting compassion as well as political savvy, the president warned Clifford that the resignation would probably mark the end of Clifford's public career, because his opponents would charge that he had not been qualified for the job. By the end of their heartfelt exchange, Clifford had decided to remain at his post, to the delight of a gratified and relieved Polk. As a result of their conversation, Polk surmised that Clifford had felt inadequate to compete with the other luminaries in the cabinet and therefore had wanted to step aside.[17]

Eventually, about fifteen months later, Clifford did leave the cabinet, but under entirely different circumstances from those mentioned above, for in March 1848 the president tapped his attorney general for a special assignment to Mexico. As the Senate neared the ratification of the Mexican treaty, discussions arose in the cabinet about an appropriate person to travel to Mexico with the approved treaty for purposes of securing the final ratification from the Mexican government. Polk informed the cabinet that he preferred Louis McLane for the assignment, to which there was general concurrence. But McLane declined the appointment, mainly because of the ill health of his wife. Shortly thereafter, Polk reopened the discussions, after lamenting on 8 March that he was "wholly at a loss to know whom to select." The president soon sought and received cabinet acquiescence in his recommendation of Senator Ambrose H. Sevier, chairman of the Foreign Relations Committee, as treaty commissioner to Mexico. Although reluctant at first, Sevier consented to take the assignment. But the story then took a sudden, unexpected twist when Sevier became quite ill, so ill that his physician reported to Polk that it would be days before Sevier would recuperate sufficiently to leave Washington for Mexico. In that emergency, both Buchanan and Polk shared the view that someone else needed to be appointed immediately and sent on to Mexico with the ratified treaty. Interestingly enough, Polk right away thought of Clifford as the man for the mission, and Buchanan concurred. Taken completely by surprise on 17 March, when Polk asked him to serve in the capacity of commissioner to Mexico, Clifford nonetheless agreed. On the next day, Polk asked the Senate to confirm Clifford as the associate commissioner, with the authority to act unilaterally or in concert with Sevier, should the latter recover quickly enough to depart for Mexico within a reasonable amount of time. Polk confided to his diary the reasons for his turning to Clifford in this situation: the attorney general was completely familiar with Polk's views regarding the treaty; and "he is, too, a very discreet, sensible man." Congratulating himself upon this appointment, the president concluded by writing, "There is no other person out of my Cabinet, who could have been so well prepared to carry out my views." The attorney general submitted his resignation, but Polk declined to act on it, deciding instead to hold the post open he hope that Clifford would return soon enough to resume his duties.[18] In the meantime, Polk, not surprisingly, turned to Mason to be the ad interim attorney general while continuing as navy secretary. Mason always seemed to answer Polk's call for service.

One month after Clifford's departure for Mexico, Polk revealed his intention to name a permanent head of the Attorney General's Office. This decision launched the quest for the eighth person to serve in the official family. Polk had not had time to consult with his cabinet in

March when urgent circumstances had necessitated the selection of Clifford, but he now sought its advice openly on the matter of naming a new attorney general. In a later meeting, for example, on 30 May, Polk informed the cabinet that he had narrowed the consideration to two men: Gov. Isaac Toucey of Connecticut and Gov. Peter D. Vroom of New Jersey. Although Polk did not mention it to the cabinet, he doubtless was thinking that Toucey would meet the geographical requirement of a New Englander, whereas Vroom would not. In any event, Polk did profess his preference for Toucey, because he "knew him to be my personal & political friend." The cabinet, however, favored the appointment of Vroom on the grounds that his state had not been the recipient of any significant jobs from the administration, whereas Connecticut had been. Thinking over the matter later during the day, Polk was persuaded of the important merits of the cabinet's argument and therefore wrote to Vroom that night, offering him the attorney generalship.[19]

Another installment of the story began when the president received Vroom's letter of 5 June, declining the position, although not out of public or political considerations. Instead, Vroom pleaded personal ones: "My professional engagements are so extended that I could not abandon them, at this time, without great sacrifice. The duties also, which I owe my family are such as I may not neglect." Polk evidently was not dismayed at this rejection, for he recorded the declination in only one noncommittal sentence in his diary. The next day, 8 June, the president acted with alacrity and without additional consultation of his cabinet when he penned a letter to Isaac Toucey, the man he had originally wanted, offering him the headship of the Attorney General's Office. In language almost identical to that in his letter to Vroom, Polk noted Toucey's devotion to Polk's administration and its policies and then praised Toucey's qualifications to fill the post of attorney general. Toucey responded enthusiastically in his letter of 12 June, pledging his devotion to the Polk administration and his willingness to undertake the duties offered to him "in such flattering terms." (Obviously Toucey did not know that Polk had used the same "flattering terms" in his letter to Vroom!) Toucey promised to leave Hartford the next week to take up his new responsibilities in Washington. Curiously, although Polk received this letter two days later, there is no mention of its receipt or his reaction to it in his diary. Instead, the diary simply reports on 15 June, the following day, that Polk had forwarded Toucey's nomination to the Senate.[20] With that done, the president, nine months away from the end of his administration, brought to a conclusion the realignment of cabinet personnel.

It is certainly worthy of reiteration that Polk was blessed by very few alterations in the composition of his cabinet. But there were some possible turnovers along the way. James Buchanan, for example, wanted to leave the cabinet in the fall of 1845 and again in the summer of 1846 to accept a seat on the Supreme Court bench. Yet, as noted below in chapter 6, patronage and other considerations finally did not permit him to make that enticing move, and Buchanan consequently remained in the cabinet for the entire four years. From time to time, however, being agitated over some real or imagined slight or over some clash with the president, Buchanan talked rashly of resigning; but Polk stubbornly refused to give Buchanan the satisfaction of taking such threats seriously. After a flap over some derogatory material that appeared in the *New York Herald* in February 1848, Buchanan, an acquaintance of the newspaper reporter involved, suspected that Polk would oust him from the cabinet. Buchanan told Clifford, however, that he would resign and take Walker with him before Polk would have a chance to fire him. When Clifford informed the exasperated president about this, Polk assured him that "there was not the slightest danger of his [Buchanan's] resigning." Then the president lambasted his secretary of state with these scathing words: "He cares nothing for the success or glory of my administration further than he can make it subservient to his own political aspirations."[21]

During a fleeting squabble over patronage in March 1847, concerning the appointment of generals from New York, an episode that is treated in chapter 6, Secretary Marcy attempted to utilize the threat of resignation. Both Marcy and Senator Dickinson made menacing noises about resigning their posts, but Polk was so "indignant at this attempt to bully" that he became "perfectly indifferent" about whether the two men left their positions. Of course, neither man carried out such uncharacteristic threats. One cabinet member who thought he might depart for greener political pastures was John Y. Mason. In late November 1848, as he began to make serious plans for his political future, the navy secretary contemplated running for governor of Virginia, a move that Polk encouraged. Had Mason done so and been successful, he would have had to resign before completing his full term.[22] Except for occasional flare-ups or ambitions for political rewards elsewhere, the remarkable stability and the admirable harmony of the cabinet seem not to have been disturbed.

Polk deserves more credit than he has sometimes been given for fostering continuity and concord in his official family. Although seemingly incapable of much affection, he was at least capable of demonstrating respect, and this he did with his cabinet members. Naturally there were disagreements; but considering the magnitude of the problems with which this administration dealt, it could not have been otherwise. Polk never embraced the authoritative style of leadership within the executive branch that might have created serious breaches; instead, he adopted a somewhat "softer" style in his relationship with the cabinet, which permitted a good bit of interchange and free expression. Indeed he seemed anxious to consult the department heads on virtually every matter that came before him. Needless to say, Polk initially enjoyed the distinct advantage of being the head of the cabinet by virtue of his office; this enabled him to assert and retain leadership control. But he chose not to hold on to this advantage by simply some sort of authoritative dominance. Rather, he worked with the members of the cabinet in pursuit of a high degree of group consensus and cohesion, both of which were commonly characteristic of the cabinet during the four years.[23] The task was more difficult than it might have been at other times because of the extremely divisive issues that confronted the administration and because, as delineated above, Polk did not have a completely free hand in selecting the personnel for his cabinet. Geographical and political considerations forced the president to make choices of persons whom he might not otherwise have desired. Therefore, when the six men convened with Polk for the first of hundreds of sessions, the challenge before him was to direct and guide in such a way that the group would become a harmonious and stable one.

For information and understanding about Polk's relationships with his cabinet, one turns principally to the president's meticulous diary. From late August 1845 through the remainder of his presidential term, Polk faithfully recorded a multitude of details about his administration, including hundreds of cabinet meetings. He did not give full reports, however, on every such gathering, sometimes saying merely that the cabinet had met on that particular day. One can only wonder why he chose not to reveal the deliberations of the official family at times. Moreover, there is always the question of exactly how fair the president was in writing about the discussions that had taken place at a specific meeting. Finally, one should understand that from the outset, Polk possessed a special sensitivity to Buchanan, which may have caused Polk to report much more about Buchanan's thoughts and actions than was warranted.[24] There is no denying, however, that even a somewhat hasty reading of the diary conveys the distinct impression that Buchanan was the man to watch in the cabinet.

One index of the cabinet's functioning is attendance. Polk firmly established the policy that all members should attend all sessions, unless some important and legitimate reasons precluded them from doing so. It is not surprising, therefore, that the president was usually careful to record who was absent from any of the cabinet meetings. Because of this practice, it is not difficult to establish some impressions, as well as data, about cabinet attendance. It is readily evident, for example, that the department heads were extremely faithful in attendance; personal illness and out-of-town trips were the only noticeable explanations for absences. Polk dutifully reported on the travels of all cabinet members whenever they left town for whatever reason. Two long periods of absence from Washington by Robert J. Walker irritated the president considerably. During the first of these, in October 1846, Walker actually was conducting official business for the Treasury Department; but during the second, in July and August 1847, he was away on vacation. During the latter, Polk became so agitated about excessive expenditures in one of the governmental departments that he ordered Walker back to Washington from his vacation. In a more compassionate vein, the president evinced continuing concern for the health and well-being of his cabinet members; he seemed to have genuine empathy for them when they were ill, frequently visiting them at their lodgings. On one occasion, in May 1847, he even urged Walker, who had been sick, to go on a vacation![25]

From the beginning, Polk established that there should be two cabinet meetings every week—one on Tuesday morning and one on Saturday morning. In addition, he felt compelled to call special gatherings from time to time. Combing through the diary, one is able to account for at least 364 cabinet meetings during the four years. Very rarely did Polk choose to cancel a regular meeting; and since he made only four out-of-town trips during his entire presidency, his own absences from Washington accounted for probably no more than twelve regular cabinet meetings' not being held. In any event, the fact is plain: Polk and the cabinet had an abundance of opportunities to deal with each other in the somewhat formal and official setting of a cabinet meeting. Given the fact of faithful attendance by all members, it was not possible for special relationships to develop between or among certain members without everyone else being aware of them. Likewise, the president was not able to cater to specific persons, had he been so inclined, because they were present for the deliberations more often than others were. Consequently, a sort of democratizing impact was presented by an excessive number of cabinet meetings and by an extraordinary attendance record of all members (they attended 88 percent of all meetings).[26]

Another measurement of the cabinet in relationship to the president is to note the contributions that were made by various persons in the formal meetings of the official family. A search of the diary's reports on cabinet sessions enables one to detect significant participation in the group discussion. While a heavy rate of contributions may not spell dominance, it does at least indicate a desire to participate actively in the group. It was not necessary, however, for Polk to contribute heavily in order to retain his decision-making power, but he chose to do so. Without doubt, Polk and Buchanan led the rest of the group in terms of contributions, for when the four years are considered, the two men together accounted for nearly 66 percent of all the contributions. Over time, however, both men moderated the rate of their contributions; Secretaries Walker and Marcy took up the slack, thanks to the onset of the war with Mexico. No other member of the cabinet made an appreciable rate of contributions during the deliberations of that body, with Cave Johnson proving to be the most quiescent during the four years.[27]

In Polk's view, every cabinet member was entitled to contribute to the discussion of any topic that came before the group. The Treasury secretary, for example, was not restricted to financial matters, or the attorney general to specific legal concerns. Therefore the cabinet was free, under Polk's tutelage, to contribute opinions and ideas on a vast array of issues and problems. They discussed such matters as appointments, even to their own body, and removals throughout the federal government's patronage network; relations with Congress; the details of military strategy during the Mexican War; the shifting of military commanders; the panoply of considerations surrounding the acquisition of Oregon and the subsequent establishment of territorial government there; each year's annual message from Polk to the Congress; and even the admission of California. No wonder that in the spring of 1848, when Polk needed a special treaty commissioner to go to Mexico, he picked a cabinet member. For either by participating actively or simply by listening, a member of that group had to be well informed about many aspects of the federal government.

Closely related to active participation in cabinet sessions is initiative taking, a third measure of the functioning of that forum. Here the term refers to persons who brought up points that became the focus of debate or comment by others in the cabinet meetings. There is, not unexpectedly, a connection between initiative taking and overall contributions to the deliberations. Moreover, as one might imagine, Polk dominated the initiative-taking index throughout the four years, especially from September 1845 to December 1846. Buchanan and Walker were notably active in initiative taking, however, when Polk's rate fell below the 50 percent mark. Other members of the cabinet were conspicuous by their lack of taking initiative, although they at times participated actively in the debates of the forum. The strongest personalities, Polk and Buchanan, were the persons who were most eager to take the initiative; furthermore, their roles as president and secretary of state gave them additional advantages. At times, however, both Walker and Marcy challenged them.[28] In sum, there was a healthy modification in the rate of contributions as the members of the cabinet became more and more accustomed to one another and to the cabinet's duties and responsibilities within the administration.

Moving outside the cabinet room itself, one is able to examine the initiative taking that members of the group exhibited by calling upon the president at the White House to discuss matters with him. His diary again provides the most consistent and reliable information about this. One clear conclusion is that the secretaries felt at liberty to call upon their leader frequently and regularly, and he responded by always being willing to receive them, even when he had closed his doors to all visitors. One must not discount the mutual trust and respect that seemed evident in the numerous consultations and discussions that transpired between the president and his men. The increasing contacts with Polk indicated the generally active involvement of members of the official family in the life of the administration.

Searching through the diary, one is able to derive specific references to various secretaries' calling upon Polk. Buchanan, at the outset, made the most calls upon the president, both relatively and absolutely; but subsequently, his percentage dropped in relation to that of his colleagues. Buchanan never regained his earlier high percentage, as other cabinet members demanded access to the president at the White House. In fact, during two extended periods, Secretary Marcy exceeded Buchanan both in the actual number of his visits to Polk and in percentage (or relative terms), which was a direct result of the outbreak of war with Mexico. As secretary of the navy, Mason also made more visits and had a higher percentage than did Buchanan in the January–September 1847 period. Part of Mason's access was not related directly to his Navy Department responsibilities but to the reality that Polk frequently wanted his political advice. Similarly, Bancroft took the initiative to see Polk at a level that was out of proportion to the demands of his position, a circumstance that has customarily been attributed to the unusual Bancroft-Polk connection, which seemed to entitle the former to give frequent counsel to the president. Despite claims made by others about Cave Johnson's status in the administration, the figures on visits made to the president's office on business indicate that he had less access to Polk than did anyone else in the cabinet.[29] The above discussion should enable one to visualize a steady stream of cabinet visitors who took up parts of 1,079 days of the president's time during a period of three and a half years.

Without doubt, some of those special visits to Polk's office were for purposes of voicing an opposing opinion. In the cabinet meetings themselves, there was a divergence of views; therefore the divisions in those sessions, plus a few that occurred elsewhere, constitute a fourth point of analysis of how the cabinet functioned. It should be understood that when the president reported a division, it might range from a serious direct clash to a relatively minor disagreement. The term is consequently broadly construed to encompass all references to differences within the official family. The major point that emerges from such an analysis is that there were remarkably few divisions, perhaps testimony to Polk's skill at avoiding them while at the same time permitting wide-range participation in the debates and discussions. It seems evident that antagonisms and divisive tendencies among the cabinet members did not receive much ventilation during their formal sessions.

Several noticeable things emerge from an investigation of divisions. There is no question that Polk was the man with whom to agree or disagree, though Buchanan became something of a focal point himself. When examining the proportion of agreements between the president and his men, in relation to the total number of agreements and disagreements reported, Polk and Buchanan had the worst percentage, 12.5, while Polk and Mason had the best, 82.4. As a rule, however, for most of the term, Buchanan played an independent role of opposition, especially on the Oregon controversy and again in the latter stages of the Mexican War. His isolation in the cabinet divisions did not foster reticence on his part, however, for he continued to articulate his views forcefully.[30] Indeed, at times one can only marvel at Polk's patience and tolerance. It is a tribute to both men that they were able to work together so effectively. Suffice it to say, Polk had to learn to live with challenge and conflict during his four years; certainly there was plenty of it from the Congress and from the nation at large. In the official family, however, he had a haven of support, though not without some exceptions and some tensions.

It is both fascinating and informative to turn again to the president's diary, this time for illustrations of specific ways in which he and the cabinet functioned together. Polk and his secretaries dealt with every significant matter, plus numerous insignificant ones, that came before the administration. It probably understates the situation to say that all of these men were diligent workers, not mere figureheads. One impressive example of how Polk utilized the cabinet, especially as a sounding board, was their joint effort to produce annual budgets and the president's annual message to Congress. The diary reported on each of the four experiences that the administration had with these assignments.

With an eye toward the convening of Congress in December 1845, Polk stirred himself on the matter of the annual reports from his departments and the preparation of his own first annual message. At the end of September, for example, the president devoted time in a cabinet meeting to reminding his secretaries of the importance of completing their departmental reports as soon as practicable and to warning them to make their budget appropriations estimates ''on the most economical scale, and to be as small as the public service would permit.'' In addition, Polk cautioned the cabinet members to watch carefully the estimates that were submitted to them by their bureau heads, who ''were favourable to large expenditures, and in some instances included objects which were unconstitutional, especially in regard to internal improvements.'' Apparently the secretaries were by no means prompt in complying with the president's request, because a month later he reminded them again of the necessity of submitting the reports, preferably before 15 November, so that he could ''examine them fully and minutely before they were communicated to Congress.'' Several days later an increasingly frustrated president once more begged for the reports. Evidently the department heads sent the requested information to Polk in time to be incorporated into the annual message.[31]

While fretting over the problem of a procrastinating cabinet, Polk turned his energies to the preparation of his first annual message. Seemingly, at each step of the way, Polk consulted with his secretaries about various portions of the message. As early as the cabinet meeting on 30 September, they, in the absence of Buchanan, discussed in a preliminary fashion the tariff views that might be included in the annual message. They returned to that particular topic on 1 November, when Polk read his draft dealing with the tariff and the proposed Independent Treasury. On the latter occasion, Buchanan, who was always nervous about the president's low-tariff views and about Pennsylvania's affinity for protective tariffs, raised objections. Two weeks later the president again read aloud to the cabinet all sections of the message that he had completed, including the one on the tariff. On 25 and 26 November, Polk presented his message to the cabinet for its final perusal and commentary, but the record does not reveal its specific response. After the message had been sent to Congress, a rumor that Secretary Walker had written the tariff section floated around Washington. When Mason reported this allegation to Polk, the president emphatically declared: "The fact is that the tariff part of the message and every other part of it is my own." The president admitted, however, that the cabinet had been heavily involved, for it had "closely scrutinized, discussed, and examined in all its parts." Nevertheless, Polk insisted that the results from this were only "changes of phraseology in some of its parts."[32]

The other topic, included in the message, that disturbed the harmony a bit was Oregon, largely because Secretary Buchanan attempted to moderate Polk's bold claims. Apparently on 25 October, when the president first read to the cabinet his section on Oregon, Buchanan remained quiet. Instead, the secretary chose to confer in private with Polk, rather than utilizing the public forum of the cabinet sessions; at least that is the strong impression conveyed by the diary's entries. On 4 November and again on the twentieth, Buchanan went to Polk's office to talk to him about the Oregon portion of the proposed message, both times trying to get the president to soften some of his statements. During the two days that the cabinet reviewed the entire message, Buchanan submitted some penciled modifications of the section treating the Oregon question, most of which Polk rejected. No wonder "Mr. Buchanan seemed to be depressed in spirits." In any event, the annual message went forward to Congress with Polk's views indelibly stamped upon it.[33] Although the cabinet did not shape the final document in major ways, still it must have appreciated being a vital part of the consulting and revising process.

When the fall of 1846 arrived, both the tariff question and the Oregon issue had been resolved, much to the delight of Polk and many others. Nonetheless, when the cabinet began discussing the proposed second annual message, Buchanan, saying that it did not reflect his views, took the occasion to object to Polk's section on tariffs. The president simply conceded the difference of opinion and moved on to other matters. Upon reading a paragraph about providing for the surveying of the Oregon boundary line, Polk was advised by Buchanan that it would likely revive hostile debates in Congress over Oregon; whereupon the president, apparently lacking a strong commitment to the project, deleted the paragraph. Naturally, the Mexican War was of primary concern to the president and his men, but the sketchy extant record in the diary indicates that there was little discussion about it in the formal sessions of the cabinet that were devoted to a review of the annual message. Instead, several secretaries, especially Buchanan and Walker, conferred with Polk privately about territorial ambitions. Unless the president simply failed to render a full report of what transpired, it appears that the cabinet devoted less time and energy to the 1846 message than had been true in 1845.[34]

In 1847, unlike the preceding year, Polk exhibited great concern over the annual reports of the cabinet members, especially their estimates of budget appropriations. Presumably, since the actual fighting in Mexico had already ended by fall, Polk was extremely anxious to pare federal governmental outlays. He began asking his secretaries in late September for their annual reports and budget estimates, but he received no tangible response until early November. Throughout the latter month, Polk had continuing conversations with cabinet members about their reports and budgetary requests, particularly with Secretary Marcy, whose estimates alarmed both the president and the Treasury secretary. At Marcy's suggestion, Polk called in various bureau heads from the War Department and pressured them to reduce their projections of financial needs; and needless to say, these subalterns yielded to the president's insistence upon restraints. By the time the annual message neared its final phase of preparation, Polk had received reports from all of his cabinet secretaries.[35]

The 1847 annual message spawned some controversy and debate within the official family, nearly all of which revolved around Mexico and the continuing prospect of warfare. Polk followed his customary pattern of consulting both with the cabinet as a whole and with individual members. Such approaches brought him into conflict with Buchanan and Walker. The dispute raged essentially over the question of the future of United States involvement in Mexico, especially as it related to territorial acquisitions. Polk staked out his traditional position that California and New Mexico were definitely to be retained by the United States, whereas Buchanan opted for the "All Mexico" position, or something closely akin to it. When this discussion first erupted in a cabinet session on 9 November, Polk noted in his diary Buchanan's changing position, adding the analysis that "since he has considered himself as a candidate for the Presidency it is probable he looks at the subject with different considerations in view from those which he entertained before that time." Nevertheless, Polk resolutely concluded, "His change of opinion will not alter my views." A single paragraph— an important one concerning the future policy of the United States toward Mexico if no peace were forthcoming—absorbed the attention and literary talents of Polk, Buchanan, Mason, and Clifford. Walker sided with Buchanan's version, not unexpectedly, and Polk surmised that the majority of the cabinet temporarily did. He therefore worked in consultation with two or three members to revise and rewrite his draft, eventually being confident of support from Johnson, Clifford, Mason, and later Marcy. By 4 December, the date of the last formal cabinet consultation, Polk had satisfactorily worked out the impasse, at least in his own eyes, by stating that if Mexico continued to fight, the United States *might* establish control over more than California and New Mexico.[36] With that, the third annual message was ready to be laboriously copied by clerks and then forwarded to Congress.

There is no question that Polk lavished attention and effort upon the departmental annual reports and upon his own fourth and final annual message. Doubtless he sensed the importance of leaving his presidential term with as impressive a budget and speech as possible. Before everything had been completed, the cabinet had become more involved than it had been in previous years. Much as in 1847, in the fall of 1848 Polk began to pressure his secretaries for their annual reports, with the stern admonition to keep budget estimates "as small as was compatable [sic] with the absolute necessities of the public service." As before, he warned his cabinet members about the inflated budget requests that various bureau heads submitted, "calculating that they will be cut down and reduced by Congress." Moreover, as the president observed, sometimes the bureau heads believed that their own prestige and status depended on the monies they had at their disposal. In his final cautionary reminders, the president asserted that these bureau heads were not responsible to the public and that they were "generally Federalists, and in favour of large expenditures." As in 1847, Polk once more had problems with Secretary Marcy's departmental requests, which Polk deemed excessive. His greatest irritation arose over the violation of his directive that no monies should be appropriated for internal improvements. Upon closely examining certain budget requests, the president discovered several hundred thousand dollars that were to be reappropriated, from previously unspent funds, for support of river and harbor improvements. Indignant that such "had been smuggled into the estimates," Polk "at once directed them to be struck out." Having resolved that difficulty, the president continued to stress to the cabinet the importance of positioning the government so that it could begin to pay off some of the national debt. Eventually, Secretary Walker, after scrutinizing the budget estimates, calculated that there would be enough money available to designate about a half million dollars for debt payment. The whole cabinet unanimously agreed that this should be provided for in the proposed annual budget, a position that immensely pleased Polk, who wanted to leave office in true Jacksonian style by attacking the problem of governmental indebtedness.[37]

As the president and the cabinet worked together on the fourth annual message, November 1848 turned out to be a very busy month for them, because they were unpleasantly aware that their party had just lost the presidency to the Whigs, who would assume control the following March. In fact, on election day, 7 November, Polk made his first presentation to the cabinet of portions of his proposed message to Congress. On that occasion, Buchanan raised some objections to the views expressed on such economic questions as the tariff and internal improvements, his perennial areas of disagreement with Polk. Secretaries Marcy and Toucey made some minor comments, whereas Secretary Mason, who could always be counted upon by Polk, praised the message as "the ablest & most interesting" that the president had sent to Congress. It is perhaps no surprise that Mason, sometimes accompanied by Walker, spent a good bit of time at the White House, working directly with Polk on the rewriting and condensing of the various drafts. Ten days after the president's initial presentation of the message to the cabinet, Buchanan spent nearly four hours at Polk's office, reading and examining it; the next day he returned with suggestions for modifications. On two separate occasions, Secretary Marcy visited the White House for extended periods of reviewing the manuscript; on the second visit, he was joined by Attorney General Toucey. Before the month had ended, every secretary had become actively involved in the final preparation of the annual message. But Buchanan, who left town for a visit to Pennsylvania at this juncture, removed himself from participating as much as he might have desired. As soon as he returned, however, he was once more busy consulting and being consulted in regard to Polk's proposed document. The only apparent hitch in progress toward the final draft was the tardiness of the receipt of various pieces of statistical information from the secretaries, a problem that had been rectified by 29 November. Finally on 1 December, almost an entire month after the first presentation, Polk read the revised version to his official family. Much to the president's dismay, Buchanan revived his earlier misgivings about the inclusion of the economic portions, a position that gained the support of Secretary Walker but no others. Marcy was the only cabinet member who refrained from jumping into the lively and extended exchange that day, which Polk terminated with his contention that it was now too late to make significant changes in the final draft. Three days later, Mason, along with various clerks, assisted Polk with proofreading the message before it was sent over to Congress.[38] That having been accomplished, the president and his men could relax briefly, content that for the last time they had succeeded in producing a worthy report to the nation.

Over the course of four years, the president also sent a number of special messages to Congress; almost without exception, cabinet members were involved in being Polk's sounding board, by listening and then by making specific contributions to the wording and the substance. Unlike more modern presidents, who have surrounded themselves with a small army of aides and writers who prepare statements and speeches, Polk had no such staff; therefore he utilized his cabinet in this manner.

As further indication of their close dependency and involvement, Polk made a practice of assisting cabinet members in their duties and responsibilities when appropriate. This was done continually during his term, but there were special times when he took a more direct hand in the conduct of the departments. One such instance occurred in the spring of 1847, after Secretary Marcy had brought a great amount of detailed information about his department to the president's attention. Polk took pity, believing that the secretary was "greatly oppressed with the duties of his office" and that his subordinates were not very dependable. Naturally the conduct of the war itself forced the president to be intimately acquainted with the functioning of the four most pertinent departments—War, Navy, State, and Treasury.[39]

Having an apparently prodigious mind for minute details and an accurate memory, the president astounded his cabinet members and others with his knowledge of the bureaucracy of the federal government. On one occasion, in July 1847, Polk even managed to gain the upper hand on Buchanan. At issue was a *pro forma* letter, prepared at the State Department for Polk's signature and addressed to the emperor of Brazil, concerning the recall of the Brazilian minister from Washington. Polk objected to a portion of the letter, which assured the emperor that he could place full credence in whatever the minister might say in Polk's behalf. Buchanan insisted that this was the customary statement and had therefore been routinely included by one of the clerks in the State Department. Whereupon Polk, in an unusual teasing mood, declared that he would give Buchanan a basket of champagne if the secretary was correct. Buchanan eagerly accepted the friendly wager and rushed off to the State Department to find the appropriate precedent in the files. Buchanan soon returned to Polk's office and, in the presence of other cabinet members, read aloud a letter written by President Jackson to the king of France. Upon reading it, however, Buchanan quickly realized that it was not a correct precedent for the letter to Brazil, and thereafter he searched the letter book in vain for an accurate model. Finally conceding, the secretary offered the president the gift of champagne, but Polk laughingly refused it, content enough with having proven his mastery of "the forms & details" of the various departments. Later,

Buchanan returned with a newly drafted and revised letter to the emperor of Brazil, which Polk promptly signed.[40]

Some fourteen months later (in September 1848) the president was perturbed when four of his cabinet members departed on trips, leaving only Mason and Toucey behind. Even though Cave Johnson had returned by mid month, Polk found himself handling a tremendous number of details, made necessary by the absence of his departmental secretaries. Near the end of the month, Polk was moved to brag about how well he had administered the government without the aid and assistance of his full cabinet: "Indeed, I have become so familiar with the duties and workings of the Government, not only upon general principles, but in most of its minute details, that I find but little difficulty in doing this. I have made myself acquainted with the duties of the subordinate officers, and have probably given more attention to details than any of my predecessors." Even allowing for some hyperbole, Polk's statement contained a considerable amount of truth.[41] Although historical evidence does not definitely make the point, it appears that the secretaries did not bristle at the president's intervention in their departments while they were away on vacation or perhaps even while they were in town at their respective desks. Assuming that to be true, it is further testimony to the impressive mutual respect and dependency that Polk and his men had for each other.

One final relationship between Polk and the cabinet to be considered, and only briefly, is social contact. By this is meant those occasions when the president and one of his secretaries were together in a social, nonofficial, nonworking context. It is admittedly difficult to discern with great precision when Polk and his cabinet members were merely enjoying fellowship and hospitality without governmental concerns bothering them, but the diary does record many instances that apparently were simply social meetings. Going to church with the president, taking a carriage or horseback ride with him, dining with him, or even going on vacation with him are examples of areas of social contact. Cabinet members, of course, frequently accompanied Polk on ceremonial occasions, such as funerals, cornerstone layings, and college commencements, but these are omitted from consideration here. The many opportunities for socializing with the president gave his secretaries further access to him. It is virtually impossible to know if any of the cabinet members actively sought to cultivate friendly, personal relations with Polk; if so, they evidently met with little success. To some extent, perhaps protocol dictated; but more than likely, Polk's personality demanded that the initiative come from him in almost all instances.

On the basis of a survey of the president's diary, it should not be surprising to learn that among the departmental heads, Mason appears to have had the most social contact with Polk, while Cave Johnson was second. These two men already had friendly relationships with Polk before he became president, and these connections did not alter during the four years. Repeatedly, Polk turned to these two old comrades for companionship and hospitality. The president only took four trips outside of Washington during his administration; and he invited Mason to travel with him on two of them, the August 1846 vacation at Fortress Monroe, Virginia, and the May–June 1847, trip to Chapel Hill, North Carolina. A few weeks after returning from the latter jaunt, Polk went on a tour of northeastern states, accompanied by Attorney General Clifford and part of the time by Secretary Buchanan. But that was a ''working'' vacation, in the sense that Polk was trying to bolster party support in that region and to improve his own standing there. The president's final trip was to Bedford Springs, Pennsylvania, and Berkeley Springs, Virginia, in August 1848, on which no cabinet members accompanied him, a break with his customary pattern.

Although Cave Johnson did not travel with Polk on any of these occasions, he has the distinction of probably having dined with the president more often than any other member of the cabinet. Perhaps Polk reckoned that Johnson and he shared similar Tennessee culinary preferences.[42] All members of the cabinet, of course, dined with the president on occasion, some events being more formal than others. Curiously enough, they were usually not very successful in getting Polk to share their table, for there are only two recorded examples of the president's having gone out to eat at the residence of one of his secretaries: a January 1846 dinner at Bancroft's and an April 1847 repast at Mason's. So while the breaking of bread was one form of socializing with cabinet members, it was customarily done in the setting of the presidential mansion.[43]

Other than his daily walks, Polk's only other recreational activity was horseback and carriage rides. Slightly more than a dozen instances when cabinet members joined Polk for such outings appear to have been merely social events. Cave Johnson won this race also, although Bancroft, had he remained in the cabinet longer, would probably have emerged as the most frequent equestrian adventurer. Of the original six members of the cabinet, Walker and Buchanan never had the pleasure of a carriage or horseback ride, for social purposes, with the president—at least there is no mention of such in Polk's diary. Although Johnson had more such outings than did any of his colleagues, Mason and Bancroft seemed to have had adventures that were slightly more interesting. On a Friday afternoon in late April 1846, Mason picked up the president for a carriage ride out to watch the fishermen on the Potomac; afterwards, Polk visited at Mason's residence. About four months later, Bancroft took Polk on a carriage ride out to the Maryland home of Francis P. Blair, for an extremely interesting visit with the deposed newspaper editor. Incidentally, this trip was only the second time that the president had been outside of the District of Columbia since arriving in Washington in February 1845. In May 1845 he had visited Mount Vernon.[44] Generally speaking, the horseback and carriage rides were uneventful outings, opportunities to get away momentarily from the press of duties. Strangely enough, there is no record of the president's having gone with any cabinet member on such excursions during 1848, his last full year in office. As a matter of fact, Polk's social contacts with the cabinet in that year appear to have been fewer than in earlier years, for no apparent reason.

Throughout his presidential tenure, Polk was a faithful and regular churchgoer, usually attending Presbyterian services. It is noteworthy, however, that there are only three recorded instances of cabinet members' accompanying Polk to church. Buchanan went in November 1845 and again in November two years later; Clifford accompanied Polk in September 1847 to the Episcopal church to hear Bishop James H. Otey of Tennessee preach.[45] The paucity of examples suggests that Polk preferred not to mix religion with professional personages; indeed, he almost always went with some family member, usually his wife. Further, one might note that his secretaries evidently chose not to take advantage of the opportunity to have access to him through church services. Perhaps Polk made it clear to them, directly or indirectly, that he did not look kindly upon such maneuvers. Finally, one could wonder whether the cabinet members had any intention of following Polk's noble example of attending Sunday worship and therefore stayed away, lest they be pressured into going to church with him.

Curiously enough, the personal illness of the secretaries offered opportunities for contact between them and the president. There were repeated instances of cabinet members being afflicted with maladies of various kinds. Of the six original members of the official family, only Johnson and Buchanan seemed to have escaped illness—according to the president's accounts in his diary.[46] During the year 1846, both Mason and Bancroft suffered on occasion, a fact that brought the president repeatedly to their doors on errands of compassion. In the following year, Polk was faithful in calling upon Marcy and Walker, especially the former, who received four presidential visits in the month of August. Polk went to check on both Marcy and Walker in early 1848, when they again were stricken by some malady.[47] From the recorded examples of the president's going out to call on his ailing brothers, one senses that he did this not simply as an official duty but instead out of genuine concern for them. He worried about his cabinet members, and he expressed this concern in an unassuming ministry of visitation. The cold, calculating, indifferent man that has so frequently been depicted is not evident here; perhaps his own sometimes frail health engendered sympathy for the members of his cabinet.

In sickness and in health, Polk and his men stayed together and worked harmoniously during four immensely trying years. It is no secret that Polk's effective administering of the government was heavily dependent upon the cabinet, whose advice, aid, and support he constantly sought. There were differences, suspicions, and antagonisms from time to time, to be sure, but the prevailing theme was loyalty and duty. All of these feelings and attitudes were exhibited somewhat poignantly during the week before Polk and his cabinet were to vacate their offices to Zachary Taylor and the Whigs. There arose among the cabinet secretaries the delicate question as to whether they could, with propriety, call upon Taylor, who had just arrived in town, before Taylor had paid a formal visit to Polk. Buchanan, not surprisingly, was the only one to hold to the view that the cabinet members were free to do as they chose on this matter. But as a sort of last request, the soon-to-retire Polk pleaded that it would indeed be improper for any of his men to visit with president-elect Taylor before Taylor and Polk had officially conferred, for "if my Cabinet called on Gen'l Taylor before he called on me, I should feel that I had been deserted by my own political family." The record shows that the cabinet members did not abandon their respected and admired leader; instead, they followed the protocol he requested.[48] In other words, here, as in a multitude of other examples across the years, the cabinet members did their duty and remained loyal to Polk. Throughout his tenure as chief executive, he derived added confidence from his "own political family," thereby enabling him to wage congressional wars, diplomatic wars, shooting wars, and patronage wars and "to be *myself* President of the U.S."

3

★ ★ ★ ★ ★

PRELUDE TO
EXPANSIONISM: TEXAS

Polk became an expansionist leader, whether he had intended to be or not. The "problem" of Texas forced him to confront the matter of the West even before he had been inaugurated as president or had selected his cabinet members. Luckily for expansionists, Polk was an avid supporter of most, if not all, their plans and aspirations. The annexation of Texas set the new president on an expansionist course from which he did not deviate and secured for him the reputation of being a foreign-policy president. For his activities and accomplishments in expanding the geographical boundaries of the nation, Polk is remembered—sometimes with admiration, sometimes with harsh criticism.

The acquisition of the Republic of Texas by the United States occurred before the ideas of Manifest Destiny had been fully refined and completed. Even prior to the implementation of other expansionist enterprises, there were particular concerns and motivations that impinged upon and influenced the Texas story. In that regard, one recent study has boldly concluded: "The intensity and extent of white racism throughout the nation created a climate of fear that facilitated the addition of the lone star of Texas to the flag of the United States."[1] Racial considerations were readily apparent on the part of most southerners who desired the Texas region in order to assure the expansion of slavery and thereby guarantee its preservation. Such advocates were understandably disturbed by rumors that British abolitionists were seeking to convince Texans to eliminate slavery in their republic. Meanwhile, various northern leaders were attracted to annexation. The appeal here was that Texas would function as a magnet to draw away slaves from the older states, those closest to the nonslave states; in the process, or so the argument went, free blacks would likewise follow the migration of slaves to the western region. The perpetuation of slavery there would assure northerners that they need not fear being inundated by slaves who would move into their states after gaining freedom as a consequence of the economic collapse of slavery. Hence, northern racial prejudice could be dealt with by the prospect of the removal of the possibility of having large numbers of blacks congregate in cities of that region. Senator Robert J. Walker of Mississippi did much to convince northerners of the validity of this view of Texas annexation.[2]

Bigotry played a key role in the movement to bring Texas into the Union, but there were also economic motivations. Many supporters expressed the conviction that the development of a cotton empire in Texas would enable the United States to obtain a monopoly on raw cotton. Such a situation would thereby make Britain dependent upon America and would assure the future economic prosperity and development of America. Later, President Tyler claimed that economic concern, rather than the protection of slavery, was his primary interest in Texas.[3] Be that as it may, some supporters of annexation undeniably had pocketbook interests for motivation, more than world politics or domestic racism. As with most momentous developments, the Texas story had a mixture of rationales in its background.

Ever since the days of its successful though bloody quest for independence in the 1830s, Texas had desired linkage with the United States; but as president, neither Jackson nor Van Buren gave encouragement to this goal. Instead, it was John Tyler, the Virginia Democrat turned Whig, who fostered overt maneuvers to bring about annexation. Tyler utilized Duff Green, first as a secret agent to Great Britain and then, in 1844, as a consul in Galveston, to promote the annexation cause; Green warned repeatedly about British interference in Texas and particularly about the threat of abolitionism. Meanwhile, Tyler's secretary of state, Abel P. Upshur, a rigid Virginian with strong concerns about the preservation and encouragement of slavery, made moves to bring Texas to the treaty table. Eventually succeeding in his endeavors to negotiate, Upshur was on the verge of the actual signing of an annexation agreement with Texas when he was killed in a freak accident on the Potomac River.[4]

In the wake of that tragedy, President Tyler turned to John C. Calhoun to head the State Department. Calhoun successfully concluded the treaty with Texas, but then he destroyed its chances for ratification. His letter to the British minister in Washington became the rallying point for all those who opposed the acquisition of Texas out of fear of the further expansion of black slavery. Once annexation had become yoked to the slavery question, the treaty was placed in great jeopardy. Consequently, probably few political observers were surprised when it failed to secure the two-thirds vote required in the Senate.[5]

Equally important to the unfolding of the Texas story was the simple reality that 1844 was a presidential election year. Democrats took a bold stance in favor of western expansion, including the "reannexation" of Texas; shoved aside the tainted Van Buren; and embraced James K. Polk, a representative of the expansionist wing. The Whig party, under the leadership of Henry Clay, tried to walk the tightrope on the Texas question, fearing defections from both of the regional components of the party. As the campaign progressed, Clay modified his position to be slightly more favorable toward Texas, in the hope of attracting support in the South and the West; by doing so, however, he impaired his chances in the Northeast.

Polk's victory in November was interpreted by many as an endorsement for expansionism, particularly the annexation of Texas. Although there is room for disputing this assessment of the election results, nevertheless President Tyler and Secretary Calhoun apparently saw it this way and therefore took action to stir the Texas cauldron again. Meanwhile, outside of the United States, opinion varied about the prospects and merits of Texas annexation. The Mexican minister in Washington was so alarmed by Polk's election that he feared an imminent threat of annexation and advised his government to provoke a confrontation with the Tyler administration. Notable Texas leaders had continued to cling to the hope that an alternative to annexation would be found, whereby Mexico would recognize the independence of Texas, and Britain and France would assist in additional negotiations with Mexico. Some political leaders in Texas opposed outright the annexation to the United States, while others straddled the fence or remained undecided. The majority of public opinion probably favored linking up with the United States, particularly after the election of Polk.[6] Britain and France seemed confused as to their precise role in the continuing drama of Texas; whereas both countries hoped to bring about Mexican acceptance of the independence of Texas, neither wanted to become involved in a war or in overt conflict to protect Texas and guarantee its sovereignty. Britain, especially, urged the Texans to resist annexation to the United States. Ironically, the more that was learned about European interest in and involvement with the Texas-Mexico problem, the more agitated many American leaders became about pushing for bringing Texas into the Union.[7]

Andrew Jackson Donelson, who had been sent as chargé to Texas by the Tyler administration in the late fall of 1844, pressed upon Calhoun and the president the urgency of immediately annexing Texas. They seemed to need little encouragement, for, in fact, emboldened by the election outcome, they opted to seek the passage of the earlier discredited treaty through the device of a joint resolution of both houses of the Congress. In his annual message in December, Tyler urged the immediate annexation of Texas, because the election of Polk had proved that the American people desired it and because Texan interest in annexation had not changed. It can easily be argued that Tyler and Calhoun needlessly complicated the annexation question by embracing the strategy of dusting off the old treaty and pushing for its acceptance. Such a move caused the animosities of the spring to reemerge and old wounds to be reopened.[8] In any event, the legislative branch of the federal government quickly became the battleground over competing ideas about the admission of Texas.

The intricacies of the debates and the parliamentary maneuverings need not detain us, but one important point should be emphasized: namely, that the House and the Senate were not in agreement on the process of annexation. In the House there was noticeable criticism of the proposed legislation that the Tyler administration was offering; consequently, various proposals circulated as possible strategies for the admission of Texas. In late January, by a fairly close vote, the House finally agreed to bring Texas in as a state right away but to leave the boundary question to a later settlement and to ask the Texans to handle matters in regard to debt and public land themselves. Rejoicing over the passage of this measure was short-lived, however, in light of the reality of a tough fight in the Senate.[9]

Although the Whigs enjoyed a slight edge in the Senate, the focal point of the controversy there lay, not with them, but with Democratic Senator Thomas Hart Benton of Missouri. Senate Democrats obviously had to unite before they could have any hope of passing a resolution on annexation. It was almost predictable that the Senate would refuse to accept the House-endorsed annexation measure, so Benton reintroduced his earlier scheme, which required that a new treaty with Texas be negotiated and that Mexico consent. But under intense pressure from Democrats back home and from Democratic leaders in Washington, Benton changed his course and presented a new proposal, which called simply for the president to appoint five commissioners to negotiate the terms of annexation with Texas. While many Democrats rallied to this new Benton measure, Calhoun voiced his strong opposition to it, a move that threw the Senate into further disarray. Suddenly the focus shifted from Benton to Senator Robert J. Walker of Mississippi. Realizing the impasse that was currently characterizing the progress of Texas legislation, Walker took steps to devise a compromise. Simply stated, he advocated that the House-passed resolution on annexation be accepted, as amended by the Benton proposal. The president therefore could opt for either the immediate admission, as provided in the House bill, or for a new negotiation with Texas, as stipulated by the Benton proposal. It was a masterful compromise, though troublesome to different persons and factions within the Senate. Finally, on the night of 27 February, the Senate accepted the Walker-inspired compromise, and on the following day the House gave its approval.[10]

On 1 March, President Tyler signed the Texas-annexation measure. But surprising almost everyone in Washington, he did not stop merely with the formal signing of the bill. Instead, Tyler decided, during the closing moments of his presidential term, to take decisive action, thanks in large measure to Calhoun's persuasive arm twisting. Grasping for some share of historical immortality hours before his successor was to take office, Tyler sent instructions to Donelson to notify Texan officials that Texas was to be annexed immediately (if they approved) under the terms of the House resolution, not under the Benton proposal for commissioners and new negotiations.[11] Neither Benton and his supporters nor Polk were quite prepared for the elusive move that Tyler made. But such were the vagaries of personal vanity and domestic politics.

In fairness to the record, however, it must be quickly acknowledged that Polk was not an innocent, uninvolved spectator during the closing days of debate in the Congress or during Tyler's decision to act promptly on the matter of annexation. In truth, there was much argument, then in Washington and subsequently among historians, over the exact nature and character of Polk's influence upon the outcome of the legislative story. It is undeniable that he dipped his oar into the streams of the Texas controversy upon arriving at the capital in mid February; but what is debatable is to what extent he did so during those anxious days.

Contributing significantly to the confusion ever since are letters written by Senator Benjamin Tappan and by Francis P. Blair in the summer of 1848, in which they accused Polk of having led them and others, in February and March of 1845, to believe that he preferred the Benton plan of new negotiations with Texas. How much credence one should lend to letters penned three and a half years after the fact in the midst of an increasingly controversial presidential campaign is a bothersome problem. Polk naturally defended himself in 1848, primarily in his diary and in conversations with cabinet members, by dismissing the public letters written by Tappan and by Blair as political devices, designed to aid the Free Soil candidacy of Van Buren. Moreover, Polk correctly noted that at no time prior to the publication of these letters had either man raised any objections to the Texas-annexation procedures or made any accusations that Polk had deceived them.[12] One cannot help wondering why, in the summer of 1848, this now ancient and almost irrelevant issue surfaced, unless it was for some political motivations.

Clearly, Polk arrived in Washington in mid February 1845 very much supporting congressional action on Texas annexation; political leaders would have been duly shocked if he had not given strong endorsement to bringing Texas into the Union. He, in fact, did have conversations with a number of influential members of Congress in the hectic days immediately prior to his own inauguration. He claimed later, probably too innocently, that he had not had the time or inclination to study either the House resolution or the Benton proposal and that he was simply anxious that one of them be adopted by both houses of the Congress. He subsequently conceded that he had indicated that if the Benton plan were endorsed, he would accept it and would appoint an outstanding group of treaty commissioners. Some people thought, and understandably, that he thus was in favor of the Benton proposal for new negotiations, and they conveyed that impression to other members of Congress. There is also some likelihood that Polk had a hand in working out the elements of the Walker compromise and that he exerted pressure upon Walker to introduce it into the Senate deliberations.[13]

It is obvious that congressional politicos were treated to a sort of preview of the caginess and craftiness of the man who was about to become president, for he kept everyone in Washington guessing about his precise views on how best to annex Texas. At that time, as on later occasions, some of these legislative notables thought that they heard one thing, only to be surprised and dismayed later. Suffice it to say, the story took a sudden unexpected twist when Tyler acted with uncustomary decisiveness and stole some of Polk's thunder. Tyler sent Calhoun over to confer with the president-elect, but Polk characteristically refused to comment one way or the other on the matter of preference between the Benton approach or the House resolution. When he was inaugurated, however, some people thought he would immediately countermand the instructions and orders that had been sent to Donelson in Texas. He certainly could have done so, but he deliberately chose not to. As he explained later in the summer to his friend Senator William Haywood, he accepted Tyler's decision and saw no reason to scuttle it.

It appears that Polk was content to let Tyler take some of the heat off of him, for Polk got what he wanted without having to take a bold stand in favor of the House version of annexation. Once he had assembled his new cabinet, Polk laid before that body the matter of how to proceed on the Texas question; whereupon the cabinet agreed unanimously that the plan that had already been implemented by Tyler should be followed. Polk and his advisers had their hands strengthened by the reaction of the Mexican minister in Washington, Juan N. Almonte, who delivered a strong note of protest against the annexation resolutions of Congress and vowed that Mexico would continue to seek to recover Texas. Thereafter Almonte asked for his passport, and the break with Mexico was henceforth unreconcilable.[14]

Without hesitation, President Polk took charge of the Texas matter. Even before all of the members of his cabinet had been confirmed by the Senate, he wrote an informal letter to chargé Donelson, advising him to wait for further word from the new administration before taking any actions in Texas relative to annexation proceedings. As noted above, Polk did convene the cabinet, as soon as it had been officially approved, to discuss the urgent problem of Texas. Although agreeing with Tyler's decision, the cabinet decided to modify slightly Donelson's original instructions, to the effect that now he was to insist that the Texans accept the terms of annexation unconditionally. Calhoun and Tyler had earlier indicated that Texan leaders might amend the annexation resolution in some manner. Meanwhile, as time drew near for the adjournment of the special session of the Senate on 20 March, Benton men became increasingly suspicious of Polk, for he had not yet forwarded any nominations for Texas treaty commissioners to the Senate. It was then that they realized that the new president was not going to overturn Tyler's plan of following the House alternative.[15]

Polk, however, did not have leisure moments to worry about the Bentonians and their hurt feelings, for he was busily formulating his tactics to accomplish the admission of the Republic of Texas. Apparently not content to rely solely upon Donelson, the president sent special agents to Texas. Congressman Archibald Yell of Arkansas, a long-time political confidant of Polk's, and Charles A. Wickliffe of Kentucky, formerly a member of Tyler's cabinet, rushed to Texas to assist Donelson in efforts to whip up a clamor among the residents there in behalf of immediate annexation. A fourth man joined the other three to round out Polk's Texas quartet; he was Robert F. Stockton, a young and aggressive commodore in the navy. Much of the president's haste about promoting an agreement was related to repeated reports and fears about British and French involvement in the Texas-Mexico sphere. During the critical spring and summer months of 1845, these servants of the Polk administration played a highly visible and somewhat controversial role in regard to matters in Texas.

When Donelson visited Texas in April, he was cautious and circumspect, especially on the matter of what western and southern boundary the United States might support for Texas. But when he returned to Texas in May, now in the company of the special agents, the message to Texan leaders was different, for the Polk quartet sang assurances to President Jones and others that the Rio Grande would be guaranteed by the government in Washington. In addition, Yell and Wickliffe, in particular, sometimes aided by Stockton, attended annexation meetings in various Texas villages and did all that they dared do to sway public opinion in favor of immediate union with the United States. Their eagerness to carry out Polk's directives was enhanced by continued rumblings of possible British arrangements with Mexico, whereby that country would recognize the independence of Texas, at long last. Warming to the challenges of the Texas environment, Polk's servants made extravagant promises to the officials and the citizenry— primarily promises of substantial federal monies to promote important internal improvements in Texas (rivers, harbors, fortifications, lighthouses, etc.) and assurances of federal patronage.[16] Such inducements must have turned the heads of a number of important and lesser persons, but more captivating for many perhaps was the allure of possible military action and adventure seemingly promised by Commodore Stockton.

Stockton is one of those minor flamboyant figures who struts across the historical stage for a moment or two, leaving confusion and controversy in his path thereafter. Ever since 1845, historians have tried to fit the pieces of the puzzle together in some meaningful pattern, but without much success. This much seems to be above dispute, however: the Polk administration sent Stockton and his ship to Texas, much as it commissioned Yell and Wickliffe, to ascertain what was going on in that republic and to make regular reports of his findings to Washington.[17] Imbued with excessive zeal, Stockton went beyond his apparent instructions, although some claimed then and do so now that he had special secret directives—for which there is no extant evidence. The young commodore no doubt was a troublemaker, and he relished the role of alerting Texans to the imminent danger of a possible Mexican invasion of their borders. Perhaps Polk, much like President Monroe, who sent Jackson to Florida in 1818, figured that Stockton would be a man of action, even without specific encouragement or official instructions.

In that regard, Polk could not have been disappointed. Stockton talked boldly with President Anson Jones and others, especially Gen. Sidney Sherman of the Texas militia, about recruiting an expeditionary force for purposes of seizing the Mexican port of Matamoros and of securing the Rio Grande boundary for Texas. Historians have been dependent upon Jones's account of the story, there being no other available source. Accusing Stockton and his adventurous allies of trying to manufacture a war with Mexico, Jones reached the not-unexpected conclusion that this is what Polk wanted. Jones wrote his version of this controversial matter some five years after the fact, at a time when he was bitterly disappointed over the misfortunes of his own political career. One's attitude toward Polk invariably determines how seriously Jones's statements are to be treated. Granted the cunning, calculating ways of the president, it still seems to be asking too much to insist that Polk wanted a war with Mexico in the summer of 1845, even before Texas had formally entered the Union. Stockton was guilty of improprieties and zealousness as he whipped up military enthusiasm among the Texans, to be sure, but his words were louder than his actions. As a matter of fact, his reconnaissance voyage along the gulf to the Rio Grande was a comical failure that found him returning to Galveston after only a short venture. Given the immense problems of communication between Texas and Washington, Polk and his cabinet could not have been aware of exactly what Stockton was doing—that is, in time to order him to cease or else to add further encouragement. Thus the commodore was relatively free to improvise and to act on whims, and he seemed to be disposed to do so. The only restraint upon him was the presence of Donelson, who in fact did move to curtail Stockton's boisterous statements and potential actions. Ever the careful diplomat, Donelson warned Stockton that he must not engage in any kind of quasi-military activities and must instead adhere to the clear-cut defensive policy of the Polk administration.[18] Considering Donelson's consistent position, one is persuaded that it was he, rather than Stockton, who reflected the actual views of Polk, Bancroft, and Buchanan. In any event, Stockton's days were numbered in Texas, and by midsummer his theatrics were over as he headed away from the Gulf Coast to the Atlantic. Eventually, Stockton reemerged in the drama of the winning of the West, when he appeared off the coast of California.

In addition to being troubled by Stockton's antics, Donelson was perturbed by the initial resistance that he met among certain Texan leaders when he discussed the annexation proposal with them. Especially bothersome were Sam Houston's objections, though he mainly quibbled over details; it appeared that Houston actually favored Benton's approach, which would have given Texan officials some leverage in pushing for certain considerations. Within a few weeks, however, Houston had changed his position, evidently in response to the recognizable ground swell of proannexation opinion in Texas. As a matter of fact, Houston set out in early May on a trek to Tennessee to visit Jackson, doubtless to confer with him about annexation. After a conversation in Galveston with Houston, Yell reported to Polk that the former president of Texas, "the Power behind the Throne, greater than the Throne itself," was supportive of annexation; *"he is now safe."* Likewise, President Jones felt the impact of public pressure, although he continued to stall and delay, hoping for British successes in dealings with Mexico over the promise of recognizing Texas independence. Apparently even threatened with physical harm, Jones, in mid April, decided to call a special session of the Texas Congress to consider the annexation proposal from the United States; subsequently, he also summoned a special convention to ratify or reject annexation. But before either of these two bodies could assemble, word arrived from Mexico that Texan independence was now recognized. An elated Jones made a public announcement of this development, declared an end to war between the two countries, and laid plans to present an option to the legislative groups: annexation to the United States or continued independence, supported by Mexican recognition.[19]

The dramatic message from Mexico did not appear suddenly, without a great deal of intrigue and negotiation. For some time the French and British chargés in Texas had been advised by their European governments to intervene in the longstanding dispute between Texas and Mexico. Therefore, when it was learned in Texas that the annexation resolutions had passed Congress, the two chargés initiated intensive conversations with President Jones and his aides, which resulted in a memorandum that provided for Texas' rejection of annexation, recognition by Mexico, and an agreement to negotiate boundaries and other disputed issues. At the end of March, the two envoys left Texas for New Orleans, but they encountered the arriving Donelson before they got safely out of Texas. From New Orleans the British chargé, Charles Elliot, left for Mexico City; en route, his identity was discovered by curious observers, and newspapers in the United States made much of the episode of "the man in the white hat." Elliot's arrival in Mexico City created quite a stir, for the news of the United States annexation resolutions had preceded him. Once there, Elliot conferred with representatives of France, Spain, and Britain in an effort to devise an approach to the agitated Herrera government. After many delays, both deliberate and unavoidable, by mid May the Mexican congress had consented to the memorandum that Elliot had brought with him from Texas. Immediately the British chargé embarked for Texas with the remarkable news of his accomplishments. Meanwhile, Donelson was in New Orleans, where he picked up reports of Elliot's activities in Mexico City, including the agreement to extend recognition of independence to Texas. Hastily writing to Buchanan, to whom he gave assurances that Texans would not fall for this latest trick, Donelson left for Galveston, prepared for all sorts of possibilities. Upon his return to Texas, Elliot made his way immediately to President Jones, but it was too late, for events had outrun both Jones and the British chargé. Prudent and sensitive, Elliot realized that his efforts had been in vain, that he could not divert the forces of historical allegiance between the Texans and the Americans. He therefore departed from Texas, having done his very best to give the European powers the final word on the West.[20]

While that dramatic scenario was evolving, Polk also had his diplomatic but calculating hand in Mexico itself. Giving evidence of a fondness for secret agents, the president sent William S. Parrott to Mexico City at the end of March. It was believed that Parrott's claims against the Mexican government were both enormous and extravagant. Parrott was instructed by Secretary Buchanan to inform Mexican leaders that the annexation of Texas was a reality that could not be altered and to urge quietly the restoration of diplomatic relations between the United States and Mexico. Arriving at Mexico City a month later, Parrott there joined the American consul, John Black, in trying to assess the situation. The Herrera government, disturbed by the news of Texas annexation, could not afford politically to have anything to do with Parrott at this juncture; therefore Polk's secret agent made no progress at first. After the Texas government had formally accepted annexation, a clamor for war broke out in Mexico. Nothing actually came from such noises, however; and by the end of the summer, Parrott reported an increasing degree of optimism about United States–Mexican relations.[21] Such encouragement soon led to overt attempts by the Polk administration to deal directly with the Mexican government in the fall months of 1845; but the Slidell Mission, as it has ever since been called, was an abortive one, sadly reflecting the deteriorating, rather than improving, relations between the two countries—a topic to be discussed later.

Although European diplomatic initiatives and Polk's quasi-secret dealings with Mexico were important parts of the Texas story in 1845, certainly an equally vital and volatile component was the matter of military protection of Texas by the United States. Donelson, having made no headway with President Jones, who defiantly refused to entertain notions about United States troops in Texas, turned to Texas' secretary of state, Ebenezer Allen. Both Donelson and Allen agreed that the likelihood of an invasion from Mexico was serious and threatening, particularly if Texas embraced annexation with the United States. Consequently, Donelson apparently persuaded Allen to draft a memorandum requesting military protection in order that a Mexican invasion could be repelled. Polk and Buchanan eagerly responded in late May by informing Donelson that Zachary Taylor's forces, which were currently stationed at Fort Jesup in Louisiana, would be moved to the Texas border and held in readiness. But this was not enough to satisfy Donelson, who was increasingly worried about the tinderbox atmosphere he perceived in Texas, which was largely attributable to chargé Charles Elliot's arrival with reports that Mexico would recognize Texas if Texas refused to be annexed to the United States. Donelson was almost certain that the British would encourage military action by the Mexican army somewhere in the vicinity of the Rio Grande. He asked Buchanan if in the event of such an invasion of Texas, the United States would "stand still" and would not counter with military force. In fact, Donelson recommended that a U.S. commander be stationed near him, so that the two men could immediately confer on strategy and deployment.[22]

In response to Donelson's letters of early June to the Polk administration, the government at Washington decided to escalate U.S. involvement. General Taylor was therefore ordered to move his troops from Louisiana to Texas, and additional naval forces were directed to the Gulf Coast. These were the "prompt & energetic measures" that Polk promised to Donelson in his letter of 15 June. The president also pledged, in that same letter, that Texas boundary claims to the Rio Grande would be upheld and that an invading army would not be permitted "to occupy a foot of the soil East of the Rio Grande."[23]

Although the Polk administration seemed clear and resolute about where a Mexican army would not be allowed to move, it was vague about where the United States Army might go. The orders to Taylor did not specify a place for him to make camp; this was either intentional, so that the Polk administration would not have to take full blame for whatever resulted from Taylor's maneuverings, or else it merely reflected the abundant ignorance of Texas geography that prevailed at this time at the White House. In any event, once Taylor and his troops had arrived in Texas, Donelson and Texan officials debated over the exact location deemed best for them. Donelson, who had genuine misgivings about claims of the Rio Grande boundary, favored stationing Taylor's troops along the Nueces, lest a movement beyond that point unduly provoke an invasion by Mexican soldiers. Bending to pressures from within Texas and from without, Donelson finally, at the end of June, directed Taylor to take up positions at San Antonio and Corpus Christi, the latter being adjacent to the Nueces. At this juncture, Donelson was unwilling to push farther, for he viewed these moves as leaving the boundary question open for eventual negotiation. But in July, Polk and some members of his cabinet interpreted Taylor's presence at the Nueces as supporting and guaranteeing claims of the land between that river and the Rio Grande. As a matter of fact, Taylor was specifically told that he could move as close to the latter river "as prudence will dictate"; but for the time being, the general refused to budge from Corpus Christi. President Polk was engaging in a risky game of deploying military troops to *deter* Mexican aggression, not to *invite* it; and the strategy worked, at least for a while.[24]

In August, however, Polk was alarmed by rumors that reached Washington reporting that Mexican troops were on the march toward the Rio Grande, where they would soon assemble a fighting force of some nine thousand soldiers to confront Taylor's little band of approximately fifteen hundred. Because by then both the Texas Congress and the convention had already accepted annexation, the president felt even more determined to rush additional troops to the aid of Taylor. Even under these new tense circumstances, however, Secretary Marcy instructed Taylor not to advance, but rather to wait for a Mexican invasion across the Rio Grande. Shortly thereafter the Polk administration learned that the rumors were without foundation, but it did not revoke its decision to increase military strength and to toughen its posture in Texas. Indeed, by the end of the month, Taylor had been told, first, that an actual crossing of the Rio Grande would be considered the commencement of hostilities and, later, that even "an attempt" to cross the river would begin the war. Meanwhile Polk was writing to and consulting with various persons, mainly to praise the build-up of American troops in Texas as an effective obstacle to military action by the Mexican government. He reiterated his defensive policy, perhaps endeavoring to convince himself of its validity, and his pledge that the United States would not be the aggressor against Mexico.[25] Aggression, like beauty, may often be in the eye of the beholder, but Polk sincerely interpreted his policies as nonaggressive, basing that view partly upon his belief that the Rio Grande rightly constituted the southern and western boundary of Texas. Suffice it to say, by the fall months there was something of a military stalemate on the Texas border, and the Polk administration was breathing easier in light of the evidence that its policies had been effective and successful. The president and his cabinet could not know at that time down exactly what road its Texas strategy would take the nation.

They could rejoice, however, and justifiably so, in the accomplishment of bringing Texas into the Union. The actual process whereby the Texas Congress in June and the convention in July approved of annexation was uneventful and almost anticlimactic. Annexation sentiment was so strong, thanks in part to the labors of Donelson and Polk's secret agents, that there was little debate or disagreement. Perhaps the timely arrival of U.S. troops, prior to the convention, lent support to the annexation cause. At any rate, the convention quickly set its hand to the task of devising a state constitution, which was subsequently approved by the voters in October. Therefore, when the United States Congress assembled in December, it was ready to receive committee reports recommending the formal admission of Texas into the Union. Although the resolution for admission met with noticeable opposition in both houses, it cleared Congress by a substantial vote. Even some senators who had originally opposed annexation now went on record in favor of the admission of Texas.[26] With that, Texas at long last entered the Union on an equal footing with all other states, thereby ending an exciting chapter in its brief but illustrious history.

Polk is due ample credit for having dealt effectively with the Texas "problem," which he inherited the moment he took office as president. There were days during this saga when he surely had just cause to curse Tyler's precipitous actions, but he did not. He doubtless refrained, because most things went his way and neatly fell into place, although there were moments when no one could be certain about the eventual outcome. Few things are inevitable, but the inclusion of Texas into the United States comes very close to being one of those things. In fact, as historian David Pletcher has noted, one may well wonder "why the Texas question persisted as long as it did, and why it involved the foreign offices of five countries in a tangle of communications and proposals." Nevertheless, it did, partly because abolitionists had been convinced by Calhoun that the annexation of Texas was a scheme to expand slavery.[27] As events turned out, 1845 was a very important year for the United States and for Texas. The story of expansionism was only beginning, however; much excitement and trauma lay ahead.

4

★ ★ ★ ★ ★

POLK AND THE WINNING
OF THE SOUTHWEST

In the mid 1840s John L. O'Sullivan, editor of the *United States Magazine and Democratic Review,* coined the phrase Manifest Destiny. To him these words seemed to be an appropriate label for the spirit of expanionism that boasted about the dream of the territorial extension of the United States westward, perhaps as far west as the Pacific Coast itself. Since those days until now, almost a century and a half later, many observers and historians have pondered the origins and meaning of Manifest Destiny and have calculated its ramifications.

To some people in the decade of the 1840s the term served as a convenient rationale—a sort of justification of bold adventures (even war) in behalf of the expansion of the United States. To them, Manifest Destiny had a belligerent, militant tone, which endorsed running roughshod over obstacles that stood in the way of extending the nation's boundaries. It also was the cloud by day and the pillar of fire by night that guided the westward thrust of the nation. Indeed, the United States had been providentially blessed by being presented with the opportunity to appropriate new expanses of space; a sort of geographical predestination was pushing the nation westward.[1]

The impulse for territorial enhancement was readily apparent before Polk took the oath of office—witness the Texas-annexation movement and the presidential election of 1844. Upon becoming president, he tapped that nationalistic desire for expansion, capitalized upon it, and carried the country to the fruition of many of its territorial aspirations, but not without difficulty and even war.

Greatly advancing the spread of the doctrine of expansionism was the technological development in the printing and newspaper industry that made possible inexpensive newspapers—the penny press, as it was frequently called. There is no denying that expansionism in its various manifestations made "good copy" for the editors. In fact, one historian has concluded that the whole notion of Manifest Destiny was the creation of newspapermen and politicians and that it did not reflect true national sentiment.[2] Be that as it may, newspapers, particularly in the Northeast and the Northwest, were vigorous proponents of territorial expansion. One wonders if Polk could have thwarted the movement for geographical extension even if he had wanted to do so.

Whether the newspapers shaped public opinion or reflected it, there is little question that advocates of Manifest Destiny were numerous, influential, and successful. The riddle of what motivated leaders, as well as plain folk, to embrace the western expansion of the United States is not easily solved. The complexity of this matter becomes more apparent as one delves into statements made by politicians, journalistic leaders, and others. Indeed, it is no easy task to fathom Polk's own motivations and commitments to national expanionism. This much seems certain, however: some proponents shared economic concerns as a primary stimulus to their involvement in Manifest Destiny. As historian Norman Graebner pointed out more than thirty years ago, northeastern merchants and shippers eagerly eyed the development of United States ports on the Pacific Coast.[3] Theirs was a concern about developing trade with the far western regions and, more important, with the Orient. Territorial expansion excited the economic interests of other Americans, who believed that the life line of the country was dependent upon finding new markets for agricultural products. As a matter of fact, anxieties over farm surpluses stirred the conviction that expansionism was the answer. Thereby, American agricultural producers might also gain monopolies against foreign competition.[4]

Closely akin to such economic concerns were the more philosophical or ideological ones about industrialization and urbanization. Many of the expansionists of the 1840s were in reality neo-Jeffersonians, who depicted the potential disadvantages of factory and city. To them, territorial extension would negate the appeal made by some Americans for a move toward industrializing and urbanizing the nation, because newly opened expanses of regions would offer new opportunities for farmers and rural dwellers. The neo-Jeffersonian arguments attracted considerable attention and support among the ardent expansionists; it was a position with which many Jacksonians, including Polk himself, could identify. It was their hope that the geographical extension of the nation's boundaries would summon the people to a renewed commitment to an agrarian life style.[5]

Other motivations apparently were at work throughout the 1840s. For example, as discussed in the previous chapter relative to Texas, racial concerns entered the picture. With regard to the acquisition of the Southwest, most expansionists evidently believed that racial and cultural homogeneity could be achieved and ensured by extending the boundaries all the way to the Pacific Coast. Nonwhites, whether Indian or Mexican, were considered to be obstacles to the realization of such a goal. Concerning the Southwest (California and New Mexico), there was not any serious argument about providing for southern slavery, in contrast to the situation surrounding the annexation of Texas.[6] Another major ingredient in expansionist thought was the conviction that geographical aggrandizement was linked with the nobler desire to spread American liberty and freedom. Several scholars have noted that the unusual yoking of the two concepts was peculiar to the 1840s; one historian has recently labeled this "exceptionalism." Somehow, American imperialism would be different from that seen elsewhere in the world. Expansionism by the United States would, it was argued, be more benign, more tolerant, less revengeful; and it would be accompanied by the dispersal of lofty ideals of republicanism and liberty. In addition, some of the expansionists strained to contend that democracy within the United States itself would be enhanced by a program of territorial extension.[7]

Considering the ferment that surrounded expansionism during the decade of the 1840s, it is not surprising that Tyler and, to a much greater extent, Polk were able to launch ambitious imperial programs. Polk gave strong indication of his goals in his Inaugural Address, which echoed the Democratic party's platform. In private, he evidently elaborated upon his public statements so as to include California. In any event, the annexation of Texas set in motion an almost irrepressible movement to stretch the nation's boundaries. The bold ambition to acquire the Southwest proved to be an elusive and costly one, for it required a war against a foreign power. As noted in the preceding chapter, the annexation of Texas in 1845 and the question of its southern and western boundary set up notable and perhaps irreconcilable differences between the United States and Mexico, especially when the latter severed formal diplomatic relations. The story of Texas did not end with its admission into the United States; as a matter of fact, the defense of its disputed boundary line led almost naturally into an armed confrontation between the United States and Mexico, which in turn became a larger battle to strip Mexico of even greater possessions, particularly New Mexico and California.

In addition to the lingering disagreements and squabbles over Texas, the matter of unpaid Mexican debts proved to be conveniently bothersome to the Polk administration. United States claims against the Mexican government amounted to something in excess of $3 million by the mid 1840s; and apparently Mexico was in no position or disposition to make further payments on the indebtedness. It was a relatively harmless issue during normal times, to be sure—a matter that could have been worked out, given ample patience on both sides. But these were not normal times, and the question of Mexican claims played into the hands of an expansion-minded Polk administration. Unfortunately, the Mexican government almost fortuitously offered an issue to Polk and his aides upon which they could focus their grievances.

Of greater importance, however, was the desire for ports on the Pacific Coast. This dream was not confined to the White House and its executive departments, for as noted above, merchants and shippers in the Northeast had frequently expressed their desire for new trading centers on the California shores. Likewise, other expansionists in the 1840s leapt to the vision of extending the nation from sea to shining sea. Much like Henry IV of France, who avowed that Paris was worth a Mass, expansionists implied or stated that California was worth a war.

But even the primitive maps of the day revealed a vast tract of land that stood between Texas and the Pacific Coast. Known generally as New Mexico, it soon became an object of Polk and the expansionists, for they would not condone a gaping hole in the continental-extension program. New Mexico was a large piece of the puzzle of Manifest Destiny during the 1840s, and there were those who intended to possess it. Considering all of these circumstances, one wonders how war, or some sort of armed confrontation, with Mexico could have been avoided in this decade.[8] This is not to sanction what happened or to imply that there were no other alternatives; rather, it is to acknowledge quite simply that the United States' continental impulse sought gratification. Besides, not far beneath the surface of the collective consciousness was the reality that some Americans had already fought Mexico in the 1830s and had won.

Although Polk was a visible and vocal spokesman for expansionism, he preferred channels other than war to acquire the Pacific Southwest. The first president to preside over a full-scale war since the days of James Madison more than a quarter of a century earlier, Polk had sought peaceful means to achieve his territorial objectives. As a matter of fact, he launched at least three recognizable peace initiatives during the two years of the struggle with Mexico—the first of which has been known ever since as the Slidell Mission.

As noted in the previous chapter, Polk had sent William S. Parrott to Mexico City in the spring of 1845, in hopes that Parrott might succeed in encouraging the Mexican officials to accept the inevitability and reality of Texas being annexed to the United States. Parrott had little or no success on this front; nevertheless, as the months went by, he became increasingly sanguine over the prospect of the reopening of diplomatic channels between the two countries. So much so that by late August, he reported to Polk and the State Department that an appropriate envoy from the United States might be able to meet with Mexican officials *"over a breakfast"* and settle issues with comparative ease. His optimism was confirmed by dispatches received in mid September from other U.S. officials in Mexico.[9]

Fortified by such encouragement, Polk and his cabinet determined in September to take the bold step of appointing and sending John Slidell, a former congressman from Louisiana, to Mexico. Ever mindful of the delicate nature of relations with Mexico and the possibility of European interference, Polk wanted Slidell's venture "to be kept a profound secret." Polk's inherently cautious nature prevailed the very next day when the receipt of New Orleans newspapers indicated a hostile and warlike attitude on the part of Mexican leaders; this information caused the president first to wonder whether Parrott and others had been correct and then to decide to delay the commissioning of Slidell. The president notified Slidell of the pending appointment and urged him to be ready to depart whenever the appropriate time should arrive. Meanwhile, Secretary of State Buchanan penned a letter to Consul Black in Mexico City, asking Black to ascertain, with some degree of reliability, whether Mexico was ready to receive a representative from the United States. Buchanan observed somewhat ominously that the president was "anxious to preserve peace, although prepared for war."[10]

The Polk administration could do nothing at this juncture but wait for further information from Mexico. This arrived in early November in the form of a message from Black and the appearance of Parrott in Washington. On the basis of these new reports, Polk was ready to commission Slidell. Significantly, Slidell was to carry the title of envoy and minister plenipotentiary and was empowered to deal not only with the Texas boundary dispute but also with United States claims and the territorial desires of the Polk administration. Polk and his cabinet agreed upon the monetary payments that might be offered to the Mexican government for New Mexico and California and for the American claims. From the vantage point of the White House, it was an eminently fair and generous proposal. In a private letter to Slidell, the president urged him to strike a quick agreement with Mexico and added that should Slidell fail in his mission, Polk would call upon Congress "to provide the proper remedies." Although that phrase had a bellicose ring to it, the president assured his brother several days later that there would be no war with Mexico, because there would be the resumption of diplomatic relations instead.[11]

The details of Slidell's venture need not detain us for long; a brief summary will suffice. The envoy arrived in Mexico during the first week in December, shortly before Gen. Mariano Paredes y Arrillaga proclaimed a revolution against the government of Gen. José Joaquín Herrera—hardly the most propitious time to seek a reopening of diplomatic channels. Slidell nonetheless persisted in his efforts to establish communications with the foreign minister, Manuel de la Peña y Peña, who immediately raised several objections to the new United States minister. As it turned out, the most important of these was the protest that Slidell had been given a higher title than what the Mexican officials had stipulated; the least important objection was that Slidell had arrived several weeks earlier than had been expected. The real problem was that the tottering Herrera government did not dare treat with Slidell, for to do so would cause it to lose face through the easy resumption of diplomatic relations and thus hasten its own collapse. In fairness to the record, however, it appears that the Mexican government, even in its rapidly deteriorating condition, did not intend to close the door to Slidell's mission entirely. Unfortunately for Slidell and the Polk administration, Paredes marched into Mexico City on 2 January, and the Herrera government fled; whereupon the still optimistic Slidell withdrew to Jalapa, with the expectation that he could shortly deal with the new Paredes government.[12]

Messages from Slidell, in which he depicted his problems with the Herrera government, began arriving in Washington in mid January. Buchanan and Polk therefore devised new instructions, which took a tougher stance toward the Mexican government by warning that U.S. patience would soon be exhausted; at the same time, they urged Slidell to continue his honorable efforts to establish channels of communications. Polk speculated, in a letter to his brother, that Paredes's strong anti-American tone was probably not genuine but, rather, was a temporary political prop.[13]

The next development in the saga occurred in February, when Alexander J. Atocha called upon the president in Washington. Reputedly representing the views of Antonio Lopéz de Santa Anna, Atocha held several conversations with Polk in which he pressed the contention that Santa Anna, if he were to gain control of the Mexican government, would favor a treaty with the United States. Territorial cessions would be made and the boundary question would be resolved, in exchange for approximately $30 million. While expressing his conviction privately that Atocha was not a trustworthy or reliable man, Polk nonetheless appeared to be quite taken with Atocha's visit, particularly when he relayed the contents of his conversations to the cabinet. Before that group, the president stiffened his attitude and tone toward the Mexican government, demanding that the government receive Slidell and that it pay the U.S. claims immediately. If nothing else seemed to work, Polk proposed that Slidell retire to a warship off the coast of Mexico and await further word from Washington. Whereupon, the president pledged, he would issue a strong message to Congress, seeking authorization for another demand by Slidell and then, if that was not successful, authorization for the executive "to take redress into our own hands by aggressive measures." Buchanan vigorously took exception to Polk's projected scenario, rightly pointing out the dangers of gunboat diplomacy; other members of the cabinet, however, sided with the president. Two days later, Polk thought better of the whole matter and cautiously elected to take no action until the receipt of further word from Slidell.[14]

Meanwhile, the tempo of events was quickening in Mexico, where Slidell, still residing in Jalapa, decided on 1 March to present the Mexican government with a new demand: it must choose between peace with the United States or the complete rupture of relations. His message was accompanied by the added verbal insistence that a reply be made within two weeks. The Paredes government, after discussing Slidell's note, conveyed both its intention to refuse the reception of Slidell and its attribution of all blame upon the United States, should war result. Slidell did not resist the urge to respond; consequently, he issued a defense of his country. Thereafter he requested his passports, which were eventually sent, and he departed from Vera Cruz on 15 March.[15]

A week later the Polk administration received dispatches from both Slidell and Black, which indicated the diminution of all hope for any agreement or settlement with Mexico. The president told the cabinet that if Slidell returned without such, he would ask for legislative measures that would "take the remedy for the injuries and wrongs we had suffered into our own hands." No one in the cabinet dissented; Buchanan was absent from the meeting, however. About ten days later, Polk wrote to Slidell, summoning him to Washington immediately for purposes of bringing fresh information from Mexico.[16] Without question, tensions were mounting as the realization of the failure of the Slidell Mission sank in: whether Polk wanted war at this juncture is debatable; that he was becoming more aggressive is almost beyond dispute.

Meanwhile, much excitement was already occurring in California, the *pièce de résistance*. From the very earliest days of the Polk administration, it had been widely known that the president coveted California. In fact, the *Washington Union* had sounded the clarion call for possession of California about three months after Polk's inauguration.[17] Fortunately or unfortunately, Thomas O. Larkin was ensconced in California as consul even before Polk's term began, a fact that caused the president to be quite dependent upon him. Larkin seems to have been principally concerned about British activities in California and the consequent threat to United States' goals that such involvement represented. Although the preponderance of evidence indicates that the British had no serious intentions of acquiring California or of intriguing with the Mexican government, the belief persisted, nonetheless, that they were a formidable obstacle to United States desires on the Pacific Coast.

In July 1845, Larkin sent to the State Department a dispatch that reflected this apprehension. Received in Washington three months later, Larkin's message warned that Mexican troops, financed and backed by British businesses, were advancing toward California. Naturally alarmed about this state of affairs, neither Buchanan nor Polk questioned whether Larkin had exaggerated. Therefore, in response to what it thought was a worsening situation on the coast, the administration sent new instructions. Taylor was told to move as close to the Rio Grande as circumstances would permit; Commodore Robert F. Stockton was urged to proceed to California as quickly as possible; John D. Sloat, commander of the Pacific Squadron, was advised to keep his forces ready, while also conciliating the natives in California; finally, Larkin was appointed as a confidential agent, to keep the administration apprised of events on the West Coast. Moreover, Larkin was entreated to pay particular attention to actions of foreign powers in California and to warn the residents there of the dangers of such.[18] Apparently, Polk was attempting to have his administration prepared for any one of three possibilities: continued Mexican rule in California, local revolt for independence, or actual warfare.

The president and his secretary of the navy elected to send a young marine, Archibald H. Gillespie, to the West, with the instructions for Larkin and Sloat and with communications for John C. Frémont, an army officer who was already on an exploring and scientific expedition in California and adjacent areas. The administration's decision to include Frémont in matters concerning the future of California was a questionable one indeed; had Polk wanted to foment trouble there, he could not have been disappointed in Frémont, who operated as a sort of law unto himself. Besides, Frémont had powerful connections in Washington, the most important of which was his father-in-law, Senator Thomas Hart Benton. We cannot know exactly what message Gillespie gave Frémont, because no evidence is available. Therefore, contemporary persons, as well as later historians, have busily constructed various possibilities, which largely depend upon attitudes about Polk and his aims in California. The somewhat erratic and independent Frémont stood poised to make trouble on the West Coast, a posture seemingly at odds with that of Larkin or even of Sloat. Suffice it to say that the whole region would be in turmoil before Frémont had finished his activities. Oddly enough, Gillespie did not arrive in California until April 1846, six months after he had departed from Washington; by then, Frémont had already succeeded in stirring up Mexican officials throughout California as he moved about the area with his troops.

Larkin was quite pleased with Gillespie's message to him, for he was in complete agreement with the order to encourage the peaceful attraction of the Californians toward United States control. Months earlier, in late September 1845, Larkin had written to Polk that the situation in California was not as threatening as he had earlier believed. Of course, by the time the president received this message, Gillespie had already been on his western trek for slightly over a month. By early May, rumors and reports had begun to circulate along the coast about the military activities that had commenced in the Rio Grande area. Neither Larkin nor Sloat knew exactly what response to make to this news;[19] but naturally, Frémont was not as indecisive.

During the first week in May, Gillespie finally caught up with Frémont, who was encamped far to the north, near the Oregon border; whereupon the young marine gave the army officer the communications, both written and verbal. Eager for action, Frémont, accompanied by his troops and also by Gillespie, quickly moved south, where they would begin to rouse the natives and others with the notion of revolt against Mexican authority. Unknown to them was the fact that at almost exactly this same time, Congress had approved a declaration of war against Mexico. In June and July, certain Californians rebelled and established the so-called Bear Flag government. Larkin, although he was not happy with Frémont's activities in fostering this revolt, decided to accept the situation as it was rapidly unfolding; he commented: ''If they have started the big Ball to roll forever and thro & thro' C[alifornia], I

73

can not stop it." Some have argued that Commodore Sloat might have stopped it, if he had moved his ships in immediately and if he had taken charge of the fluid military situation. But Sloat was unusually cautious.[20]

Finally, in early July, Sloat and Larkin conferred and agreed to present a declaration, announcing that California had been annexed to the United States. Shortly thereafter, Commodore Stockton, ready for action and influence, arrived off the coast of California, took over command from Sloat, and issued a proclamation to the Californians. In it he contended that the capture of San Francisco and Monterey had been in reprisal for Mexican actions against both Taylor along the Rio Grande and against Frémont. Moreover, Stockton threatened, he intended to conquer the rest of California. Giving reality to his warnings, Stockton, along with Frémont and Gillespie, entered Los Angeles in mid August and proclaimed United States authority over the entire province.[21] Subsequent events would spell additional trouble for the U.S. coup in California, however; but for the moment, Polk's desires for that coast had been affirmed, and the eventual likelihood of American domination and possession had been assured.[22]

In the meantime, Congress had actually declared war against Mexico in May, and the Polk administration was mapping its strategy for a decisive victory. Naturally, there had been a number of steps toward the climactic war message and declaration. In January, for example, Secretary Marcy had sent new orders to General Taylor, instructing him to move his troops to the Rio Grande itself, a maneuver that the general had requested earlier. About a month later, Taylor had received the new directives, but he had waited until early March before he finally had moved his troops toward the Rio Grande, a destination he had reached by the end of that month.[23]

As events unfolded, the spring months of 1846 were critical. Taylor established himself with his troops at the Rio Grande in March, the same month in which Slidell finally surrendered his hopes of a successful mission in Mexico and left the country. Interestingly enough, throughout the month, Polk remained mainly optimistic about his peace initiatives and clung to the expectation that the Mexican officials would receive Slidell, not knowing that his envoy had already given up. In a regular cabinet meeting on 28 March, for instance, the president shared his belief that Slidell would succeed, claiming that the only genuine obstacle might be the availability of money with which to pay the Mexican government. In fact, Polk averred that the prompt payment of a sum of money might enable Slidell to obtain an actual treaty and to secure the territorial acquisitions being sought by the administration. The president speculated that if Congress would make such an appropriation, $1 million might accomplish the task. The cabinet joined Polk in his views, with the exception of Secretary Buchanan, who thought it unlikely that Congress would provide such money. But Buchanan, along with the other cabinet members, did support the president's intention to confer with several senators about the likelihood of a special appropriation. Accordingly, Polk consulted with Benton and William Allen of Ohio, who, along with others, endorsed the president's tentative proposal. But Benton and Allen urged Polk to talk with Calhoun, who was then summoned to the president's office. On 30 March the president and the senator had an amicable conversation, as they studied maps of the West and conferred about possible western territorial acquisitions. Calhoun was unwilling to commit himself, however, to the support of a special appropriation to facilitate treaty negotiations, although he favored a quick treaty with Mexico. Promising to give the matter further thought, Calhoun departed, only to return four days later, at which time he advised Polk that it would be inexpedient "at present to move in the matter" of the appropriation. Later on that same day, Senator Allen, when informed of Calhoun's opposition, warned the president that "the measure would meet with serious embarrassments in the Senate" without the South Carolinian's support. Therefore Polk postponed his plan for enticing the Mexican government to negotiate in the spring.[24]

By the end of the first week in April, Polk and his administration had learned of the failure of Slidell's venture. The president was inclined toward the conviction that this unfavorable turn of events warranted a movement toward a declaration of war against Mexico, but the enormity of such an action encouraged caution and delay. Moreover, the critical prominence of the debates over Oregon at this juncture would not permit agitation in Congress over problems in Mexico. In his introspective moments the president apparently reasoned, however, that Slidell's lack of success was not sufficient grounds for a declaration of war; something greater, more dramatic was needed. He therefore elected to wait, still hoping for more recent and reliable news from the Rio Grande front.[25] While he delayed, warfare broke out along that river border.

Ironically, on 25 April, the very day that hostilities commenced between Taylor's reconnaissance patrol and a contingent of Mexican troops, the cabinet was talking about a declaration of war, with Buchanan being one of its principal supporters. Three days later the cabinet again returned to this proposition; but they hesitated, waiting for Slidell to arrive in Washington and waiting for the Oregon matter to be disposed of. There is no room for doubt that by the end of April the

Polk administration wanted war—even before receiving actual information about the fighting that had begun on the Rio Grande. Conferring on 8 May, John Slidell and Polk readily agreed upon war with Mexico as the only alternative now available to the United States. This conversation was followed by an extremely important discussion by the cabinet the next morning, at which time there was unanimous concurrence that if Taylor were attacked, Polk should immediately send a war message to Congress. The president then solicited the cabinet's assistance in framing such a message—whether there were any skirmishes along the Rio Grande or not. Secretary of the Navy Bancroft, however, preferred to wait until some definite action had occurred on the border. The cabinet adjourned, having agreed to reconvene on 12 May for a discussion and consideration of a war message.[26]

The tempo of events accelerated so quickly, however, that by the latter date, Congress had already received Polk's war message. On the fateful night of Saturday, 9 May, Taylor's dispatch, giving the details of the commencement of hostilities, arrived in Washington. The president therefore immediately reconvened the cabinet, whose members unanimously favored sending a war message to Congress on Monday. After the cabinet adjourned at ten o'clock, Polk began to work on the document, assisted by both Buchanan and Bancroft. By then, word was flying through the streets of Washington, which brought various congressional leaders to the White House to confer with the president. On Sunday, except for a two-hour break to attend church, as was his custom, Polk labored all day on the message. Numerous visitors arrived at the White House to consult with the president, while clerks scurried back and forth, copying portions of the document. Finally, at 10:30 that night, Polk ceased his work and retired, but not before recording in his diary this assessment: "It was a day of great anxiety to me, and I regretted the necessity which had existed to make it necessary for me to spend the Sabbath in the manner I have."[27]

The following day was likewise "a day of great anxiety," reported Polk. By noon the president had forwarded his war message to Congress, after revising and working on it that morning. Polk was particularly concerned by the lack of full support from Benton, with whom he had conferred on that day. Fretting would do no good, however, for the matter was in the hands of Congress. Informing the members of Congress that war had already begun, the president traced the history of the difficulties with Mexico, noting especially the claims question. Nowhere in the message, however, did he indicate his great desire for California, a strange and perhaps deliberate omission. Naturally he offered a strong contention for the Rio Grande as the traditional southern and western boundary of Texas, a position that lacked convincing evidence. Whatever the validity of the president's arguments, the House seemed determined to have war with Mexico, as it gave a resounding affirmative vote to the declaration of war—only about five hours after having received Polk's formal message. The situation in the Senate, however, was quite different, for there a cadre composed of Calhoun and Whigs stood poised to block the declaration of war, or at least to stall and delay its approval. Eventually, proadministration Democrats prevailed, however, and managed to bring the declaration before the Senate for a vote. Much like the House, the Senate condoned the war message with an overwhelmingly favorable vote—partly the result, as Polk had predicted, of fear of public sentiment, which was deemed to be supportive of war. The president's private secretary brought news of the Senate action and pronounced the vote and the "whole debate as a great triumph for the administration."[28] Events and the passage of time might render a different verdict, however.

Two days after first sending his message to Congress, Polk received the declaration bill and signed it. As the opponents would say, he now had his war. A mass meeting in Philadelphia on that same day adopted resolutions in support of the declaration of war; similar meetings and demonstrations occurred elsewhere, particularly in the Ohio Valley and in the South.[29] Likewise, however, voices of protest were almost immediately raised, much as had been heard in the chambers of Congress. Patriotic fervor obscured some of this dissent for the moment, but increasingly the nation would become divided over "Mr. Polk's war."

Although inching toward war over a period of weeks, if not months, the Polk administration was manifestly ill prepared to launch an all-out struggle against Mexico when the declaration of war passed. Despite that obvious reality, the president was determined to wage a vigorous war, to the end that the conflict might be concluded speedily— since political considerations dictated a short, rather than a prolonged, war. If anyone had questioned the intention of Polk in May to embark on a decided bid to defeat Mexico, he needed only to have read the pages of the president's newspaper, the *Union*, which editorialized near the end of the month: "We mean to conduct war against Mexico with all the vigor in our power. . . . *We shall invade her territory; we shall seize her strongholds; we shall even* TAKE HER CAPITAL, *if there be no other means of bringing her to a sense of justice.*"[30] Editor Thomas Ritchie exaggerated Polk's position at the moment, to be sure, but in the process he swept away any lingering concerns about whether the administration had a strong-enough commitment to victory.

Taylor rendered an invaluable service to Polk and to the nation by his string of impressive victories. One wonders what the administration might have done if United States troops had suffered defeats. To the relief of the president and his secretary of war, successes in Mexico permitted them time to plan and prepare without unusual panic. Had they been as intent upon full-scale war as some people argued, then and subsequently, surely they would not have been caught as completely unprepared when the hostilities actually commenced. In any event, the top priority for Polk and Marcy was to select someone to assume overall command of the American troops. Undeniably the only available choice at this juncture was Gen. Winfield Scott. The story of his appointment and removal two weeks later is a familiar one, but it bears further scrutiny in order to illustrate the adversarial relationship between the civilians and the military that characterized much of Polk's conduct of the war effort. Unfortunately for all concerned, the nagging question of politics entered into the Scott-Polk imbroglio from its genesis in 1846 until its conclusion in 1848. Polk was not just an average Democrat; he was a fiercely partisan, avid Democrat, who, as president, was head of the party. On the other hand, Scott was a firmly committed Whig, who had already given ample evidence of his political ambitions. The differences put them on an unavoidable collision course from the outset; in addition, their personality quirks ensured conflict, even if they could have skirted around political matters from time to time. Luckily for Polk and for the nation, Scott was a tremendously capable general, as he was to prove, once he was given the opportunity in 1847.

Trouble brewed from the beginning, for on 13 May, Polk, after offering the command to Scott, who accepted, confided to his diary his own lack of respect for the general. The president had felt obligated to appoint Scott solely because he was the top officer in the Regular Army. On the following day, Polk, Scott, and Marcy engaged in a lengthy strategy session; afterwards the president recorded that he had been unimpressed with Scott, whom he deemed to be "rather scientific and visionary in his views." The realities of politics compelled both Polk and Marcy to rush Scott in his planning and preparing for his expedition to Mexico, where he would take command; but the realities of military logistics demanded that it would take months before Scott and the new recruits would be ready to embark for the war front. On 21 May, one week after the initial strategy meeting, Polk became highly incensed over a minor matter concerning a Captain Hutter, who wished for an appointment that Scott refused. The overly sensitive president interpreted the affair as an indication of the general's hostility toward the appointment of Democrats and of his antagonism and recklessly vindictive feelings toward the administration. Polk immediately complained to Marcy that he had no confidence in Scott's willingness to carry out the administration's plans and views, and he lamented that he was being compelled to wage war with Scott as overall commander. On the following day, Polk protested that Scott and some other generals were attempting to block legislation before the Congress that called for the appointment of additional generals to the army. Polk condemned them as being "all whigs & violent partisans, and not having the success of my administration at heart [they] seem disposed to throw every obstacle in the way of my prosecuting the Mexican War successfully." He hoped for a speedy end to such difficulties; he very quickly got his wish.[31]

The explosion occurred on 23 May, when Polk went before his cabinet to read Scott's famous letter, in which he protested against the pressures being put upon him to embark for Mexico. Or as the general so graphically put it: "I do not desire to place myself in the most perilous of all positions, a fire upon my rear from Washington and the fire in front from the Mexicans." It is not difficult to imagine Polk's lips snarling as he read these stinging lines. The cabinet reacted strongly, as the president spelled out his conviction that Scott wanted to avoid going to the battlefield and that his partisan attitudes made him unfit for command. Whereas Polk wanted "a prompt and energetic movement" of the general and his troops to Mexico, Scott intended to remain in Washington until September. The discussion was interrupted, but two days later, in a special meeting, the cabinet resumed its consideration of Scott's incredible letter. Polk informed the members that he and Marcy had prepared a letter by which they removed Scott from his command—an action that the cabinet approved of unanimously.[32]

Marcy took this letter to Scott at about 5:30 P.M. on 25 May, just as Scott was taking "a hasty plate of soup." Immediately after reading the letter of removal, Scott wrote a reply in which he attempted to defend himself in a rather conciliatory mode. This was to no avail, for Polk subsequently insisted that there was nothing in this new letter "which changes my determination to order Gen'l Scott to remain in Washington instead of taking command of the army on the Del Norte," although the letter contained "a high compliment" about the president. By the beginning of June, the president had conveyed to the wounded general his refusal to reconsider the removal order.[33] As gracefully as possible, Scott took the rebuke like a real soldier, biding his time in Washington until months later, when the president picked him to lead the Vera Cruz expedition.

In the midst of Taylor's skirmishes with the Mexicans and Polk's skirmishes with Scott, the administration managed to piece together a strategy for the war against Mexico. Before he was summarily removed from command, Scott had exerted a helpful influence upon Secretary Marcy and Polk, as the three of them fashioned the plans for a victorious campaign. Essentially they agreed upon a simple strategy to conquer the northern provinces of Mexico, particularly California and New Mexico, as well as the area of Taylor's campaign. Polk insisted that the war be waged with volunteers, rather than a large regular army, a decision that had more political overtones than military ones. Moreover, reliance upon citizen-soldiers accorded well with the beliefs of the day that were antagonistic toward a professional army. Indeed the citizen-soldier became a symbol of American democracy and, as Robert W. Johannsen has argued, perhaps one of the foremost symbols of the Mexican War. In any event, General Scott determined that twenty thousand such volunteers would be needed immediately, most of whom would come from the states in the South and in the Ohio Valley. Subsequent volunteers would be drawn from all states (Congress had authorized up to fifty thousand volunteers).[34] Polk's cabinet approved—as did Senator Benton—the strategy to conquer and control the northern provinces and to send Scott to the Rio Grande and then into the interior, taking command from Taylor. Typical of Polk, he urged upon the secretaries of war and navy "the necessity of giving their personal attention to all matters, even of detail, and not confiding in their subordinates to act without their supervision. I required of them, too, to keep me constantly advised of every important step that was taken."[35]

At the end of May, after Scott had been relieved of command, Polk and his cabinet considered the possibility of dispatching a mounted group of soldiers to California, to help hold that province for an extended period of time, should that become necessary. The president had already been in consultation with Senator Benton about the proposal; the only hitch was whether such an expedition could be launched soon enough to enable it to reach the coast before the beginning of winter. Agreement was reached that Col. Stephen W. Kearny, who had already been ordered to take Santa Fe, could move on toward California after securing New Mexico. A cabinet meeting on 2 June considered these strategies once again and confirmed them, with the added proviso that Kearny might receive Mormon volunteers who were on their way to California. By the middle of the month the cabinet had listened to Polk's scheme to send a regiment of volunteers from New York to California by sea, in hopes that they would arrive there in time to join Kearny's command.[36] The president's lively interest in the conduct of the war continued to produce plans and strategies, but there were no important deviations from the original concept set down in mid

May, until the decision in the fall of 1846 to launch the Vera Cruz expedition.

Meanwhile, Taylor had been advised to push into Mexico, although how far was not made clear by Secretary Marcy. In fact, the War Department inquired of Taylor whether his campaign should extend as far south as Mexico City. For a time, Taylor appeared to be somewhat on his own, improvising strategy as he went, while the Polk administration was waiting for Scott to depart from Washington for the Rio Grande front—an eventuality that did not happen. Secretary Bancroft alerted Commodore Sloat, who was off the California coast, to blockade the coast, to seize port cities if possible, and to conciliate the natives. The navy secretary likewise ordered Commodore David Conner to blockade as much of the Gulf Coast as he could, to seize Tampico, if this seemed warranted, to maintain communications with Taylor, and to encourage secessionism in the Mexican states along the coast. The administration, seeking to escalate the war effort, offered considerable latitude to the officers at the scene.[37]

In May, during much of the original planning and plotting, the president turned his attention to an unusual aspect of strategy—namely, the conciliation of the Catholic Church in Mexico. To that end, he conferred with the bishop of New York and the bishop of Missouri. To both of the prelates, Polk stressed the desire to eradicate the rumors, which were already circulating widely in Mexico, that the United States intended to destroy the Catholic religion and church property in that country. The president suggested that Catholic priests from the United States be assigned to accompany the United States troops as chaplains and that perhaps some priests should go immediately to Mexico in advance of the soldiers. Clearly, Polk hoped to win the propaganda war as a means of facilitating the winning of the shooting war. Both bishops pledged their support; in fact Bishop John Joseph Hughes of New York even offered to go to Mexico himself, since he was a personal friend of the archbishop of that country. The president was immensely satisfied with these interviews.[38] Credit must be given to him for his perception of this delicate matter, his handling of it, and his apparently genuine concern for the traditional U.S. commitment to the freedom of religion.

As strategy evolved quickly during the critical weeks of May and June, no one did more than Secretary Buchanan did to smoke out the president on the vital matter of territorial aims and objectives. Whether it was an inadvertent action or a deliberate one is an unresolved question, though doubtless Polk was convinced it was the latter. In any event, on 13 May, the very day that the president signed the declaration of war, the cabinet held a special meeting to review Buchanan's draft of a letter to be circulated to all United States ministers serving in foreign countries. The secretary of state read aloud his message, in which he disavowed any territorial ambitions, beyond the obvious one of securing the Rio Grande as the boundary of Texas. Not surprisingly, this epistle ignited a heated discussion that evening, bringing forth Polk's withering comments, directed at Buchanan, as well as strong statements from other members of the cabinet. The secretary's somewhat lame defense centered upon his fear that Great Britain and France might enter the war on the side of Mexico, if they suspected territorial goals on the part of the United States. In response to this, the president, with dramatic flair, declared that before he would disavow territorial ambitions, he "would meet the war which either England or France or all the Powers of Christendom might wage, and that I would stand and fight until the last man among us fell in the conflict." Near the end of the heated two-hour debate, Polk stepped to his desk, quickly wrote out a substitute paragraph for the circular letter, and handed it to Buchanan, with the admonition to use it in place of the controversial paragraphs.[39] There could no longer be any doubt that the war aims of the Polk administration were territorial, especially in the Pacific Southwest, a position that was consistent with Polk's earliest pronouncements about western expansion.

The letter that eventually circulated to the United States diplomats spoke eloquently: "We go to war with Mexico solely for the purpose of conquering an honorable and permanent peace. Whilst we intend to prosecute the war with vigor, both by land and by sea, we shall bear the olive branch in one hand and the sword in the other; and whenever she will accept the former, we shall sheath the latter." With regard to foreign countries, Polk obviously wished to play his cards close to his vest: these nations would not be privy to knowledge about territorial goals and desires; by the same token, they would not ever hear of any disavowal of territorial ambitions, for Polk was never one to paint himself into a corner, if he could possibly avoid doing so. In subsequent cabinet deliberations over the next several weeks, Buchanan continued to express his apprehension about territorial annexations, particularly excessive ones, such as those advocated by Walker and Bancroft. Polk intervened with the observation concerning California that he wished to press as far south as the twenty-sixth parallel but would accept a boundary as far north as the thirty-second parallel. Flexibility seemed to be his motto, as long as Upper California, as well as New Mexico, became a part of the United States.[40]

While his time was occupied almost daily with the onerous task of planning for war, Polk turned his attention during the summer months of 1846 to the challenge of developing a strategy for peace. After his first peace initiative—the Slidell Mission—had failed, the president next offered a three-pronged approach to the peaceful resolution of the difficulties: the Mackenzie Mission to Santa Anna and its aftermath; the July dispatch to Mexico in behalf of peace negotiations; and finally, the request of a $2 million appropriation from Congress to purchase the coveted territory from Mexico. Regrettably, like the first overture, the second also ended in failure.

Having apparently never completely discarded the suggestions made to him by Atocha in February, Polk took action in the summer to establish direct contact with the exiled Mexican leader, Santa Anna. The man designated to lead this possible peace mission was Alexander Slidell Mackenzie, a brother of the leader of the first peace initiative, John Slidell. But weeks before this unique venture was to take place, the president had already instructed Commodore Conner to permit Santa Anna to enter Mexico, should he attempt to do so in the spring months. Comfortably situated in Havana, however, Santa Anna did not stir himself to return to Mexico, obviously waiting for a more propitious moment. In any event, Polk met with Mackenzie and instructed him to ascertain if Santa Anna would negotiate peace with the United States, if he could manage to assume leadership of Mexico. The enthusiastic young navy commander arrived in Havana in early July and shortly thereafter arranged an appointment with the former Mexican general. For whatever reason, Mackenzie put down in a memorandum the three alleged desires of President Polk: the restoration to power of Santa Anna, an insistence upon the Rio Grande as the Texas boundary and upon part of California, and a willingness to pay handsomely for territorial cessions. About a year and a half later, Polk claimed that he had not sent any specific message to Santa Anna, that he had sent no written instructions with Mackenzie, and that the latter had in fact exceeded his authority by composing the memorandum and presenting it to Santa Anna. At any rate, the exiled general responded with professions of peaceful desires, coupled with some support of territorial cessions to the United States. Mackenzie was delighted further with Santa Anna's words of military advice about how Taylor and others might best prosecute the war. Completely convinced of the success of his mission to Havana, Mackenzie made haste to visit with Taylor at his headquarters in Mexico and to relay the Mexican general's recommendations.[41]

Meanwhile the situation in Mexico had become increasingly favorable to Santa Anna's successful return, particularly since Gen. José Mariano Salas had arrested Paredes, assumed power, and issued an invitation for the exiled general to come home. Therefore, at the end of the first week in August, Santa Anna left Havana, bound for Vera Cruz. The week-long trip by British steamer was delayed by mechanical problems on board ship, but by 16 August, Santa Anna had reached his destination, having been permitted safe passage by United States Navy ships. Shortly after his arrival in Mexico, Santa Anna betrayed the Polk administration's incredible hopes that he would sue for peace. Instead, he assumed command of the Mexican army and, largely through his determined efforts, managed to prolong the war by more than a year. Polk's assistance in restoring Santa Anna to power in Mexico haunted him repeatedly and created the greatest irony of the entire war experience.

As Mackenzie set out for Havana, the president launched the second part of his summer peace initiative, namely, a new dispatch to the Mexican government. Having heard from Consul Black that the Mexican officials might be receptive to a peace commission, Polk and Buchanan leaped at the opportunity. After consulting with Senator Benton, who gave his approval, the secretary and the president readied the dispatch to Mexico in which they professed their readiness for peace negotiations, either in Mexico or in Washington. Unfortunately, once more an overthrow of Mexican officials worked against the hopes for negotiations, for by the time the new dispatch had reached Mexico, Salas was in the presidential chair. The new government rejected the Polk overture, principally on the grounds that such important matters had to be submitted to the congress, which would not convene again until early December. Meanwhile there were some fleeting hopes on the part of the Polk administration that Taylor and his troops might successfully foster secessionism in the northeastern provinces of Mexico and thereby stimulate the peace movement. But such dreams proved abortive.[42]

On the evening of 19 September, Nicholas P. Trist, chief clerk in the State Department, took to the president the Mexican answer to Polk's dispatch. Translating on the spot, Trist gave the gist of the decision to the discouraged president, who concluded that the message was in effect a rejection of the peace overture. In the light of this development, Polk informed his secretaries of navy and of war that ''the character of the war which we were waging in Mexico should be in some respects changed.'' Accordingly, he began to hasten aggressive movements against the enemy, devoting much energy during the next few days to war and naval preparations. In the midst of these stirrings, Polk revived his criticisms of officers in the War Department, obviously Whigs, and of General Scott in particular, who ''is of no aid to the Department, but his presence at Washington is constantly embarrassing to the Secretary of War." Although in a difficult mood, the president was receptive to Buchanan's effort to send a reply to the Mexican government. Originally the secretary of state had wanted to inform the Mexican officials that their country must compensate the United States for all expenses of conducting the war; but the president, as well as Secretary Marcy, objected to such a blunt demand. As eventually composed, the letter from Buchanan to the foreign minister of Mexico warned that the war would be vigorously prosecuted; at the same time the letter soothingly claimed that "the President will now await with patience and with hope the final decision of the Mexican Government."[43] Thus the door to peace negotiations was not firmly closed but remained at least slightly ajar.

In Polk's scheme of things, an integral component of his peace program during the summer of 1846 was his request for $2 million from Congress, which might enable the United States to purchase outright the coveted territories and thus end the strife between the two countries. The president revived this plan in late July, having let it remain dormant since April. On 4 August he sent a confidential message to the Senate, in which he asked for the special appropriations, because the acquisition of territory through purchase would be "the best mode of securing perpetual peace and good neighborhood between the two Republics."[44]

After rather quick approval in the Senate, the matter went before the House, where Congressman James I. McKay of North Carolina presented the appropriation request. Heated debate immediately ensued in that chamber, however, as Congressman Hugh White of New York charged that the real purpose of the bill was to extend slaveholding territory. To meet that accusation a young Democratic congressman from Pennsylvania, David Wilmot, proposed his now famous resolution—namely, that slavery should not be permitted in any territory acquired from Mexico. The House then passed the appropriations bill with Wilmot's amendment attached, but the Senate was not able to deal with this new version of the proposal before the session adjourned.[45]

A very disappointed president confided to his diary that had the appropriations bill passed Congress, "I am confident I should have made an honorable peace by which we should have acquired California, & such other territory as we desired, before the end of October." Polk was also perplexed, for he could not grasp why Wilmot had placed his "mischievous & foolish amendment" to the Two Million bill, for "what connection slavery had with making peace with Mexico it is difficult to conceive." Perhaps this was difficult for the president to comprehend, but it was not difficult for the antislavery elements in Congress and in the northern states to understand.[46] From this point forward, Polk's opponents would utilize the Wilmot Proviso to harass his administration and to foster their conviction that the Mexican War was unconstitutional, corrupt, and, in fact, immoral. They henceforth waged an unrelenting war upon a beleaguered president, who continued to maintain that he wanted peace—nothing more and nothing less.

The years of Polk's presidency were marked by a stirring of dissent and opposition throughout the American nation. Much of it was confined to the halls of Congress, to be sure, but wherever located, it was directed at the controversy over the Mexican War. The War of 1812 had certainly generated its share of critics and dissenters, but the war against Mexico fostered an even-more-widespread spirit of opposition, although it is easy to exaggerate the breadth and depth of dissent in the 1840s. In the long perspective of history, of course, opposition to the Mexican War pales in comparison to the strident voices and activities of dissent during the much-more-recent Vietnam War. In any event, it is important to examine briefly the character and nature of opposition as it manifested itself during the 1840s.

The president felt most acutely the criticism, directed at him and his conduct of war, that circulated in the national legislative branch. Not surprisingly, Whigs led much of the attack for a period of some two years. But the Whigs had to tread very carefully at times, lest they be depicted as friends of the enemy and lest they damage their party in a manner similar to what the New England Federalists had done in the days of their dissent against the War of 1812. The party of Clay, Webster, and others was trapped in the uncomfortable dilemma of voting for men, weapons, and supplies, while at the same time protesting against the war effort. They were also caught by the disagreements among themselves over the proper course of action to take in regard to the war.

Greatly hampering any effective opposition by the Whigs was the simple reality that they did not control a majority of the votes in either house until the Thirtieth Congress. Their role then became essentially one of delaying, stalling, criticizing, and hampering the administration whenever possible. Even at that, not all congressional Whigs reached agreement. The more radical element in the party, for example, staked out a strong antiwar position, coupling it usually with an antislavery position; but more conservative Whigs shrank from such an identification. Eventually, by 1847, the Whigs had hammered out a tentative compromise that embraced the "No Territory" pledge. As historian John H. Schroeder has observed, however, this agreement was essentially "a political strategy designed to protect the Whig party rather than a means of ending the war." It became patently unreasonable to expect that the United States would, after winning a victory over Mexico, walk away from an extraordinary opportunity to enlarge its boundaries. Whigs could find little support outside of the narrow confines of Congress for the "No Territory" position. Later, in the closing months of the negotiations with Mexico as the All Mexico movement blossomed, Whigs closed ranks to protest against extravagant territorial ambitions; but in this they were joined by many Democrats, including the president himself.[47] In sum, Whig leaders in Congress made life miserable for Polk, by raising significant questions about policies and even about morality; but beyond that, they did little to stop the war effort or the march toward territorial goals. Moreover, whatever they did or said was easily interpreted as raw politics, devoid of loftier principles.

Although Whig rhetoric and Whig actions in Congress tormented Polk, dissent on the part of some Democrats sentenced him to an even greater number of sleepless nights. As already mentioned, David Wilmot's proviso stirred controversy within the Democratic party and within Congress. But the president adopted an attitude of minimizing its importance, choosing instead to view the whole matter as tangential at best. Polk did not perceive the enormity of the meaning and ramifications of the Wilmot Proviso to the nation at large; few political leaders did so at the moment. The Democratic opposition that troubled him the most came from none other than Senator John C. Calhoun, the erstwhile leader of Texas annexation. The president should have antici- pated difficulties with the South Carolinian from the outset, since Calhoun refused to vote in favor of the declaration of war, ostensibly on technical grounds. Leader of the peace coalition on the Oregon matter, Calhoun feared what Mexican disruptions might do to the prospects of a final resolution of the Oregon controversy. Moreover, he apparently sensed that his political fortunes could not prosper if Polk were fully in command of situations; therefore, challenges and criticisms might be beneficial. It is not easy to escape the interpretation that Calhoun was seeking some sort of southern coalition on the question of the Mexican War, to offset the southern influence that was being exerted by the president.[48]

As the time neared for the beginning of the 1846/47 session of Congress, Calhoun began to contemplate his position on the war with Mexico. Friends and allies urged him to declare himself, especially regarding a plan to end the war. Calhoun needed little encouragement, for he was becoming increasingly pessimistic about the war and its consequences for the South, as well as for the Democratic party. One of Calhoun's friends, James Hamilton, who conferred with Polk in September, stressed, however, that Calhoun must not break with the president, for Polk bore no ill feelings toward Calhoun and in fact "cherished for your character the most unbounded respect, and for your talents the highest admiration."[49] Calhoun, who was becoming more and more concerned about the future of slavery in the West and was sensitive to the Wilmot Proviso, feared that an eventual treaty with Mexico might be silent on the question. In a "frank & pleasant" conversation in mid December, the president sought to woo Calhoun's support for the administration's conduct and plans on the war front. At that time, Calhoun warned against a treaty that might restrict slavery in the newly acquired territories, although both men agreed that slavery could not exist in those areas. Unlike Polk, Calhoun was extremely worried about the principle that was involved; both agreed upon the remoteness of the likelihood of the existence of slavery in the western lands. On that same occasion, Polk sought Calhoun's support for a proposal to create a lieutenant generalship, with Senator Benton as the candidate for that appointment, but to no avail. The South Carolinian evidently feared that such a military office would create the next president, and he viewed Benton as an antagonistic rival. Polk did not give up easily on this matter, however; on Christmas Eve he again entreated Calhoun's backing, but once more the senator expressed his opposition. Moreover, Calhoun did not favor the planned expedition to Mexico City, believing it to be a highly risky campaign and one that would prolong the war indefinitely. Instead, he supported the proposal to establish a chain of military posts in Mexico to enable the United States to hold enough territory for purposes of indemnification. Within a few days after this conversation with the president, Calhoun notified his friends about his plan for a defensive strategy.[50]

Calhoun's opposition to Polk accelerated and intensified in January and February 1847. The two men publicly separated when Calhoun spoke out against the president's request for the creation of ten regiments of regular soldiers. Believing that the bill had therefore been doomed in the Senate by his own Democratic party, Polk castigated Calhoun as "the most mischievous man in the Senate to my administration." Two days later the bill passed both houses of Congress, but irreparable damage had already been done to the relationship between the president and the South Carolinian. Calhoun followed his dangerous course by next opposing the request for $3 million to enhance negotiations with Mexico. In his mid-February speech, Calhoun elaborated upon his defensive-line strategy, while at the same time he attacked the Wilmot Proviso. Administration supporters Senators Houston and Benton rose in the chamber to attack Calhoun and his strategies.

Eventually the Three Million bill cleared Congress, without the Wilmot Proviso's being attached. The president therefore got the two vital pieces of legislation that he had lobbied for, despite the difficulties presented by Calhoun's heavy-handed opposition. In some quarters the senator's activities were viewed simply as political ploys, designed to promote his presidential ambitions. Not the least of those who clung to that understanding was Polk himself, who told Secretary Mason that "Mr. Calhoun had become perfectly desperate in his aspirations to the Presidency." Polk commented further: "I now entertain a worse opinion of Mr. Calhoun than I have ever done before. He is wholly selfish, & I am satisfied has no patriotism."[51]

In the ensuing months, Calhoun did nothing to shake the president from this critical assessment. In his December 1847 annual message to Congress, Polk categorically rejected the proposal for a defensive line, which Calhoun had offered earlier, and in fact warned that additional territory might be required if the war were to continue and if no treaty were forthcoming. Displeased with the president's message and fearful that Polk was about to embrace the All Mexico movement, Calhoun stirred himself to prepare an attack. Shortly thereafter he presented resolutions against the conquest and annexation of Mexico. In a well-received speech in January, Calhoun reiterated his defensive-line strategy, warned against the All-Mexico enthusiasm, and chided the Whigs for their No Territory proposal. Subsequently, Calhoun immodestly took credit for eliminating both the Wilmot Proviso and the All Mexico movement, while fostering support for his defensive-line stance.[52] The arrival of the peace treaty in Washington, however, ended Calhoun's hopes for determining the United States' dealings with Mexico.

While braving the criticism in Congress, the president was likewise subjected to opposition and dissent in the country at large, particularly in the northeastern region. Whig newspapers, for example, kept up a relentless attack upon Polk and his administration. Critical of virtually everything he did, but especially of his conduct of the war, they found no merit in the president. Victories and successes met with criticisms of Polk, coupled with praise for Taylor and Scott. The political motivations of the Whig journals were transparent. Interestingly enough, when the treaty provided for the payment of $15 million to Mexico, the *National Intelligencer* concluded that the United States had taken nothing by conquest but instead had compensated Mexico for the limited amount of territory that had been claimed. The Whig press, like Whig politicians, had to be careful about an overly strong stance against the war, for most readers fully supported the war as a natural by-product of Manifest Destiny.[53]

Many groups, some of which were well organized and some not so well organized, rallied dissent against the war. The chief geographical locale was the northeastern states, and the chief group was the abolitionists. With an almost fanatical interpretation of the war as an effort to enlarge the slaveholding regions of the country, the New England antislavery leaders were the most vocal opponents of the war. They urged their followers not to cooperate with the national government, and in their most radical moments, they wished for the success of the Mexican troops. William Lloyd Garrison, when he learned about the final assault upon Mexico City, editorialized in the *Liberator*: "We only hope that, if blood has had to flow, that it has been that of the American, and that the next news we shall hear will be that General Scott and his army are in the hands of the Mexicans. . . . We wish him and his troops no bodily harm, but the most utter defeat and disgrace." Naturally, members of the pacifist movement raised their objections to the war, although division crept into the ranks of the American Peace Society. One group, led principally by George Beckwith, opposed war but allowed for the possibility of a defensive war; whereas another group, under the leadership of Elihu Burritt, radically opposed all war. Closely allied to both the abolitionists and the pacifists were the clergy and their churches. Again, one must remember that official opposition to the Mexican War among religious denominations was largely confined to the northeastern region and was restricted to the Unitarian, Congregational, and Quaker churches. Elsewhere, religious dissent against the war was virtually nonexistent; in fact, in the South and in the West, pulpits offered support and sanction for the war. On the war question the American churches followed, rather than led.[54]

The fundamental problem with all of the war protesters was that they had no acceptable alternative to offer. In the face of public enthusiasm for the war and, particularly, for the acquisition of Pacific Coast lands, there was in reality little that the dissenters could do, except register their protest and seek to raise the moral consciousness of the United States. The fact that they expressed themselves freely and without fear of reprisal from the government must not be ignored. Never during all of the exasperating months of the war did Polk attempt to take any steps to quell the dissent outside of Congress.[55] The string of military victories made war protest more palatable, to be sure, but the president deserves credit for accepting the legitimate rights of those who wished to protest—something that such presidents as Lincoln and Wilson had great difficulty with. As events turned out, it was the opponents of war who were out of step with the American temperament, not the president.

Perhaps one of the accomplishments of the war dissenters, unintentional though it was, was to pressure the president toward seeking a more effective military solution. Certainly by the fall of 1846, Polk and his administration had committed themselves to the daring gamble of opening a second front in the military campaign, believing that perchance this would constitute the shortest road to peace. Even months before the outbreak of actual hostilities, Secretary Bancroft had inquired of Commodore Conner about the logistics of capturing Vera Cruz. And in June and July of 1846 the president had sought information from General Taylor about a possible attack upon Vera Cruz as the commencement of the adventuresome plan to capture Mexico City. Yet afterwards the matter of a second front disappeared from the topics of discussion at the White House until the fall months. Such a campaign would not have been necessary if Taylor had forced the surrender of Mexico by his various victorious battles; the administration waited in vain for the nearly impossible to happen. General Taylor won an impressive victory over the Mexican forces at Monterrey in late September but granted an armistice, which permitted the enemy to evacuate and to enjoy the advantages of an eight-weeks' truce. When word of the victory and the armistice was received by Polk and his cabinet, there was unanimous agreement that Taylor had fumbled a great opportunity to end the Mexican War. The president therefore ordered that the general should be instructed to terminate the armistice immediately and to resume the prosecution of "the war with energy and vigor."[56]

Receipt of news of the Monterrey victory/armistice coincided conveniently with renewed interest in administration circles in the strategy of a second front. In fact, on 10 October, the day before news of Taylor's battle at Monterrey reached the War Department, the cabinet and the president had discussed the prospects of an expedition to Vera Cruz but had postponed further consideration until F. M. Dimond, a former United States consul at Vera Cruz, could be brought to Washington for consultation. Exactly one week later, Dimond arrived in the capital from his Rhode Island home to advise the president, the cabinet, and certain military leaders about the logistics of landing at Vera Cruz and establishing an effective beachhead there. All were suitably impressed, and they asked Dimond to put the information and drawings on paper for them. Eventually there was unanimous agreement about the reasonable likelihood of a successful expedition at Vera Cruz. Subsequently the cabinet decided that Taylor should be instructed not to move beyond Monterrey; and the president picked Robert M. McLane of Baltimore to deliver this message directly to the general. As the administration became excited about the opening of a second front, General Scott was informed of the tentative plans, whereupon he raised some objections about the details but also expressed his desire to command the expedition. Telling his secretary of war that he had no intention of appointing Scott, Polk complained that the general's criticisms were "intended to embarrass the administration."[57]

What actually became embarassing was the simple fact that Polk lacked a commander for the proposed campaign at Vera Cruz. As the president commented regarding a cabinet discussion of this matter on 14 November: "All were at a loss to designate who should be the chief in command in the expedition against Vera Cruz." But Polk and his secretaries were not uncertain about their conclusion that Taylor must not be given the appointment, because "he was unfit for the chief command, that he had not mind enough for the station, that he was a bitter political partisan & had no sympathies with the administration." Senator Benton, who had arrived in town a week before this cabinet discussion, immediately sought out the president, to whom he advocated, in the strongest terms possible, that "a bold blow should be struck at once." By this he endorsed the capture of Vera Cruz and, from there, "a rapid crushing movement made . . . on the City of Mexico." Three days later, Polk and Benton conferred again, at which time they considered possible generals to lead this expedition but rejected both Taylor and Scott, among others. Finally the senator declared that the campaign "required a man of talents and resources as well as a military man for such a command, & that with a view to obtain peace more depended upon the talents & energy of the officer than upon mere bravery." Then, with notable immodesty, Benton professed that he would be willing to take the position, if Congress would create the special post of lieutenant general. By the next day, Polk had apparently recovered enough from Benton's temerity to be able to tell the senator about his doubts that Congress would agree to a lieutenant generalship, to which Benton replied that it seemed unlikely to him also.[58] The matter did not end there, however.

Meanwhile the Polk administration wrestled in mid November with the requirements that a prospective expedition to Vera Cruz would place upon the government and the military. Polk and his advisers reached consensus upon the absolute necessity for additional troops to be called out for the establishment of a second front. The president clearly stated at this juncture that he had not committed himself to a cross-country invasion of Mexico City as a by-product of the invasion of Vera Cruz. But Buchanan continued to voice his objections to any proposals for the capture of Mexico City: it would be too expensive, its success was doubtful, and it would not "facilitate peace." In a very important cabinet meeting on 17 November, Polk and his secretaries again reviewed strategy and again agreed that the possible invasion of central Mexico toward Mexico City was still a matter that was open to further debate and consideration. They spent a good bit of their time once more deliberating over the choice of a commander for the expedition to Vera Cruz. Finally, four members of the cabinet, professing much reluctance, concluded that General Scott should be offered the position. The president, in response, asked for additional time to consider this matter, for he had "strong objections to Gen'l Scott," acknowledging that "nothing but stern necessity and a sense of public duty could induce me to place him at the head of so important an expedition." Not surprisingly, on the next day, Polk summoned Benton to his office to obtain his reaction to the possible appointment of Scott. Both men agreed that they must surrender their objections to Scott, since he constituted "the best we could do." The president then promised Benton that if he could get Congress to establish the position of lieutenant general, he would appoint the senator as overall general commander. With pedestrian phrasing, Polk reported in his diary that Benton "said he would take such a command."[59]

Thursday, 19 November became one of those turning points that Scott had been waiting for. On that day the president summoned the general to his office to bestow upon him the command of the Vera Cruz campaign, but only after he had extracted professions of loyalty and cooperation. With seeming magnanimity, Polk declared that he "was willing that by-gones should be by-gones," whereupon a "deeply grateful" General Scott "almost shed tears." In this exhilarating moment of gratitude and appreciation the general offered to take with him any of the volunteer generals that Polk might wish to designate, a proposal that Scott would have ample opportunity to regret later. There was no reluctance to leave for Mexico on the general's part now, as there had been back in the spring, nor was there any "hasty plate of soup" letter; perhaps both men had reached a mature accommodation of each other's views. At any rate, a bemused president recorded that Scott left his office that morning "apparently the most delighted man I have seen for a long time."[60]

The seeming harmony did not last long, however. By the time that Scott had reached New Orleans from New York City, word was out about the planned invasion of Vera Cruz—despite all efforts to maintain secrecy. Polk naturally jumped to the conclusion that Scott had leaked the news of his special mission to the press. Or as Polk said to Benton, "He has from his inordinate vanity or from some other cause given it out, so that it has gotten before the public.[61]

Another disruptive factor in the relationship between the president and Scott was Polk's pursuit of the Benton-inspired proposal to create a lieutenant generalship. Without ever having informed Scott of his intentions but having promised Benton, on 9 December, that he would consult with members of Congress, Polk began to seek support for it. Evidently the first was Senator Lewis Cass, who reluctantly assented to the proposal, while at the same time warning about its slim chances of approval in the Congress. Secretary of War Marcy gave little evidence of enthusiasm for the bill either; in fact, Benton later charged that Marcy had opposed it. Senators John M. Niles and Ambrose H. Sevier appear to have been among the very few congressmen consulted by the president who supported the appointment of Benton. Considering the lack of backing expressed by most of his advisers, it is remarkable that Polk persisted with stubborn determination on this matter. Evidently the depth of his hostility toward both Taylor and Scott became the principal motivation behind the pursuit of a futile cause. Benton continued to pressure Polk, however; and apparently the president feared the loss of the senator's friendship and support if he did not push the lieutenant-general bill. In any event, on Christmas Day, Polk committed himself to this bill, a position that he informed the cabinet about on the next day. On the twenty-ninth the president's private secretary took a special message to the Capitol, which included the recommendation for the creation of the lieutenant generalship; but because the Senate had already adjourned, the message was not finally delivered until 4 January. A week and a half later the Senate tabled the proposal for a new general, thus bringing to an abrupt end this questionable episode, which did nothing to enhance Polk's relationship either with Congress or with Scott.[62]

Meanwhile the general was preparing for the all-important invasion campaign of Vera Cruz, a project that he carried out with dazzling success in early March. By then the commitment had been made to escalate the war even further by launching a march toward Mexico City. Indeed, such an attack upon the capital became inevitable once Vera Cruz had been secured by the U.S. forces, for there simply was to be no turning back.

With the sword in one hand, Polk pursued the second-front campaign; at the same time he held the olive branch in the other hand, anxious once more for peace negotiations. The widening of the war effort in 1847 was accompanied by the opening of another peace initiative. Moses Y. Beach played a minor role in this, as did the ubiquitous Alexander J. Atocha; mostly, however, it was Nicholas P. Trist's show. In November 1846, the same month that Scott assumed command of the Vera Cruz expedition, Secretary Buchanan wrote an official letter to Beach, who was anxious to depart for Mexico as a facilitator of peace discussions and also of private business matters. The Polk administration appointed him as a special (secret) agent to Mexico, without any specific instructions other than that he must not let anyone know that he had such an appointment. Buchanan and Beach conferred several times before the latter's departure for Mexico, and apparently both men considered that Beach had been given diplomatic powers—a point that Polk later denied. Nevertheless, Beach, his daughter, and Mrs. Jane Storms, an editorial writer for Beach's paper, the *New York Sun*, went first to Charleston, then to Havana, where they remained for about three weeks, and finally, in January, to Vera Cruz and eventually to Mexico City itself.[63]

Little is known about Beach's activities during the period of some nine or ten weeks that he spent in the capital city. He was in communication with Consul Black, as well as with high Mexican officials, before hastily leaving Mexico City in April. Beach claimed to have exerted influence over the Catholic clergy there to the extent that he was instrumental in obtaining a commitment from them for certain specified peace terms. In mid March he wrote a letter to Secretary Buchanan in which he avowed that Mexican leaders were ready for a treaty of peace. When informed of Beach's letter a month later, Polk fretted that the secret agent might be exceeding his authority and might attempt to press a treaty upon the Mexican officials. But "should he do so, and it is a good one, I will waive his authority to make it, and submit it to the Senate for ratification. It will be a good joke if he should assume the authority and take the whole country by surprise & make a Treaty."[64]

Beach had no such remarkable luck, however. Instead, he left Mexico City empty-handed and arrived in New Orleans not long after Buchanan and Polk had received his March letter. The editor-businessman appeared in Washington during the second week of May, visited with the president, and gave him "valuable information." Two days later, his appointment officially ended, and he collected nearly $3,000 from the State Department for his services. In early June, Beach submitted the official report of his activities while he was in Mexico, the only available information about his adventures. Despite its claims, however, the fact remains that Beach played an inconsequential role in the Polk peace initiative and that, some have argued, he did more harm than good while in Mexico.[65]

Equally difficult to assess was the handiwork of Atocha, whose timely arrival in Washington in January stirred the Polk administration to revive its hopes for peace negotiations. The president, although he did not confer directly with Atocha, believed the information that was relayed to him by Buchanan and Benton, who discussed at length the letters in Atocha's possession from Santa Anna, Manuel Crescencio Rejón, and Almonte. Polk, Benton, and Buchanan concluded that the documents were genuine and that the expressions in favor of treaty talks were valid. Atocha reported that these Mexican officials desired immediate peace negotiations, that they were ready to accept the Rio Grande as the Texas boundary, although they would stipulate a neutral zone between it and the Nueces, and that they were ready to sell California for $15 to $20 million; they furthermore requested that the United States lift the blockade of Mexican ports and that it send peace commissioners to Havana. Polk, however, wanted New Mexico in addition to California, so he would not consent to a cessation of the blockade or of the military effort until a treaty was actually in hand. These reservations, which Secretary Buchanan communicated to Atocha, presented no obstacle to the Mexican emissary.[66]

Meanwhile, Polk clung to the conviction that Atocha had been sent directly to Washington by Santa Anna and others and that successful negotiations were feasible. Accordingly, he and his cabinet agreed to send Atocha to Mexico City with a sealed letter (from Secretary Buchanan) to the high government officials there, indicating United States interest in treaty talks. The document that Atocha took back to Mexico promised that the United States would send peace commissioners to Jalapa or Havana with the full power to negotiate and with discretionary powers to suspend hostilities and lift the blockade. To hasten Atocha's journey, the United States provided transportation for him from Washington to Vera Cruz. By the time that Atocha had reached Mexico City, the political situation there had changed again, however, the results of which were the acting presidency of Valentín Gómez Farías and a stiffening of attitudes toward the United States. As a matter of fact, Farías had Atocha placed under house arrest after the latter had delivered the sealed document from Secretary Buchanan. The acting president subsequently issued a published version of the document, which he had modified and altered to make the U.S. demands appear unreasonable, thereby eliciting negative responses from Mexican political leaders. Afterwards, Farías's foreign minister penned a reply to the Buchanan overture in which he rejected the proposal for peace commissioners and discussions until such time as the United States had lifted the blockade and withdrawn its armies. Atocha subsequently left Mexico for Washington, where he arrived on 20 March, after Congress had adjourned.[67]

Atocha's message of rejection greatly disappointed the president and his cabinet, so much so that it prompted the decision to send Scott's army all the way to Mexico City. As Polk expressed it: ''No alternative was now left but the most energetic crushing movement of our arms upon Mexico.'' When Buchanan raised objections, the president responded even more strongly: ''I would not only march to the City of Mexico, but . . . I would pursue Santa Anna's army wherever it was, and capture or destroy it.'' Polk concluded by averring that the proper military commander ''who would lay aside the technical rules of war to be found in books'' could accomplish the goal of ending the war with Mexico.[68] While the president was understandably upset by this latest rejection from Mexico, he nonetheless did not abandon his quest for peace negotiations and therefore looked to the State Department to find someone who could depart for Mexico and accompany Scott's army as it moved toward the capital city.

On Saturday, 10 April, several sources conveyed the ''joyful news,'' as Polk described it, of Scott's successful capture of Vera Cruz. Immediately the president began conversations about his ultimate peace initiative—sending a commissioner, armed with a draft treaty, to accompany Scott's army. Buchanan and Polk had conferred on this matter earlier, but now the victory gave great urgency to it. Informing the cabinet of Scott's successes, the president indicated his desire to dispatch a peace commissioner at once to Mexico. Factional jealousies within the Democratic party precluded the possibility of sending a prominent politician, whereas the likelihood of great delays in the negotiations prevented sending Buchanan. The secretary of state therefore suggested to the cabinet meeting the name of his chief clerk, Nicholas P. Trist, ''an able man, perfectly familiar with the Spanish character and language.'' Quickly, all agreed to the designation of Trist for this extremely significant mission, one that the president hoped to keep ''a profound secret.''[69]

In the course of subsequent discussions within the Polk administration, the terms of the proposed draft treaty were hammered out. The president and his cabinet readily agreed upon demands for the Rio Grande boundary and for the cession of New Mexico and of both Lower and Upper California. Secretary Walker pressed his proposal that any treaty also should provide for transit rights for U.S. citizens across the Isthmus of Tehuantepec. Although Polk agreed that this demand might be included in Trist's instructions, he clearly stated his position that Tehuantepec must not be construed as an absolute necessity for any treaty with Mexico. On the other hand, he continued by declaring forthrightly that the acquisition of New Mexico and Upper California must be a *sine qua non* of a Mexican treaty. The president and his advisers juggled payment figures; apparently there was no dissension over the proposition that Mexico should be compensated for the lands that it would cede. Buchanan's initial draft of instructions to Trist provided that the United States would pay $15 million for Mexican cessions, but the president was willing and even anxious to increase that amount if necessary. As he argued cogently before the cabinet, the prolongation of the war would cost the country far more than $20 or $30 million. All eventually agreed that if Trist were able to acquire all the terms mentioned, the price tag should be $30 million; if, however, the Tehuantepec matter fell through, the payment should not exceed $25 million. Furthermore, if Lower California could not be obtained in the treaty, then the compensation should be $20 million. Near the end of this discussion, Polk emphasized that all of these figures represented *maximum* payments; consequently Trist should exert himself to settle for much less. Two days later, on 15 April, the cabinet held a special session to complete the final review of Trist's instructions; thereafter Polk signed the clerk's letter of appointment. On the following day, Trist left Washington, bound for Mexico.[70]

As the peace commissioner departed, Polk worried lest the general public, and particularly the Whig press, learn about this dramatic initiative. His concern revolved around his warped notion that Whig leaders, upon hearing of Trist's mission, would seek to sabotage it by sending a delegation to Mexico to entreat that country not to negotiate. After all, the president was confident that articles in the Whig newspapers had done "more to prevent a peace than all the armies of the enemy." But his anxiety about leaks to the press did not apply to friendly newspapers. The very day that Trist left Washington, for example, Polk summoned Editor Ritchie to his office in order to inform him of this secret peace venture, justifying his conversation on the grounds that "it was necessary that he should know it in order to shape the course of his paper in reference to it." The president's consultation with his editor was followed on the next day with another meeting between these two allies.[71]

Historian David Pletcher has observed: "The auspices for peace seemed favorable: the Mexicans badly beaten, the Americans receptive, the British complaisant."[72] It was unlucky for the Polk administration's quest for imminent negotiations that Trist turned out to be a quite difficult emissary—not necessarily for the Mexicans but for General Scott. By the time the peace commissioner arrived at Vera Cruz on 6 May, he was already suffering from delusions of grandeur. Very soon, all of his liabilities as a person and as a diplomat became painfully evident, much to the dismay of Polk, Buchanan, and other cabinet advisers. As events developed, Trist and Scott matched each other in terms of extreme personal pride, thin-skinned sensitivity, fierce independence, and an irrepressible propensity for letter writing. Sharing so many negative traits, both men instantly disliked one another. Emotionally wounded and resentful over the reality of Trist's appointment, Scott was in no mood to receive Polk's representative or to cooperate with him. After the two men launched their famous antagonistic epistolary campaign, Polk was ready to declare a plague on both their houses and to recall them from service in Mexico. Only the lack of acceptable alternatives at the moment stayed the president's hand.

Fortunately, Scott and Trist would eventually accomplish the defeat of the Mexican armies and the negotiation of a peace treaty; but it would take months. After having poisoned the atmosphere with their accusatory and heated letters, the two men refused to speak to one another, the sort of predicament that no one in Washington had contemplated. A young British attaché, Sir Edward Thornton, was shocked to discover this state of affairs when he journeyed out from Mexico City to confer with Scott and Trist at Puebla and to relay the encouraging news of peace sentiment at the capital city. Eventually, in early July, Scott befriended an indisposed Trist with a box of guava marmalade, a gift that brought peace at last to the two feuding Americans; subsequently they were able to turn their attention to the far-more-significant matter of seeking peace with the Mexicans. In the meanwhile, however, the Polk administration had fretted over the conflict between Scott and Trist and had been shocked and dismayed when Scott had written to Washington in early June asking to be recalled, because of "the many cruel disappointments and mortifications I have been made to feel since I left Washington." Polk's absence from Washington during part of the summer of 1847, because of two different trips, may have saved the professional hides of both the distraught Scott and the temperamental Trist. In any event, the president kept his secretary of state and his secretary of war busy trying to resolve the embarrassing and exasperating difficulties between Trist and Scott.[73] As indicated, the two prima donnas finally effected a genuine truce and became fast friends, much to the puzzlement of Washington observers.

As Scott was preparing for his final move toward Mexico City from Puebla, Trist was holding conversations with Mexican officials, initially through the good offices of the British. Both the general and the peace commissioner agreed to the highly risky course of yielding to a bribe proposal, whereby they would agree to release $10,000 as a down payment toward an eventual figure of $1 million. Scott first sought

Gideon J. Pillow's approval (an important gesture in light of Pillow's personal friendship with President Polk) and then the support of all his generals. Whereas Pillow at first endorsed the bribery attempt, he changed his mind when his colleagues condemned it. The money was sent forward to Mexico City anyway, but instead of becoming bread upon the waters, as Scott had prophesied, it did not result in any immediate peace talks and therefore caused criticism to be directed at both Scott and Trist. At the end of August, after the battles of Contreras and Churubusco, Trist held his first meeting with Mexican commissioners, at which time he revealed the draft treaty that had been prepared by the Polk administration. He also confided that there might be some flexibility in his instructions, particularly with regard to the amount of payment for ceded lands. Acting within his prerogatives, Trist likewise abandoned the demand for Lower California. About a week later, Mexican officials returned with their answer: they rejected the treaty as outlined by Trist; instead, they proposed the Nueces as the Texas boundary, California above the thirty-seventh parallel, and no part of New Mexico. Greatly disappointed, Trist broke off the negotiations, thus setting the stage for the assault upon Mexico City.[74]

Meanwhile, in Washington, the administration was worrying about the progress that both Scott and Trist were making toward ending the war, either through military might or through peace talks. In an important cabinet discussion of these concerns on 7 September, Secretary Buchanan took the initiative by suggesting that the compensation offered to the Mexicans should be reduced to a maximum of $15 million and that some readjustment of boundary lines would be warranted. Quickly Secretary Walker and Attorney General Clifford joined in to make demands for additional territory. Cautiously the president sided with Buchanan and refrained from endorsing the bolder position of Walker and Clifford. Secretary Mason urged that nothing be done, however, until further word had been received from Mexico regarding Trist's progress or lack thereof. Although there was concurrence on this proposal, Clifford, followed by Walker, declared that if the Mexicans still refused to agree to a peace treaty, Trist should be recalled. Polk disagreed with this more radical proposal on the grounds that it was advisable to keep Trist with Scott's army in case the Mexicans should decide to make peace overtures.[75]

Exactly one week after this cabinet meeting, Scott marched into Mexico City. Unaware of this dramatic victory, the Polk administration continued to fret over the prospects for peace. As a matter of fact, on the very day of Scott's entry into Mexico's capital, Polk received word about the mid-August battles of Contreras and Churubusco, the brief armistice that followed, and Trist's conversations with Mexican commissioners at the end of that month. Quite naturally regretting the armistice, Polk expressed his hope that Trist might be successful. After being distracted by several days of illness, the president, on 4 October, finally decided to recall Trist from Mexico. He directed Buchanan to prepare such a letter, a decision that was based upon information received from a Mexican pamphlet concerning the proposal of that government. The cabinet unanimously agreed upon the propriety of recalling Trist, and on 6 October, Buchanan forwarded a letter to him. The secretary informed his chief clerk that if he had already negotiated a treaty by the time he received the recall notice, he should bring it with him to Washington; otherwise, he must immediately suspend talks and depart from Mexico.[76] Evidently the Polk administration had by now despaired of negotiations that would bring an immediate and acceptable end to the war.

Later in the month of October the president received word about Scott's capture of Mexico City and also reports from Trist about his discussions with Mexican officials subsequent to Scott's remarkable victory. By that time, Polk had begun to question Trist's capabilities—a return to his earlier views about the peace commissioner—and consequently to find further reason for recalling Trist. The president was quite irritated, for example, with Trist's indications of some flexibility on his part concerning the Texas boundary and the acquisition of all of Upper California. By 23 October, Polk had concluded that "Mr. Trist has managed the negotiation very bunglingly and with no ability. He has done more. He has departed from his instruction." The cabinet agreed with the president's assessment of the situation and supported Polk's directive to Secretary Buchanan to prepare another letter, insisting upon the immediate recall of Trist. Corresponding with these actions was the decision to send stronger messages to General Scott, urging him to clamp down upon the Mexican people, principally by obtaining supplies and money from them. Moreover, he must take whatever steps were necessary to eradicate guerrilla warfare. Clearly, the victory at Mexico City brought bittersweet messages. Polk now seemed more determined than ever to take a harsher stand against Mexico and perhaps to take direct charge of the peace negotiations. He and others had justifiable reasons to regret that victory after victory had not yet brought a cessation of hostilities. In those moments of exasperation, Polk told his cabinet that he intended to recommend to Congress that California and New Mexico should be annexed as territories and that appropriate governments should be established in each of them—a bold, if not dangerous, position for the president to hold.[77]

Polk was spared such drastic actions by the eventual successes of his negotiator, Nicholas P. Trist. It is common knowledge that Trist ignored the recall letters and proceeded through months of agonizing discussions and deliberations with Mexican officials, which resulted in a treaty in February 1848. Curiously enough, the Polk administration remained oblivious to Trist's efforts during much of this time, for communications apparently were exceptionally slow and infrequent. Although Trist received his instructions to return to Washington in mid November, he elected to disobey them, after an initial impulse to break off negotiations and leave Mexico. As a matter of fact, on 27 November he wrote to Secretary Buchanan, describing the favorable chances for successful peace negotiations but also reporting that he would depart within ten days. About a week later, however, Trist yielded to pressures in Mexico to remain and therefore pursued the difficult quest for a treaty. Unfortunately for him, the Mexicans devised new ways to stall and procrastinate. Meanwhile, in early January, his November dispatches were finally received by the Polk administration; ironically, by that date the president had decided to recall General Scott, replacing him with Gen. William O. Butler. Much of the concern about Scott revolved around the sparring among the generals, which resulted in charges and countercharges involving the commander and his generals—a matter that greatly distracted and annoyed Polk during December and January. By January the president had also become increasingly exercised about Trist's decision to ignore the recall messages; he was convinced that Trist was acting upon advice from Scott.[78] After all, Polk was predisposed to believe that conspiracies existed.

The December messages from Trist began to arrive with some frequency in Washington in early and mid January. One of them was a letter to his wife; it contained a special postscript for Buchanan, which reported the reopening of negotiations and possible terms of agreement. His dispatch of 6 December greatly offended Polk, for it was ''arrogant, impudent, and very insulting to his Government, and even personally offensive to the President.'' The entire cabinet shared Polk's sense of outrage, or at least bruised feelings, and supported the president's orders to Buchanan to prepare a stern rebuke for Trist. Near the end of the month, Polk sought support among senators for his plan to have General Butler evict Trist from Mexico and levy some sort of punishment against him. Finally, Polk, Buchanan, and eventually the whole cabinet wrestled with the possibility that Trist might actually secure an acceptable treaty, despite his lack of authority, and forward it to Washington, whereupon the administration must have a previously agreed-upon strategy about how to handle the arrival of such a document. The president and his secretary of state cautiously elected not to commit themselves one way or the other, although each confessed his inclination to reject Trist's handiwork. On a closely related front, the administration deliberated over sending a letter to General Butler, authorizing him to oust Trist and send him home. The issue became clouded with the potential for embarrassment, should the negotiator truly succeed with a treaty that accorded with his instructions. The cabinet was painfully divided on the matter, much to Polk's dismay, but the president decided to send the letter anyway. Accordingly, a special courier was dispatched to Mexico on 26 January. On 2 February, the very day that Trist secured the signatures of the Mexican peace commissioners to the final version of the treaty, Polk, who was naturally unaware of events in far-off Mexico, engaged in a conversation with Senator William Allen about "the unpardonable conduct of Mr. Trist and Gen'l Scott."[79] Within a short time thereafter, the abstractions about Trist's conduct, his questionable legal authority, his alleged conspiring with Scott, and other grievances were swept away by the receipt of a copy of the actual treaty. Now the moment of truth had finally arrived for the president and his advisers: would they accept the treaty and forward it to the Senate for ratification, or would they reject it summarily, because it had been devised by the tainted Trist?

The treaty actually arrived in Washington on 19 February, a scant two and one-half weeks after it had been signed at Guadalupe Hidalgo. Shortly before its appearance, however, Polk had fretted about the lack of letters or dispatches from Trist and Scott, naturally concluding that such neglect "was undoubtedly from design." He was confident "that there is a conspiracy between Scott & himself [Trist] to put the Government at defiance & make a Treaty of some sort." The president was particularly upset because Alexander Atocha, "a great scoundrel," had written to Buchanan, urging that he be given money by the United States with which to bribe the Mexican congress to approve a peace treaty.[80]

Several days later, with the arrival of the treaty, Polk had the opportunity to turn his attention to more significant matters. He was initially pleased with the treaty, for its terms were within the instructions given to Trist. Although complaining once more about Trist's conduct, the president acknowledged that the treaty should not be rejected simply on that basis. At a special Sunday meeting, the cabinet discussed and debated the treaty, with only Buchanan and Walker recommending that it be rejected. On the following day, 21 February, Polk called another special session of the cabinet, at which time he elaborated upon his reasons for being favorably disposed toward the treaty and toward submitting it to the Senate for ratification. He rightly reasoned that it represented what the administration had been seeking and that further delay, especially in light of the possible outcome of the presidential election, would lose all that he had worked for. Buchanan nonetheless again sparred with the president, arguing that the United States should hold out for additional territory, a position that was in contradiction to the one that he had held months earlier, as Polk carefully pointed out. The president confided afterwards: "I cannot help laboring under the conviction that the true reason of Mr. Buchanan's present course is that he is now a candidate for the Presidency, and he does not wish to incur the displeasure of those who are in favour of the conquest of all Mexico." Undeterred by his secretary of state, Polk made ready to forward the treaty to the Senate, with an accompanying presidential message, after having first presented a copy of the treaty to Senator Ambrose Sevier. The death of John Quincy Adams ironically intervened to delay the Senate's consideration of the treaty for a day or two.[81]

In the days that followed, Polk and his advisers were kept on tenterhooks as they heard predictions that the Senate would reject the treaty, only to be assured next that the Senate would ratify it. Apparently, Postmaster General Cave Johnson was the first person to warn the president that the Senate might not approve the treaty. Johnson also ominously noted the rumors that both Buchanan and Walker were working behind the scenes to bring about the rejection of the treaty. Such reports from Johnson reached Polk's ears on the same day that Attorney General Clifford informed the president that Buchanan and Walker were planning to resign from the cabinet, a prospect that Polk minimized. Three days later, on 28 February, Senator Sevier brought the disturbing news that his Foreign Relations Committee would recommend that the treaty be rejected and would instead approve the appointment of a new treaty commission, largely on the grounds that Trist had not had the authority to negotiate the treaty. Jolted by this news, the president immediately and shrewdly analyzed why different members of that committee were supporting such a position. He was particularly struck by the fact that Daniel Webster, who advocated that no territory be taken from Mexico, had lined up with Senator Edward Hannegan, who was an All Mexico proponent. As Polk wisely observed, "Extremes sometimes meet and act effectively for negative purposes, but never for affirmative purposes." Doubtless he was relieved and pleased when Buchanan and Walker went out to lobby with senators against the proposal of a new treaty commission. As Polk continued to confer with senators, he continued to receive predictions of defeat for the treaty, but suddenly on 2 March, the president concluded that the treaty would indeed be ratified, albeit by a close vote, an opinion that was shaken two days later by reports from the senators that the ratification of the treaty was doubtful. Polk noted that ''the Presidential election has too much to do with the question of the ratification of the Treaty.'' No sooner had the president become doubtful about the treaty's prospects than Senator Thomas Jefferson Rusk, on 6 March, predicted that it would be ratified—a view that others reiterated during the next few days.[82]

Accordingly, Polk set himself to the task of selecting someone who would be designated to carry the treaty to Mexico for the purpose of seeking its acceptance there. The cabinet deliberated over the matter, but Polk made clear his preference for Louis McLane, a veteran of the Oregon treaty negotiations in London. But McLane's son brought news of his refusal to serve. Therefore, on the day after the treaty was ratified, Polk and his cabinet once more considered the appointment of a special commissioner, at which time the president indicated his desire to nominate Senator Sevier. At first, Sevier rejected the appointment, but subsequently he agreed to take it; and on 14 March, Polk forwarded Sevier's name to the Senate, which approved the nomination promptly. Probably a shrewd move on the part of the president, it was upset by Sevier's sudden illness, which forced Polk to seek someone else to go to Mexico, in the event that Sevier did not recuperate right away. The president turned to a cabinet member, Attorney General Clifford, who accepted.[83]

Meanwhile the Senate, by a wide margin of 22 votes (36 to 14), ratified the treaty. Polk had little time for rejoicing, however, for he had to secure a special commissioner to take the treaty to Mexico, had to relay the news to General Butler, and had to attend to many other chores. In the pursuit of such matters he was alarmed by reports that the Senate intended to remove the injunction of secrecy from the treaty-ratification proceedings, an unprecedented action. Fearing the likelihood of rejection on the part of the Mexican government if such information became publicly known, the president quickly conferred with several senators to head off this possibility. He was successful in blocking the lifting of secrecy, a move that he interpreted as one that ''could not be otherwise than mischievous.'' But no sooner had he put out that fire than another erupted—the publication in the *New York Herald* of the treaty and other confidential documents. The Senate launched an investigation of this breach of security and secrecy, but to no avail.[84]

Fortunately for the president, the arrival of the treaty in mid February undermined the All Mexico movement. The campaign to acquire even more territory than the Polk administration had long advocated began to gain momentum during the fall of 1847, aided and abetted by Buchanan from time to time. It could have been exceedingly dangerous to Polk and his plans for an end to the fighting in Mexico, for it almost inevitably meant continued hostilities. The president quite sensibly never supported the All Mexico enthusiasm, but such unbridled expansionism was not an unnatural extension of the position that he had promoted in behalf of the acquisition of western lands. Ironically, the All Mexico movement reached its peak at about the time when Trist's treaty arrived in Washington. Although there were some lingering expressions of the movement during the Senate's deliberations, it faded rapidly, partly because of fears about incorporating nonwhite people into the United States.[85]

Controversies surrounding the two heroes of the treaty negotiations, Scott and Trist, would not fade rapidly away, however. As noted earlier, in January, Polk and his cabinet agreed upon the removal of Scott from command—the result of his having court-martialed Pillow, William J. Worth, and James Duncan. The president, in response, ordered a court of inquiry. Had Polk's personal friend Pillow not been involved, perhaps the entire matter could have been dealt with in a less controversial fashion. Suffice it to say that the swirling currents of dispute detracted somewhat from the success at the peace table in Guadalupe Hidalgo. With regard to Trist, the president directed General Butler to send him home immediately—to receive, not accolades, but reprimands instead. Yielding to petty impulses, Polk decreed that Trist could not be paid for his services beyond the date of his receipt of the letter of recall—about mid November. Therefore the exceedingly tough months of negotiating in December and January were to remain unrewarded, from a monetary point of view. Years later, long after Mexico had formally accepted the Treaty of Guadalupe Hidalgo, Congress voted the necessary funds to remunerate Trist for his labors in behalf of the treaty.[86]

During the early months of 1848, problems with the All Mexico campaign, with Scott, and with Trist were not the only disturbances that seemed to keep Polk from savoring the triumph of arms and talks. The almost insatiable appetite of expansionism turned its attention toward Yucatan and Cuba. Admittedly postscripts to the story of California, the Yucatan and Cuba chapters gave vent to further desires for territorial greed and gains.

In late April the Polk administration received word from Yucatan about the Indian atrocities and the general situation of civil war on that peninsula. Yucatan governmental officials begged for assistance, in exchange for which they offered the dominion and sovereignty over Yucatan to the assisting nation. But as the president shrewdly observed, "The subject is environed with difficulties." During a cabinet discussion of the Yucatan situation, Polk revealed his apprehensions about letting some European power intervene and thereby achieve possession and/or sovereignty. Subsequently the president began to prepare a special message to Congress in regard to Yucatan, because he had been displeased with the draft penned by Buchanan. After conferring with Buchanan, other cabinet members, and several congressmen on 28 April, Polk sent his Yucatan message to Congress on the following day. In this document the president made no specific proposal concerning aid to that stricken peninsula, leaving that matter to the wisdom of Congress. But after claiming that the United States did not desire to take actual possession and control over the Mexican peninsula, he made clear his aversion to the prospect of having some European power gain dominion over Yucatan.[87]

In response to the president's message, the Senate became the forum for much debate and disagreement. Calhoun and Whig leaders voiced their opposition to any involvement in Yucatan. Meanwhile the arch expansionist, Senator Hannegan of Indiana, introduced a resolution providing for the temporary military occupation of Yucatan and the distribution of arms and ammunition to the whites who were attempting to repel Indian attacks there. But an even stronger stance was taken in Polk's cabinet by Secretary Walker, who advocated that the United States annex Yucatan, a position that was vigorously opposed by Secretary Buchanan in a cabinet discussion on 6 May. Eventually, Senator John A. Dix attempted to alter Hannegan's resolution by deleting the commitment to a military occupation of Yucatan and by substituting merely an authorization of aid to the people of Yucatan by the United States military. Evidently Dix did not know, at the moment of his speech and proposal, that word had been received in Washington of peace, or at least of a truce, in Yucatan. Senator Hannegan thereafter withdrew his original resolution, and the whole Yucatan matter collapsed, not to be revived even when civil warfare resumed in the Mexican peninsula shortly afterwards. Interestingly, Polk made no mention of any of these discussions or the changing developments in Yucatan in his diary, for there is no further reference to such matters after the cabinet discussion on 6 May. One later interpretation of the excitement over Yucatan assesses it as evidence of Polk's inability to control the Democratic party.[88] More likely, however, the president and many others were simply distracted in May by the pending Democratic

National Convention in Baltimore and also by a general war-weariness, which precluded a genuine commitment to intervention in Yucatan.

But despite such distractions, interest in the acquisition of Cuba blossomed in May and June 1848. John L. O'Sullivan, a prominent journalist and western expansionist from New York, was probably the first to push the State Department in the direction of developing an interest in the future of Cuba; but his memorandum of 1847 came in the midst of the great struggle for military victory over Mexico and hence could not be acted upon. Persistent as he was, O'Sullivan penned another memorandum to Buchanan, this time in March, and then in May he appeared at Polk's office, accompanied by Senator Stephen A. Douglas. The president gave them a polite hearing but would not make any commitment, except in the pages of his diary, where he recorded his support of a plan to acquire Cuba by purchase and to annex it to the United States at some future date.[89]

Not until the end of the month, however, did the president bring before the cabinet the idea of acquiring Cuba, a topic that consumed the attention of at least five cabinet meetings from 30 May through 17 June. From the outset there was a notable division of opinion within the cabinet, with Secretary Walker being the most enthusiastic and Secretary Buchanan being the most reluctant on the matter. At the very first cabinet discussion the president disclosed his support of the immediate purchase of Cuba. Before the second cabinet meeting devoted to Cuba (on 3 June), dispatches were received from the United States consul in Havana, depicting the volatile situation there and the likelihood of a revolution and the overthrow of Spanish authority. O'Sullivan paid a second visit to Polk, at which time he informed him, much like the consul's dispatches, of the revolutionary environment in Cuba. He pressed the possibility of some military action in Cuba by returning U.S. soldiers, but Polk categorically rejected this, declaring "that as President of the U.S. I could give no countenance to such a step, and could not wink at such a movement." Instead, contended the president, Cuba must be obtained only "by amicable purchase." Also prior to the second cabinet discussion of Cuba, the president had intentionally sought out the views of presidential nominee Senator Lewis Cass, who revealed his strong backing for the purchase of Cuba and his conviction that this proposal would in no way jeopardize his presidential campaign. Therefore when the cabinet convened, Polk was able to defuse one of Buchanan's main arguments, namely that the pursuit of the acquisition of Cuba might be detrimental to Cass's candidacy. But Buchanan continued to play the role of the reluctant and difficult member of the

Polk family, while Walker, on the other hand, continued to press the urgency of the purchase of Cuba.[90]

The third cabinet debate on Cuba occurred on 6 June, at which time Polk unveiled his strategy—namely, that the prospective purchase of Cuba must be handled through Romulus Saunders, the U.S. minister to Madrid. Members of the cabinet continued to voice divided sentiments over any plan to acquire Cuba, however, with Buchanan maintaining that the United States must await the appropriate time to purchase Cuba; Walker, joined by Secretary Mason, continuing to campaign for immediate action; and Postmaster General Johnson once more expressing his opposition. Three days after this discussion, Walker conferred privately with Polk to express his concerns that any notions held by U.S. soldiers (volunteers) in Mexico that they might go to Cuba to foment revolution should be headed off by explicit instructions to General Butler. Walker rightly feared that all hopes of purchasing Cuba would be ruined by any military involvement, whether authorized or unauthorized. The president concurred, sent for Secretary Marcy to prepare orders to Butler, and then called a special meeting of the cabinet.[91]

The fourth cabinet discussion (on 9 June) brought at last harmony and unity of beliefs within the official family, thanks to Walker's efforts. The Treasury secretary stressed to his colleagues that the most auspicious approach would be to assure Spain of the United States' friendly attitudes by emphasizing the nonsupport of any revolutionary activity in Cuba. Furthermore, argued Walker, Spain should be offered the opportunity to sell Cuba to the United States. The reasonableness of this approach struck all members of the cabinet, including Buchanan, as the best way to proceed, and everyone therefore agreed. The head of the State Department even avowed that "he heartily approved the plan suggested, and if adopted he would cheerfully prepare the necessary instructions to Mr. Saunders." Delighted with this turn of sentiment and opinion within the cabinet, Polk immediately declared that he would support this procedural strategy. The elated president even decided to cancel the regular cabinet meeting that was scheduled for the next day.[92]

Nothing more remained to be done except for having Buchanan draft the instructions to Saunders. This he did, as promised, and read them aloud to the cabinet at its fifth and final consideration of Cuba, on 17 June. The minister to Madrid was authorized to assure Spanish officials of the United States' peaceful intentions regarding Cuba and of the United States commitment to prevent any other European power from gaining control of Cuba. If Spain would be willing to cede Cuba to the United States, a sum in the amount of $100 million would be offered.

To that end, Saunders was to be given the power to devise a treaty with Spain. Although the president was ill, he stirred himself to describe Buchanan's instructions to Saunders as "an able and well-written despatch"—a very rare compliment from Polk, especially to his secretary of state. The cabinet adjourned, with Polk hoping for secrecy. He had already concluded that he could not trust O'Sullivan (who, after all, was a member of the Barnburner faction of New York Democrats) with any clues about the intentions to purchase Cuba. Except for Senator Jefferson Davis's bringing three Cuban citizens to confer with the president on 23 June, nothing more was heard of the Cuba strategy for a while.[93] Eventually, however, Spain turned down Saunders's overtures, for a variety of reasons, thus putting an end to this attempt at territorial expansion.

As the summer breezes of 1848 wafted across the Potomac, Polk could easily lay aside momentary concerns about Cuba and Yucatan to luxuriate in his accomplishments. Europe, beseiged by revolutions in that year, had little to offer to the history books in comparison to the saga of the winning of the Southwest, which was finally completed during Polk's last year as president.

With the official termination of the Mexican War and the consequent acquisition of both California and New Mexico, as well as the resolution of the Texas boundary problem, the president and the nation took stock of themselves. Polk singled out his conviction that the war "fully developed the capacity of republican governments to prosecute successfully a just and necessary foreign war with all the vigor usually attributed to more arbitrary forms of government."[94] Much like America's experience in the War of 1812, the conflict with Mexico during the 1840s strengthened the United States in ways beyond the obvious military ones. To Polk and others of like mind, the Republic was stronger as he prepared to depart from the presidency than it had been when he had assumed office. Certainly he had demonstrated in the winning of the Southwest that he had the capacity to function effectively as the nation's executive and as commander in chief, in noted contrast to President Madison's handling of matters during the War of 1812.

There was opposition to the Mexican War, to be sure; indeed, one should not gloss over that reality. But throughout the nation there was widespread and impressive support of the war. The winning of the Southwest tapped the notions of romanticism and chivalry that were abundant in the country. Remarkable feats of communication were accomplished by the newspapers; new literary productivity, fostered by the experiences of the war, helped to create heroes for an enthusiastic America. Soldiers who served in the Mexican campaign reaped the benefits that travel in a foreign country and contacts with foreigners often bring. So, Southwest expansionism, even though it forced the nation into a war, contained much that was positive.[95]

Geographical extension, via New Mexico and California, fitted neatly into the aspirations of many Americans, not the least of whom was President Polk. Although he had helped to "conquer" the Southwest, the problems in regard to slavery in the West would eventually conquer the nation and push it toward intense sectional rivalry and then war. Yet to the people who lived during the 1840s, such an evolution of circumstances was unknown and largely unanticipated. Instead, they rejoiced in the bold expansionism of the Polk administration, whether in the Southwest or in the Pacific Northwest.

5

★ ★ ★ ★ ★

POLK AND THE WINNING
OF THE NORTHWEST

President Polk secured the Pacific Northwest in 1846. Although not as controversial as the conquering of the Southwest, the acquisition of Oregon nonetheless stirred the nation in many ways. Polk took the nation to the brink of war with Great Britain, but he managed to avoid an actual shooting war. Instead, Polk waged a war of nerves, of diplomacy, and of skillful political intrigue. His endeavor to expand to the far reaches of the Northwest was furthered by his own clear determination to do so and also by the national mood, which encouraged and indeed seemed to demand territorial extension.

Advocates of Manifest Destiny included Oregon on their list. Sentiment in the old northwestern states, such as Michigan, Ohio, Indiana, and Illinois, was strongly disposed toward the acquisition of Oregon—perhaps all of Oregon. Political leaders in Congress from those states were quite insistent upon expanding to the Pacific Northwest. They and others of like mind felt a strong affinity for that region, partly because they perceived of the Oregon country as fertile soil for the nation's agricultural development and for future markets for the farm surpluses of the northwestern states. Many exponents of the Oregon crusade also shared a common hatred or hostility toward Great Britain; they looked for opportunities to cause trouble for the British and to acquire economic advantages over them.[1]

Motivations and rationales similar to those invoked in behalf of southwestern expansion were active in the Oregon story. There was one significant difference, however, for the slavery question apparently played no part in the desires for the Pacific Northwest. Most expansionists readily conceded that the Oregon region would never be hospitable to slavery, and southerners seemed content to accept this reality. Given the absence of the troubling question of slavery, therefore, the expansion to the Pacific Northwest captured the imagination and devotion of large groups of Americans.

The major controversy that disturbed an otherwise harmonious campaign was disagreement over how far north the United States claims should go. Some Oregon advocates thought that the traditional historical boundary of the forty-ninth parallel should be moved west from the Rocky Mountains region to the Pacific Coast. Yet even that claim was bold, in light of the sparse settlement of Americans who hovered around the Columbia River, far to the south of that parallel. An audacious, loudly vocal group of Oregon supporters insisted upon a boundary that soared recklessly up to the 54°40' line. Known as the All Oregon men, this band of expansionists listed among its chief leaders the Democratic congressmen from the states of the old Northwest. Eventually they embraced the shibboleth "Fifty-four forty or fight." They probably did not mean it, however; that is, they truly did not want war with Britain. At any rate, the Pacific Northwest figured much into the plans of the expansionists of whatever hue and figured prominently into the goals of the new president who was elected in 1844.

The vast and alluring Oregon country had been jointly occupied, in an official, diplomatic sense, by the United States and Great Britain since a mutual agreement had been signed in 1818 and then renewed in 1827. This unusual arrangement could be ended, according to the understanding, whenever one country notified the other that it wished to terminate the joint occupation. Once such notice had been given, the two countries were obligated to work out a division of the Oregon tract along a boundary line to be defined. The expansionism of the decade of the 1840s fed renewed interest in claiming as much of Oregon as possible for the United States and bringing an end to the joint occupation.[2]

Consequently, when Polk became president, he took advantage of this intensification of desires for Oregon, and he inherited a history of active negotiations, which were already in progress between the United States and Great Britain. As in the matter of the annexation of Texas, Polk, in the Oregon controversy, did not initiate the intention to define and expand the territorial boundaries. In fact, shortly before Polk assumed office, the Tyler administration and Congress had both been noticeably involved with the Oregon question; but certainly the new president must be credited with having forced the matter to a quick and successful resolution. That was truly one of the major goals of his new administration. But the Oregon "problem" was infinitely more complex than Polk initially realized; hence it admitted of no quick solution. Instead, Polk and his administration had to wrestle with negotiations over Oregon—both within the federal government and within the British government—for some sixteen months.

At first confident that Congress would do his bidding without much difficulty, the new president had not reckoned on rejection from the British, an accelerating tempo of demands for all of Oregon, a conflict of personalities within his own cabinet and certainly within the Congress, or the sectional tensions that might be aggravated by this controversy. Believing that American public opinion preferred a satisfactory resolution of the joint occupation, Polk directed his early attentions to accomplishing just that. But from the British viewpoint, he got off to a somewhat shaky beginning with his Inaugural Address, which was apparently designed to placate, if not encourage, extreme western expansionists in the United States. From that moment on, Polk's bold moves on the Oregon front became more and more beset with difficulties. If only the British had cooperated in the summer of 1845, Polk could have presented a *fait accompli* to the Congress when it convened in December of that year; but that is not the way things evolved. Instead, he had to admit setbacks and a shift in policy which, in turn, fostered resistance on the part of some prominent congressmen. It then took the national legislative body some five months to agree finally on giving notice to Great Britain that the joint-occupation arrangement was to be terminated. Meanwhile, negotiations between the diplomats on both sides of the Atlantic followed a tortuous path toward concurrence. One should appreciate the reality that during the involved process of working out the Oregon controversy, the Polk administration was simultaneously dealing with the deteriorating reactions and with the looming threat of war with Mexico. Whatever else one might say about Polk's handling of foreign policy—and there is ample room for dispute—it surely must be credited to his account that he managed things as well as he did, especially since there were moments when he got little aid from his secretary of state, from members of Congress, or from international developments.

It is important to establish the background of events and situations that immediately preceded Polk's assumption of office. As noted earlier, the decade of the 1840s ushered in a revived determination to settle the Oregon issue—favorably for the United States if possible. In fact, the Tyler administration's minister to London, Edward Everett, made a proposal to the British government in late 1843 to end the joint occupation and to draw the boundary along the forty-ninth parallel, bending it so as to grant all of Vancouver Island to the British. Had both governments been ready at that juncture for a final resolution of the Oregon debate, it could easily have been over with even before Polk launched his presidential campaign. Certainly one of the most notable ironies in the Oregon story is that the final agreement in 1846 was essentially the proposal that Everett had made nearly three years earlier. In his annual message of December 1843, President Tyler muddied the diplomatic waters by asserting American rights to the 54°40' parallel in Oregon. In the early spring of 1844, the British foreign secretary, Lord Aberdeen, sent Richard Pakenham to the United States as his official representative and charged him with the prime responsibility for conducting negotiations with the Tyler administration over Oregon. Curiously, at about this time, Congress went through its ritual of debating about the Northwest, during which Senator James Buchanan took a public stand in favor of the United States' title to all of Oregon, up to the northern boundary of 54°40'. When Pakenham arrived in Washington, the State Department had been taken over by Calhoun, upon the death of Abel Upshur. Throughout the year, Calhoun and Pakenham waltzed around the Oregon question periodically, but without making noticeable progress; although Pakenham hinted that the British might soften their demand that the Columbia River constitute the line of division in Oregon. Finally, in the last days of the Tyler administration, Pakenham proposed that the Oregon-boundary question be resolved by arbitration, an offer that Calhoun rejected immediately.[3] The British nevertheless stubbornly clung to their arbitration proposal during much of the Oregon negotiations, apparently not being willing to accept the repeated negative responses of American presidents and diplomats.

Oregon took on additional coloration in 1844 because of the presidential campaign and election, although it must be conceded that the Democratic platform in favor of an extreme claim for Oregon did not seem to have much influence upon the election in most quarters of the nation. What it lacked in actual impact, however, it could claim as a symbolic issue, for it distinctly bespoke the expansionist spirit that was steadily moving across the land. The Democratic party linked Texas and Oregon together, not without reason or strategy, because it wished to identify issues of concern to both southwestern and northwestern expansionists. With victory in November, Polk and his party were expected to cast covetous eyes upon possible western expansion.

As with the question of the annexation of Texas, the Tyler administration almost stole the Oregon issue before Polk took the oath of office.

As mentioned, Tyler and Calhoun engaged in continuing talks with Pakenham about a feasible answer to the riddle of an acceptable boundary for Oregon. Indeed, these two Americans boasted about their anticipation of some dramatic breakthrough during the last two or three weeks of their term. Had it not been for Prime Minister Sir Robert Peel's opposition to Everett's formula, such a breakthrough might have occurred. The lame-duck session of Congress became involved with the Oregon question, much as it did with Texas annexation. Senator David Atchison of Missouri stirred the expansionists when he introduced a bill providing for a territorial government in the entire Oregon country, as well as a string of American forts and a land-allotment program from the United States government. Naturally excited about Atchison's bill, Pakenham made haste to confer with Secretary Calhoun, who reassured Pakenham that nothing would come of the measure. But the House passed such a bill by an overwhelming vote, even larger than that on the Texas bill. Consequently, Tyler and Calhoun rushed to convince the Senate that a new positive development was about to occur on the Anglo-American diplomatic front. With time literally running out, the Senate failed to bring Atchison's bill to a vote.[4] With the expansionist sounds of Congress ringing in his ears, Polk prepared his Inaugural Address.

He did not lack for advice and encouragement as he drafted the document, both from individuals and from population data. As Polk made ready to take the reins of government, approximately thirty-one hundred settlers had already located in various parts of the vast Oregon country, of whom some twelve hundred were United States citizens living south of the Columbia River. During the following autumn a heavy influx of Americans swelled the region's population substantially. Even at that, the American presence in Oregon was slight, compared to what it was in Texas at the same time. Oregon represented great potential, however, more than anything else; Polk and the expansionists understood that quite well. Departing Secretary of State Calhoun felt it was incumbent upon him to advise Polk and Buchanan to pursue a conciliatory path on matters of Oregon policy, perhaps even to leave the current joint occupation undisturbed. By the time of the final draft of the inaugural speech, Polk had moderated the section on Oregon somewhat, possibly in response to advice that had been given to him. Although softened to a degree, the address still staked out a fairly bold position on Oregon, as Polk quoted the Democratic party's platform to communicate the conviction that the United States' title to Oregon was "clear and unquestionable." He could have said more; he could have announced a commitment to the 54°40' cause. Some thought that he implied as much, but he was shrewdly trying to compel the British to recognize that they must abandon the notion of the Columbia River and prepare to accept the forty-ninth parallel.[5]

Speaking before the houses of Parliament, both Aberdeen and Peel reacted rather strongly to Polk's address; they seemed shocked and dismayed by the new president's language and position. Once their response to the Inaugural Address became known in the United States, the American press, especially in the western states, reacted to the British with increasingly warm rhetoric. In fact, an Oregon fever swept through those areas in the aftermath of these developments. In other locales, however, there was a shaking of disapproving heads by those who adhered to the belief, expressed by none other than Calhoun, that Polk's inaugural was ''a profound blunder.''[6]

The actions that followed the new president's speech were perhaps more important than words. Buchanan, for example, immediately held interviews with Pakenham to give repeated assurances of the desire for good relations between the two countries. The British minister was likewise eager to establish friendly rapport with the new administration. Yet in the early days, Pakenham offered up the favorite British fall-back position—namely, arbitration. Buchanan parried that indirectly, however, by expressing his hope for a negotiated settlement. Encouraged by supposedly knowledgeable persons in town, among them being Senator William S. Archer, Pakenham was led to believe that Polk would consent to arbitration; therefore, Pakenham pressed this proposal more than once on Buchanan. But to no avail, for after weeks of studying the Oregon files, the president and his cabinet had become convinced that the government in London still liked the Everett proposal of 1843; they therefore unanimously agreed to reject arbitration. Buchanan so informed Pakenham in mid May.[7]

Meanwhile the British minister had been receiving new instructions from Aberdeen, mainly to the effect that he should hold to the Columbia River line if possible by offering free ports for both nations south of the forty-ninth parallel. Aberdeen also naturally advised that arbitration could be offered again. Most important, however, he told Pakenham that if the Americans were to offer the forty-ninth parallel to the Pacific, with all of Vancouver Island for the British, he would be favorably inclined to support such a proposal. At this juncture, the government in London wanted to compel the new Polk administration to present some sort of firm offer, rather than allowing Polk and Buchanan to respond to a concrete British proposition. Optimistically believing that it could manage the Oregon problems early on, in the harmonious days of its term, the Polk administration set its hands to the task. The immediate hitch to forward movement, however, was the president's need to secure a replacement for Everett in London.[8]

After some offers to and refusals from other persons, Polk finally enticed Louis McLane, a veteran diplomat and cabinet member during the Jackson presidency, to take the London mission. There is reason to suspect that the president picked McLane, who was known to be an opponent of extreme Oregon claims, in order to utilize him as a compromiser and negotiator with the British officials. In any event, McLane arrived in Washington in late June to receive his instructions and to be informed by Buchanan and Polk specifically of the proposal that was about to be presented to the British. The administration planned to delay submitting the proposition to Pakenham, however, until McLane had embarked for Britain, so that his arrival there would coincide with the arrival of Pakenham's dispatch bearing the terms of the United States recommendation.[9]

It therefore was mid July before Secretary Buchanan sent to Pakenham the new proposal, to which McLane had already been privy, outlining the offer of the forty-ninth parallel all the way to the Pacific but with free ports for the British south of that parallel. There was no mention of free navigation of the Columbia River for the British, as had been customary in negotiations prior to Polk's presidency. In a subsequent dispatch from Buchanan, McLane was told that he might offer all of Vancouver Island to the British, if this was required by the London officials. Evidently the Polk administration had some hesitancy about the terms being presented to the British and was therefore willing to bend and yield slightly. Suffice it to say that the president made this proposal in the summer because he felt duty-bound to do so, that is, he believed that he had an obligation to pick up the situation where Tyler and Calhoun had left it several months earlier.[10] Not surprisingly, he displayed little enthusiasm for the whole business of compromising with the British.

Whatever his true feelings or beliefs may have been, Polk was hardly prepared for the reaction of Pakenham, who after receiving Buchanan's letter, penned a reply in which he firmly rejected the American offer. He thus violated both the spirit and the letter of his instructions in this instance by not submitting Polk's proposal to his superiors in London, a regrettable mistake indeed. There was a flurry of agitated and angry feelings at the White House and at the State Department when the contents of Pakenham's letter became known. Suspicious and skeptical by nature, Polk quickly assumed that the British minister had acted on instructions from Aberdeen and Peel. Moreover, Polk believed that he had been duped by the British into thinking that they would be receptive to an American offer. Although embarrassed and hurt by this sudden turn of events, Polk also felt a sense of relief—relief that perhaps the British rejection had spared him considerable political damage from the western extremists in his party had the proposal gone through. Not unexpectedly the president decided to withdraw, firmly and completely, any proposition for the settlement of the Oregon situation.[11]

Two things kept Polk from moving more precipitously. One was Buchanan's entreaty to delay and wait for a signal from London that might indicate a further desire to pursue compromise; and the other was the disturbing rumor that Mexico was sending troops to the Rio Grande. By 26 August, however, the president, who was ready for action on Oregon, pressured the cabinet into agreeing that a withdrawal of the American proposition was the correct procedure. Buchanan attempted to hedge on the matter by insisting that a sentence be included in the withdrawal statement to welcome a discussion of a future British proposal. A resolute Polk would not permit such an invitation, how-ever, for he was fearful that the British might offer terms that would be less desirable than those already presented to them in his July proposi-tion. Prodded by the president, who wished no further delay lest an impression of weakness be conveyed to the British, Buchanan reluc-tantly drew up the withdrawal document. On 30 August the secretary delivered to Pakenham a statement rescinding the earlier offer and articulating a renewed and bold claim to all of Oregon. It appeared that the Polk administration was engaging in bluster and bluff again, for it truly did want some compromise on Oregon, not a war or even a struggle over the exaggerated demand for 54°40'.[12]

Meanwhile, on the other side of the Atlantic, both McLane and the British officials were dismayed to learn about Pakenham's unilateral actions. Aberdeen informed the United States minister that if Pakenham had forwarded the Polk proposal, he (Aberdeen) would have utilized it as the basis for discussion and possible agreement. Moreover, Aberdeen reassured McLane that Pakenham's rejection should not be interpreted as an ultimatum to the United States government, for the British were anxious to continue negotiations with a view toward a reasonable settlement in the near future. McLane transmitted these ideas and statements back to Washington in the hope of encouraging compromise and discouraging unfortunate responses from the Polk administration. But the president had already committed himself to an absolute with-drawal of the American offer. When McLane eventually learned about this action, he was further chagrined, partly at the breakdown of diplomacy and partly at the diminishing prospect of acclaim for himself as the skillful and successful negotiator of the Oregon compromise. Certainly McLane was mindful of the extremely difficult situation that the British had been put in by Polk's vigorous reaction to Pakenham's rejection.[13] McLane and all others who desired a sensible compromise on Oregon had their work cut out for them.

From September through November the impasse over Oregon became more visible; both sides seemed to be willing simply to let matters drift for a while. Throughout these months, Buchanan tried to maintain his optimistic view that breakthroughs would occur, whereas Polk was certain that his pessimistic outlook was the only proper view of Anglo-American relations. The secretary continued to encourage McLane and even Pakenham to believe that compromise was feasible and possible, while Polk continued to demand substantial concessions from the British. In the meantime, Pakenham attempted to defend himself to his British superiors, and they, in turn, reprimanded his unilateral rejection of the Polk offer. The president smugly seemed to be enjoying Pakenham's discomfort.[14]

In October there were some false moves toward a resumption of negotiations, first with Aberdeen's new instructions to Pakenham that he should approach Buchanan with an offer to withdraw the July rejection. The foreign secretary was hoping thereby to ease some of his minister's discomfort and to push both countries toward open discussion once again. Behind the scenes, meanwhile, Aberdeen was trying to persuade Prime Minister Peel that the earlier proposal by Everett was acceptable, both politically and diplomatically, to the British. An important consideration of the Oregon problem occurred at a meeting of Polk's cabinet on 21 October, when the president and Buchanan again found themselves at odds. Polk announced that since the British had broken off discussions about Oregon, he had no intention of renewing them, unless the British were to offer definite terms in a new proposal. Protesting that further delay on the Oregon controversy might lead to war, the agitated Buchanan implored that progress be sought and that Pakenham be assured that any proposition the British might present would be respectfully considered and would be submitted to the Senate for its advice. But Polk drew a sharp line of refusal on this point, lest it appear that too much was being conceded to the British. Furthermore, the president declared to the cabinet his intentions to take a bold stand on Oregon in his forthcoming annual message to Congress. The secretary of state left the meeting in an unhappy frame of mind, carrying further instructions to inform Pakenham that the United States would not resubmit its original offer or make any new proposal. Thereafter both the secretary and the British minister held conversations about the stalemate or impasse over Oregon, a consequence of which led Buchanan to suggest that Pakenham might make some sort of unofficial proposal which could be shown to the president privately. Buchanan carried such a written message to Polk and the cabinet; but the president absolutely refused to play this cagey game, taking instead the high ground that he would not traffic in unofficial notes.[15] With that, the hoped-for resumption of negotiations collapsed, at least for the time being.

Other things happened, however, to demonstrate that Oregon was still very much a viable issue. The president, for example, summoned Senator Thomas Hart Benton to the White House in late October to confer about Oregon matters. The senator, already having had privileged access to Oregon files in the State Department (courtesy of Buchanan), was well versed on the topic. Polk successfully endeavored to build support for the strategy of proposing, in his annual message, that notice of the abrogation of the Oregon treaty should be given to Britain. In a wide-ranging conversation about questions of western expansion, the Missouri senator concurred. Shortly thereafter, Polk's newspaper, the *Washington Union*, took up the cry for all of Oregon, an extremist position that many assumed had been sanctioned by the president himself.[16] Apparently Polk was beginning to orchestrate the initial stages of his new offensive on the Oregon front.

In any event, as time approached for the convening of Congress, both Buchanan, in Washington, and Aberdeen, in London, expressed the belief that the two countries were closer than ever to successful negotiations, a strange notion in light of the reality of the stalled condition on both sides of the Atlantic. In a letter to Aberdeen, Edward Everett added some murkiness to the already cloudy atmosphere by assuring the British leaders that no bill would pass Congress in favor of taking all of Oregon, for Calhoun's group would hold the balance of power in that body. But he also warned Aberdeen that even Calhoun and his allies would not accept a boundary line south of the forty-ninth parallel. And so, on the eve of the convening of Congress, confusion and uncertainty about the future of the Pacific Northwest seemed to prevail, except in the mind of the president, who had a clear strategy prepared. He called for increasing pressure upon the British by pushing a notice resolution through Congress; the lion's tail would be twisted again.[17]

December brought the congressmen to Washington for a new session and concurrently launched the commencement of a new phase of the Oregon controversy, one that was characterized by an unsteady movement toward the notice resolution that Polk was advocating. The president, who was in command of the situation at the outset, established his position with clarity and firmness in his first annual message to Congress. After presenting a brief historical review of the negotiations that had transpired, including the days of the Tyler administration and concluding with a reminder of what had happened during the summer relative to his proposal to the British, Polk invoked Monroe's earlier noncolonization principle in support of his view that North America was off limits to any European power. Not surprisingly, the president asked Congress to give formal notice to Great Britain that the joint occupation was to be terminated. Incorporating ideas from both Benton and Buchanan, Polk produced a message that took a fairly tough stance toward the British. Interestingly, the day after the document was presented to Congress, Aberdeen, who could not have had any knowledge of the contents of the message, wrote to Pakenham, professing his admiration for Polk's tactics but also expressing his perceptive observation that Polk was probably more fearful of the Senate than he was of the British government. Aberdeen correctly surmised that the president would have trouble with the 54-40 men in Congress. Meanwhile, loyal Democrats flooded Polk's office for the next couple of days to declare their approval of his message; and the president dutifully made note of who appeared. Western expansionists from across the nation wrote letters to the president, commending his firm stand.[18]

During the remainder of the month, however, there was more give and take on the diplomatic front, as Buchanan strove to keep the negotiating door open, while Polk and the cabinet periodically closed it. About four days after Polk's message was delivered, Senator Benton told the president about a conversation he had had earlier with Pakenham, who had hinted at a compromise solution endorsing the forty-ninth parallel, with Great Britain retaining Vancouver Island and free navigation of the Columbia. At the cabinet meeting of 9 December, Buchanan, who also had heard about the Benton-Pakenham conversation, urged Polk to declare whether he would submit such a proposal to the Senate for its advice; but the president refused to make a commitment. The secretary was not to be dissuaded, however, so he prepared instructions for McLane in which he asserted that Polk would be "strongly inclined" to forward a compromise proposal to the Senate. Striking that sentence out of the Buchanan document, the president substituted words to the effect that he would submit a British proposal if he thought it justifiable.[19] Neither the secretary nor the president knew that important dispatches from McLane, dated 1 December, were on their way to Washington at this time.

McLane's communications, which arrived two days before Christmas, correctly predicted that Pakenham had been instructed to offer an arbitration proposal and warned the administration not to reject it outright. McLane also encouraged Polk to speak in bold and decisive terms and disclosed that the British were counting on Calhoun and the moderates to thwart the extremists in Congress. On the day of their arrival, McLane's dispatches and letters were read aloud to the regular meeting of the cabinet; they stirred considerable discussion about Oregon. There was unanimity that any arbitration proposition should be turned down and that the country's defenses would need to be strengthened (Buchanan's recommendation). At the cabinet meeting, the secretary of state attempted, without success, to persuade Polk to let him make conciliatory statements to Pakenham; the president did concede, however, that he might consult the Senate, or at least some senators, if the British were to offer the forty-nine parallel while retaining Vancouver Island.[20]

Taking steps to prepare for whatever the British were about to propose, the president summoned Senator Allen, of the Foreign Relations Committee, to his office on Christmas Eve. After reading McLane's dispatches aloud, Polk solicited the senator's opinion. While concurring with the rejection of arbitration, Allen advised that a compromise proposal along the forty-ninth parallel should be presented to the Senate for consultation. Later on that same day the president was a bit more cautious in his conversation with Senator Hopkins Turney of Tennessee, who asked what Polk would do with a British compromise proposition, after Turney had warned Polk about a potential split in the Democratic party over the Oregon question. Polk told Turney that he "would feel inclined to take the advice of the Senate confidentially" before he took any actions on a proposal. Three days after these conversations, Polk asked the cabinet again if a British compromise arrangement should be offered to the Senate for advice. All members agreed that it should be, while they also reaffirmed that arbitration should be refused.[21]

Immediately after the adjournment of this cabinet meeting on 27 December, Buchanan went to the State Department offices, where he found Pakenham awaiting him. The British minister quickly removed the suspense by making a formal recommendation for arbitration to draw a compromise boundary line. Perhaps Buchanan's recognition of the futility of such a proposal caused him to feel humorous, for he jokingly told Pakenham that the pope should be considered as an arbitrator; and a less casual British minister took the secretary seriously for a moment. After this diversion, Buchanan informed Pakenham that even if Polk were to accept arbitration, it was extremely doubtful that Congress would. That night, Buchanan and Bancroft went to Polk's office to share Pakenham's arbitration proposition with him; all three men immediately agreed that it must be rejected. Subsequently, Buchanan drew up an official refusal, as amended by Polk, of the British proposal, and the entire cabinet endorsed it. Interestingly enough, Pakenham was not distraught over this turn of events; doubtless he had sufficient grounds to have anticipated the outcome. He was, in fact, cheered by private assurances from several senators, who claimed that there was a group in Congress that was supportive of the forty-ninth parallel as the boundary, with all of Vancouver Island going to the British. Historian Charles Sellers has contended that by its outright rejection of arbitration, the Polk administration committed a faux pas, much as Pakenham had done in July when he had turned down the Polk proposal; this was so because Aberdeen really sought a statement from the Americans that they preferred continued negotiation, which he did not get.[22]

Sentiments for mediation were readily apparent at least in certain quarters, particularly in the new Congress. A substantial group of moderates—Whigs and a number of Democrats, galvanized by the spectacle of John C. Calhoun at the head of a peace coalition—desired a suitable and reasonable compromise with the British. Most moderates were not opposed to acquiring territory, as long as it could be done without armed conflict; but they feared that the abrogation of the joint-occupation treaty was a step toward war, not peace, with Great Britain. Calhoun arrived in Washington after the congressional session had begun, but he immediately exerted his leadership capacities and took charge of the moderates. He visited Polk at the White House on 22 December, for example, in an effort to persuade the president either to delay or to surrender altogether his recommended termination of the joint occupation. The two men agreed only when they both professed to be in favor of peace; otherwise their conversation ''was not a satisfactory one.'' The president correctly surmised that in Congress, Calhoun would lead the opposition to Polk's Oregon program. Exactly what motivated the South Carolina senator and southern apologist to embrace a cautious, moderate course on Oregon, after having stirred bellicose sentiments on the matter of Texas annexation, is not easily comprehended or explained. Perhaps he saw the Oregon controversy as the only available avenue for him to combat the Polk administration and thereby attempt to solidify his southern base in the Democratic party, which was temporarily being threatened by Polk, a southern president. In any event, during the early weeks of the session, Congress witnessed the remarkable spectacle of northern and eastern legislators aligning with Calhoun, their nemesis on many other issues, to thwart the president's plan for a notice resolution. But at the end of the month, when Calhoun was attempting to unite his followers in support of his resolution in opposition to Senator Hannegan's (which denounced the surrender of any part of Oregon), the faction was unable to entice Whig colleagues to join it.[23]

Both the Hannegan and the Calhoun resolutions were tabled on 30 December; but on the next day, Congressman James A. Black (from Calhoun's state) began to work on a bargain with western extremists, whereby they and the moderates would agree to drop the notice resolution, in exchange for which the Calhounites would oppose any boundary compromise and would back bills for courts, land grants, and military protection in Oregon. Black went to the White House on 4 January to lay his scheme before the president, who sized Black up as "a sensible & patriotic man" with good motives, though doubtless sent over by Calhoun. Polk lent no overt or actual support to Black's plans and used the occasion to make his famous declaration: "I remarked to him that the only way to treat John Bull was to look him straight in the eye; that I considered a bold & firm course on our part the pacific one; that if Congress faultered or hesitated in their course, John Bull would immediately become arrogant and more grasping in his demands." Six days later, Calhoun, perhaps hoping to cause the president to blink an eye, insisted that the western extremists construed the notice resolution as a war policy and therefore urged that it should be abandoned. The president did not avert his eyes from the British, however; he held firmly to his previously announced course and employed some of the exact words that he had spoken in the earlier conversation with Black.[24] Hence, as the old year ended and the new one began, it was evident that the moderate cause would be strongly tested in the congressional session.

Naturally, those who exasperated and frustrated the moderates, other than the president himself, were the extremists, or 54-40 men, in Congress. Articulating the vision of Manifest Destiny that continued to sweep large segments of the country, they were determined to have their way on the Oregon controversy, especially since Polk seemed to be in their camp. Lewis Cass of Michigan, certainly one of the foremost leaders and spokesmen for this expansionist cause, galvanized the Senate in mid December with his resolution calling upon congressional committees to investigate the state of military preparedness, which was approved by a unanimous Senate vote, and with an accompanying speech, described by one historian as "the first of many Western war whoops'' and by a contemporary observer as ''a thundering declaration of war.'' It is likely that during the early weeks of the session, Cass, Allen, and other extremists from the West were attempting to create something of a crisis climate, an atmosphere that would be more hospitable to their exaggerated claims in behalf of 54-40.[25] At any rate, once their voices had been heard, to be answered by the resolute cries of the moderates, the battle was joined. The president quickly perceived that the simple request for a notice resolution would not glide through Congress; instead, it would follow an uncertain and difficult path.

The initial strategy of the Calhoun moderates was to postpone any consideration of the notice resolution. In the Senate, Calhoun success-fully maneuvered a resolution stipulating a delay until early February of any debate on notice, but the peace bloc was unable to stall the deliberation in the House. Consequently, throughout January, members of the latter body dealt with Polk's plan for notice. During the House debates, probably the most dramatic occurrence was the speech by John Quincy Adams in which he staked out a position, much to the dismay and shock of his northern and eastern colleagues, advocating that the United States acquire all of Oregon. By majority vote, the House eventually set 9 February as the date for a vote on the notice resolution. Just prior to that day of decision, however, the House received from the president (in compliance with congressional resolutions) State Depart-ment correspondence relative to Pakenham's arbitration proposal and the rejection thereof. After the receipt of these documents, Whig representatives were especially vocal in their denunciations of the administration's actions, accusing if of making war inevitable. What was clearly unavoidable, however, was a final vote on the notice resolution, which carried by a 163 to 54 vote, after having been amended by moderates to read that notice was not intended to block the pursuance of continued negotiations for ''an amicable settlement.''[26]

Attention then shifted to the Senate, which was in no hurry to deal with the notice proposition. Instead, moderate leaders there effectively waged a stall-and-delay strategy, awaiting hopeful news from the diplomatic front. From the time of the abortive arbitration offer in December through the month of April, there was much activity and there were some breakthroughs in the field of Anglo-American diplo-macy. The new year began auspiciously enough with the London *Times*, for the first time, embracing a position favoring compromise on the Oregon question; though that striking conversion was offset somewhat by Aberdeen's unhappiness when he received documents indicating that the Polk administration had categorically rejected arbitration. At about that same time, however, Pakenham made a second arbitration offer, which differed only in that it proposed to arbitrate the matter of title rather than of boundary. Not surprisingly, Polk and Buchanan quickly agreed about refusing this latest proposition. Yet in their communications to McLane, explaining their rejection of the second arbitration scheme, they authorized him to inform Aberdeen that Polk was willing to submit a compromise proposal to the Senate, despite his notable stand in behalf of all of Oregon.[27]

If one had to single out a particular month as the most significant one for diplomatic breakthroughs on the Oregon controversy, it would unquestionably be February. Diplomatic waters were stirred up in ways that they had not been since Polk had become president, and McLane was the first to agitate them. In an extremely important dispatch and letter of 3 February, McLane optimistically depicted Aberdeen and Peel as poised to make a reasonable compromise on Oregon. All that was needed, in effect, was an encouraging word from Washington, preferably from Polk rather than from Pakenham. The paragraph that grabbed the attention of both Polk and Buchanan, however, was the one in which McLane, in an almost offhand fashion, mentioned that British warships had set sail for North America. Once McLane's dispatch had arrived in Washington, Polk and some of his cabinet members huddled immediately at the White House, although it was a Sunday, to pore over it. Excitedly, they read the lines about British war vessels; ironically, McLane had not intended that to be a very important part of his message. Two days later, on 24 February, the cabinet agreed that McLane must inform Aberdeen right away that Polk was ready to submit to the Senate, for its advice, a compromise for the forty-ninth parallel as the boundary, as well as temporary navigation rights on the Columbia. On 26 February the president and his secretary sent new instructions to McLane, conveying the agreement that had been reached by the administration.[28]

Any surprise that Aberdeen and Peel might have felt when learning in March about the new stance of the Polk administration was certainly equaled by McLane's sense of surprise. In fact, he was amazed that so much significance had been attached to the disembarkation of British warships to Canada. News that the House had passed the notice resolution had the desired impact upon the foreign secretary and others by convincing them that the time was drawing nigh for the British to make a definite proposal to the Polk administration. They decided not to rush the matter, however, preferring to let circumstances drift for a while, until it could be ascertained what action the Senate would take on the notice resolution.[29]

As already mentioned, the Senate was in no hurry to act, for the peace coalition believed that delay was its best policy. This bloc succeeded initially in postponing consideration of the notice resolution until February and then in dragging the deliberations out for weeks. Senator Allen of the Foreign Relations Committee presented the resolution calling for giving notice to the British for the abrogation of the joint-occupation treaty. Senator John J. Crittenden, a Whig of Kentucky, then countered with a proposal that the president be permitted to give notice at his discretion, but not before the end of the congressional session. With these two resolutions and with the actions of five state legislatures calling for support of the president's Oregon policies, the stage was set for a full-scale debate in the Senate.[30]

In early February, two western extremists, Allen and Hannegan, launched the Senate deliberations with speeches in which they attempted to stir sentiment in behalf of the All-Oregon movement. Both senators already knew that Polk was inching toward compromise and away from the 54-40 position (if indeed he had ever truly occupied that stance), but they persisted in promulgating the extreme expansionist cause. As one historian has observed, the real question before the Senate was whether the notice resolution was to be "an invitation to negotiate . . . or a shout of defiance." Nevertheless, in late February, the Calhoun bloc escalated the struggle in the Senate a bit by pushing for a resolution that would urge Polk to negotiate a compromise settlement. Calhoun had not calculated, however, upon rejection by the Whig caucus, a group that was not willing to trust the president. Having been rebuffed by the Whigs, Calhoun and his ally Walter T. Colquitt of Georgia went to the White House to seek Polk's endorsement of their proposal. The president, who had been warned in advance by Senator Haywood, turned a deaf ear to their plan. Polk used the occasion, as he was to do repeatedly, to inform both senators that he would submit a compromise proposal from Britain to the Senate for advice, while specifying his objection to navigation rights on the Columbia River. Eventually, in mid March before crowded galleries in the Senate, Calhoun announced his support of a notice resolution, since it was now obvious to him that compromise was favored by the Senate and by the British government.[31]

Other notable developments in the Oregon story occurred in March. For one, Senator Haywood, while declaring his support of a compromise line along the forty-ninth parallel, contended that the president favored it. Moreover, he asserted that some of the 54-40 men in the Senate were merely using that cause to foster their presidential ambitions. In a heated rejoinder to Haywood, Senator Hannegan categorically insisted that if Polk endorsed Haywood's views, then the president had betrayed the Democratic party and its platform. Afterwards, Hannegan and Atchison made their way to Polk's office to determine his true convictions about the Oregon matter. But the president stiffened his neck, refused to be bullied by the extremists, and shrewdly evaded their difficult questions. A parade of senators of various political hues soon followed, all vainly seeking to ferret out Polk's intentions about Oregon. While refusing to disavow Haywood's speech, the president intimated that no one had authority to speak for him; he also informed one and all that he probably would submit to the Senate a British compromise offer.[32] On 11 March, in a private conversation with Senator Benton, Polk further encouraged the moderates, even to the point of expressing interest in Crittenden's resolution, which was pending before the Senate. A week after Calhoun's mid-March speech, the president sent a special message to Congress, in which he noted British military activity and claimed that a notice resolution was not a war measure. Interestingly, in cabinet discussions that led up to the issuance of this message, Buchanan had taken a more aggressive stance, one that was more disposed toward the western extremists and one that expressed a desire for a statement of censure of the Senate for its failure to act on the notice resolution. It was commonly believed, however, that Buchanan's political aspirations were clouding his vision at this point, since he was already mindful of the jockeying for position in preparation for the 1848 presidential sweepstakes.[33]

Spring brought the Senate to its final month of deliberation, and fortunately, April saw the notice resolution clear the congressional hurdles. But as different factions sought to have an impact upon the shape of the final resolution, parliamentary maneuverings proliferated. In the middle of the month the Senate, with Polk's blessing, overwhelmingly endorsed a slightly modified Crittenden version of the notice resolution. Immediately thereafter the House and Senate engaged in some sparring over the exact phrasing of a resolution that would be acceptable to both bodies. The president utilized his cabinet members to lobby the House members in behalf of the Crittenden resolution that had been embraced by the Senate. The legislative tug of war finally ended on 23 April, when, by substantial margins, both chambers approved the Senate version, with minor alterations.[34] Congress had taken five months to answer Polk's request for notice, a period that was prolonged by the tactics of the Senate's peace coalition and by the unwillingness of western extremists to accept the realities of compromise. Now, having at long last taken decisive action, Congress looked across the Atlantic to see what the response would be.

The ball was in London's court in May, as Pakenham immediately notified Aberdeen about the decisions made by the United States Congress. Pakenham was more confident than ever that the Oregon controversy was now susceptible of amicable agreement. Meanwhile, in Britain, pressure was building steadily for Peel and Aberdeen to resolve the impasse on Oregon, lest they leave office shortly with a major diplomatic problem still pending. Therefore, when Aberdeen and McLane received word of the congressional action on notice, both men accepted the challenge to hammer out a British proposal without delay. The foreign secretary and the United States minister pledged that they would have a proposal ready by the time the trans-Atlantic steamer left Liverpool on 19 May. The only troublesome issue was navigation rights on the Columbia River, a dispute that had affected the negotiations since the very beginning. Aberdeen's proposal stipulated that the British, as well as the Americans, have free navigation of the Columbia, a concession to which Polk had repeatedly objected. Fearful of being deprived of a last-minute opportunity to reap success in the field of diplomacy, McLane prevailed upon Aberdeen to alter this clause to provide, instead, that there would be free navigation only for Hudson's Bay Company; yet McLane doubted whether Polk would accept even this. Otherwise, the British proposal contained no surprises, for it drew the boundary line along the forty-ninth parallel, detouring south around Vancouver Island so as to preserve that domain for the British. With that, Aberdeen penned his instructions to Pakenham, accompanied by the formal proposal; and on the next day the steamer left for the United States.[35]

About two weeks later it became the United States' turn to act. Both a letter from McLane and the formal proposal, which was presented by Pakenham to Buchanan, removed all doubt as to what the British intended to do about Oregon. When Polk first received McLane's letter, he was disturbed by the minister's discussion of the terms that Aberdeen and McLane had worked out. Nevertheless he discussed the matter with his cabinet on the next day, 4 June; and the members were favorable toward its being submitted to the Senate, although Buchanan refused to commit himself. Two days later, Pakenham made the official presentation to the State Department, whereupon Buchanan immediately took the proposal to a meeting of the cabinet. Evidently the only question of concern was the relatively minor one of whether navigation rights would expire when the charter of the Hudson's Bay Company ended. Then, as the president surveyed the cabinet on the major issue of submitting the proposal to the Senate for advice, Buchanan was the only one to balk, saying that he would wait for Polk's message transmitting the proposal before he would take a stand. The secretary then startled his colleagues by declaring that "the 54°40' men were the true friends of the administration and he wished no backing out on the subject." After smoothing the ruffled feathers, particularly Walker's, the president asked Buchanan to draft the message that should be sent to the Senate; the secretary refused, agreeing only to comment subsequently upon one drawn up by Polk. As Secretary of War Marcy remarked to the president after the cabinet had adjourned, "Mr. Buchanan's course was a very queer one, for . . . he had been for a long time the most strenuous advocate of settling the question on the basis of the 49°."[36]

There seems to be little doubt that Buchanan suddenly felt threatened by the final solution to the prolonged Oregon question, lest his own political future be jeopardized by this blatant retreat from the extremist position. In any event, in a private conversation on 8 June, the secretary and Polk once more clashed when Buchanan declined to assist the president with the preparation of the message for the Senate. In a somewhat sarcastic tone, the secretary commented: "Well! when you have done your message I will then prepare such a one as I think ought to be sent in." Stung by that remark, the president exchanged harsh words with Buchanan, accusing him of trying to make public issue with him, to which the secretary quickly offered a denial. Eventually they worked out a temporary truce, at the end of "a very painful and unpleasant" conversation. On the following day, 9 June, Polk took his draft to the cabinet meeting, and when Buchanan raised objections to it, the president sent him off to an adjoining room to compose a draft of his own. Eventually the cabinet members and Polk made alterations and deletions in the president's version so as to satisfy everyone, including Buchanan, who finally consented to a public declaration of his support for the document.[37]

Therefore, on 10 June the president was ready to transmit his message to the Senate, revealing the British terms and asking for the Senate's advice. Shrewdly, before sending the document, Polk had conferred privately with at least nine senators—first, Cass, Allen, and Turney; then, Haywood; and finally, Benton, Dickinson, Houston, Arthur P. Bagby, and Niles—to ascertain their reactions. Interestingly, only Senator Allen advised the president not to forward the British proposal to the Senate; and only Senator Cass indicated at this time that he would vote against accepting the terms of the proposition. Benton and the president apparently discussed the entire membership of the Senate in an effort to calculate whether a safe two-thirds vote in favor was possible. Polk's message of 10 June indicated his own continuing belief in an extreme boundary claim for the United States; concurrently he indicated his willingness to conform to the consensus of the Senate on this matter. Furthermore, he made a case for his strategy of seeking the prior advice of the Senate, appealing to long-standing practices of the executive branch of the government dating from the days of George Washington's administration. Once the Senate had received the message, it made short order of the whole matter, although Allen attempted, without success, to have it bottled up in his Foreign Relations Committee. On 11 June, Senator Haywood introduced a resolution calling for acceptance of the British proposal, and the Senate concurred by a vote of 38 to 12. Curiously, Polk recorded the receipt of the information about the Senate's action without any elaboration or hint of jubilation.[38]

Buchanan and Pakenham met on 13 June to draw up the actual treaty. Two days later it was sent to the Senate to be either ratified or rejected. There the western extremists, through the device of amendments, made their last valiant effort to thwart the compromise. But their attempts were to no avail, as the Senate on 18 June overwhelmingly, and not unexpectedly, approved the treaty by a vote of 41 to 14. The fallout from this procedure was antagonism that was directed at the president by the All-Oregon men, who felt truly betrayed. Allen, for instance, resigned his chairmanship of the Foreign Relations Committee in bitter protest; he also tried to get others on that committee to follow his example. In a lengthy conversation with Senator Sidney Breese of Illinois on the day before the final vote on the treaty, the president defended his actions by indicating his long-standing approval of the forty-ninth parallel as an acceptable boundary. Breese was satisfied, but he admitted that some of the 54-40 men were not. As with the information about the Senate's vote on advice, the president did not permit himself the luxury of expressing elated feelings about the ratification of the treaty.[39]

Perhaps there was little room for rejoicing, for the successful completion of the Oregon question contained bittersweet results. True, a vast new expanse had been added to the nation at very little cost; expansionist Polk was elated with this accomplishment. But the Oregon debates and strategies had divided the Democratic party, because most of the southern Democrats opposed extreme expansionism, for fear of war with Britain, while northwestern Democrats wanted all of Oregon. Other Democrats tried to take a moderate stance or else moved with the shifting winds. In any event, Polk was discouraged by such overt disharmony. Party unity became an increasingly elusive goal. Some northwestern Democrats denounced the president; but shortly thereafter the situation cooled, and there was no actual revolt of Democratic congressmen—much to Polk's relief.[40]

To claim that there was divisiveness is not to maintain that Polk's leadership was badly shaken by the Oregon controversy or that the president lost control of the Oregon question because he had politicized it unnecessarily.[41] Such contentions ignore the two and one-half years of Polk's administration that yet remained, during which time the president, for example, successfully prosecuted an extremely difficult foreign war. With regard to politicizing the Oregon matter, surely ample credit must be given to the northwestern Democratic expansionists and even to the Calhoun Democrats and the Whigs who opposed them. Somehow one must make allowance, in addition, for Buchanan's last-minute political maneuvering to position himself with the All Oregon men—for which he was understandably rebuked by Polk. Concerning leadership, one should not overlook the important accomplishments that followed in the summer of 1846: the enactment of the Independent Treasury bill and the passage of the new tariff. These achievements, coming fast on the heels of the resolution of the Oregon dispute, do not bespeak a president whose leadership was faltering. Finally, one must remember the overwhelming votes of approval given in June by the Senate, first on the matter of advice and then on the treaty itself.

Evidence of Polk's successes and of congressional support, however, has not deterred at least one scholar from arguing that Polk escaped great political harm during the summer of 1846 by goading Mexico into war. The president thereby "mollified the All Oregon men," so the contention goes, "with another nationalistic crusade"—this one in the Southwest.[42] A simple reminder of the sequence of events should be offered in rejoinder. For example, the declaration of war against Mexico came before, not after, the arrival of the British proposal on Oregon. Whether Polk "goaded" Mexico into war has been much discussed; I have treated it above, in chapter 4. Finally, what proof exists to substantiate that Polk sought war with Mexico so as to lessen or remove the attacks of the 54-40 men upon him? Withholding recognition from Polk for the political acumen that enabled him to negotiate the churning waters of the Oregon controversy seems unjustified and unfair.

The basic truth is that Polk brought about an amazing and bloodless conquest of territory in the Pacific Northwest. He was doubtless a wiser man in the summer of 1846 than he had been a year earlier, when he had made the proposal that Pakenham, acting without authority, had rejected. Moreover he was perhaps a more honest man; unfortunately, the Oregon episode revealed the president's inclination toward disingenuousness, directed both toward members of Congress and toward the British government. Blame for a seeming lack of candor and forthrightness should not be assessed too harshly against Polk, however, for circumstances and situations at times did not permit complete honesty. Doubtless there were times when the president did not truly know his own thoughts and opinions. He was, after all, engaged in a game of high-stakes diplomacy with the powerful rival Great Britain during a time of intense nationalistic feelings in America. At any rate, he convinced at least himself that his position on Oregon was essentially a consistent one and, of course, a correct one.

Nevertheless, the arguments linger, though no one has proposed then or since that Oregon should have been surrendered to a continued unsatisfactory joint ownership. Instead, Americans quickly expressed their views in the 1840s by rushing to the Pacific Northwest to occupy that lush and alluring wilderness. Manifest Destiny was certainly more than mere rhetoric to them. Expansionism was a challenge both for the nation and for its president. Polk would find additional worries, however, as he attempted to carry the burdens of presidential patronage.

6

★ ★ ★ ★ ★

PATRONAGE
AND THE PRESIDENT

Nearly two years after he had assumed office, Polk confided to his diary: "If God grants me length of days and health, I will, after the expiration of my term, give a history of the selfish and corrupt considerations which influence the course of public men." The president repeated this same vow in April 1848, when he specifically declared that he would "write the secret and hitherto unknown history of the workings of the Government." Polk had more than ample reason to want to set the record straight. The exasperations and frustrations that he had experienced in dealing with public patronage had driven him to distraction. Even a simple, cursory reading of the president's voluminous diary convinces one of the crushing weight involved in making federal job appointments. Constantly striving to use the patronage tool to strengthen his administration, Polk found instead that most often he was beating his head against the walls of factionalism, pettiness, selfishness, and suspicion. For a man who had imbibed the harsh tenets of Calvinism from his youth up, Polk actually was not surprised at the blatant examples of human corruption and depravity. More than ever before, however, he distrusted "the disinterestedness and honesty of all mankind." His chief regret was that he, because of being president, had to deal with the fallen state of man almost on a daily basis.[1]

Several factors were responsible for imposing upon Polk an unusually heavy burden of patronage problems. Obviously the Democratic party, having been out of power for four years during the Harrison-Tyler administration, was extremely anxious to pluck the fruits of victory from the patronage tree in Washington. Scores of hungry Democrats therefore stormed into that city in early 1845, ready to make their special pleas to the new president. As if that were not enough to worry about, the retiring president, John Tyler, during the closing four months of his administration, had chosen to make many federal appointments, perhaps with a view toward enhancing his misplaced presidential ambitions for 1848. Thus, when Polk arrived in town, he was greeted by loud clamors to engage in a wholesale ousting of officeholders. The young president set his hands first to the compelling matter of choosing a cabinet (discussed in chapter 2); in the process, he set the stage for a continuing saga of trouble for his administration in regard to the distribution of patronage.[2] Afterwards, he turned his attention to the hundreds of federal jobs that it was his prerogative to fill immediately upon taking the oath of office.

Perhaps Polk was not fully aware of the forces that, over the past ten years, had been operating to give the presidency special power and concern in the area of job appointments. The development of the two-party system in the mid 1830s had fostered a mad scramble for patronage, with Congress, the president, and the party organizations all vying for the right to make the final decisions. The three-way struggle would be especially conspicuous during Polk's term. The old "career system" of federal officeholding had split up under the pressure of two-party politics, so that by Polk's time, there were two clearly established tracks of officeholding: the career system and the newer partisan system. The latter group aroused attention and excitement, certainly for Polk and also for other presidents in the ante-bellum period. It must be said, however, that career clerks furnished a source of continuity, despite the removals and replacements carried out by the Polk administration; they stayed on through many exigencies and kept the government functioning regardless of who was occupying the presidential chair. The agents of change, on the other hand, were the "party clerks," those who came and went at the whims of the president and his aides. This open and much-traveled avenue of service had the presumed advantage of enabling many citizens to participate in government.[3]

In fairness it must be conceded that Polk brought a good bit of his patronage woes upon himself by his own decisions and actions. Even before he was inaugurated, he had already determined that he was going to keep a tight rein on his administration. He wanted to run an efficient, politically adroit executive branch of the government. He also had decided, many months before his actual election, that he would serve only one term. Because he did not intend to seek reelection, he did not want to have anyone around the executive departments who would be running for the presidency four years hence. He could not afford, therefore, to let members of his own administration have a free hand in patronage matters, lest they use federal appointments to boost their climb to the presidency. He felt compelled to look over the shoulders of his cabinet leaders and also to view with suspicion the entreaties of members of Congress, for they might be angling to replace him in the presidential office. No wonder that Polk once lamented that the presidency was "no bed of roses."[4]

After taking office in March, Polk embarked upon the tasks of removing federal officials and of replacing them with loyal Democrats. Rumors were rampant throughout the city that the president would engage in what the *Madisonian* called a "sanguinary proscription, unprecedented in the annals of our Government." After discussing matters with his cabinet, a group that seemed to be curiously divided on the topic of a clean sweep of offices, Polk launched his removal policy in a fashion befitting the days of Andrew Jackson's presidency. He apparently decided to make extensive removals, but in the words of one observer, he "would not tomahawk beyond what might be considered Christian ferocity." The first removal notices hit the desks of Washington clerks on 29 March; the new broom intended to sweep clean. The president ordered all department heads to submit to him detailed lists of all employees, with information about their political loyalties, the circumstances of their original appointment, and recommendations to retain or dismiss said employees. With that available data, the president would be able to proceed with a systematic realignment of personnel in the Washington offices.[5] Federal employees who were located elsewhere would happily have a bit more time before the new administration would reach them. All in all, it was a truly serious business that the Polk crowd set about doing. Once the president had launched removal procedures during the very first month, office seekers began to descend upon Washington like the plague of locusts in Biblical Egypt.

Four months after his inauguration, Polk confessed to Governor Silas Wright of New York that he wished he had no offices to bestow, a sentiment that he repeated in his diary on the first anniversary of his administration. Several things soured the president on the matter of patronage, not the least of which was the incessant flow of persons to his office in search of federal appointment. According to his carefully kept diary, 3 September 1846 seems to have been the only regular day of business during his entire four-year term on which no office seekers appeared. Presumably, on all the other days he had to deal with patronage applicants. Needless to say, the efficiency that he had hoped for was seriously compromised and eroded by this intrusion of the multitudes. Polk knew this, but in the best spirit of Jacksonian democracy, he continued to open his doors to these people.[6] It was his duty, however painful and repugnant it might be.

Polk, who grew to detest the job seekers, became bitter and sarcastic. His frustration and exasperation are evident in virtually every reference that he made to them in his diary. He described them, for example, as being "so patriotic as to desire to serve their country by getting into fat offices"; they are "a set of loafers without merit"; "professional office-seekers . . . have become in my estimation the most contemptible of our race"; they merited Polk's "sovereign contempt"; finally, they were "the very scum of society."[7] He learned to deal firmly and sternly with this unpleasant crowd, who dogged his steps every day; but no amount of rejection by him could stop the daily barrage of applicants. In fact, in October 1846, Polk admitted that one unusually persistent office seeker had been troubling him for a year and a half. The president mused that he might have to give the man a position just to get rid of him. No wonder that after nearly two years in office, Polk declared: "I am ready to exclaim God deliver me from dispensing the patronage of the Government." And near the close of his administration, the president in jest thought of getting "one of Colt's revolving pistols to clear my office of the office seekers." What particularly exasperated Polk during the final months was that the number of office seekers greatly increased, rivaling that seen during the early weeks of his administration. The president attributed this distasteful turn of events to the rumors around Washington that President-elect Zachary Taylor intended to make very few removals once he assumed office.[8] In any event, Polk ended his term much as he had begun it, besieged by persons clamoring for public appointments.

Among those who plagued the president throughout his four years, several types of office seekers received special comments from him. One such group was women. Polk never seemed to be quite sure about the females who showed up in his office, looking for positions for their husbands, sons, and brothers. He revealed his skepticism when he noted that the women arrived "in the garb and appearance of ladies." The president was disgusted even when "two ladies of respectability" implored him in behalf of their worthless drunken brother, for he had already concluded beforehand that when women seek offices for members of their families, the presumption is "that the persons for whom they apply are unworthy of public employment." Polk's annoyance and irritation were apparent when a woman who "shed tears freely" pleaded for an appointment for her poverty-stricken husband; but when a woman sought a better-paying job for her fiancé, who was already a government clerk, the president seemed somewhat amused rather than agitated. Perhaps he was intrigued by her audacity and charmed by the fact that she "was rather a pretty woman." Certainly one of Polk's most awkward and embarrassing interviews was with an English lady, Mrs. Sarah M. H. Maury—a year later he described her as "a gossipping woman of a Foreign Kingdom"—who sought the president's support in behalf of the appointment of John C. Calhoun as minister to Britain. Polk, who was extremely careful in making his response to her pleas for Calhoun's assignment, was very glad when she left his office. The chief executive was puzzled and a bit unprepared when Mrs. Lewis Cass arrived at his office door in May 1846, seeking a diplomatic appointment for her son.[9] Apparently, women in the patronage marketplace made Polk, who would today be called a male chauvinist, uncomfortable, for it was simply not a woman's place to bargain in a man's world for federal positions, even when she was seeking jobs for men, not for herself.

Another group that earned the president's attention quite naturally was formed by those who solicited military appointments. In the spring of 1846, when hostilities with Mexico erupted, swarms of office seekers arrived, particularly because the democratic-minded president had decided to appoint officers from among civilian applicants. Again in February 1847, after Congress had authorized ten additional regiments, Polk was beset by scores who were hoping for officer appointments. The president became increasingly perturbed with such blatant opportunism, lamenting that "the City is crowded with young men, many of them loafers without merit, seeking military appointments."[10] Because the president had to preside over the conduct of war, he carried the extra continuing burden of army and navy patronage.

One peculiarly vexing problem for Polk was the presence of greedy office seekers who were waiting for someone to die so that they could pounce on the vacated position. In February 1848, for example, when a federal marshal in the district became ill and was confined to his house, a dozen persons sought his job, *"if he should die."* About a year later, when the death of a certain army paymaster was rumored, applicants showed up in the president's office in less than an hour after the telegraphic message had been received. That evening and the next day, even more patronage vultures circled around the paymaster's job. At that same time, in early January 1849, news arrived telling of the death of former Senator Ambrose H. Sevier, who had been nominated to serve as a commissioner to establish the new boundary line between the United States and Mexico. Immediately, several congressmen appeared, urging that one of their friends replace the deceased Sevier. As Polk sarcastically noted, as soon as an officeholder dies, applicants seek the vacancy without waiting decently enough for the funeral ceremonies to be held.[11] Hardly a more crass illustration of human avarice can be found in the patronage story than in this unseemly quest for the offices of the dead or the nearly dead.

Perhaps more complicated was the question of what to do with the Whigs. The president did not remove all the Whig clerks already in office; "moderate and deserving" Whigs, for example, were retained, though they were not to be promoted. Polk was clear in his policy to get rid of all violent and obnoxious Whigs, but even after a year in office, he was still receiving complaints from Democratic members of Congress about the number of Whig officeholders, "whilst worthy and competent Democrats who desired the places were excluded." Armed with "a list of very obnoxious Whig clerks," the president summoned the Treasury secretary to his office and demanded that the secretary take action. Polk was careful to make a few occasional appointments of Whigs to office, despite his own inclinations and pressures from his party. He decided, for example, at the outbreak of the Mexican War, that some Whigs should be appointed as officers. When the two Kentucky senators, both of whom were Whigs, asked the president to designate a Whig friend of theirs as paymaster in the army, Polk, who wanted "to prove to them that I was not proscriptive in my appointments," promptly complied with their request. On balance, the chief executive followed the tactic of removing and excluding Whigs, but he did make exceptions from time to time (crumbs from the table), a somewhat surprising strategy in light of his fierce partisan leanings. At the very end of his presidency, many Whig officeholders called upon Polk "to express their gratitude & to take leave" of him.[12]

One major policy decision that Polk adhered to with notable consistency was that members of Congress should not receive federal appointments from him. He reiterated this principle several times, but he enlarged upon it so as to make congressmen eligible for elevation to the cabinet, to the Supreme Court, or to the ministry of a foreign country. The president quickly discovered the thirst for federal appointments that members of Congress had; especially were they desirous of various and sundry military positions. Polk resisted these pressures admirably well, citing constitutional proscriptions against congressmen being eligible for offices that they themselves had voted to create. All along, he hedged on the matter of appointment to some high military station, however, arguing that he did not want his hands tied completely on this situation. He did make one abortive effort to have Senator Thomas Hart Benton placed in a generalship. By January 1847, Polk judged that he had incurred the wrath and political opposition of no fewer than twenty members of Congress who had approached him for specific federal appointments.[13] By and large, Polk successfully warded off the entreaties of members of Congress by making his rule early in the patronage game and by sticking with it, although it cost him support from time to time. His dealings with members of Congress were troublesome enough (as discussed elsewhere) that he did not need the additional problem of handing out federal jobs to them. He was both wise and circumspect to deny them routine governmental appointments.

The final observation of a general sort to be made about Polk and the patronage is that he recognized, however painfully, that the dispensing of appointments weakened both his office and his party. Judging from a survey of his diary, it appears that Polk was more concerned about the erosion of the presidency than of the party; perhaps that is to be expected. At least as early as June 1846, Polk began to confide his damning thesis that the patronage and its distribution sapped the strength of the presidency and the presidential administration, a view that he repeated a number of times throughout his tenure in office. By December 1846, Polk was so convinced of the correctness of his interpretation that he began to make the prediction that no president would ever be reelected. For the mid-nineteenth century, he was remarkably accurate in this prognostication, although failure to be reelected was not always tied to patronage woes. As Polk aptly pointed out in the following month, every time he made an appointment to a federal post, he created several enemies from those disappointed office seekers who had hoped for the job. The applicants are so numerous, wrote Polk, that "they hold the balance of power between the two great parties of the country." A very discouraged chief executive lamented almost a year later that even if he could put ten persons in every office available, he still would not be able to satisfy all the applicants for office. In the closing months of his term, Polk still claimed that the presidency and its administration were greatly harmed by the whole patronage business. In December 1847 he specifically acknowledged that patronage "does more to weaken the democratic party than all other causes combined." He returned directly to this theme immediately after Taylor's victory in November, when he warned that the party in power would always be hurt in elections by the thousands of unhappy office seekers who turn against the party.[14] Although such claims as these are not susceptible to precise proof or documentation, nevertheless they seem at least plausible. One must grant, of course, that Polk naturally wanted to explain away his failures and those of his party by pointing to patronage woes. Even allowing for some exaggeration on his part, the persuasive point remains that the awarding of federal offices was a two-edged sword, whose destructive edge was sharper than its constructive one.

Not unexpectedly, the president devoted quite a bit of his time and effort to his relationship with Congress vis-à-vis patronage. As already mentioned, he established the rule that members of Congress were not themselves eligible for routine federal appointments; this did not stop some of them from seeking office, however, nor did it halt a steady progression of legislative leaders from interceding in behalf of family members and constituents. Although Polk was thoroughly exasperated by the pressures and demands from members of Congress, he handled the relationship fairly well. He did, in fact, consult frequently with congressional leaders about patronage in their home states, and he permitted them to name their preferences for appointments. While doing so, he also clung tenaciously to his independence as chief executive, thereby making some degree of conflict unavoidable. The two states of New York and Pennsylvania caused more patronage problems for Polk than all the others combined; therefore they will be dealt with separately. Congress blocked some of the president's nominations, but what is surprising is that it did not reject more of them, given the tense relations between the executive and legislative branches over many issues. Strange as it may seem, Polk was more successful with nominations requiring senatorial confirmation than President Jackson had been. Viewed in that light, "Young Hickory" must be credited as being an astute and adept master of patronage relations with Congress.[15] Unfortunately, Polk complained more about his infrequent setbacks than he praised his numerous victories; but then, that was his basic nature.

The scores of congressmen who visited the president in search of choice federal appointments mainly did so in behalf of friends and constituents; some, however, sought positions for themselves or for members of their families. Jacob Brinkerhoff of Ohio and James Semple of Illinois, for example, both requested military appointments for themselves, but Polk refused to bend his rule against positions for members of Congress. Both men shortly thereafter caused problems for the president on various pieces of legislation.[16] In the summer of 1848, John D. McCrate, a former congressman from Maine, used his connections with colleagues on the Potomac to push his bid for appointment as a Mexican-treaty commissioner. Polk, unimpressed with this approach, made no promises to McCrate. On the other hand, when the name of Senator Edward Hannegan surfaced for consideration for a diplomatic appointment, Polk took cognizance of bipartisan support for Hannegan and, on the next-to-last day of his presidential term, nominated him for the Prussian post.[17]

Somewhat embarrassing were the attempts by certain congressmen to obtain federal positions for family members. Probably the most difficult situation for the president was when Senator Thomas Hart Benton, in March 1847, pressed for a diplomatic appointment for William Carey Jones, who had married Benton's daughter just a week and a half earlier. Polk did not like Jones, who had formerly been the editor of an opposition newspaper in New Orleans; but he feared Benton's "violent outbreak" if he did not grant a post to Jones. Slightly over a month later, Jones appeared at Polk's office to reiterate his desire for a diplomatic assignment but also to indicate his preference for appointment as postmaster at New Orleans. Polk abruptly informed the applicant that there was no vacancy in New Orleans, nor was there likely to be one. The chief executive had not seen the last of the Benton family, however, for in October, John Randolph Benton, the senator's son, entreated Polk for an appointment as a lieutenant in the army. The president carefully explained the reasons why such a position could not be offered to young Benton, but to no avail, for the senator's son bolted for the door "very rudely, swearing profanely." Witnesses in the president's office were shocked at the young man's conduct, and more than one of them claimed that Benton reeked of alcohol. Justifiably troubled by his dealings with the Benton family, Polk predicted that the senator would turn against him.[18]

Another son of a prominent family who sought patronage favors from the president was Lewis Cass, Jr. As early as 1846 his mother had promoted his claims, but the matter lay dormant for two years before being revived. In September 1848, two days after it was learned that Jacob L. Martin, the chargé d'affaires at Rome, had died, young Cass, along with others, showed up at the president's office, seeking the vacated post. Polk's interview with Cass was very painful; he expressed his belief that an appointment on the eve of presidential election would be detrimental to Senator Cass's chances. Young Cass then tried, without success, to extract a promise from Polk that the post would be given to him once the election was over. Three days after his father's defeat in November, Cass reappeared at Polk's office to beg for the Rome assignment. The president refused to give him any satisfaction but confided to his diary that he would probably appoint him out of respect for the senator, who had urged Polk to find a position for his ambitious son. The following month, when Polk did indeed submit young Cass's nomination, two senators spoke to the president about their opposition to him and their desires to see Senator Hannegan appointed instead. Luckily, Polk was eventually able to work himself out of the dilemma by sending Lewis Cass, Jr., to Rome and Hannegan to Prussia.[19] The Benton and Cass families were not the only ones to push for patronage, but they serve as notable illustrations of the unusual kinds of pressures that members of Congress exerted upon the president.

More often, however, Polk was besieged by congressmen trumpeting the capabilities of their friends and constituents, rather than family. This was nothing new, of course; Polk had done the same thing when he had served in Congress. It was of such magnitude and frequency, however, that the president believed that he was more harassed by this than any of his predecessors had been. He seemed not to appreciate the reality that congressional egos were wrapped up in the quest for patronage; instead, Polk apparently saw only unmitigated selfishness on the part of members of Congress. Particularly annoyed when they arrived at his office accompanied by a train of friends and constituents, the president blamed the congressmen for bringing in unworthy applicants and for putting him in an unpleasant situation. Polk complained even more vigorously about the deceptive recommendations that congressmen sometimes gave him, which forced him to make bad appointments. Salt was added to the wounds when these same congressional leaders tried to deny or obscure their involvement in the appointments that turned sour. The president, who was himself not always known for his candor, frequently lamented the lack of candid recommendations from the congressmen. Chastened by the appointment, upon the insistence of Senator John M. Niles, of a collector at New Haven whose unpopularity subsequently had negative political repercussions in Connecticut, the president refused Senator Benjamin Tappan's nominee for postmaster of Steubenville, because local Ohio Democrats did not want the man. Meanwhile Senator Sidney Breese of Illinois received Polk's top award as "the most troublesome and inveterate seeker for office for his friends in either House of Congress." The president blamed Breese for being the cause of a number of bad appointments; and wearied by the senator's incessant quest for jobs, Polk declared that Breese "has always an axe to grind."[20] So did a majority of the members of the legislative branch, especially the Democrats.

In January 1847 the notorious Breese teamed up with his colleague, Stephen A. Douglas, to push Richard M. Young of their state to become commissioner of the General Land Office. Polk yielded to their demands, although he actually preferred another man for the post. The president sent Young's name to the Senate, which, with extraordinary rapidity, confirmed him before the end of the day. When it became

known that Young had been approved, however, three Illinois representatives hastily made their way to the president to voice their unhappiness. Although they had no objection to Young, they were perturbed
for having been kept in the dark about the matter. Polk had innocently
assumed that Breese and Douglas had cleared everything in advance
with their Illinois cohorts. The revelation that Douglas and Breese
earnestly desired the appointment of Young in order to prevent him
from opposing either one of them in their reelection bids further
shocked the president. Realizing how he had been tricked, Polk wished
that it were possible for him to withdraw Young's name, but it was
already too late.[21]

A year and a half later an unhappy group of Michigan congressmen
descended upon the president to protest because their candidate for a
second lieutenancy had not been appointed. Polk saw this instance as a
pointed illustration of "the importance which is attached by members of
Congress to petty offices." He became harshly indignant, noting that
"many members of Congress assume that they have the right to make
appointments, particularly in their own states, and they often . . . fly
into a passion when their wishes are not gratified." He castigated
congressmen who forget "that they were sent to Washington by their
constituents to legislate, & not to usurp the functions of the Executive or
to dictate to him in matters of appointment to office."[22]

They never stopped trying to "dictate" to the president, however.
A good example of the swirling controversy that sometimes greeted the
efforts of congressmen to get positions for their constituents is the case
of James H. Tate of Mississippi. Members of Congress from that state
had urged that Tate be appointed as consul to Buenos Aires, but shortly
thereafter, Congressman Jacob Thompson changed his mind and
wanted Tate's name withdrawn. Whereupon both Mississippi senators
strongly urged Polk to retain the Tate nomination. The confusing
situation was further clouded by Thompson's attacks upon Tate as an
indirect way of criticizing Treasury Secretary Robert J. Walker, also of
Mississippi. The story had a somewhat happy ending, at least for Tate,
who arrived in Washington to find that Thompson's charges against him
had been dropped and that the Senate had confirmed his nomination.[23]
To be sure, the president made scores of nominations and appointments
that elicited no public conflict, only approval. The point remains,
however, that many members of Congress devoted some part of almost
every waking day to efforts and schemes to obtain patronage plums for
their hungry friends and constituents.

Needless to say, there was some dissatisfaction within the Congress
over Polk's distribution of patronage. Whig congressmen understand-

ably were left out of the president's plans for appointments, but some Democrats also were ignored or deliberately thwarted by the chief executive. With a degree of exaggeration, Francis Blair reported to Martin Van Buren in early 1846 that unhappiness was rampant in Congress over the administration. A few other observers likewise believed that the president had little control over the legislative body. Granted, he had problems with the Calhoun element, the New York contingent, and the Pennsylvania delegation; but with the exception of occasional disputes with certain other Democrats, Polk managed Congress very ably, thanks in part to his use of the patronage. Among the difficult Democrats was Senator James D. Westcott of Florida. Benton and Polk also had their differences from time to time; and Senator Thomas J. Rusk of Texas fumed about the lack of patronage caused by his having been categorized as one of Calhoun's friends.[24]

There were others who troubled Polk, but probably no one agitated the president as much as did his fellow Tennesseans George W. Jones and Andrew Johnson. Early in his administration, Polk had shut off the patronage valve to them, and when Johnson finally complained to him in person in July 1846, the president delivered a bitter lecture to Johnson. He issued a bill of grievances against both Jones and Johnson for their actions and statements in the House. The president also admitted that he had not consulted with them about recent military appointments, although he had indeed conferred with other congressmen from the state. Very pointedly, Polk told Johnson that there would be no patronage rewards unless Johnson and Jones mended their ways. Professing to be a good Democrat and a supporter of the administration, a somewhat chastened and sobered Johnson left after Polk's hour-long tirade. The president rushed to his diary at the first opportune moment to record his version of the tension-filled conversation. He boasted that he possessed the power to ruin both Johnson and Jones in Tennessee, if he merely told their constituents the true story of their opposition to him and his administration. Of these two men, Polk complained: "They seem to assume to themselves the right to judge of the appointments in Tennessee, and to denounce them among members of Congress and in boarding houses." While concluding his entry with a slight hope that Johnson and Jones might reform, the president offered this indirect condemnation: "I would almost prefer to have two Whigs here in their stead." Two and a half years later, Polk indicated that Johnson had not changed, declaring that "he has been politically if not personally hostile to me during my whole term."[25]

Offsetting these difficulties with the obstreperous Johnson and Jones was the immensely satisfying relationship with another Tennessean, Cave Johnson. As postmaster general, Johnson played an influential role in the patronage story. For sheer quantity of jobs to be filled, no one could rival Johnson. But the remarkable thing about this long-time friend of Polk's is that his patronage duties were not confined solely to the Post Office Department. Instead, Johnson emerged as the president's man to see about practically all patronage concerns; he conferred with members of Congress, with colleagues in the cabinet, and with non-Washington political leaders about far-ranging matters of federal positions. One scholar has described Johnson as Polk's "patronage broker"—the man who did most of the investigative leg work for the president and who relayed messages about appointments all around Washington.[26] Polk had complete trust and confidence in Johnson; their relationship dated back many years, to their political apprenticeships in Tennessee and their service together in Congress. He was therefore the natural choice for assistance in such sensitive concerns as the federal patronage.

Cave Johnson seems to have been a man of few words but much action, especially when he set the example for patronage sweepstakes in the Post Office Department. As one might expect, Democratic congressmen immediately pounced on the challenging excitement of determining the appointment of postmasters in their districts. With his customary political savoir-faire, Johnson heeded many of the congressional recommendations for removal and replacement. He was, of course, particularly anxious to remove Whig postmasters; but he tried to retain many of the Democrats who already held positions, and he attempted to steer clear of factionalism in making new appointments. During the first year of the Polk administration, Johnson superintended the removal of some 700 postmasters across the nation. He made sure that the Democratic party would reap a bonanza in post-office patronage, with the result that by the end of the administration, there had been an astounding 13,500 appointments as postmasters. More than 10,000 postmasters had resigned during the four years, for some reason or other, and 1,600 had been removed outright.[27] One marvels that the mail was ever delivered in those days of disruption and turmoil in the post offices.

Cave Johnson was more than ably served by his second assistant postmaster general, William Medill of Ohio, an officer who was in charge of the thousands of postmasters whose appointments did not require the consent of the president and the Senate. Senator William Allen had insisted upon Medill's appointment, using the argument that Medill knew how to carry out a vigorous proscription policy. Polk, evidently convinced by Allen, gave the post to Medill, although Senator

John Niles of Connecticut had pushed for the appointment of Gideon Welles from his state. Both Medill and Johnson seemed to have had a natural instinct for the distribution of patronage. It is worth noting that on one day in September 1845, when Polk was considering a new commissioner of Indian Affairs, he consulted first with Medill and then with former Senator Benjamin Tappan and Cave Johnson concerning Thomas L. Homer of Ohio. In late October, however, Polk named Medill, not Homer, to head the Office of Indian Affairs, obviously a reward for his effective work, as well as a recognition of political pressures.[28]

Secretary of State Buchanan and Secretary of War Marcy, due to the circumstances of their own appointment to Polk's cabinet, were intimately involved in patronage in their home states, but their duties as heads of their respective departments also thrust upon them the task of making appointments. Buchanan set about designating his own team to work under him in the State Department, although he retained some of the incumbents at least for a time. Not surprisingly, anyone who thought that he had the slightest connection with Buchanan wrote to him or visited him in behalf of some kind of federal job. Buchanan created something of a mild stir in 1845 when he asked Francis P. Blair if he would like to go to Spain as United States minister; Blair, thinking that Buchanan had offered the post to him, wrote a note declining it. Afterwards the president and the secretary had a candid discussion in which Buchanan denied that he had actually told Blair that he could have the diplomatic assignment. Marcy apparently was much more careful not to overstep his prerogatives as head of an executive department. In fact, he was very cautious about changing the personnel in the War Department; he made virtually no changes in the Washington office. Indian agents who were under the supervision of this department, however, proved to be a ripe field for removal and replacement by the new administration. Once the Mexican War had begun, Marcy had his hands more than full in working with the president on officer appointments. In February 1847, for example, after Congress had approved ten new regiments, Marcy and Polk were in daily contact about filling the leadership positions. With some four hundred appointments to be made within a short span of time, the president and the secretary had their work cut out for them, and it was a strain on both of them.[29]

Polk's victory in Massachusetts enabled George Bancroft to position himself to control state politics and also to reap high political reward. The president selected Bancroft to serve as head of the Navy Department, a post that he held until he departed for London in the fall of 1846.

Like other cabinet members, Bancroft was inundated with letters and requests from far and wide, all seeking federal jobs. The secretary heeded the pleas in behalf of Nathaniel Hawthorne by obtaining posts for him, first in the Boston customs house and subsequently as surveyor of the port of Salem. Bancroft evidently used his influence with Polk to secure for Marcus Morton the lucrative assignment of collector at Boston, although not without some controversy.[30]

Treasury Secretary Walker also could not avoid being drawn into patronage considerations. He quickly discovered that Democratic politicians across the nation expected a sympathetic hearing and the implementation of their requests for jobs. Gideon Welles in Connecticut and Elijah Haywood in Ohio, for instance, early let it be known that they were prepared to give Walker advice on appointments and removals. Senator David Levy Yulee pledged that he would support the administration if Treasury Department patronage were used to keep Florida Democratic. As earlier noted, Walker was pulled into the controversy over the James Tate diplomatic appointment, but he managed to extricate himself in a fashion that pleased Polk. A rude office seeker who wanted a position as keeper of a lighthouse on the Great Lakes was turned away by Polk with the declaration that Secretary Walker had the legal power to make such appointments and therefore the president would not intervene. In April 1846 the president issued orders to Walker to clean house of the Whig clerks who were still on the payroll in his department. On that same occasion, Polk also told the secretary that Walker's brother-in-law, William W. Irwin of Pennsylvania, would have to be removed as chargé d'affaires to Denmark, a post he had received from President Tyler. Pennsylvania Democrats, reported Polk, were up in arms over the retention of Irwin, an avowed Whig.[31]

With all the disturbances over patronage that characterized the Polk administration, it should be noted that the president occasionally told the cabinet in advance about appointments that he intended to make and asked for their support. He did this, for example, in September 1845, when he secured the cabinet's endorsement of his nomination of Senator Levi Woodbury of New Hampshire to the United States Supreme Court. In June 1848, when he unilaterally decided upon Senator Arthur P. Bagby of Alabama to be United States minister to Russia, he turned to the cabinet to seek its approval. In the following month, Polk yielded to the advice of his cabinet members, who urged him to submit to the Senate his nominations for generals, appointments that the president did not think were necessary, since the war had ended.[32] Both collectively and individually, the cabinet influenced patronage, sometimes directly, sometimes indirectly. Yet to Polk, these department heads were often simply another source of irritation and exasperation in the continuing quest for chairs at the federal banquet table.

Certainly this was true of Secretary Marcy, whose original appointment to the cabinet had galvanized disputes in New York over federal patronage. Polk's efforts to enlist someone from the Van Buren–Silas Wright wing of the New York Democrats had been thwarted, and he therefore had turned to the conservative "Hunker" group. Once the president had named Marcy to the War Department, the "Barnburner" element declared unofficial war on Polk.[33] Acutely aware of the dangerous pitfalls in handling New York appointments, the president went out of his way to give assurances to the Van Buren faction, while at the same time trying to maintain something close to parity in patronage. He even offered the London post to Van Buren, who, although tempted, refused it, and promised several prominent party leaders, such as John L. O'Sullivan, Samuel J. Tilden, John A. Dix, and Van Buren's son John, that he would clear the distribution of patronage with their segment of the New York party. Some were impressed with Polk's intentions, while others remained suspicious. Polk swung into action by parceling out jobs to both groups but favoring the Van Buren–Wright clique. Benjamin F. Butler, for example, was offered an appointment as federal district attorney, which he accepted; there was even some talk of making Azariah C. Flagg the collector at New York City; Wright's protégé, Ransom H. Gillet, was designated as register of the Treasury; other Van Burenites were awarded jobs as postmasters, marshals, and surveyors of customs. Other than the cabinet post itself, the Marcy group initially received appointments only of a district attorney in western New York, a navy agent (Marcy's friend Prosper M. Wetmore) at New York City, and a few minor posts.[34]

Diligently though he tried, Polk could not walk the tightrope between the warring factions. As subsequent examples will show, both groups registered their dissatisfaction. By and large, however, the Van Burenites proved to be the most contumacious crowd. After the dust from early skirmishes had settled, John Van Buren arrived in Washington and criticized Polk's distribution of patronage by saying that Governor Wright and others had not been fairly treated. The president responded to this November 1845 visit by maintaining that the Van Burenites would be content only if he eliminated Marcy's Hunker wing of the party. But, avowed Polk, "I will do, as I have done, Mr. Martin Van Buren's friends full justice in the bestowal of public patronage, but I cannot proscribe all others of the Democratic party in order to gain their good will." In letters to Cave Johnson and to Polk, Governor Wright protested against their appointment policy in New York, which, in his opinion, favored the Marcy faction.[35] A year later, when Wright and the Democrats suffered defeat in New York elections, the Barnburners blamed Polk's catering to the Marcy group for fracturing the state party and thereby making victory impossible. As a matter of fact, Polk confided to Secretary Buchanan his evaluation that the Hunkers had been responsible for Wright's defeat in 1846. He therefore pledged: "This faction shall hereafter receive no favours at my hands if I know it." In early 1847, James K. Paulding castigated the Polk administration for having warred against Governor Wright by giving the patronage to Marcy and his cohorts. An exasperated president later told a New York congressman: "Both factions of the Democratic party complained that I had given too many appointments to the opposing faction." Polk further observed that the factional disputes were not over principles or policies but rather were over who should receive "the larger share of the 'loaves & fishes.'"[36] The president seems to have been perceptive enough in analyzing the New York situation, but trying to treat each group equally was beyond his capabilities.

The imbroglio over the office of collector of the New York City Customs House demonstrates Polk's extreme difficulties in keeping peace in that state's Democratic family. When the president took office, Cornelius P. Van Ness, who had been appointed in 1844 by Tyler, was the collector. Partly because of Marcy's advice and guidance, Polk agreed to retain Van Ness, at least for a while. News of this decision reached the Van Burenites shortly, and they howled in dismay, causing Polk then to ask Benjamin F. Butler to consult with fellow members of his faction for purposes of making a recommendation. Accordingly, Butler reported to the president in early April 1845 that the Van Buren faction favored Jonathan Coddington for collector and Michael Hoffman for naval officer. In the conversation about these proposed appointments, however, Butler indicated that there was not a great deal of enthusiasm for Coddington, a revelation that sent up warning flags to Polk. He therefore balked at the appointment of Coddington; he agreed, however, to designate Hoffman as naval officer; and he delayed on the collector's post, while keeping Van Ness. Various New York leaders meanwhile had been going about the state giving assurances to everyone that Polk was on the verge of removing Van Ness and of replacing him with a Van Burenite.[37]

The more pressure and intimidation that the president felt, the more reluctant he became to give the Barnburners the position of collector, so much so that he finally announced that he would find a person of his own choosing for the post. By June, Polk had his man,

Cornelius W. Lawrence, a former congressman, a former mayor of New York City, and a businessman who was identified with the conservative and banking interests. Marcy, who was delighted with the decision, hastened to New York City to persuade Lawrence to take the collectorship. Lawrence eventually consented, whereupon Polk arranged for Van Ness to resign. Barnburner Democrats were pleased with the removal of Van Ness, of course, but they were not happy with Lawrence's elevation, declaring that Lawrence was part of Polk's strategy to build up the Hunker faction in New York. Sensitive to these outcries, the president wrote to Silas Wright in an effort to explain and defend his actions; he even offered the ministership in Russia to a New Yorker. But Wright responded by noting that Lawrence was identified with banking interests and that he had resisted banking reforms in the state. Although Treasury Secretary Walker commended Polk for having successfully navigated "the whirlpools of N. York politics," bitter feelings within the state offset such congratulations.[38] By the summer months of 1845 the chief executive had reason to regret the necessity of becoming involved in the factional politics of New York.

This is not the end of the story, however, for there were other patronage struggles between the president and that state. In early July 1846, with Secretary Marcy's approval, Polk approached Senator John A. Dix, a Van Burenite leader, with the possible offer of the job of United States minister to Great Britain. Evidently Polk was still trying to make amends with the Barnburner group. The appointment of Dix did not develop, however, because in a few weeks the president gave the post to Bancroft, who was anxious to leave the cabinet for some attractive foreign assignment.[39] In August a controversy began to develop over the appointment of a postmaster for Buffalo. With the support and prompting of Secretary Marcy and Senator Daniel S. Dickinson, the president agreed to name Henry K. Smith to the position. The cabinet discussed the legal questions about making a temporary appointment to fill the vacant post, and the members, with the exception of Buchanan, concurred in the belief that Polk had the power to make such an appointment. When Congress reconvened in December, the president submitted Smith's name, this time as a permanent postmaster. Senator Dix, however, visited Polk's office to register his great dissatisfaction over the nomination of Smith and to hint that he might attempt to block Smith's confirmation. When thinking about this matter some months later, Polk was moved to express his disgust "with the petty local strife between these factions. There is no patriotism in it on either side."[40]

The best example of conflict with Marcy and the Hunker Democrats occurred at the very end of the session of Congress in the spring of 1847.

Polk went to the Capitol, ready to sign legislation and to nominate five generals to command the ten new regiments that Congress had authorized. Having already decided in advance that the only way he could deal with the factional conflict in New York was to appoint no generals from that state, the president was prepared when Secretary Marcy approached him with much fervor to entreat the nomination of a General Clark from New York. Polk informed Marcy that he did not believe Clark to be qualified for such a command and, furthermore, that no appointment he could make would satisfy both groups in the state. Marcy, much disturbed by the president's strategy, went out to consult with Senator Dickinson and other allies. Meanwhile, Polk dispatched Attorney General Clifford to the Senate chamber to confer with Senator Dix about Clark. Denouncing Clark as "the most obnoxious man in N. York," Dix declared that he "& his faction were bitterly & uncompromisingly opposed to him." Polk was not suprised at this reaction.[41]

Finally the president, apparently troubled by Marcy's unhappiness, hit upon a different tactic; he would indeed name a general from New York, but it would be Enos Hopping, rather than Clark. Hopping was a personal and political friend of Marcy's and earlier had been recommended by both factions of the New York delegation for an appointment as colonel. Believing therefore that Hopping was the nearly perfect nominee, the chief executive presented the new plan to the sad-countenanced Marcy. The secretary was not pleased with the nomination of Hopping and argued that he and his friends in Congress would accept no one but Clark, whereupon Polk insisted that it either had to be Hopping or New York would be by-passed. Senator Dickinson rushed in to see the president and excitedly declared that he would resign his seat if Clark were not appointed; Dickinson also claimed that Marcy's friends would demand that he resign from the cabinet. Indignant at such efforts to bully him, Polk dug in his heels and "resolved not to be driven from my purpose." At the appropriate moment, therefore, he instructed his private secretary to insert Hopping's name as one of the generals. Trying to do a personal favor for Marcy had turned into a detestable conflict with him; to be sure, Polk eventually appointed Marcy's friend, rather than a Van Burenite, but he won only criticism for doing it. No wonder the bewildered and frustrated president expressed himself to be "perfectly indifferent whether Mr. Dickinson and Mr. Marcy resigned or not."[42] Doubtless he regretted having abandoned his original strategy of nominating no New Yorkers for generalships.

The last important chapter in the story of patronage for New York showed the triumph of Secretary Marcy and his associates. It began in the summer of 1848, when Barnburners broke with the Democratic party in preparation for the presidential election, a turn of events that greatly alienated President Polk. He therefore resolved to retaliate with the most available weapon at his disposal, namely, the federal patronage. Not surprisingly, Polk was particularly anxious to remove Benjamin F. Butler as district attorney in New York, for Butler had emerged as one of the most vigorous and strident leaders of the Barnburner faction. In early July, when Congressman Ausburn Birdsall urged the dismissal of Butler and other Van Burenites who were holding federal appointments, Polk gave Birdsall a sympathetic hearing. Nevertheless, the president was fearful of acting immediately, lest the removals work against Cass's presidential chances. On the following day, Polk discussed the matter with his cabinet, most of whom were in favor of ousting the Barnburners; he told them about his conversation with Birdsall and read them a letter from Senator Dickinson, recommending that action be taken against Butler and others. Polk informed the cabinet that he intended to consult with two of Cass's stalwarts, Senator Alpheus Felch and Congressman Robert McClelland, before reaching any final decision. Although agreeing that there needed to be a housecleaning of the Barnburners, these two congressional leaders from Michigan entreated Polk not to make any removals before the election. At the end of the month the president conferred with William O. Butler, Cass's vice-presidential running mate, about the appropriateness of taking immediate action against the Barnburners. Even after reviewing a petition from prominent Democrats in New York City, requesting dismissals, both Butler and Polk agreed that the implementation of such a policy might jeopardize the Democratic campaign.[43]

By early August the president's position began to stiffen, however, for he was determined to remove Benjamin F. Butler. Polk again discussed the topic with his cabinet, all of whom, save Buchanan, approved the immediate ouster of Butler. Secretary Walker suggested, however, that Polk should wait until after the Buffalo convention, scheduled for 9 August; and Polk acquiesced, but not before saying of the Barnburners "that I ought no longer to retain them in office, and by retaining them thus give to them the apparent countenance of my administration in their treason to the principles they formerly professed to the party to which they formerly belonged." A week after the Free Soil Convention at Buffalo, Secretary Marcy escorted to Polk's office John McKeon, who was somewhat startled to learn that the president was ready to appoint him that day to Butler's post as district attorney. McKeon, a former New York congressman, declined the offer, however, on the grounds that he was already holding a public office in New York and could not abandon it. A frustrated Polk, anxious to leave on a rare vacation trip, admonished Marcy and McKeon to identify a suitable candidate, but McKeon begged the president to wait until after he had returned to Washington to make the appointment. Polk reluctantly consented and then charged Marcy and McKeon, in the meantime, to consult with prominent New York leaders. Ready to depart from town, the president instructed Secretary Marcy to make the final decision about the proper person for the post.[44]

The story took an unexpected twist when McKeon changed his mind, visited Polk at his vacation spot in Bedford Springs, and asked for the appointment. The president, somewhat taken aback, now told McKeon that he could make no decision until after consulting with Marcy. Immediately upon his return to Washington, Polk convened the cabinet and engaged the members in a further conversation about the situation in New York. Informing them of McKeon's desire for the appointment, Polk professed doubts about McKeon because of his involvement with the Irish directory in New York City, a connection that could prove to be quite embarrassing to a federal official. All cabinet members agreed that McKeon should not be appointed for fear of potential trouble for him and the administration over his support of the Irish against British authority. Whereupon Secretary Marcy recommended that McKeon be invited to come to Washington immediately for an explication of why he had been rejected.[45]

Two days later, when McKeon arrived, Polk and Marcy outlined the problems that they saw in regard to his nomination. While confessing his private sympathy for the Irish patriots, the president quickly noted that his public position had to be that of complete neutrality on the matter. McKeon reluctantly swung around to Polk's and Marcy's viewpoint and surrendered his ambitions for the appointment. Then both McKeon and Marcy offered to the president the names of some possible candidates, and all eventually concurred in the selection of Charles McVean, a former congressional colleague of Polk's. Finally on 1 September, the president officially removed Butler and nominated McVean to replace him. Polk could not restrain himself from writing in his diary a fairly lengthy condemnation of Butler and the Barnburners.[46] At long last it seemed as though Marcy and his Hunker allies had finally won the patronage warfare, but it was something of a hollow triumph, since the November election yielded a Whig victory in New York and across the nation.[47]

Any headaches that Polk experienced in dealing with New York were certainly matched or superseded by problems with Pennsylvania, especially since he had representatives of the two rival factions within his own administration: Dallas and Buchanan. At the simplest level the two men became competitors for the presidential succession, which made it therefore crucial for one of them to control, or at least to seem to control, the federal appointments in Pennsylvania. Unlike the factions in New York, those in Pennsylvania appear not to have had an ideological basis; they seem essentially to have resulted from struggles for elected office and patronage. In any event, prominent leaders generally lined up either with Dallas or with Buchanan. A small group of Democrats did not fit into either camp; instead, it charted a somewhat maverick course, with Simon Cameron as its helmsman. Because of the unorthodox circumstances of Cameron's election to the Senate, many of Pennsylvania's Democratic leaders wanted Dallas and Buchanan to condemn him and read him out of the party. Neither man would do so, although they generally refused to help him with federal patronage. Eventually, Polk sided mainly with Buchanan in the distribution of appointments, a strategy about which he later expressed some regret. One of the fruits of the patronage rivalries in the state was the unhappiness of Congressman David Wilmot, who felt blocked in his quest for jobs for his constituents. His Wilmot Proviso, which was introduced first in the summer of 1846, became one of the hallmarks of party revolt against the Polk administration.[48]

Polk had two major battles with his Democratic friends in Pennsylvania: the appointment of the customs collector at Philadelphia, and the selection of a United States Supreme Court justice from the state. Just about every conceivable aspect of patronage squabbles was wrapped up in these two conflicts, which raged during 1845/46. Before delving into them, it would be instructive to examine briefly some of the lesser struggles. Polk got a small taste of the internecine strife among Pennsylvania Democrats when Vice-President Dallas approached him in December 1846 with a letter from John K. Kane, a federal judge in the state, asking that the president find an appointment for Governor Francis Shunk. Dallas and Kane were members of the same faction, whereas Shunk belonged to the Buchanan camp. They wanted to keep Shunk from seeking reelection as governor by arranging a federal position for him and thereby, in their opinion, promoting "the harmony of the Democratic party in Pennsylvania." The president's response to this touchy situation was to say that he considered Shunk a worthy man and would find a federal post for him if there were a suitable one available, but that Secretary Buchanan would have to be consulted first, before any action could be taken. An uncomfortable Dallas consented to Polk's suggestion and promised that he would ask Kane to come to Washington to confer with Buchanan regarding a possible federal appointment for Shunk. Polk asserted afterwards that he had made no promises to anyone, which was the only safe tactic for him to follow.[49]

The president's efforts to award a diplomatic post to Congressman Charles J. Ingersoll, a Pennsylvania Democrat, turned out to be one of the most exasperating and prolonged of all the patronage conflicts. The story, though tedious, provides insight into Polk's handling of difficulties in regard to a high-level appointment. Both Dallas and Buchanan were involved in the unfolding saga at one time or another, as were several other people, mostly Pennsylvanians. Early in Polk's administration, Ingersoll indicated his desire for a foreign appointment, and he enlisted Dallas to convey his wish to the president. Eventually Polk informed the Pennsylvania congressman that he would be nominated as United States minister to Russia, but in July 1846, Ingersoll declared his preference for the French mission instead. The latter was simply not available. As the congressional session neared its conclusion, Polk warned Ingersoll that the Senate might reject his appointment to Russia. Fearful of this possibility, Ingersoll asked the president not to submit his name to the Senate. That is where the matter rested when Congress adjourned in early August.[50]

A week later, Ingersoll wrote a letter to Polk, in which he inquired about an appointment as minister to France. The president did not answer the letter; apparently he thought little about it until late October, when Buchanan asked Polk to return Ingersoll's August letter to the congressman. Offended by this request, the president harshly criticized Ingersoll. Buchanan claimed that the congressman simply wanted the letter, so that it would not be in the record to show that he had applied for the French post. Polk, still annoyed, searched for Ingersoll's letter, found it, and handed it over to Buchanan. Two months later, in December 1846, Ingersoll visited Polk to ask again for the diplomatic appointment to France, a request that the president denied. Evincing a somewhat unusual flexibility, however, Polk, near the end of the session of Congress, made up his mind to designate Ingersoll as the minister to France "and thus gratify his most ardent wishes as repeatedly expressed to me."[51]

The president therefore submitted Ingersoll's name to the Senate on 3 March, the last day, but the nomination was rejected by a narrow margin. Because time was about to elapse, Polk hastily decided to appoint Richard Rush, a Philadelphia lawyer and former diplomat, to the post in France, and the Senate confirmed the nomination. The president expressed regrets to Ingersoll, who seemed not to be overly disappointed with the sudden turn of events. Ingersoll could not or would not accept the finality of the situation, however; instead, at the end of March 1847, he wrote a strong letter to the president, reprimanding him for appointing Rush and criticizing him for not waiting to resubmit Ingersoll's name.[52]

Ingersoll's epistle enjoyed important, if not wide, circulation, for Dallas, Mason, Buchanan, and Rush all read it. But by the time these men had seen the infamous letter, Polk had already declared Ingersoll *persona non grata*, complaining that he "has shown that he is selfish & without principle. I have profound contempt for him, and shall never have any further intercourse with him, unless he withdraws his letter and makes suitable explanations." Because the four men vigorously disapproved of Ingersoll's course of action, Polk let them see the letter that he had drafted in response. Buchanan asked for both of the letters so that he could write an appropriate reply to Ingersoll. He returned the next day with his response, but Polk quietly filed it away because "it was much more intemperate and violent than my own draft." The president then revised his original version and sent it to Ingersoll at the end of April.[53]

Nothing more was heard about the Ingersoll case until the fall of 1847, when Polk and Robert Armstrong, the consul at Liverpool, engaged in a conversation. Armstrong added fuel to the fire by informing the president about yet another letter penned by Ingersoll; this one was critical of Polk for not having appointed Ingersoll's son as an officer in the army. Despite this, the president and the congressman attempted to patch up their differences. After all, explained Polk, Ingersoll "is a democratic member of Congress supporting the principles of my administration, and I was willing to overlook the past follies." Polk was perturbed, however, when the congressman, during a January 1848 conference, complained about his rejection by the Senate and the unfitness of Rush for the post in France. In February, Ingersoll returned to Polk's office to ask again for appointment to France, whereupon the president understandably declared the impossibility of this request, since he had no intention of recalling Rush. Ingersoll concluded the visit with a hint that he might be interested in the proposed mission at Rome, a suggestion that must have caused Polk to be amazed at the temerity and tenacity of this Pennsylvania Democrat.[54] After two years of bargaining and campaigning for a diplomatic assignment, the story ended with Ingersoll's still being in Congress, far away from France or Russia.

As alluded to earlier, one of Polk's major patronage battles with Pennsylvania was over the lucrative collectorship in Philadelphia. In that contest, Ingersoll, Buchanan, Dallas, Cameron, and others were all involved to varying degrees. The early stages began almost as soon as the president had taken office, with different Pennsylvanians campaigning for their favorite candidates. No fewer than four men were advocated: Buchanan backed George F. Lehman; Dallas supported Richard Rush; John K. Kane and the state administration favored Henry Welsh; and Hendrick B. Wright and Simon Cameron pushed for Wright. In the midst of these competing claims, the president decided that the best way to deal with the dilemma was to ignore these four candidates and find one of his own, in consequence of which he turned to his long-time friend and former congressional colleague Henry Horn. Ironically, Horn, a member of the Dallas wing in Pennsylvania politics, did not have the support of the vice-president. Sensitive to these difficulties and striving to satisfy Buchanan in a number of other appointments, Polk elected the strategy of stalling and waiting to decide on the collectorship, especially since he was also embroiled in the problem of choosing someone from that state to elevate to the United States Supreme Court. Eventually, by the time Congress was ready to begin its 1845/46 session, Polk had managed to swing Buchanan around to a tentative endorsement of Horn for the Philadelphia post. In the meanwhile, the president had taken care of two of the prospective candidates, Lehman and Welsh, by securing the postmastership at Philadelphia for the former and the position of naval officer there for the latter.[55] And as mentioned above, Richard Rush, by virtue of a diplomatic appointment, was provided for at a much later date.

What Polk apparently had not taken adequately into account was the opposition of Senator Cameron. Having been ignored and rebuffed by the president on patronage matters, Cameron retaliated by working to block the collectorship appointment, as well as the Supreme Court nomination. In early February 1846 the president and the senator had a candid conversation about the collectorship, in which Polk strongly defended Horn, while Cameron forcefully expressed his opposition. In fact, the senator revealed his unhappiness with nearly all of the Pennsylvania appointments that had been made, especially since most of them had been Buchanan's choices. Cameron concluded his visit by saying that perhaps if Horn would confer with him in a congenial way he might withdraw his objections, but Polk refused to become involved in any kind of possible deal between Horn and Cameron. Not surprised when Dallas warned him in early March that Horn's nomination would probably be blocked in the Senate, the president placed the blame upon those who were displeased with his Oregon policy.[56]

The showdown came on 25 May, when Cameron engineered a rejection of Horn's appointment by taking advantage of a small attendance in the Senate and by enlisting a few Democrats along with Whig senators. Outraged, Polk excoriated Cameron as "a managing, tricky man in whom no reliance is to be placed." To the president, Cameron was "little better than a Whig." As a consequence of the Senate's action, Polk shifted to James Page, a former Philadelphia postmaster, as his nominee for the collectorship. In the next couple of days, however, several senators visited the president to say that either they had been absent when the vote on Horn was taken or else they had changed their mind and would now support Horn. These revelations naturally encouraged Polk to resubmit Horn's name to the Senate, instead of pushing for Page. But the president had at least two direct warnings that there would still be trouble with the nomination of Horn. One was another visit from Senator Cameron, who indicated that he would support Horn for any appointment other than collector, a stand that disgusted Polk. The other warning was Congressman Ingersoll's report that the Pennsylvania congressional caucus had reached agreement upon a Mr. Elred for the collectorship nomination. But Polk would not be moved from his renewed determination to have Horn, a man who was so trustworthy that the president claimed, "I could sleep sound on my pillow & know that the public money was safe in his hands." Polk renominated Horn on 29 May, with a warning that no one who sought Horn's rejection would benefit by having his own candidate appointed.[57]

About two weeks later, Buchanan, whom Polk suspected of having indirectly encouraged Cameron's opposition, entered the picture by disclosing that Cameron might now be friendly to the Horn nomination. Buchanan therefore recommended that the president have Secretary Walker write to Horn, inviting him to Washington for a conference with Senator Cameron. Polk consented, the letter was written, Horn arrived, and the meeting with Cameron took place; but evidently to no avail, for eleven days later the Senate once more turned back the Horn nomination. On the following day, the incensed president sent the name of James Page to the Senate; but Secretary Buchanan objected because of Page's bitter opposition to him in Pennsylvania. Buchanan recommended, instead, that Polk consult further with the state's congressmen. The president resolutely declared, however, that since his independence as president was at stake, he was therefore required to "show to Mr. Cameron and others who had made a factious opposition . . . that by their rejection neither they nor their friends should be profited by it." Yet during the day, Polk did seek the opinion of several leaders, including Secretary Walker, all of whom were favorable toward Page. Before the day had ended, Buchanan had sent a note to Polk, recommending Thomas McCully; but the president, who had already submitted Page's name, refused to be swayed. With the confirmation of

Page, success at long last crowned Polk's quest for a reliable and suitable person for this important post in Pennsylvania.[58] That ended the story until a year and a half later, November 1847, when Buchanan complained to Polk that persons in the Philadelphia customs house had been personally abusive to him and that he and his friends would seek the removal of James Page as collector if such conduct did not stop. Secretary Buchanan, certain that the rude customs personnel were friends of Dallas, insisted that Polk protect members of the cabinet from being subjected to such treatment. Polk concurred and asked Secretary Walker to forward Buchanan's grievances to Page.[59] That action apparently settled the matter, although the Buchanan-Dallas rivalry continued to intensify.

The secretary of state and the vice-president certainly had ample opportunity to parade their strengths and weaknesses in the fight over the Supreme Court appointment, a battle that was waged concurrently with that over the Philadelphia collectorship. Justice Henry Baldwin had died in the spring of 1844, but President Tyler had not been successful in his attempts to pick a Pennsylvanian to fill the vacancy. Polk therefore had two positions on the bench to fill, Justice Joseph Story's death in 1845 having created the other one. As noted earlier in this chapter, the president nominated Levi Woodbury to replace Story; but his plan to save Baldwin's seat for a suitable Pennsylvanian proved to be a difficult strategy to implement. Evidently he could not turn his attention to this matter until the late summer of 1845, because the press of other appointments and duties had distracted him until then. Just three days after Polk had announced his intentions to elevate Woodbury to the nation's highest court, editor Thomas Ritchie confided to the president that Buchanan would like to leave his cabinet post and take the other vacancy on the bench. On 29 September, Polk and Buchanan therefore talked over the Court nomination. The secretary argued that perhaps he should depart from the cabinet because of fears that in the forthcoming session of Congress, the Pennsylvania delegation would not support Polk's measures to revise the tariff, thereby making Buchanan an embarrassment to the president. Buchanan pledged that if war with Mexico or Britain should threaten, he would of course continue as head of the State Department. The conversation ended civilly enough, with both men agreeing to think further about the matter. Nothing more was said until mid November, when the secretary notified Polk that he did not want the Supreme Court appointment but instead would remain in the cabinet, a decision that the president received with gratitude.[60]

The next installment of the story occurred in the early days of the new session of Congress. By that time, Buchanan was busily promoting his friend John M. Read of Philadelphia for the Court nomination; but Polk steadfastly resisted this recommendation on the grounds that Read had formerly been a Federalist and therefore his political views could not be trusted. Turning a sympathetic ear to Dallas and other prominent Pennsylvanians, the president heeded their endorsement of George W. Woodward. Because Cameron had defeated Woodward in the recent senatorial election in Pennsylvania in a somewhat questionable or unsavory manner, Woodward's nomination offered a sort of reprimand to Cameron. Certainly the aggravated Senator Cameron interpreted it thus. Without consulting Buchanan, Polk submitted Woodward's name to the Senate two days before Christmas. Ironically, the president had informed the cabinet of his plans, but Buchanan had not been present when Polk had made his brief announcement. In any event, on Christmas Day, Buchanan stormed into the president's office to express his great discontent, not necessarily with Woodward per se but with not having been consulted in advance. After all, snapped Buchanan, he had had to learn of the nomination by receiving a penciled note at the Capitol from Dr. Joel B. Sutherland. After icily reminding the secretary that he did not need cabinet approval of his appointments, the president then expressed regrets that his procedures had angered Buchanan. Polk also took exception to Buchanan's complaint that "the impression was becoming general among his friends in Pennsylvania that the patronage of the Government here was wielded against him." Having probably succeeded in ruining the president's holiday, Secretary Buchanan then left, saying that he had been satisfied with his conference with Polk.[61]

Almost exactly one month later the Senate rejected the nomination of Woodward, with Cameron playing the major role in this turn of events. Distressed at this news, Polk was quick to implicate Buchanan in the failure, charging that Buchanan could have prevented at least three or possibly four senators from voting against Woodward. On the next day the president declared that if he could be certain that Buchanan had caused the rejection of Woodward, he would dismiss him from the cabinet. Dallas and several senators expressed both their indignation at the rejection of Woodward and their hostility toward Cameron. Polk was dismayed and perplexed when he received word from Senators Cass and Benton that they were recommending Buchanan for appointment to the bench. In fact, it swiftly became common talk around town that Buchanan would soon be leaving the cabinet and taking the Supreme Court appointment. Polk confided to his diary that he had been overly generous in naming Buchanan's friends to various federal positions, and yet the secretary was still not completely satisfied. Polk promised that he would not surrender the appointing power to anyone.

Four days after the rejection of Woodward, Attorney General Mason, as an emissary from Buchanan, visited the president. Mason bore two messages: Buchanan's denial that he had interfered with the confirmation of Woodward and his desire to be appointed to the Court. Informing Mason that he intended to make no nomination for a while, the president professed "that Mr. Buchanan had brought all his troubles on himself." Furthermore, Polk announced, any member of the cabinet whom he discovered working to secure a rejection of nominations "would find me a lion in his path." Later, when Polk heard more reports of Buchanan's pending resignation from the cabinet, he bluntly replied, "I will accept it and will not regret it," and added sarcastically, "If he chooses to retire I will find no difficulty in administering the Government without his aid."[62]

In February, Polk had an opportunity to confer with some of Woodward's opponents, including Cameron. The president stoutly defended Woodward as the best nominee he could find in Pennsylvania and gave lectures on his right to nominate persons for office. In the middle of the month, Polk, complaining about the bad mood that Buchanan had been in since the rejection of Woodward and since the revelation that Buchanan himself was not to move up to the Court, suspected that Buchanan was seeking some grounds for breaking with the administration. The president was sure, however, that he knew the formula that would restore his secretary's friendly feelings: "If I would yield up the Government into his hands & suffer him to be in effect President, and especially in bestowing the public patronage so as to advance his own political aspirations, I have no doubt he would be cheerful and satisfied." Of course, Polk had no intention of doing this.[63]

Despite the strained relationship with Buchanan over the Court appointment, by late spring, Polk had decided to nominate him to the bench. Near the end of June, Cave Johnson, the liaison man, carried a note to the president from Buchanan, stating that Buchanan would gladly accept the Supreme Court nomination, unless his departure from the cabinet would create problems for Polk. Johnson forthrightly stated his own view that Buchanan should remain in the cabinet and not be named to the judiciary. At any rate, the story became more complicated in July, as Polk and Buchanan tried to reach an agreement about the timing of Buchanan's appointment. In the simplest terms the problem was that Buchanan wanted an immediate nomination, whereas Polk wanted to delay it until near the end of the session of Congress, since he felt the need of the secretary's services for a while longer. In their conversations, Buchanan voiced the concern that postponement might permit opposition to his appointment to build up or else that some international problem might arise that would preclude his nomination. On the other hand, Polk feared that a public announcement of his intentions to nominate Buchanan might endanger his pending measures before Congress and would surely cause all the patronage woes to devolve upon him. The president characteristically wanted to play his cards very close to the vest, particularly because it would be ''impossible to select any man who breathed who would be satisfactory to all the factions of the Democratic party.'' Their negotiations therefore remained at an impasse until 1 August, when Buchanan announced to Polk that he did not want to be named to the Court but instead preferred to remain in the cabinet, a decision to which Cave Johnson had already alerted the president. In response, Polk informed Buchanan that he would nominate Robert C. Grier of Pittsburgh to fill the vacancy on the Court, and the secretary graciously gave his approval. Accordingly, two days later the president forwarded Grier's appointment to the Senate, where it was confirmed, thus bringing to a conclusion the sometimes acrimonious struggle between Polk and Pennsylvania Democrats over the nomination to the Court.[64] The president seems to have won the battle, though harsh feelings towards him on the part of some political leaders were among the fruits of the conflict.

As though Polk did not have enough problems with Pennsylvanians during the summer of 1846, another situation presented itself because of the sudden death in early June of federal district judge Archibald Randall. With the Supreme Court matter still unresolved at that date, the president calculated that he had to act swiftly to fill the judgeship of the eastern district of Pennsylvania. At least three candidates immediately appeared: Edward King, Thomas Petit, and John K. Kane. Vice-President Dallas and Senator Daniel Sturgeon seemed to back Kane, while notable political and business leaders supported the other two prospects. Kane's brother-in-law, William J. Leiper, traveled to Washington to urge Polk and Buchanan to endorse Kane, who, it was said, had Cameron's approval. The president held a hasty conference with Buchanan on 10 June, in which he assured the secretary that he intended to recommend Kane, unless Buchanan ''had insuperable objections to him.'' The secretary, who apparently had no candidate, admitted that Kane was not his first choice but consented to support him. Buchanan, in return, pressured Polk to seek to have John M. Read, an unsuccessful aspirant to the Supreme Court appointment, named as Pennsylvania's attorney general, to replace the departing Kane. Buchanan affirmed that this ''would harmonize and reunite the party in the State.'' On the next day, Polk sent Kane's name to the Senate, where Cameron immediately raised objections. This time the obstinate senator was not able to enlist enough opposition, however, and Kane's nomination was confirmed within a few days.[65] Afterwards, Polk still faced struggles over the Philadelphia collectorship and the Supreme Court vacancy before the summer ended. Luckily for the president, once all of these conflicts were resolved, he had no further important patronage controversies with Pennsylvania Democrats.

This discussion of court appointments in Pennsylvania leads to a brief, general consideration of the judiciary in relationship to Polk's concerns over patronage. Determined at the outset of his administration to appoint to federal judgeships only those persons who had had previous judicial or legal experience, the president was quite successful in realizing this goal, unlike many of his predecessors and successors, some of whom expressed no interest in designating experienced persons to the bench. Polk also wanted appointees to be "original Democrats" who possessed a strict constructionist point of view. The three beliefs that he deemed essential for his judicial nominees were States' rights, unionism, and a limited government. Polk discovered, however, that sometimes those persons who most aptly fitted his criteria had to be eliminated because other considerations, such as political pressures, crowded in. More than his predecessors, Polk relied on the legislative branch of government to fashion the selection of the district-court judges, although he never entirely surrendered his independence or freedom. As a general rule, however, Polk preferred to cooperate with the Senate and the House in making judicial appointments, rather than to confront them. One thing was certain, however, he ignored hostile congressmen who tried to press candidates upon him. As he and the Congress moved toward what has been called the party-directed mode of selection, they did not abandon the traditional patron-client influences upon patronage. This is to say that Polk personally knew some of his court nominees and that fully one-fourth of the appointees had family ties to the persons who were promoting their candidacies. Personal connections therefore continued to be an ingredient in the selection process, although it was not always the dominant one. Finally, it should be noted that from an administrative point of view, Polk exercised firm and almost complete control of the selection process, refusing to share it with his secretary of state, an officer who had traditionally been involved in the details of identifying and scrutinizing prospective judicial nominees. The small number of vacancies on the bench, plus Polk's own disinclination to trust Buchanan very much on such matters, led to the president's tight grip on patronage in the judicial branch.[66]

With regard to federal district judges, Polk made eight appointments during his term as president, five of which were to the four new states that were admitted during those years. He therefore named only three replacements to established district courts, one in Pennsylvania, which has already been discussed, one to the circuit court of the District of Columbia, and one to the western district of Virginia. In all of these he recruited experienced persons, while trying to strike a balance between the demands and pressures of congressional Democrats and rival factions of the state party. At the end of August 1845, one of the three judges of the circuit court in the District of Columbia died, whereupon Democratic lawyers in the District as well as Democratic leaders in Virginia and Maryland all tried to sway Polk to their candidates. The latter group maintained that there was not a lawyer in the District who was qualified to handle the complex matters that came before the court, whereas the former contended that the court was merely a local office and therefore suitable only for a lawyer from the District. When the bar association in the District united in recommending James Dunlop, a Georgetown lawyer, for the post, Polk, who was favorably impressed, nominated him, and the Senate confirmed the appointment in December.[67]

In that same month the judge of the western district of Virginia resigned to enter the United States Senate, thereby stirring a patronage scramble for his replacement. As it worked out, Polk engineered a skillful blend of cooperation between the executive and legislative wings of government. The first inclination of the Virginia congressional members was to turn to one of their own for the judgeship—either George W. Hopkins or William Taylor. Polk immediately let it be known that neither of these men was acceptable, because of his general rule against bestowing federal offices upon members of Congress and, second, because he deemed one of them to be a Whig (i.e., a leader of conservative Democratic revolt in the 1830s) and the other was a sick man. The congressional delegation therefore responded immediately by looking elsewhere for an appropriate nominee. Two more emerged: John W. Brockenbrough, a man of excellent legal credentials and important political support, and Benjamin R. Floyd, a former governor's son and a member of the conservative Democratic wing. Brockenbrough unquestionably benefited from the intervention of two of his uncles, Thomas Ritchie and John Brockenbrough. But the president refused to move on the nomination until the Virginia congressmen had reached a decision among themselves, which they finally did in late December, when they sided with Brockenbrough. Immediately thereafter, Polk nominated Brockenbrough, and the Senate concurred. The successful nominee had been aided by family connections, to be sure, but in Polk's mind these were of secondary importance in this instance.[68]

Judges, generals, postmasters, collectors, diplomats, and petty clerks—these constituted the heart and soul of the quest for patronage. And these were the problems that helped to age the president and to impair his health. On balance, it appears that Polk weathered the patronage storms reasonably well, though there were contemporary critics who held the opposite view. Francis Blair, certainly not one to have reason to be favorable to the president, criticized Polk's handling of his administration, including patronage, and held him accountable for the Democratic defeat in 1848.[69] Such assessments seem severe and unwarranted. Certainly there is little denying that the above review of the patronage story has indicated mistakes that Polk made along the way, and one could easily second-guess him on some of the appointments. But the forces that split the Democratic party and troubled the regions during the late 1840s were beyond the control of any president and his patronage policies.

An evaluation of Polk on the basis of the distribution of federal positions would in fairness render the judgment that he was a mixed success. Obviously he was not able to keep the warring factions satisfied with his nominations, and he failed ultimately to unite his party. But can one seriously argue that a few more postmasterships, collectorships, or judgeships would have salvaged the situation? It seems plausible to maintain that if Polk had steered clear of the morass of New York and Pennsylvania squabbles over patronage, he would have emerged with more strength and fewer enemies. The fact remains, however, that he simply could not avoid these situations. About all that he could have hoped to do there was to miss most of the land mines that were planted in the patronage fields. Perhaps Polk, in dealing with recalcitrant Democratic congressmen, could have been more generous; one thinks, for example, of his Tennessee colleagues Johnson and Jones. But Polk, with occasional exceptions, was not inclined to be a magnanimous person; moreover, how could he build strength for his program and his administration if he were handing out awards to those who were voting against him in the Congress? Certainly such a policy would not have encouraged his political friends in the legislative body to remain loyal.[70]

Perhaps Polk should have delegated more of the patronage chores to the members of his cabinet, thereby letting them take more of the heat and him less. This appears to be a reasonable tactic, except that Polk remained basically suspicious of most of his cabinet members and could not therefore trust them with such significant responsibilities. The president tended to be wary of most people; it was his nature.

Moreover, his apprehensions about cabinet members' fostering and promoting their presidential ambitions continually got in his way, an unfortunate development, to be sure, but perhaps an understandable one.

Upon examination it looks as though Polk was a trapped president on the matter of political appointments, and several things ensnared him. The circumstances of his nomination by the party in 1844 and then his election stirred hostilities within the Democratic camp that were not of his own making. Van Buren Democrats, for example, bitterly resented Polk's nomination and apparently intended to do little to help him as president and party leader. When they prophesied that Polk would have trouble with patronage, it was a self-fulfilling prophecy. His efforts to form a cabinet unleashed many of these antagonisms, even as he was striving to restrain them. The president furthermore was trapped by his one-term pledge, an affirmation in the noblest of Jacksonian traditions but hardly a politically shrewd one. Instead of generating party unity and harmony, as Polk intended, it merely hastened and fed the ambitions of leaders within the party to work toward the goal of replacing him. Patronage fights were colored frequently by the desires of some to position themselves so as to enhance their chances for the 1848 nomination. Finally, the president was fettered by major foreign-policy disputes that rocked his party and troubled the nation at large. When Democrats concluded their fights with the president over the Oregon question and over the Mexican War, one saw only a divided and weakened party. The palpable split in 1848, which resulted in the Free Soil movement led by Van Buren, confirmed everyone's fears. The conflicts made it increasingly difficult for Polk to use patronage distribution to heal wounds and to bind up the party. No credence can be given, however, to the claim that the president was guilty of not giving enough appointments to northerners and that he thereby jeopardized his administration.[71] As noted earlier, if there had been a few more federal positions to distribute, this would probably have done little to quiet the raging unhappiness in certain quarters of the party.

Polk knew that patronage was crucially important to his administration; therefore he devoted excessive hours and energy to it. But he was deeply troubled by the parceling out of federal positions, perceiving the malevolence of man more often than not. The incessant daily clamor for jobs by political leaders and by ordinary folk took its toll on the president; he emerged from it drained and enervated. A compassionate analysis of his handling of patronage suggests that Polk did admirably well, given the magnitude of problems that plagued his presidency.

7

★ ★ ★ ★ ★

THE PRESIDENT, THE PRESS, AND THE CONGRESS

In the spring of 1845 the *Washington Globe* died and Andrew Jackson died. The former had been Polk's nemesis; the latter, Polk's mentor. Although Polk had nothing to do with Jackson's death, he had everything to do with the *Globe's*. The *Globe* had long been the spokesman for Democratic principles and party, while Jackson had long been the embodiment of these principles and that party. The demise of these two remarkable institutions shortly after Polk became the nation's eleventh president heralded a new day, perhaps even new life, for "Young Hickory" and for the country. Polk would remain true to Jacksonian principles, especially in the realms of domestic economic legislation and of territorial expansionism, but not without difficulty.

In order for Polk "to be *myself* President of the U.S.," he had to gain quick control over the press and over the Congress. As noted in chapter 2, he had barely been able to choose his own cabinet, a situation that repeatedly tested Polk's ability to assert dominance over that group of six men. With regard to the press, the new president reckoned that he had to be in a position to choose, as well as control, the editor. Flowing from that determination came the actions that ended the *Globe*. Certainly Polk had not been able to select his own Congress, for that was simply beyond his prerogatives. The real question, however, was, Would he be able to "manage" an unwieldy group of approximately three hundred men? The ensuing four years of tension and struggle between the national legislature and the national executive yielded a somewhat mixed report, although it appears that Polk held the upper hand for most of the time. Polk evidently calculated that unless he could dominate the principal party organ in Washington, he would have little hope of working effectively with a malleable Congress.

Ironically, Polk's actions, which were strongly opposed by Jackson, to terminate one newspaper and give life to another bore strong resemblance to what President Jackson himself had done in the early 1830s, when he had eliminated the *United States Telegraph* and installed the *Globe* as the administration's organ. Thus, Polk was imitating Jackson's own model of how to seize control of the press in Washington by creating a new journal. Often overlooked is the fact that Polk came well equipped for this task, because ten years earlier, in 1835, he had been instrumental in establishing the major Democratic newspaper in Tennessee, the *Nashville Union*. Being no stranger to the business of controlling the press for partisan reasons, Polk therefore had little hesitation about the course he must follow once he arrived in Washington. And in the opinion of some, he very wisely chose to eliminate the *Globe* in favor of a journal and an editor who would do his bidding. One scholar has claimed that the new *Washington Union* "represented the peak of presidential control over an administration organ." Still another has noted that "had it not been for the press, James K. Polk might as well have retired to a monastery instead of occupying the White House." Obviously, Polk understood clearly what was widely comprehended, namely, that an effective, even aggressive, president had to "manage" the news to build support for his administration and to gain leverage with the Congress.[1]

No great mystery surrounds Polk's decision to oust Francis P. Blair from the comforts of his editor's chair. Bluntly stated, Polk did not like Blair. Over the years, Polk had compiled a list of grievances against the editor of the *Globe*, which he nursed and harbored, so that he could seek retribution when the opportune moment came. Polk's election to the presidency offered such an appropriate time. He had been particularly troubled by the way in which Blair had treated Polk's political setbacks in Tennessee, notably his gubernatorial defeats in 1841 and 1843. In Polk's eyes, the *Globe* had summarily dismissed him from any future political considerations, including his vice-presidential aspirations. In January 1844, Polk wondered if Blair would suppress the news of Polk's being endorsed by the Mississippi Democrats or else "stick it in an obscure corner as he did the Tennessee and Arkansas nominations." By the time of the national convention in the spring, Polk was convinced that the *Globe* would oppose his selection, because it had always favored Van Buren. Afterwards, Polk had no difficulty in believing that after he was nominated in Baltimore, the newspaper "was cold and lukewarm in its support." Scarcely one month after his victory in November, the president-elect entertained various strategies relative to the future of the *Globe* and its editor.[2]

During the period between the election and the inauguration, Polk and his closest advisers contemplated several solutions to the "Blair problem." Playing critical roles in the unfolding drama were Aaron V. Brown, Polk's political confidant, and John P. Heiss, the publisher of the *Nashville Union*. At crucial moments they made decisions and took actions that led to a final resolution of the journalistic imbroglio. Along the way, some thought was given to retaining the *Globe*, but with Blair and John C. Rives simply as owners and with a new person as editor, possibly Aaron Brown, who was not above mentioning himself for the position. Both Polk and some of his advisers gave serious consideration to Andrew J. Donelson as a prospective editor. Simon Cameron of Pennsylvania, himself a veteran of the newspaper business, made overtures to Donelson, hoping to enlist him as the new editor; but Donelson was wary and reluctant, fearing that he might unwittingly become part of a distasteful conspiracy. He therefore sought assurances from Polk and also begged for time to think over the matter. The new president granted his wish, doubtless knowing that time would in effect remove Donelson from contention. Other candidates who received fleeting consideration as editor of the *Globe* or else as head of an entirely new journal included Cameron; J. George Harris, the former editor of the *Nashville Union*; and Edmund Burke, a former New Hampshire congressman and the top candidate in 1838 for editorship of the *Nashville Union*. Finally, all eyes focused upon Thomas Ritchie, the elderly and infirm editor of the *Richmond Enquirer*.[3]

The Virginia editor was soon subjected to something like a fraternity rush by Polk's associates. Cave Johnson, who first boasted about his intention to travel to Richmond for purposes of enticing Ritchie, soon was seized by timidity after rumors of the "plot" to replace Blair with Ritchie began to circulate in Washington. As Johnson reported, "Even old J.Q. A[dams] asked when we were going to Richmond." As an alternative to Johnson's visit, Congressman Thomas H. Bayly of Virginia was enlisted to write to Ritchie about becoming the president's new editor. Polk's strategists were not fully prepared for Ritchie's hesitancy about moving to Washington to compete against his old friend Blair. Actually, Ritchie was planning to get out of the newspaper business altogether when representatives of the new Polk administration began to offer blandishments to him to take up the editor's pen at the nation's capital. Not willing to accept a negative answer as final, they applied additional pressure upon Ritchie. Some of this came in the form of a curious letter from the Washington journalist W. D. Wallach, who, acting under authorization from a Mississippi congressman, offered the Richmond editor large amounts of money, as well as a furnished house in the District. The prospect of financial gain in Washington, something that he had not enjoyed at Richmond, ''softened'' Ritchie's resistance to the temptation of becoming Polk's editor. Eventually, in March, John Heiss took the initiative by traveling to Richmond to confront the old editor in person, hoping thereby to persuade Ritchie to agree and to give him further assurance of financial security.[4]

Meanwhile, Polk had arrived in Washington and had already begun dealing, somewhat gingerly, with Blair. The latter was immensely pleased when Polk gave him a copy of the Inaugural Address before distributing copies to the other Washington papers. The editor remained optimistic, but not for long. About three weeks after Inauguration Day, Blair called on the new president in an effort to assess the situation, only to discover that Polk was firm in his determination to have a new editor. As the president put it on that occasion: ''I must be the head of my own administration, and will not be controlled by any newspaper, or particular individuals whom it serves.'' Three days later, Ritchie arrived at the nation's capital, ready to talk directly with Polk about the proposed editorship. The Richmond editor and the president quickly reached a meeting of the minds, whereupon Polk called in Blair to tell him that he was out and Ritchie was in. On the following day, 28 March, Ritchie and Blair met together to discuss the sale of the *Globe*. Rives and Blair asked for time to ascertain the views of Jackson and Van Buren relative to the sale of the paper, whereupon Rives left immediately for Albany to confer with Van Buren and Silas Wright. The latter pair, as did a reluctant and sad Andrew Jackson, endorsed the lifting of the *Globe* from Blair's shoulders.[5]

With that, only the complicated financial arrangements remained to be perfected before a new paper could be born. Assisting as midwives were such persons as Simon Cameron; Lewis S. Coryell, a Pennsylvania financier and political playboy; Robert J. Walker; William Selden, treasurer of the United States; and Thomas Green, Ritchie's son-in-law. During the first two weeks of April, much financial maneuvering took place, after a group of appraisers had set the value of the *Globe* at $35,000. John P. Heiss, who was anxious to run the business side of the proposed paper, made most of the arrangements. Ritchie and Heiss would each own one-fourth of the operations, while Cameron would have one-fourth, and J. Knox Walker, Polk's nephew and private secretary, would hold the remaining fourth. Later, Heiss bought out both Cameron and Walker. The exact origins of the initial down payment and of other monies that were necessary in order to launch the paper remain unknown and apparently unknowable. By 12 April, all appropriate arrangements having been made, Blair and Rives had transferred their paper and its physical facilities to Ritchie.[6] Two-and-a-half weeks later, the last issue of the *Globe* appeared.

The *Washington Union* made its appearance on 1 May. Sometime prior to that, Ritchie and others had settled on the new name for the paper, possibly hearkening to the highly successful *Nashville Union*, which Polk had helped to establish and Heiss had helped to publish. With the new label went the apparent requirement of a new motto. First leaning toward the classic Andrew Jackson declaration ''The Union, it must be preserved,'' the editor and associates then switched to a more Calhoun-like expression, ''Liberty, the Union, and Our Country,'' a concession that was intended to enlist the approval and backing of the more conservative element of the party. Although a new paper, the *Union* was paradoxically also a continuation of the old *Globe*, for it took over the latter's presses, type, furniture, building, subscription list, and even most of its employees.[7]

The first issue staked out the paper's stance. In so doing, the *Union* reiterated ideas that were contained in the prospectus that Ritchie had earlier written for Polk's inspection. The president gave his sanction to it and handed it to William Selden, the very helpful United States treasurer, charging him with the responsibility for preparing its publication. In his first editorial, Ritchie graciously lauded the work of Blair and Rives and acknowledged their magnanimous spirit in carrying out the sale of the *Globe*. The new editor then placed his paper in opposition to the loose construction of the Constitution and to a national bank. He promised to assist in the quest for a new tariff and to accept the annexation of Texas as a *fait accompli*.[8]

During the months that followed, Ritchie and Polk worked both sides of the independence-dependence street. It was periodically to the advantage of each to assert independence from the other, thereby enabling Ritchie to pose as a champion of the free press and Polk to absolve himself from certain statements that appeared in the *Union*. Such claims, however, were largely grandstanding, for the president and the editor were undeniably dependent upon each other. As noted earlier, no other president had so directly and distinctly controlled an administration organ as did Polk. He gave meticulous attention to the details of the operations of the *Union*, so that the paper served as a conduit of presidential news and opinions. Ritchie was, in the analysis of one recent scholar, the equivalent of a modern-day presidential press secretary. Or as Buchanan expressed it to Bancroft in 1847, when the organ fell out of tune, the president adjusted its pipes. Although Polk's diary indicates that he and Ritchie had frequent contact, both professional and personal, the editor never became a key adviser, in the same mold as Blair had been with Jackson and Van Buren. Ritchie did function, however, as a significant line of contact with members of Congress, for he had a number of friends in the national legislature, and he enjoyed a remarkably active social life in Washington.[9]

A number of specific instances illustrate the relationships between the *Union's* editor, the president, and members of Congress. Although Polk became thoroughly exasperated at times with Ritchie, nonetheless he defended his editor and excused his faults. In this regard the president seems to have been more tolerant and generous than is expected from a man who is usually portrayed as being one who did not suffer fools gladly. At times when Ritchie's editorials did not suit Polk, Polk himself would simply intervene and write one, to be inserted in the *Union*. An example of this occurred in September 1845, when a correspondent for the *Charleston Mercury* circulated the rumor that Robert J. Walker, not Polk, had actually authored the famous campaign letter about the tariff to John Kane of Pennsylvania. Ritchie published what, in Polk's view, was a weak denial of the allegation. Therefore, Polk summoned Walker and Ritchie to his office to confer about an appropriate response to the false claims and read to them his "authorized contradiction." Polk's private secretary thereafter copied the new article so as to prepare it for publication in the *Union* that very day.[10]

Another example of the president's picking up the pen to provide editorial matter took place some seven months later, in April 1846. The Senate had just passed the notice resolution on the Oregon question, but Polk was not overly pleased with the Senate's version, for he did not believe that the Senate had assumed enough responsibility. In any event, Ritchie wrote and published an editorial, "The Deed of the Day," in which he strongly commended the Senate's action. Postmaster General Johnson was the first to approach Polk about possible repercussions from the article, and Buchanan followed shortly thereafter. Polk confessed that he had not known anything about the editorial prior to its appearance in the 23 April issue. When editor Ritchie called at the White House, the president immediately informed him that the editorial was "exceptionable," whereupon Ritchie pleaded that he had hastily prepared it late at night. When Buchanan hotly insisted that Francis Blair be brought in to help Ritchie edit the *Union*, Polk rebuked Buchanan and defended his editor as one who "meant well, but might occasionally make mistakes." Then the president asked to see the secretary of state's essay on the Oregon resolution; but after both men had read it, they agreed it was too harsh on Calhoun and his followers. Buchanan consequently tore it up and threw it into the fire. Polk then read aloud "an explanatory article" that he had just written, which Buchanan agreed should be published. Ritchie, returning later that evening for another conference with the president, was given Polk's essay to print in the *Union*, the second or third time that the president had "sketched an article for the paper." This editorial, which appeared in the 24 April issue, clarified matters somewhat, after apologizing for the previous day's carelessly written essay, by stating a definite preference for the notice resolution that the House had passed.[11]

The relatively mild flap in the official family over Ritchie's original editorial soon developed into a serious protest from certain senators, who called for the editor's head. Senator Allen of Ohio, chairman of the Foreign Relations Committee, served as the chief spokesman, when he went to Polk's office to complain strongly about Ritchie's conduct of the *Union*. Like Buchanan, Allen recommended that Blair be brought in to assist the paper, to which Polk responded with a long dissertation about his grievances against Blair and a brief defense of Ritchie. When Senator Allen retired, Polk thought that he had smelled a conspiracy, "some understanding and concert between them [Buchanan and Allen] on the subject" of Blair's being added to the *Union* staff. Polk suspected that what was truly desired was domination over the paper as preparation for the next presidential campaign. Lewis Cass reported to Polk two days later, on 27 April, that Allen had conferred with him about the possibility of starting a new Democratic journal in Washington, with Blair and Rives in charge of it. Both Cass and Polk readily agreed that such a move would be destructive of Democratic-party unity and harmony and that in fact it would be viewed "as the beginning of the next Presidential campaign." Subsequently, Cass, having promised to try to persuade Allen and others to abandon their reckless strategy, approached Allen, who evidently heeded the Michigan senator's pleas.[12]

The story did not end there, however. In the fall of 1846, Ritchie found himself in difficulty with Polk, Louis McLane, and McLane's son Robert. Louis McLane, upon his return from England, had made a speech in New York in the course of which he had examined the president's position on the matter of the Oregon boundary. Polk and McLane thereafter had a rather frank discussion of the newspaper accounts of the latter's New York speech, in which both men reached an understanding about the ideas that McLane had intended to convey. Both were anxious to offset the accusation of the *Intelligencer* that regarding the Oregon boundary, Polk had taken one position publicly and a different one privately. About two weeks later, Ritchie jumped into the controversy with an editorial that, in defending the president, seemed to cast doubt upon McLane's veracity. Polk told Ritchie that he regretted the appearance of the editorial, whereupon the editor claimed that Charles Eames, his assistant, had written it and that the essay had been inserted into the paper "without much examination." When Robert McLane arrived in town the next day, he reported that his father had been annoyed by the editorial in the *Union*. In a conciliatory manner the president assured young McLane that he had "condemned and disapproved" of the essay and that Ritchie had mistakenly let his assistant write it. McLane professed to be satisfied with the explanation, and both agreed to let the matter drop.[13]

The most dramatic and exciting clash between the press, the Congress, and the president occurred early in 1847. The fundamental source of irritation was the recalcitrance of Congress regarding the war legislation that Polk had recommended. This caused both the president and Ritchie to become increasingly impatient with the dilatoriness of the legislative body; consequently the *Union* mounted strident attacks upon Congress. For example, Congressman John Wentworth's refusal to support a wartime tax on tea and coffee spawned a blistering editorial against him, in reaction to which Wentworth defended himself with the claim that his opposition to these duties was the most consistent Democratic position. Wentworth's Illinois colleague Stephen A. Douglas, who secured a House committee to investigate the *Union*, attempted unsuccessfully to pass a resolution that would have expelled that paper's reporters from the House.[14]

Shortly afterwards, controversy erupted in the Senate when it rejected the president's Ten Regiments bill in early February. Polk confined most of his comments to private conversations and to his diary, but the *Union* published a letter, "Another Mexican Victory," which excoriated the Senate's failure to provide for the ten new regiments. The thrust of the epistle was that Congress had done as much as the Mexican Army itself to undermine and harm the United States war effort. In response to the letter, Senator Yulee of Florida introduced a resolution, declaring that the *Union* had committed a libel against the Senate and that therefore its editors should be expelled from the floor of the Senate. The legislative chambers echoed with heated debate over the resolution, as Sevier, Turney, and Allen defended Ritchie, while Yulee and William S. Archer demanded retribution. Yulee declared that Polk was trying to use the *Union* to destroy the separation of powers. Similarly, Archer alleged that Ritchie, under direct orders from Polk, was seeking to compel the senators to conform to the wishes of the executive. Eventually the senators voted by a narrow margin to expell the *Union* editors, an action that Polk decried as "a blow at the liberty of the press." Evidently buoyed by public opinion, which seemed to convert him into a martyr for the free press, Ritchie launched an attack, particularly upon those Democratic senators who had voted in favor of Yulee's resolution. Moreover, Ritchie denied that either he or Polk had any direct connection with the author of the infamous letter. In the midst of the brouhaha over the *Union's* editorials and letters, the Senate, reconsidered its vote on the Ten Regiments bill, which it decided to endorse. The expulsion ended nearly a year later, when the *Union* leadership was readmitted to the floor of the Senate.[15]

As can be readily discerned from the above examples, life with "Father" Ritchie was at times difficult for Polk and his administration; but generally the president was pleased with his editor. The two men had a final clash of sorts, however, that revolved around the all-important fourth annual message to Congress, in 1848. Polk knew from prior experience that Ritchie could not always be trusted with confidential information, a fact that was reconfirmed when the editor jumped the gun on the annual message. Ritchie had been shown parts of the document in confidence and in advance by Polk, but Ritchie decided to reveal its basic tone and spirit when he became provoked by a disparaging remark made by a correspondent for the *New York Courier.* Polk was "much vexed" when he read the *Union* editorial of 29 November, which "shadows forth" what the president intended to say in the yet-to-be-completed annual message. Polk mused: "It is an infirmity of Mr. Ritchie that he cannot keep a secret," a fault that was accentuated by "his propensity to give news to the public, and to appear to the public to be the Executive organ." When Charles Eames called at Polk's office, the president expressed his "dissatisfaction at Mr. Ritchie's course in strong terms." Later that day, Ritchie sent a note to Polk, justifying the appearance of the editorial; but the president was not mollified. Finally, the next day, Ritchie went in person to Polk's office to make amends for his indiscretions. Noticeably touched by the editor's contriteness, the president told Ritchie simply to let the matter drop. Polk then sent for assistant editor Eames to beseech him not to repeat to Ritchie any of the things that he had said the day before, because, confessed Polk, he had spoken "perhaps too strongly" on that occasion. During the three remaining months in the presidential term, no additional significant tensions developed between Polk and his editor.[16]

Although the president had his share of problems with Ritchie, he faced more serious difficulties from newspapers that were unfriendly to him, particularly over the Mexican War and related concerns. Polk personally dealt with this unpleasant situation by refusing to read newspapers, unless specific things were brought to his attention by members of the cabinet or Congress. As he told one visitor in December 1845, he had "little opportunity to read newspapers, and could at no time do more than glance hastily over them." Led by the *National Intelligencer* in Washington, the Whig press was extremely critical of the president and his administration. That is why Polk decided in the spring of 1847 that the Nicholas Trist mission to Mexico should be "a profound secret . . . known only to the Cabinet." Polk feared that the *Intelligencer* and other opposition journals would try to jeopardize the peace initiative that spring. Revealing the depth of his hostility toward that segment of the press, he confided in his diary that the *Intelligencer* might attempt to send someone to Mexico to dissuade it "from entering upon negotiations for peace." Indeed, declared the exasperated and embittered Polk, "if the war is protracted it is to be attributed to the treasonable course of the federal editors & leading men." Consequently, information about Trist's assignment had to be kept from the sabotaging hands of the Whig press; only Ritchie should be informed about the mission. The *Union* editor, as noted above in chapter 4, had to know "in order to shape the course of his paper in reference to it." Thus, "in the strictest confidence," the president furnished Ritchie with the details of Trist's errand to Mexico.[17]

Polk's conspiratorial notions about the press were readily confirmed on 20 April, when two letters appeared in the *New York Herald* which provided accurate and detailed information about Trist's mission. Nothing prior to this had caused Polk to be "more vexed or excited" than he was upon reading the *Herald* that morning. "There has been treachery somewhere," the president declared; but where, he wondered. He quickly dismissed the possibility that any member of the cabinet could have been responsible for "leaking" the news to the *Herald*, which narrowed the field to William S. Derrick, a clerk in the State Department—and a Whig. In the presence of Buchanan, Polk strongly accused Derrick, to which the secretary responded that Derrick was "perfectly trustworthy." The president then called in Marcy and Mason to inquire if any clerks in their respective departments might have gotten information about Trist's activity. The secretaries assured Polk that no one in their departments had knowledge of it. On the following day the president and Buchanan had another confrontation over the *Herald* letters, with Buchanan still attesting to Derrick's innocence. The conversation became quite delicate when Polk bluntly asked Buchanan if he meant to implicate J. Knox Walker, the president's private secretary and nephew, as the person who had been responsible for truckling to the New York paper. Buchanan "promptly and with some excitement said he did not."[18]

Before dropping the episode out of frustration, Polk quizzed two more persons. He naturally had to turn to Ritchie, for the editor knew about Trist's mission; moreover, Ritchie did not have a good record for keeping secrets. Ritchie testified, however, "that he had not as much as alluded to or hinted the matter to any human being." Next Polk confronted Derrick directly, to express his indignation over the disclosure to the *Herald*. The State Department clerk made a solemn statement, however, exonerating himself from any involvement in revealing information to anyone about Trist's assignment. Polk resignedly accepted Derrick's statement and decided not to terminate him solely on the grounds of suspicion. This decision brought to a close the flap over the *Herald* letters, as Polk voiced confidence that in the future the State Department would keep all secrets.[19]

If the president believed that he would not be troubled by serious breaches in propriety by the press any more, he was unfortunately mistaken. Beginning in February 1848, Polk became increasingly agitated about letters appearing in the *New York Herald,* authored by John Nugent in Washington, that heaped criticism and abuse upon the president, his administration, and his supporters in Congress. Most distressing was the distasteful reality that Nugent was a daily visitor to the State Department. Buchanan sought to vindicate himself with the argument that he had trafficked with Nugent in order to get the *Herald* to support the Mexican War and the Polk administration. Moreover, Buchanan denied that he had in any way encouraged Nugent to write abuses of and attacks upon the president. Polk accepted Buchanan's professions of innocence but advised him "that it presented a very singular appearance that a member of my Cabinet should be holding familiar intercourse with an unprincipled newspaper letter-writer who was in the daily habit of calumniating and abusing me."[20]

Exactly one month later, Polk was astonished to discover that the *Herald* had published his confidential message to the Senate, conveying the terms of the Mexican treaty and related documents. The Senate immediately appointed a special committee to investigate this palpable breach in confidentiality. The consensus was that Nugent had obtained the documents in question directly from the State Department. Senators who conferred with Polk on the Nugent episode frequently complained that they often could not get in to see Buchanan at his office because Nugent was always closeted with him, which only added to their suspicion that the newspaper writer had gotten the materials directly from Buchanan. Nugent readily confessed that he had sent the germane materials to the *Herald*, but he steadfastly refused to reveal his source. The president, visibly upset with the thought that Buchanan and Nugent might be fellow conspirators, could not deny that the two had constantly been together of late so that Nugent might "puff him [Buchanan] as a candidate for the Presidency." Polk vowed that if there were conclusive proof of any collusion between Buchanan and Nugent, he would dismiss Buchanan from the cabinet immediately. When the president confronted his State Department head directly on 25 March, Buchanan asserted that a group of senators was conspiring to harm the secretary by pinning the publication of the treaty and related documents on him; he also reiterated that he had continued to work with Nugent in order to garner support from the *Herald* for the administration. At any rate, eventually, Nugent sent a letter to the Senate special committee, in which he acquitted Buchanan of any involvement in the *Herald* publication scheme. At the end of the month, Nugent, appearing in person before the bar of the Senate, persisted in his refusal to disclose how and from whom he had obtained the treaty and the confidential documents, whereupon the investigation could not be continued.[21]

It is certainly worth noting, in conclusion, that despite his anger and aggravation toward the press at times, Polk never took steps to censor or restrict the newspapers, other than attempting to have the news "managed" by Ritchie and the *Union*. He did not, for example, ask Congress for a Sedition Law, as had been done in 1798; nor did he invoke the 57th Article of War (1806), which provided the death penalty for reporters found guilty of publishing materials that might aid the enemy. Polk's position toward the press stands in marked contrast to that occupied later by Lincoln, who took direct action in 1861 to shut down the *New York Daily News* and who also, in that same year, imposed an official censorship upon the press. Lincoln furthermore invoked the 57th Article of War; but in fairness to him, it should be noted that he generally had little interest in press censorship. Years later, Woodrow Wilson demonstrated what a president could do with the press in times of war, the Espionage Act and the Sedition Act being obvious examples of a stringent censorship policy.

Considering the energy and attention that Polk lavished upon the administration newspaper, it is no surprise that he relied upon the *Union*'s editorials and articles as one of his strategies for "managing" the Congress. From time to time, recalcitrant congressmen, particularly Democrats, felt the pressure of public opinion that had been galvanized by Ritchie's paper. Likewise they felt the sting of his direct attacks upon them. Historian Thomas Hietala believes that Ritchie "probably exacerbated the administration's problems," because his biting editorials "irreparably damaged the party." Certainly Ritchie might have tempered his newspaper in order to push toward harmony, but that was not his style. Besides, the Polk administration had a full agenda and therefore kept up the pressure upon Democratic congressmen. It is an exaggeration, however, to blame Ritchie and the *Union* with having done irreparable damage to the Democratic party. In fairness to Ritchie, one needs to be reminded of a quite similar situation that prevailed with the tough, outspoken editor Francis Blair. Presiding over the *Washington Globe* during Jackson's presidency, Blair certainly wielded the pressure of the press in behalf of the administration—not unlike Ritchie some ten years later. In fact, as one scholar has observed, President Jackson, through Blair, achieved "the most effective employment of the press for partisan purposes in the long history of the Presidency." Not only were Blair and the *Globe* effective; they were also feared.[22] Polk knew in 1845 that he needed an editor who could establish the sort of fearless reputation that Blair had enjoyed earlier. He deliberately selected Ritchie as the man to lead the journalistic campaign in behalf of his administration and its policies. While concerned from time to time about Ritchie's foibles, Polk overall was firmly convinced that his editor had been a notable asset.

The president did not have to rely solely upon the *Union* to exert pressure upon Congress, for another arrow in Polk's quiver was the utilization of cabinet members to cajole congressmen into supporting administration measures. Moreover, as discussed in chapter 6, Polk was not above denying federal patronage to those members of Congress who failed to vote for bills that he wanted enacted. Altogether the president exerted executive muscle upon Congress in a variety of ways, the chief purpose of which was to compel Congress to deal with the program he recommended.[23] Members of Congress were seldom in the dark about what legislative enactments Polk desired, for he used the press, his annual message, and other communications to delineate his program.

Confident of what he wanted and reasonably sure of how to obtain results, Polk had little hesitation in his relations with Congress. After he had been in office for three and a half years, he set down his views in his famous fourth annual message, in 1848. More boldly and more cogently than Jackson had done earlier, Polk declared that the president was the representative of the whole people of the United States, whereas congressmen were relegated to lesser roles of representing only portions of the people. Even the passage of a piece of legislation by Congress, wrote Polk, is not conclusive evidence that those who vote for it represent or reflect the will of a majority of the people. (He could not withstand much questioning on this point, without embarrassment, for he usually had no apprehension that Congress's favorable action on his measures conformed to majority public opinion.) Polk staked out the claim that the president had a constitutional obligation not only to veto unwise and unsound legislation (a negative function) but also to recommend to Congress measures that were necessary and expedient for the nation (a positive function). In this fashion he entered a defense of his own initiative taking in the area of legislation. Moreover, he argued, Congress itself possesses veto power, in that it can refuse to enact a measure that the president recommends out of improper or corrupt motives. Clearly, Polk did not intend to wait obediently or quietly upon Congress to shape a legislative program and thereby have no greater task than that of merely signing or not signing the successfully enacted bills. Instead, he desired to guide and direct the implementation of a planned program of legislation; in so doing, "Polk was," in the words of Charles Sellers, "to display a brand of presidential legislative leadership that the country would not see again until the time of Theodore Roosevelt and Woodrow Wilson."[24]

Not everyone agreed, of course. Certainly, dissident Democrats and unhappy Whigs in the Congress thought of Polk as a president who lacked leadership or else as one who meddled in the affairs of the legislative branch. They chafed and protested against the determined and resolute occupier of the presidential chair, but to little avail. Much more recently, a student of the Polk administration, Brian Walton, has argued that the president cared only slightly about his relationship with Congress and believed that he was severely limited in the pressures that he could bring to bear upon that august body. Furthermore, alleges Walton, Polk did virtually nothing to maintain contacts with members of Congress, both during sessions and during recesses. The president, perhaps not unexpectedly, made little effort to develop bipartisan support in Congress for his program, and he lamented the cohesiveness of the Whigs in Congress. During the second half of his term, notes Walton, Polk had "considerable difficulty in handling Congress," with the Senate proving to be "unmanageable" at times.[25] Walton overstates the case, however; for a close examination of the president's diary as well as other materials builds a convincing case of a chief executive who superintended an impressive array of domestic legislation and also wars and treaties with foreign powers. None of this, of course, is intended to deny that Congress had a life of its own and that it proved resistant to Polk at times.

The Senate, perhaps more so than the House, exhibited traits of somewhat coherent and independent leadership. Much of this came through the functioning of committee chairmen, as well as certain managerial leaders. Senators in the Twenty-ninth and Thirtieth congresses had a high opinion of themselves and of their role vis-à-vis the executive branch of the government. Their six-year terms conveyed a sense of independence, allowing them to balk at party or presidential pressures. Committee chairmen often did not view themselves as being tools of the president. Senator Allen, chairman of the Foreign Relations Committee, for example, had no hesitation in resigning his chairmanship in protest against the Oregon boundary that was negotiated in the treaty with Great Britain. By so doing, he was indirectly admitting that the head of that committee should represent Polk's stance on foreign affairs.

In addition to the obvious role and function of committee chairmen, there existed in the Senate a small group of influential managerial leaders whose primary task was to seek to ensure party effectiveness and cohesiveness at a high level. At times they sought alternatives to Polk's measures. In any event, these leaders were essential to the smooth operations of the Senate. Chief in this category was Ambrose H. Sevier of Arkansas, who, according to at least one scholar, did more than anyone else in the Senate to hold the Democratic party together in that body. In functioning thus, Sevier generally tried to get along with Polk and to avoid displeasing him. Although Sevier disliked the treaty with Mexico, for instance, he agreed to go to Mexico as a special peace commissioner in the spring of 1848. His departure from the Senate at that time, argues Walton, hastened the deterioration of the Democratic party therein, for no one else stepped forward to take his place and Polk seemed to be completely incapable of handling that legislative body.[26] Suffice it to say that the president had to deal with both chambers of the Congress in his efforts to implement the measures and policies that he embraced, and along the way he enjoyed considerable success, sometimes in spite of the leadership of the Senate and the House.

The linchpin of Polk's domestic economic program was tariff reform. This had been an issue, and a particularly difficult one in Pennsylvania, during the presidential campaign. Years before he became president, Polk had been a consistent opponent of high tariff rates, and his fourteen years in Congress had given him more than ample opportunity to chart his career as a low-tariff man. Like others who shared his stance on the tariff, Polk's commitment to a tariff for revenue only was rooted in his neo-Jeffersonianism or republicanism. Just as such persons interpreted territorial expansionism as a way to diminish the threat of industrialization and urbanization, so they also perceived protective tariffs as beneficial only to manufacturers and therefore detrimental to the working classes and to the vision of an agrarian

America. Low tariff rates would restore the proper emphasis upon an agricultural economy and would directly benefit the nation's farmers, in part by expanding the opportunities to export. Essentially, Polk and other low-tariff stalwarts depicted themselves as free traders, advocates of nonintervention in the economy by the government, except for the required need to raise revenue. Southerners were more inclined to such views than were congressmen from other regions. While expressing philosophical or ideological points, such leaders were mindful of the firmly held belief in the South that protective tariffs hampered the region's economy. The tariff question, in sum, was both an intellectual concern and a pocketbook issue.[27]

When Polk assumed the presidency, the nation was operating under the somewhat controversial tariff that had been enacted by a Whig-controlled Congress in 1842. Undeniably it was a protective tariff, although its scale of duties did not differ markedly from that in the tariff of 1832. In any event, Polk's long-held views about tariffs pushed tariff reform to the forefront as a major goal of his administration. Eventually he was successful, and the resulting tariff of 1846 endured for eleven years, the longest tenure of any tariff measure in the nineteenth century.[28]

The year 1845 was an important time of preparation for tariff revision. In his Inaugural Address, Polk embraced a nonprotective, revenue only tariff. Treasury Secretary Walker, also an exponent of a low tariff, followed up immediately in the summer months by sending out questionnaires to importers and customs officials in order to accumulate information and statistics about tariffs. The purpose of such inquiries was to ascertain the level at which duties become so high as to reduce the volume of imports and, correspondingly, revenue. His investigations were followed by an extensive report, issued in early December, that became, in the words of one scholar, "one of the most celebrated documents connected with the tariff discussion in the United States." Among the principles that Walker enunciated in his report were the commitment to collecting no more revenue than was absolutely necessary for the functioning of an economical government and to the support of ad valorem duties. All in all, the secretary's treatise was a ringing endorsement of free trade, based upon financial and constitutional arguments.[29] Further buttressing the crusade for tariff reform was the appearance, also in early December, of Polk's first annual message to Congress, in which he strongly advocated a revenue-only tariff and left little hope for protectionists. Urging a repeal of the 1842 tariff and a downward revision of rates, Polk invited Congress to initiate action upon a new tariff bill.[30] Before this goal could be achieved, however, several developments and events crowded in to postpone such legislation. In the early months of 1846, for example, consideration of the Oregon notice resolution, the outbreak of hostilities with Mexico, and political dissent within the Democratic family all conspired to thwart tariff revision altogether or at least to make its passage through Congress quite difficult.

Nevertheless, the administration continued to push tariff reform, first in the House and then in the Senate. Congressman James I. McKay, chairman of the House Ways and Means Committee, turned to Secretary Walker for guidance in fashioning a lower tariff, one more or less "scientifically" based on the massive data collected by the Treasury Department and provided to Congress. Walker summoned to the nation's capital a group of appraisers and deputy collectors from the major customs houses, to work out a schedule of duties that would establish ad valorem rates that would be structured so as to produce maximum revenues. Although by mid February a bill had been devised and was ready for the House committee, McKay kept the bill bottled up in committee for nearly two months, awaiting somewhat more favorable conditions. Meanwhile, much tampering with Walker's scheduled ad valorem rates took place as political pressures impinged upon the "scientific" tariff.[31]

The tariff bill, with alterations, was reported out of committee in mid April, but it would be two and a half months later before the House would finally vote on it. As originally devised, the proposal called for seven different classes, or categories, of items upon which varying ad valorem duties would be levied. The first class—luxury items such as various distilled spirits—provided for duties at the level of 75 percent; the second category asked for 30 percent duties on such manufactured items as iron, other metals, glass, cotton, wool, paper, sugar, spices, tobacco, and wine. Schedule C, which stipulated 25 percent ad valorem duties, included raw materials such as wool, worsted yarn, silk, and cordage. The remaining four classes of enumerated goods were arranged on a descending scale: 20 percent for Schedule D, 15 percent for the next, 10 percent for the next, and 5 percent for the final category. The only amendments that the House eventually approved were to increase the duty level of the first category to 100 percent and to raise the level of the second schedule of items from 30 percent to 40 percent. Professed free traders, such as Walker and Polk, produced a tariff that certainly contained protective features in it.[32] After all, they were charged with the responsibility of proposing measures that would generate revenue for the federal government. One cannot help wondering why there was controversy over the 1846 tariff, except for the obvious political needs of posturing and of protesting against any proposal from the administration.

In any event, between the time that the bill came out of McKay's committee until the votes were finally taken, the opposing sides schemed to build support. The low-tariff crowd took over a committee room to display British manufactured goods that would be available at low prices if the tariff were revised downward, and protectionists brought their manufactured goods to exhibit at the Capitol also. From this exposition came plans for a national fair of American manufactures, to be held in Washington in late May and early June, to which Polk was escorted so as to visit a large temporary building, erected at a cost of over $6,000, which housed an impressive display of goods manufactured in America. The president commented that "the specimens of manufacture exhibited are highly creditable to the genius and skill of our countrymen," but he resented this overt attempt by manufacturers to pressure congressmen to support protective duties. Indeed, Polk was certain that various items on display had been marked with lower than usual prices, no doubt with the intention of convincing the public that "high duties make low goods," which was an "absurd doctrine," declared the president.[33]

Manufacturers' fair or not, the House continued to stall, mainly because it was waiting for news from Britain concerning the repeal of its Corn Laws. That information arrived in mid June, and the House immediately agreed to consider and vote on the tariff. During the debates, one of the contested features of the proposed tariff was the duty on tea and coffee. Ohio Democrats, chagrined over the agreement on the Oregon boundary, mounted an attack upon the tariff; this was led by Congressman Jacob Brinkerhoff, who had been disappointed in his quest for an appointment as a paymaster. Eventually this relatively minor provision was removed from the tariff schedule, so that it would not block passage. The president, fearful that the vote might go against his revenue tariff, sent cabinet members as well as senators to lobby with particular representatives. At long last, on 3 July, the House voted favorably on the Walker Tariff, an action that "much gratified" Polk, who viewed the bill as "the most important domestic measure of my administration." The measure cleared the House by a margin of nineteen votes. Altogether there had been seven separate roll calls on the tariff bill; on the basis of these, one is able to identify low, moderate, and high tariff positions. Just under 70 percent (67.4) of the Democrats occupied the low-tariff position, whereas no Whigs did; 15.6 percent of the Democrats were in the moderate category, joined by only one Whig (or 1.4 percent of the Whig delegation); an important 17.0 percent of

Democrats showed themselves to be high-tariff people, while an astounding 98.6 percent of the Whigs were found there.[34] There is no doubt that the Walker Tariff was a Democratic-party measure in the House.

The Senate proved to be a veritable battleground of opposing views and pressures. Throughout the month of July, Polk kept his finger on the pulse of the Senate and marshaled support wherever he could. Again cabinet members, as well as sympathetic senators, were admonished by the president and were sent to confer with their wavering colleagues. Three men in the Senate offered the most trouble: James Semple of Illinois, William Haywood of North Carolina, and Spencer Jarnagin of Tennessee. On 15 July, Polk's private secretary notified the president that Semple was about to leave town, an action that might eventually spell the defeat of the tariff in the Senate. Reminiscent of some modern-day "situation room" scene, Polk dispatched several members of the Illinois delegation in the House and Postmaster General Johnson to find Semple and to persuade him not to leave town. On that same evening, Semple appeared at Polk's office, where the president convinced him to remain in town and to vote in favor of the tariff. Semple had wanted to leave Washington, so he told Polk, because of some legal problems back in Illinois. The skeptical president surmised, however, that Semple's hasty departure was related to unhappiness over a possible military appointment that Polk had denied him. In any event, Semple stayed and voted affirmatively later in the month.[35]

Haywood, a long-time personal friend of Polk's, presented special difficulties. Beginning on the fifteenth and continuing for a week thereafter, Polk was continually in contact with Haywood, who had announced his opposition to the Walker Tariff. Haywood evidently opposed it because, however strangely, he perceived it to be some kind of neonullification tariff reduction. The president had Mason and Senators Bagby and Benton lobby with Haywood to induce his support, but to no avail. Other senators likewise reported to a disappointed Polk that Haywood was simply not going to vote for the tariff. The president and the North Carolina senator had two intense conversations on 23 July, both requested by Polk. Fervently the president pleaded with his obstinate friend, telling him that a negative vote "would strike a severe blow upon my administration, inflict great injury on the country, and as a friend I must say to him that I thought he would ruin himself." Haywood meekly suggested that he could vote in favor of the tariff, if the duties would not go into effect until the following March, a position the president rejected. Before Haywood left Polk's office, the president issued a final warning against any rash action, such as a rumored resignation on Haywood's part. The next day the senator escaped by going out to Francis Blair's home in Maryland, whence he returned to Washington, escorted by Blair, to tender his resignation on 25 July. When Polk learned about this astonishing development, he labeled it "a great error," expressed his personal regret, and then offered a possible explanation of Haywood's quixotic actions. The president thought that perhaps the senator had wanted to be the author of a tariff bill and because he was not, he had taken a negative position on the Walker bill and then had been too proud to alter his stance.[36]

With Haywood's unanticipated departure from the Senate, the focus shifted to Jarnagin of Tennessee, a Whig who enjoyed fairly close connections with the president. Jarnagin had been instructed by his home-state legislature to vote for the bill, but there was concern in the president's office that Jarnagin might not accede to those instructions and might thereby kill the tariff. On the day of Haywood's resignation, Jarnagin appeared at Polk's office on matters of official business, but while there, he announced that he fully intended to vote in favor of the tariff. Later that evening, however, word came to Polk from Treasury Secretary Walker that Jarnagin was contemplating resigning, the prospect of which caused the president to dispatch Senator Turney of Tennessee immediately to call on Jarnagin. (No wonder that the following day Polk reported that he was "unwell.") Although Jarnagin assured Turney that he would not resign and that he intended to remain to vote for the tariff, Polk could never quite bring himself to trust Jarnagin, fearing that he would not honor his repeated pledges. The president felt extremely uncomfortable that the fate of the bill seemed at this juncture to be in Jarnagin's unreliable hands. The Tennessee senator was also subjected to immense pressure from fellow Whigs, chief of whom was Daniel Webster. These two men actually concocted an elaborate scheme by which each would vote to effect the eventual failure of the revenue tariff bill. Their conspirings went awry, however, thanks mainly to Senator John M. Clayton, who unintentionally disturbed their plans. In any event, Jarnagin took a stand in favor of the tariff as it finally cleared the Senate on 28 July.[37]

In the midst of the drama that was staged by personalities in the tariff controversy, Polk repeatedly worried about the impact of manufacturing or high-tariff lobbyists. In his view, these protectionists were swarming all over Washington, seeking to influence members of Congress. Senator Turney's allegation that a manufacturer attempted to give him money for a vote against the tariff bill stirred dismay and astonishment on the part of the president. Given the lobbying efforts of capitalists and the emerging Whig determination to fight against the bill,

Polk seemed to have little choice but to work diligently to secure its passage. On 29 July, after the House had concurred with the Senate's version of the bill, the president depicted the months of labor in behalf of the new tariff as "an immense struggle between the two great political parties of the country" and also as "a fierce and mighty struggle," engaged in by capitalists and manufacturers. He rejoiced that the battle had been won by the low-tariff forces.[38] In the Senate, the party stayed remarkably cohesive, despite defections from Pennsylvania, Connecticut, and Mississippi. On the various roll-call votes in the Senate, a very impressive 80 percent of the Democrats emerged as low-tariff backers; only one senator (or 4 percent of the delegation) occupied the moderate-tariff rung; and four senators (or 16 percent of the delegation) advocated a high tariff. The Whigs were equally cohesive, but on the opposite side, for 96 percent of them were high-tariff supporters, only one Whig (or 4 percent of the delegation) was a moderate, and no Whig senators occupied a low-tariff position. In addition to pride in Democratic-party solidarity in the Senate, Polk also could afford to be immensely pleased with Vice-President Dallas's support of the Walker Tariff, a stance that was politically dangerous for this aspiring Pennsylvania luminary.[39] All in all, the president justifiably took pleasure that tariff reform, which was reminiscent of his mentor Andrew Jackson, had been accomplished.

The second of the twin pillars of Polk's domestic economic program was the Independent, or Constitutional, Treasury bill, which was enacted a day or two after the Walker Tariff. From the time of his Inaugural Address, in which the new president denounced national banks, until his first annual message to Congress, in December 1845, there was little doubt that Polk wanted to divorce the federal government from the banking business. The annual message decried the late Bank of the United States, as well as state banks, and expressed the view that the people and their government were fully competent to manage their money. With proper Jacksonian grimaces, Polk excoriated banks that used federal deposits to make profits for themselves and thereby encouraged inflation. Demonstrating that he was an even better Jacksonian than Jackson himself, Polk renounced the deposit of federal monies in various state banks (known derisively as "pet banks" in the 1830s) and instead embraced the Van Burenite idea of the safekeeping of governmental deposits in the Treasury itself. As president, Van Buren had first advocated this "radical" approach in 1837, in response to the economic crisis of that year. For three years, however, debate, obfuscation, and procrastination conspired to keep Van Buren's measure from passing both houses of Congress, until finally, in the summer of 1840, it

191

succeeded.[40] Not for long, however, because the Whig-controlled Congress in 1841 repealed the Independent Treasury and in the process ironically returned to Jackson's earlier despised "pet bank" scheme.

That is where the situation stood when Polk became president, a new proposal for a national bank having twice been vetoed by President John Tyler. In simplest terms the newly proposed Independent, or Constitutional, Treasury bill provided that the government should build fireproof vaults into which its monies would be deposited until they were needed for dispersal to various persons and agencies. This legislation, perhaps crafted by Secretary Walker, finally emerged from the Ways and Means Committee at the end of March, a delay that Polk was not happy about. When George C. Dromgoole of Virginia presented the bill to the whole House, its Whig opponents began their somewhat half-hearted attacks upon it. Caleb Smith of Indiana, Henry Grider of Kentucky, and Joseph R. Ingersoll of Pennsylvania all spoke in opposition to the measure, but without much effect. Democrats responded mainly by arguing that banks had no right to the federal monies in the first place, therefore no great harm or discrimination was being proposed by the administration. After about two days of seemingly unimportant debates, the House was ready to vote, but not before tacking on an amendment requiring that payments to the government be in gold or silver. On 2 April, with no Whigs voting for it and no Democrats voting against it, the Independent Treasury bill cleared the House by a wide margin, on a vote of 122 to 66.[41]

The Senate was notoriously slow in dealing with the House bill, partly because there were so many pressing matters on its agenda. Nevertheless, a four-months' delay seemed inexcusable; certainly the president thought so. The Senate Finance Committee, chaired by Dixon H. Lewis, felt no urgency about the Independent Treasury bill. Lewis publicly admitted that he wanted the warehouse and branch-mint bills to precede Polk's proposal. Near the end of April, a somewhat anxious Daniel Webster attempted to smoke out Lewis on his intentions concerning the Independent Treasury legislation, with the hope of signaling reassurances to the financial circles. In response, Lewis made his public declaration about stalling, a statement that caused the president to summon Lewis to his office. Polk chided the Finance Committee's chairman and the Senate for the delay, reminding Lewis of the importance that he, Polk, attached to this particular legislation. Adding a candid analysis of patronage concerns, the president stressed the necessity of having Lewis and like-minded colleagues cooperate with the administration. Three days later, Polk stressed to Senator Benton the importance of moving forward on domestic legislation. For a variety of reasons, however, such pleadings fell on deaf ears, as Lewis continued to sit on the bill until 8 June, when he finally reported it out of his committee to the Senate. The measure that emerged had a number of amendments attached, the most significant one being the postponement until 1 January of the requirement of specie payment to the government. For nearly two more months the bill languished in the dust bins of legislative delays before being voted on, as amended, by the entire Senate. By a strict party vote, as in the House, the Senate approved the Constitutional Treasury, 28 to 25.[42]

Remarkably, during the prolonged saga, this bill attracted little controversy or attention. Congressional debates were uninspiring but mercifully brief, quite different from the deliberations during the Van Buren administration. Moreover, Polk was unusually taciturn; without question, his time and energies were being pulled in several important directions (the Mexican War and the Oregon treaty, for example). Yet at the same time that the Independent Treasury bill was pending, he managed to devote attention to the tariff question. In the spring and summer of 1846, Polk made only two references in his diary to discussing the Independent Treasury bill with members of Congress. Furthermore, when it passed the House and later the Senate, he made no mention of these developments in his diary. Although he earnestly wanted the legislation, he did not permit himself to become caught up in its success or failure, as he did with the tariff. Avowedly one of the four major goals of his administration, the Constitutional Treasury nevertheless failed to stir within the president or within the Congress the excitement and commitment that other matters did.

One measure that generated strong reaction, however, was the proposal for internal improvements that would be backed by appropriations of the federal government. Whereas the tariff and the Constitutional Treasury had emanated from the president's office, internal-improvements bills had their genesis in the halls of Congress. In both sessions of the Twenty-ninth Congress, legislators forced the president's hand by enacting improvements measures, generally labeled ''harbors and rivers'' bills, and threatened to do so again in the Thirtieth Congress. The bills that were actually passed by Congress generated two of the three veto messages that Polk issued during his four-year term.

To an ardent Jacksonian such as Polk, federally funded internal improvements were so much out of the question that he saw no reason to make any comments about them in his Inaugural Address or in his first annual message. Since his days as a young congressman, Polk had opposed such measures. On a practical basis he linked protective tariffs and internal improvements, the latter being designed to siphon off the government surpluses produced by the former. Being a strict constructionist, Polk also could find no clause in the Constitution that authorized the involvement of the federal government in transportation projects, unless these were directly related to national defense. Polk found the so-called American System to be repugnant, for it bespoke an activist government, one with almost unlimited possibilities. To him the federal government should be as inactive as possible, particularly on matters directly affecting the economic lives of the people. Jefferson the theorist (not Jefferson the president) would have been proud of Polk's arguments and policies.

The president, however, seems not to have reckoned with western interests even within his own party that were pushing for harbors-and-rivers legislation. For example, John Wentworth, a Democrat from Illinois, was one of the ringleaders of such a proposal in the House in 1846. As passed by that body on 20 March, the bill, in a grandiose manner, designated approximately $1.4 million for a long list of river and harbor projects. A week before its successful passage, Congressman James A. Seddon of Virginia had visited Polk's office in an effort to ascertain the president's views on the pending legislation and specifically on any provision for the improvement of the James River below Richmond. Polk refused to reveal his position on the proposed harbors-and-rivers bill, except to concede that while a member of Congress himself, he had always voted against such legislation. In any event, the House approved the somewhat reckless internal-improvements plan by a vote of 109 to 90.[43] An analysis of the roll-call votes in the House discloses that only 27.1 percent of the Democrats favored the bill, while an overwhelming 87.1 percent of the Whigs approved it. A bare 10 percent of Whig representatives opposed the legislation, in contrast to an imposing 65.7 percent of Democrats. Western Democrats tended to break with Polk and with the traditional party position on internal improvements, but they were by no means united in their support of such legislation.[44] Basically then, the question of internal improvements was a partisan one rather than a sectional one.

Meanwhile, over in the Senate, strange things were happening, chief of which was Calhoun's leadership of internal-improvements legislation. His position was more narrowly focused, however, for he advocated a program of improvements for the Mississippi River system, not the more elaborate scheme endorsed by the House. Under Calhoun's tutelage the Senate approved his plan in a bill passed on 13 July; not surprisingly, however, the House wanted no part of it. The House then forced the Senate either to accept or reject its harbors-and-rivers bill, so the Senate approved it by an impressive vote of 34 to 16. On the various roll calls taken in that chamber, only 10.1 percent of the Democratic senators voted for federally supported improvements, whereas a thumping 89.5 percent of the Whigs did. Interestingly, only 51.9 percent of the Democrats were in the opposition category, while 37.0 percent of the Democrats occupied some sort of moderate stance. In the Senate, as in the House, the notable Democratic dissenters were from the western states; but as in the House, western Democratic senators were not unified on the question of internal improvements. On the other hand, Senate Whigs, regardless of geographical location, were united in support of the federal government's having a harbors-and-rivers program.[45]

Upset by the legislative enactment, Polk immediately began to work on his veto message, shortly after receiving the bill from representatives of both houses on 25 July. Four days later he called in Secretary Mason to assist him with the document, and by 1 August, Polk was ready to present it to the cabinet. When he did so, he announced in advance that he had already determined to veto the bill and therefore was not consulting the cabinet; he was merely informing it. Although all cabinet members liked the message that Polk read to them, he confided to his diary that probably as many as four of them—Buchanan, Marcy, Bancroft, and Walker—would have advised him to sign the bill, had he consulted them. Polk was certain, however, that Johnson and Mason strongly supported his opposition to the legislation. That evening, Congressman Dromgoole of Virginia called at Polk's office, as requested; whereupon the president read the veto message to him and received his approval. On Sunday night, 2 August, Polk summoned James I. McKay, John A. McClernand, Linn Boyd, and Barclay Martin to the White House in order to hear his message, so "that they might be prepared to vindicate my course if I should be assailed on the floor of the House." These congressional leaders listened attentively to Polk and promised to sustain his veto, if it were challenged.[46]

The veto message cogently set forth the traditional Jacksonian arguments against federally backed internal-improvements projects. Not unexpectedly, Polk boldly proclaimed the concept of a limited federal government, circumscribed by the provisions of the Constitution itself. Moreover, the president protested against the local nature of many of the projects provided for in the bill, saying that "to call the mouth of a creek or a shallow inlet on our coast a harbor can not confer the authority to expend the public money in its improvement." Polk further noted that some twenty projects to be funded as harbor improvements were "at places which have never been declared by law either ports of entry or delivery, and at which, as appears from the records of the Treasury, there has never been an arrival of foreign merchandise, and from which there has never been a vessel cleared for a foreign country." Among the potential evils perceived by Polk in the harbors-and-rivers bill was the likelihood that funding would produce sectional feelings that would disturb the harmony of the Union and would "produce a disreputable scramble for the public money." The president also reasoned that the measure would be unfair to states that were already actively promoting their own locally funded projects. Finally, Polk depicted the serious drain on the federal Treasury that such legislation would cause; or as he eloquently declared: "The treasure of the world would hardly be equal to the improvement of every bay, inlet, creek, and river in our country which might be supposed to promote the agricultural, manufacturing, or commercial interests of a neighborhood."[47]

Almost immediately after Polk's private secretary took a copy of the veto message to the House chamber, members of that body began a debate on the president's action. While those deliberations were in progress, Congressman David S. Kaufman of Texas appeared at Polk's office to inquire about the provision in the bill for improvements to the Red River, which traversed his congressional district. Although professing to support the president's veto, Kaufman also paradoxically indicated his desire for appropriations for the Red River project. On the following day the House vote on overriding Polk's veto was a close 95 to 91, which fell short of the required two-thirds majority. Polk's secretary arrived shortly thereafter with news of the vote.[48] It is clear that the president, assisted by his staff, his cabinet, and certain congressional leaders, had kept a close scrutiny on the Congress.

Congress adjourned a few days after the abortive attempt to repudiate Polk's veto, and nothing more was heard on the topic in the presidential quarters until October. At that time the president notified his cabinet that he had been studying the question of internal improvements and was contemplating taking "strong grounds in my [annual] message against the whole system." A lengthy discussion followed among members of the cabinet, with the surprising result that Buchanan strongly endorsed Polk's position.[49] Despite the president's declared intentions at that meeting, he did not incorporate any section on internal improvements in his 1846 annual message, perhaps having decided to let sleeping dogs lie.

They did not remain asleep for long, however, because the ardor for improvements stirred again. The push in the second session of the Twenty-ninth Congress for federally supported projects resulted in a bill that was passed at the end of the session, in March 1847. Much of the impetus for this legislation came from the internal-improvements convention, held in Chicago in early 1847, which sanctioned resolutions that demanded federal appropriations for such projects. As passed by both houses, the improvements bill of 1847 was called a bill to continue certain works in the Wisconsin Territory, but the fine print revealed an appropriation of only some $6,000 for Wisconsin projects, while more than $500,000 was stipulated for harbor and river improvements throughout the country. The day before Congress adjourned, the measure was presented to Polk, who decided to give it a pocket veto and, for want of sufficient time, to postpone a veto message until later, when the new Congress convened.[50]

Beginning in August and continuing for the next four months, the president worked sporadically on his veto message. He actually began to write it in mid August, and about a month later, he optimistically voiced his intention to complete this document before he had to commence work on his annual message. Nothing more is heard about it, however, until early December, when he indicated that he had resumed writing the veto message, the annual message having been completed and sent to Congress. Finally, on 14 December, Polk read his veto message to the cabinet members, all of whom agreed that it should be sent to the House. The president recorded in his diary that Mason, Johnson, and Clifford concurred in the views contained in the document, Marcy expressed no distinct opinion on the subject, and Buchanan strongly endorsed Polk's position, vowing that if he were president, he would veto any such bills. Walker was ill and therefore was unable to attend the cabinet session or to have his ideas reported. Evidently inspired by the cabinet discussion, Polk wrote some additional paragraphs for the message later in the day. That evening he summoned James H. Thomas of Tennessee, James Thompson of Pennsylvania, and Robert M. McLane of Maryland to the White House to hear the veto message, so that they "might be advised in advance of what it contained." Still later that same night, Buchanan, Clifford, and Mason huddled with Polk to assist in revising certain paragraphs in the message; they worked until one o'clock in the morning before finally departing. The dawn of a new day, 15 December, found Polk busily, almost frantically, polishing and revising the document still further, aided by Buchanan, Mason, and Ransom H. Gillet, solicitor of the Treasury. Eventually, at about one o'clock in the afternoon, the president completed his labors and sent his private secretary over to the House with the message.[51]

Thus, eight months after the passage and his pocket veto, the president at long last delineated for Congress his objections to the harbors-and-rivers bill of 1847. Unlike his veto message in 1846 on improvements, this one was replete with much historical discussion, obviously the result of research on the part of the president in preparation for writing the message. Polk provided a succinct and fairly accurate summary of the relationship between internal improvements and the federal government. Not unexpectedly, he made repeated references to President Jackson's Maysville Road veto and to similar stands taken in opposition to internal improvements. By so doing, Polk evidently attempted to portray himself as a guardian of the Treasury and of the Constitution, as Jackson had done. The ever-spiraling costs of improvements projects must be stopped, insisted Polk, lest great harm befall the financial security of the nation. In a creative and even eloquent paragraph, the president challenged his readers to grasp the long-range consequences of a harbors-and-rivers bill such as the one passed in March 1847:

> Let the imagination run along our coast from the river St. Croix to the Rio Grande and trace every river emptying into the Atlantic and Gulf of Mexico to its source; let it coast along our lakes and ascend all their tributaries; let it pass to Oregon and explore all its bays, inlets, and streams; and then let it raise the curtain of the future and contemplate the extent of this Republic and the objects of improvement it will embrace as it advances to its high destiny, and the mind will be startled at the immensity and danger of the power which the principle of this bill involves.

Having said this, Polk next offered a remedy to the advocates of government-sponsored improvements projects: let the states, with the consent of Congress, levy tonnage duties, the revenue from which would be applied to such programs in the individual states. To make his case persuasive, the president introduced historical examples of states that had utilized this method of obtaining monies for improvements projects. Polk concluded his message with the customary constitutional stance, namely, that the federal government possesses no powers to embrace activities such as those recommended by the 1847 bill. In a gracefully written concluding sentence, the president summarized his fundamental views: ''The investigation of this subject has impressed me more strongly than ever with the solemn conviction that the usefulness and permanency of this Government and the happiness of the millions over whom it spreads its protection will best be promoted by carefully abstaining from the exercise of all powers not clearly granted by the Constitution."[52] Jackson had not said it any better.

Although the Whigs in the House "violently assailed" the veto message upon receiving it, this new Thirtieth Congress did not seem greatly disposed to deal with a measure that had been enacted by the second session of the Twenty-ninth. Congressman Frederick P. Stanton, a Democrat from Tennessee who had supported the bill in March, visited Polk two days after the veto message had been sent. Informing the president that he would not now, in view of the condition of the federal Treasury and because of the war with Mexico, support such legislation, the congressman confessed, however, that he differed with Polk on the essential issues involved.[53] There was no attempt to override the president's veto; but before the session had ended, Congress had threatened to confront Polk with yet another internal-improvements bill.

This time the president hoped to be ready in advance. In late July, anticipating some sort of improvements legislation, Polk began composing his veto message. He had already been alarmed at the House action attaching a Savannah River improvements rider to the civil and diplomatic bill and had warned that he would veto the entire bill and call a special session of Congress to obtain the necessary civil and diplomatic bill. A few days later, the Senate struck the House rider from the general bill, thereby averting a very unpleasant showdown with the president. Nevertheless, Polk continued to prepare his internal-improvements veto message. In fact, on 8 August he informed the cabinet of his resolute intention to veto any such legislation that might emerge from the Congress; and since his mind had already been made up, he did not seek the cabinet's advice. Two days later he devoted three to four hours to the message, and after dinner he read it aloud to his private secretary, who counseled him to save the document for the next session of the Thirtieth Congress. Apparently that advice caused Polk on the next day to abandon work on the veto message, pleading that he was simply too fatigued to continue preparing it. If Congress passed a bill, he would veto it and send a message to the forthcoming session. Although the House had a harbors-and-rivers bill under consideration near the end of the session, no such bill cleared Congress to be forwarded to the president's desk.[54] An exhausted Polk was relieved that he did not have to deal with that problem; the Oregon territorial bill had been difficult enough.

The president could not relax for long, however, for a month after the adjournment of Congress he decided that he must begin to prepare a veto message in anticipation of what the second session might enact. Therefore, in September and October, Polk devoted time to composing such a message, one so strong that even if his veto were overridden, which he conceded was a distinct possibility, "I may leave my full views on record to be judged of by my countrymen & by posterity." Thoroughly "convinced that I am right upon the subject, . . . I have bestowed much labour in preparing a paper which may contribute to convince others that I am so." Whatever Polk had actually written by the end of October was set aside, once he was compelled to direct his attention to the preparation of the fourth annual message to Congress. There are no further references in his diary to his proposed veto message until March 1849, when Congress and the president were at the conclusion of their terms. Knowing that a number of improvements bills had been before the Congress, Polk went to the Capitol on 3 March, armed with a veto message in the event that one of the bills should finally clear both houses. He had already warned the cabinet and many members of Congress that he fully intended to veto any such legislation, a threat that evidently was heeded by the chambers, for no bills were passed. It is somewhat difficult to ascertain, however, whether Polk was more disappointed than relieved—disappointed because he had been denied the opportunity to make public his veto message, "one of the ablest papers I have ever prepared." He determined, nevertheless, that the document would be preserved "with my other valuable papers."[55] With that, the curtain descended on a three-year struggle over internal improvements, a battle that was won by the president, acting in the mold of Andrew Jackson himself, but at the cost of some administration support in the Congress.

As long as Polk focused on domestic economic issues, he triumphed—whether a negative victory, as in the internal-improvements question, or positive victories, such as the tariff and the Constitutional Treasury. But when he tried to push Congress in the direction of dealing with territorial acquisitions or with the administration of newly acquired regions, he immediately confronted notable complications. A cogent example of this is the controversy over organizing the Oregon Territory, a struggle that consumed the time and energy of the president and the Congress for two tedious years from August 1846 until August 1848. Presumably an official request to organize a new territory should not constitute a threatening situation for the federal government or for the Union, but the Oregon matter seemed to contain the seeds of destruction.

It did so because in 1846, for the first time, the Congress in particular and the nation in general had to think about regions that stretched beyond the Rocky Mountains, whether to the northwest or to the southwest. Virtually everyone who gave the matter serious thought began to contemplate the profound conundrum of slavery in the Far West. With that, the Pandora's box of sectional discord and national tension was opened. Perhaps Polk forced it open a bit prematurely when, in the summer of that year, he asked the national legislature for $2 million to be used in negotiating peace with Mexico and adjusting boundary disputes. This compelled that body to address the complex matter of territorial acquisitions in the Southwest. Coupled with this, of course, was the ratification of the Oregon treaty by both the United States and Great Britain. When word arrived in Washington in early August that Britain had approved the treaty, Polk immediately sent a special communication to Congress, asking for the establishment of a territorial government in Oregon.[56]

That request was overshadowed three days later, however, by Polk's plea for a special appropriation of $2 million. Three or four disgruntled Democrats, who were unhappy about the new tariff or the veto of the internal-improvements bill, plotted their strategy to upset the president's extraordinary request for funds. David Wilmot emerged from that group to attach an amendment to the $2 million bill, stipulating that slavery would not be permitted in any lands acquired from Mexico. Thereafter, this would be known as the famous, or infamous, Wilmot Proviso. A chaotic and divided House, frantically attempting to wrap up legislation in time for the 10 August adjournment, accepted Wilmot's amendment and then the $2-million measure, as so amended. The Democratic party in the House split along sectional lines, a harbinger of menacing problems for the party as well as the nation. In any event, the bill was sent over to the Senate late on the morning of the tenth, in fact only about thirty or forty minutes before the scheduled noon adjournment.[57]

Senator Dixon Lewis of Alabama took up the bill and immediately moved to strike the Wilmot clause from it. There was little doubt that opponents of the Wilmot Proviso would prevail in the Senate, for they had the votes. But they had not reckoned with Senator John Davis of Massachusetts, who immediately secured the floor and began a filibuster, albeit a truncated one, so as to prevent a Senate vote before precious minutes had slipped by and the clock had struck noon. Lewis tried in vain to regain the floor, but twelve o'clock had chimed, and the first session of the Twenty-ninth Congress had ended. A deeply disappointed Polk was especially bitter toward John Davis and the supporters of Wilmot's "mischievous & foolish amendment." The president, like many others across the nation, confessed honestly,

"What connection slavery had with making peace with Mexico it is difficult to conceive."[58]

Polk and others would soon learn, if they genuinely did not know already, because from the summer of 1846 until his departure from the White House, the slavery question arose at every turn. To be sure, the Wilmot Proviso never did pass Congress, but it was repeatedly introduced and voted upon in one house or the other. In March 1847 the second session of the Twenty-ninth Congress did, however, give Polk a $3–million appropriation, without Wilmot's amendment.[59] Yet this was something of a hollow victory, for the proviso, both as a reality and as a symbol, would not go away.

The Oregon Territory bill, regardless of when it was considered, could not escape the clutches of Wilmot's amendment, although hardly anyone, even the staunchest defender of slavery, believed that slavery would or should exist in that northwestern region. As mentioned earlier, Polk asked Congress in August 1846 to establish a territorial government for Oregon. The House attempted to do so with a bill, which was amended by Congressman James Thompson, to apply the old Northwest Ordinance to the Oregon Territory, thereby excluding slavery. The House overwhelmingly accepted the Oregon bill with the Thompson amendment attached, but time expired in the first session before the Senate could take action on the proposed legislation.[60]

Polk, who was extremely anxious to extend governmental laws and protection to the people of Oregon, turned his attention to the next congressional session in the hope that it would do his bidding. His second annual message again urged the establishment of a territorial government in Oregon. The House, in fact, did take up such a bill in January 1847, after it had been reported out of the Committee on Territories. This bill, like the unsuccessful one in August, imposed the Northwest Ordinance upon Oregon, thus prohibiting slavery there. In the middle of January, Armistead Burt of South Carolina, at Calhoun's urging, sought to amend the bill so as to read that there would be no slavery permitted in Oregon simply because the region lay north of the old Missouri Compromise line of 36°30'. Without conceding the constitutionality of that original line of demarcation, which had been drawn through the Louisiana Purchase area, Burt advocated it merely on the assumption that it was a reasonable and sensible way to deal with the Oregon matter. But a substantial number of his colleagues in the House did not agree and therefore rejected his proposed amendment. On the next day, Burt's associate from South Carolina, Robert Barnwell Rhett, spoke strongly in behalf of the proposition that Congress did not possess any power to regulate slavery in the territories; but probably few members caught the full import of what he declared. In any event, the House accepted the territorial bill on 16 January in the form in which it had emerged from the Committee on Territories. The Senate, however, did not wrestle with this matter until the end of the session. After a Senate committee had removed the slavery-restriction provision from the bill, the amended measure was tabled when it came before the entire body for consideration.[61] The president therefore once more failed to realize his goal with regard to Oregon.

Polk, who was becoming more and more concerned about the future of the Union, recognized that some way out of the apparent impasse needed to be found. During the second session of the Twenty-ninth Congress, however, he had failed to take any bold steps toward resolving the emerging sectional hostility over the extension of slavery. He did confer with David Wilmot in late December 1846, at which time the two men reached an understanding to the effect that Wilmot would not introduce his proviso again. As circumstances would show, Wilmot was not faithful to his pledge; and besides, other congressional colleagues were eager to present his amendment. Two or three weeks after the Polk-Wilmot accommodation of December, the president and his cabinet examined the idea of drawing the old Missouri Compromise line across the entire west to the Pacific Coast. Buchanan, a strong advocate of this solution to the territorial stalemate, captured the support of his cabinet associates; but for curious reasons, not fully comprehended then or now, Polk withheld his endorsement. He refused to intervene in the House deliberations as a proponent of the proposal of the 36°30' line, for example, and instead kept the members of Congress guessing about his stance.[62]

After Congress had adjourned in March without creating a territorial government for Oregon, Buchanan emerged in the public eye as the chief exponent of the extension of the Missouri Compromise line. As the months went by during the Congressional recess, the *Washington Union* backed this as the answer to the escalating debates over western territories. Shortly after the convening of the new Thirtieth Congress in December 1847, however, Lewis Cass burst upon the territorial scene with his idea of popular sovereignty, a notion fraught with inherent ambiguities, which insisted upon the right of the residents of a given territory to determine whether or not slavery would be permitted therein. When the *Union* pronounced this concept to be sound Democratic doctrine, it appeared that the Polk administration was abandoning a presumed commitment to the Missouri Compromise line. Confusion therefore emerged at a time when clarity was critically needed. Unfortunately, Polk seems to have been indecisive at this crucial juncture, perhaps the only issue he ever wavered on while serving as president.[63]

Meanwhile, Polk had sent his third annual message to Congress, in which he entreated that body to establish governments for Oregon and for California and New Mexico as well. The matter seemed more urgent than ever, for the residents of Oregon had organized an unofficial, extralegal government already and had sent a memorial to Congress, asking for confirmations of land titles. Congress seemed anxious to confront the Oregon problem: Stephen Douglas, now in the Senate, presented a territorial bill to that body in January, and Caleb Smith offered one to the House in February. But appearances were deceiving, for it would be early summer before Congress would actually be ready to swing into action. Ironically, by that date, the Democratic party had nominated Lewis Cass as its presidential standard-bearer and, by implication, had thus placed its imprimatur upon popular sovereignty. The irony was compounded by the realization that Polk had belatedly determined to take a public stand on how best to resolve the conflict over slavery in the West and in June had emerged, along with a unanimous cabinet, as an advocate of stretching the Missouri Compromise line to the Pacific Coast.[64] To him, at long last, this seemed the only feasible answer to the congressional impasse.

At least two things added to the urgency of finding a way out of the territorial stalemate. One was the receipt, in late May, of a special dispatch from the temporary, unofficial government in Oregon, reporting that the Indians there had mounted an attack upon the white inhabitants. Or as the Oregon leaders phrased it, the Indians had raised "the war whoop and crimsoned their tomahawks in the blood of their [Oregon's] citizens." In response, Polk conveyed this disturbing news from the northwestern frontier to Congress in a special message in which he again pleaded for the prompt establishment of a territorial government. The second development was the almost hopelessly deadlocked condition of Congress, a perilous situation in the eyes of the president. These circumstances galvanized Polk to take a bold stand in favor of the 36°30' solution and to intervene in the proceedings of Congress in order to help force an answer.[65]

Polk's seemingly aggressive behavior in June and July matched the gravity of the situation. In late June he conferred with several senators, impressing upon them the necessity of adopting an amendment to the Oregon bill that would provide for the extension of the Missouri Compromise line. In a meeting with Senators Henry S. Foote and Jesse D. Bright the president even dictated to them his version of such an amendment, they copied it down, and Bright shortly thereafter introduced it into the Senate. During the next two weeks or so, Polk met with various southern senators in an attempt to build support for the territorial bill as amended. Little headway was made in the Senate, however, with the result that in mid July, Senator John Clayton of Delaware submitted a proposition that a special Senate committee be named and charged with the responsibility of offering a way out of the territorial/slavery quagmire. The Senate concurred and hence created a special bipartisan committee, which wrestled unsuccessfully with the Missouri line but eventually surrendered and turned to an ingenious compromise of its own. Labeled the Clayton Compromise by the senators, it proposed that Congress would make no pronouncements about slavery in Oregon; instead, the provisional laws against slavery, which had already been adopted by the temporary government there, would remain in effect until such time as a bondsman, moving with his master into the Oregon Territory, could challenge in the federal courts of the United States the legal status of slavery there. Before Clayton presented his committee's Solomon-like proposal, Polk had huddled repeatedly with Calhoun to try initially to bring him around to the 36°30' extension and then to assist Calhoun in arranging portions of what was to emerge as the Clayton committee's recommendation.[66]

There was lively debate in the Senate as it reacted to the submission of Clayton's proposal in July. Finally, on the twenty-seventh of the month, the Senate approved the Oregon Territory bill, with the so-called Clayton Compromise attached. But on the following day, when this measure reached the House, Alexander H. Stephens immediately recommended tabling the Senate bill and managed to carry his colleagues with him. Polk, dismayed at the House action, laid blame for this development upon the reality that the nation was in the midst of a presidential campaign. As he put it, "The political factions in Congress are all at work and they seem to be governed by no patriotic motives, but by the effect which they suppose may be produced upon the public mind in the pending Presidential election." Polk concluded his private comments with a pledge to remain true to his principles and "to perform my whole duty." As usual, he had difficulty imagining or admitting that others were also motivated by principles and duty. House members, whatever their motivation, immediately began the consideration of an Oregon bill of their own making, which they passed on 2 August. This bill, not surprisingly, prohibited slavery but was nonetheless subjected to amendments when it reached the Senate. The House, standing firm with its bill, rejected the Senate's attempts to alter or modify the bill in any way. Although it appeared that the session might end without a territorial bill, Polk optimistically preferred to believe that a bill would succeed; therefore he consulted with his cabinet about whether he should sign such a bill. His official family unanimously urged him to sign it, but was of somewhat mixed opinion whether Polk should accompany his approval with a special message indicating his reasons for the endorsement. The president finally concluded that a message would be prepared with a view either toward publication in the *Union* or toward presentation to the Congress.[67]

With adjournment only one day away, the Senate returned to the territorial matter once again, this time to sanction the House version. Polk then was hounded by advisers, both cabinet members and congressmen, who urged him either to veto the bill or to place his imprimatur upon it. Also, some wanted him to spell out his reasons for approving it, while others cautioned him against making any overt statement. Calhoun and Burt of South Carolina, for example, pleaded with the president to veto the territorial bill, as did Turney of Tennessee. Buchanan did not want a presidential message that would specify that Polk would veto any congressional bill seeking to exclude slavery south of the 36°30' line, but Mason, Marcy, and Ritchie favored such a statement from the president. His mind swimming with conflicting advice, Polk turned to the convenient instrument of a special message to Congress in order to clarify his position. During the early morning hours of 14 August, Polk hastily revised the message that was intended to accompany his signature of the Oregon bill. Directing the document to the House, the originator of the present bill, he commended the Congress for finally having provided a legitimate government for the people of Oregon. Significantly, Polk declared that because the southern boundary of Oregon lay far north of the 1820 Missouri Compromise line, he had no hesitancy about approving the exclusion of slavery from the new territory. But, added the president, had the prohibition of slavery "embraced territories south of that compromise, the question presented for my consideration would have been of a far different character, and my action upon it must have corresponded with my convictions." With this solemn warning, the Oregon bill became law, and for all intents and purposes, it ironically killed the future political possibilities of the old Missouri Compromise line in the Far West.[68]

In the very month of the passage of the Oregon Territory bill, dissident Democrats, joined by Conscience Whigs, and men from the Liberty party, formed the Free Soil party, which was dedicated to the exclusion of slavery in the West. Much to the dismay of many Democrats, Martin Van Buren ("the most fallen man I have ever known," lamented Polk) became the presidential candidate of the Free Soil party. By the end of that fateful summer of 1848, it should have become disturbingly clear to Polk and to others that questions about tariffs, internal improvements, and banks were fast vanishing from the national and partisan scene, to be replaced by the all-consuming issue of the expansion of slavery. Although it is enticing to portray Polk and Wilmot as the two principal antagonists in the drama surrounding Mexican appropriations and the Oregon bill, such would be a palpable over-simplification. For one thing, many other prominent figures were involved in the controversy and, for another, the president and Wilmot were fundamentally in agreement, not disagreement. Neither man actually desired the extension of slavery into the West, and neither one wanted to disturb slavery where it presently existed. Anticipating Daniel Webster's famous argument in 1850, Polk frankly admitted that slavery would not move into an area where climate and terrain were not favorable to it. The major difference between Polk and the Pennsylvania congressman was that the president was not able to grasp the significance of the emerging debates over slavery, choosing instead to blame the controversy on perverted motives of various political leaders, whereas Wilmot accurately perceived the tremendous meaning involved in how the new western regions would be developed.[69]

The shadow of Wilmot's Proviso continued to lie across the national government until the moment that Polk vacated the presidency, giving further credence to the observation that Wilmot's perception was essentially correct, whereas Polk's was not. Somewhat lost in the stressful and tedious controversy over the Oregon Territory bill was the president's request for territorial governments for California and New Mexico, which he first proposed in his third annual message, in December 1847. In the very difficult summer of 1848, the California and New Mexico propositions were dislodged from the Oregon bill, in the hope of salvaging a legitimate government for at least the Northwest. A few weeks after Congress had adjourned, Senator Benton sent a remarkable letter to California residents, exhorting them to form their own government in view of Congress's neglectful treatment of them. At the end of September and in early October, Polk consulted with his cabinet about Benton's letter, which Polk depicted as being flawed with ''an arrogant tone and calculated to do much mischief.'' In reaction to it, Polk wanted Buchanan to write a letter to California, giving the residents there assurances of forthcoming congressional action, as again recommended by him. There was a noticeable variety of opinion within the cabinet regarding the present status of any governmental authority in California. Nevertheless, a few days later, Buchanan prepared a letter instructing the residents that they had no right to overturn the de facto government (military authority) to form one of their own.[70]

The president then focused on the preparation of his fourth annual message, in which he pleaded for the establishment of governments for both California and New Mexico, areas that were "already inhabited by a considerable population." Polk formulated his conviction that slavery would not likely ever exist in the region, yet he did not believe that Congress needed to legislate either way on the slavery question; instead, Congress could, as an alternative, leave that matter unresolved until each territory itself made a decision at the moment when it sought statehood. He clearly indicated that he did not favor any attempt to exclude slavery automatically from any territory south of the 36°30' line. Adding immense pressure to the necessity of creating a legitimate government for California was the discovery of gold. As Polk reported in his message: "The accounts of the abundance of gold in that territory are of such an extraordinary character as would scarcely command belief were they not corroborated by the authentic reports of officers in the public service."[71]

After receiving the president's message, the Senate initiated action; Douglas introduced a bill to admit California and New Mexico as a single state, not as a territory or territories. With the concurrence of the cabinet, Polk summoned the Illinois senator to the White House two days later to raise questions about Douglas's proposal and to advocate the possibility of statehood for California but territorial status for New Mexico. Douglas was receptive, but Calhoun was noncommital when he, on that same day, conferred with the president. As the lame-duck session of the Thirtieth Congress commenced, Polk articulated his private fear that Congress might do nothing about the southwestern area, thereby causing the eventual loss of California and New Mexico to the Union. On the same day that Polk first counseled with Douglas, the House again passed the Wilmot Proviso, confirming the president's suspicions that it would be extremely difficult to establish governments in the Southwest. About ten days later, Polk declared to Senator Andrew P. Butler, chairman of the Judiciary Committee, that he would veto any territorial bill that came to him with the Wilmot Proviso attached.[72]

In an apparent bid to secure a united front of southern congressmen, Calhoun sponsored a special caucus, which convened first on 22 December and subsequently on 15 January. Polk, who was kept informed about every detail of these meetings, officially stayed aloof from these machinations so as not to jeopardize his ability to deal with all groups in the Congress. To southern legislators who visited him, he candidly stated that no good would emanate from the caucus and its formal address, although he did in fact advise some to attend the meetings "in order to prevent mischief from being done." On the morning after the conclave of the fifteenth, Polk's private secretary gave him a report, the gist of which was that a number of southern congressmen had refused to sign the message authored by Calhoun, an action that seemed to justify Polk's dim view of the prospects of such a meeting. Shortly afterwards, Calhoun himself appeared at the president's office to discuss the southern caucus in particular and the slavery question in general. Polk took the initiative as soon as possible, by endorsing quite strongly the admission of California as a state, "the only practical mode of settling the slave question." Furthermore, he bluntly told Calhoun that he desired that "the agitation of the delicate and dangerous question of slavery should be arrested . . . by the organization of Governments for the territories acquired by the Treaty with Mexico." Calhoun was unbending, however, in his opposition to statehood for California and to special arrangements for a territorial government in New Mexico. In somewhat caustic words, the exasperated president summarized his analysis of Calhoun's position: "I became perfectly satisfied that he did not desire that Congress should settle the question at the present Session, and that he desired to influence the South upon the subject, whether from personal or patriotic views it is not difficult to determine."[73]

In the wake of Calhoun-inspired activity, Polk began to press members of Congress, urging the passage of a California statehood bill. Likewise he attempted to secure a unified opinion among his departmental secretaries. Probably the most important meeting of the latter group occurred on 20 January, at which time special communications that had been transmitted from California were examined and discussed. These documents depicted "anarchy and confusion," fostered by the absence of "any regularly organized Government," with the result that "there is no security for life, liberty, or property." Naturally, Polk was anxious to permit the wide circulation of these communications, particularly among members of Congress; he therefore asked the cabinet how best to utilize the documents. Secretaries Marcy and Walker preferred that they be sent directly to Congress, accompanied by a special message from Polk; but the other four members of the cabinet favored their being immediately published in the *Union*, fearing that yet another message on California might engender some negative reaction. When Marcy shortly swung around to this point of view, Polk reluctantly yielded and ordered that the documents be sent over to editor Ritchie.[74]

The president and his men next discussed the likelihood of California statehood and also Polk's observation that no territorial bill would pass the House without the Wilmot Proviso attached, a measure that Polk would veto without hesitation. The president decried the stirring up of the slavery issue by extremists from both the North and the South, avowing that "I put my face alike against southern agitators and Northern fanatics, & should do everything in my power to allay excitement by adjusting the question of slavery & preserving the Union." At the conclusion of the cabinet conference, all agreed to work for the passage of a California bill, specifically by pressuring members of Congress. Buchanan, Marcy, and Toucey were to contact northern congressmen, while Johnson, Mason, and Walker were to call upon southern brethren. Polk also pledged that he would be very active in organizing support for the bill, "an unusual step for the Executive to take, but the emergency demands it."[75]

Shortly thereafter the Senate decided to form a select committee to treat the matter of governments for the Southwest. Douglas, not unexpectedly, was named chairman, and in that capacity he finally, at the end of January, brought forth a bill providing for California statehood and a territorial government for New Mexico. Senator Isaac P. Walker of Wisconsin confused matters by attaching a bill designating temporary governments for California and New Mexico as a rider to the general appropriations bill. The so-called Walker amendment would also have permitted the president to have considerable discretion in determining which laws and regulations of the federal government should be enforced in the Southwest. Eventually on 26 February, five days before adjournment, the Senate accepted the Walker-amended bill. On the following day the House passed its own version of a territorial-government bill, one that would exclude slavery, and then on 2 March rejected the Senate bill. A conference committee of members from both houses was unable to reach any agreement on how to deal with the California and New Mexico impasse.[76]

When Polk went over to the Capitol to sign bills that had been enacted during the closing moments of the congressional session, he was told that the House had agreed to alter the so-called Walker amendment by stipulating that Mexico's laws would be in force in the Southwest until Congress modified or eliminated them. As the president quickly discerned, such a measure would have sanctioned the abolition of slavery, since Mexico had forbidden slavery throughout its provinces. Southern members of both houses hastily and in much excitement went to Polk's room, but he cleared them out so that he could confer with his cabinet about this unanticipated turn of events. Four members—Buchanan, Walker, Marcy, and Toucey—counseled the president to sign such a bill, arguing that it was not the same thing as the Wilmot Proviso, a distinction that Polk failed to perceive. Secretary Mason, however, warned Polk not to sign the bill if it came to him, whereas Cave Johnson believed that Polk's term had already expired and therefore he could not properly act upon the measure. The general-appropriations bill eventually reached Polk, but not before the Walker amendment had been stripped from it, leaving only the original bill. Meanwhile Polk had been busily revising the veto message that he had arrived with, so as to make it more pertinent to whatever bill on statehood and territorial governments might have evolved. He, of course, was determined to veto any measure bearing the Wilmot Proviso. He captured the tension of the waning hours of his term with these words: "It was a moment of high responsibility, perhaps the highest of my official term. I felt its weight most sensibly, but resolved to pursue the dictates of my own best judgement and to do my duty." But no California statehood and New Mexico territorial bill, with or without the Wilmot Proviso, emerged in the last frantic minutes of the Thirtieth Congress.[77] Therefore, as with his internal-improvements veto message, Polk was denied the opportunity to issue his Wilmot Proviso veto. His term ended abruptly and in confusion; most importantly, it concluded without a bill to determine the status of California and New Mexico, the first fruits of the war with Mexico now having been transformed into the bitter fruits of sectional discord. In 1850, with both Polk and his successor dead, Congress finally established statehood for California and a territorial government for New Mexico.

Whether in dealing with territorial matters, domestic economic legislation, the waging of war, or some other issues, the president's involvement with the Congress had breadth and depth throughout the four years. Even a cursory survey of the published diary should easily convince one of the intense and frequent contact between Polk and the members of Congress. Congressmen made thousands of visits to the president's office at the White House, particularly during those months that Congress was in session; some went on their own initiative, while others were summoned there by Polk. In any event, there is no denying that this level of contact enabled the president to keep his finger on the congressional pulse and thereby to exert powerful influence upon the national legislative body.

Given Polk's fierce partisanship, however, few Whig congressmen enjoyed access to the president, and in this regard he followed an imprudent course. The argument supposedly could be made that Polk might have been even stronger and more successful if he had courted Whig backing in Congress for his policies and programs. Yet since he triumphed repeatedly without trying to woo Whig support and since he possessed an incredible but narrow devotion to his own party, it is hardly realistic to have expected something different from him. At any rate, Polk had a few favorites among Whig senators, John J. Crittenden of Kentucky and Willie P. Mangum of North Carolina being two in this select group. The latter, for example, was called to Polk's office in March 1848 so the president could explain to Mangum, a member of the Foreign Relations Committee, that Senator Sevier would be nominated as a special peace commissioner to Mexico. Moreover, Polk authorized Mangum to tell the other senators that Sevier had been quite reluctant to take this assignment, lest Sevier's motives be misconstrued by his colleagues. In a fairly typical fashion the president praised Mangum privately with this statement: "Mr. Mangum, though a Whig, is a gentleman, and fair & manly in his opposition to my administration." Polk evidently felt similarly toward Crittenden, about whom he wrote that "though differing with me in politics [he] is an honorable gentleman, and in the confidence that ought to exist between a Senator & the President I was unreserved in my conversation." Actually there were not many Democrats who merited such a favorable evaluation from the president. A year and a half later, in June 1848, when Crittenden prepared to leave the Senate to run for governor of Kentucky, he paid a farewell visit to Polk at the White House. The senator was especially grateful to the president for pardoning his military-officer son, who had been in some serious difficulties. Polk and Crittenden had a very pleasant visit, for the president confided to his diary: "My personal relations with Mr. Crittendon [sic] have always been of a friendly character, & I am sure he parted with me my personal friend."[78]

Senator William S. Archer of Virginia also had a close connection with Polk, partly because they had been friends since beginning service in Congress together in 1825. Throughout the Twenty-ninth Congress, Archer expressed support for most of Polk's program, and from the outset he praised the president's first annual message and confessed his belief that "he was half a Polk-man." Shortly after the end of that session, Archer visited Polk to convey his regret that the $2-million bill had not been passed and to disclose his opposition to the Wilmot Proviso. This led to an extended and confidential conversation between the two men, after which the president wrote, "Although differing with me in politics Mr. Archer is an honorable man." When the second session of the Twenty-ninth Congress began, however, Archer was conspicuous by his absence from the president's office, for he waited until 23 December to call upon Polk. Although Archer explained the reasons for his tardy visit, the president seemed skeptical about the senator's explanation and behavior. There was a coolness, if not more, in Polk's assessment: "Mr. Archer is a peculiar man; but has always professed great personal friendship for me." Since the senator did not serve in the Thirtieth Congress, one can only speculate as to whether the two men would have remained on friendly terms.[79]

In efforts to reconcile himself to former political enemies from the Whig camp, the president succeeded in one instance and failed in another. In December 1845, at the commencement of the new Congress, Secretary Bancroft and Polk conversed about the president's inviting John Quincy Adams, a Whig representative from Massachusetts, to dine with him at the White House, "in consideration of his age and the high stations which he had held." Whereupon Polk asked Bancroft to approach Adams about such an invitation. The navy secretary subsequently reported that Adams was still peeved at Polk, with whom "his personal relations . . . had always been good," for statements allegedly made during the 1844 campaign that were critical of Adams's involvement years earlier with the Florida-boundary question. Adams could not therefore accept a dinner invitation until Polk had offered to him some explanation for the campaign statements. Upon hearing this, the president curtly informed Bancroft that "it was a matter of no consequence whether he was invited to dinner or not, and that certainly I had no explanations to make." Regrettably, Polk and Adams never laid aside their political differences. A year and a half later, in April 1847, Adams's granddaughter attended one of the customary Friday-evening receptions, a fact that Polk duly noted, because "it is the first that has been made by any of the family of Mr. John Quincy Adams during my Presidency."[80]

Better luck, however, surrounded attempts to reconcile Polk and the newly elected Senator John Bell of Tennessee. Long-time and bitter political enemies during heated warfare in that state, Polk and Bell had not spoken to each other since 1834, the year in which Bell had defeated Polk for the Speakership of the United States House of Representatives. Daniel Saffrons, a friend from Tennessee, and Senator Turney approached the president at the end of December 1847 about the possibility of a meeting between Polk and Bell. The president, indicating immediately that he was favorably disposed to that prospect, declared that he was "willing to let bye-gones by [sic] bye-gones, & to receive and treat him kindly; that I had no other feelings towards him personally; and that as we would probably reside near together after my term was out I desired to be on good terms with him, and with all my neighbours." The two men met on the morning of 4 January in the president's office, to talk for the first time in nearly fourteen years. Bell, at first uncomfortable and embarrassed, soon relaxed, thanks to Polk's "manner and conversation," which "put him at ease." Both men expressed a genuine desire to be personal friends, although both recognized that they still remained on opposite sides politically. At the conclusion of the meeting, Polk boasted in a restrained manner, "My whole interview with him was of an agreeable character."[81]

Additional insight into Polk's relationship with and attitude toward individual members of Congress may be acquired by scrutinizing his reports about the deaths of legislators. Altogether, ten congressmen died during Polk's presidency, two of whom were Whigs and eight, Democrats; two were from northern states and eight from southern states (there is probably no moral to be wrung from these statistics). In only four of the ten instances did Polk express in his diary any personal grief or lament over the death of a particular member of Congress. Of Senator Isaac S. Pennybacker of Virginia, for example, Polk wrote: "He was an excellent man, and was my personal and political friend. None of his friends will deplore his loss more than I do." Upon the death of Senator John Fairfield of Maine, Polk lamented: "His death was very sudden and therefore the more melancholy. I deeply deplore it as he was one of my best personal & political friends." Representative James A. Black of South Carolina, who died in April 1848, was described by the president as "my personal as well as political friend, and I deeply regret his death." Doubtless the saddest was the death of Felix McConnell of Alabama, who committed suicide by slashing his abdomen and throat with a knife. McConnell, an alcoholic, had begged Polk for one hundred dollars just two days before his tragic death, and the president, taking pity on him, had lent him the money. Polk viewed McConnell's death as "a melancholy instance of the effects of intemperance" and eulogized him as "a true democrat & a sincere friend of mine."[82]

The two Whigs who expired, Senator Alexander Barrow of Louisiana and Representative John Quincy Adams, were evidently not personal or political friends of the president. He treated Adams's death in February 1848 as a sort of historic occasion, devoid of any personal grief, and referred to the funeral ceremonies at the Capitol as "a splendid pageant." Senator Barrow died suddenly in December 1846 in Baltimore, where he had gone to assist his friend, Representative Garret Davis of Kentucky, fight a duel with Representative Thomas H. Bayly of Virginia. Actually the duel did not take place, but Polk was confident that Barrow's death "was a judgment of Heaven upon the immoral, unchristian, and savage practice of dueling."[83] Because he had been reared in a strong Calvinist tradition, perhaps the president's pronouncement was to be expected.

One senses in the references to deaths of members of Congress that perhaps there was little close personal, as opposed to political, contact between the president and congressmen. That appears to be an accurate appraisal, for social contacts were quite limited. To be sure, many congressmen dined at the White House at one or more of the numerous dinners staged there by the president. Such affairs were seldom, if ever, intimate parties, for customarily a large group attended, composed of both Democrats and Whigs, because, as Polk boasted, his dinners were "never of a partisan character." In addition, scores of congressmen went to the White House for the traditional public receptions on Tuesday and Friday evenings or for special events, such as the New Year's Day open house. The point is, however, that at none of these occasions was a congressman likely to have had intimate contact in a personal, social way with the president. Likewise it seems that no member of Congress went horseback or carriage riding with the president or went to church with him. Polk's diary contains only two references to his going out to visit a congressman; in both cases the congressmen, Senator Bagby and Representative James H. Thomas, were ill, and the president checked on them at their lodgings.[84] In sum, Polk wisely or unwisely restricted his social, personal contacts with the members of Congress; of course, this was offset to some degree by his extraordinary contact with them in an official context. It must be conceded, in the final analysis, that he could not be expected to deal socially with approximately three hundred congressmen in the way that he did with his six cabinet members.

Considering the struggles over legislation that marked much of Polk's administration, it is certainly understandable that he ran low on patience with Congress from time to time and that periodically he indulged in some caustic, if not hostile, comments about the legislators. Patronage woes particularly seemed to disturb him, a topic that is treated above, in chapter 6. In fact, in March 1847, after Congress had adjourned, Polk kept wishing that all of the members of Congress would leave town and quit bothering him about jobs and positions for their constituents and friends.[85] However one assesses the negative attitudes toward Congress that he revealed on occasion, it should be affirmed that Polk was highly effective in his working relationship with Congress across a span of four extremely difficult and challenging years. When the last session had ended, congressional leaders, as well as the rank and file, knew that they had met their match in a man who was determined to preserve, defend, and exert presidential prerogatives and power. Whether "managing" the press or the Congress, Polk succeeded in his goal "to be *myself* President of the U.S."

8

★ ★ ★ ★ ★

THE MAN
IN THE WHITE HOUSE

It would be tempting indeed to believe that the president had to deal only with winning the West, or with congressional relations and legislation, or with patronage problems, or with leading an effective cabinet and executive branch of the national government. His waking hours were certainly absorbed with such concerns, as the preceding chapters have shown. As a matter of fact, most students of his presidency focus almost exclusively upon Polk's successes and failures in the realms of diplomacy, war, and western expansion. It is a helpful corrective, however, to be reminded that there were many other claims upon the president's time and energy. Therefore this chapter proposes to examine in a somewhat cursory fashion the various demands that were made upon Polk by the ceremonial functions of his office, by family and personal concerns and activities, by bouts of illness, and, indeed, by his infrequent attempts to escape the pressures of the office. Brief attention will also be devoted to the private musings of the president on those rare occasions when he permitted himself the luxury of such cathartic or therapeutic indulgences.

Under the slightly vague heading of ceremonial functions there are several topics. One is the requirement that the president be available to receive certain individuals and groups in his capacity as chief executive of the nation. Like all presidents, Polk was compelled to devote many hours to these sorts of occasions. Unlike some presidents, who seem to have relished such activities, Polk seldom did. The visitation to the White House of foreign diplomats or dignitaries more often bothered than pleased Polk. He frankly begrudged the time spent on seemingly frivolous ceremonies—a not surprising attitude for this incredibly hard-working president; he also begrudged the reminders of European and aristocratic ways—a not surprising attitude for this staunch Jacksonian.

In his diary, Polk reported approximately twenty visitations by diplomats for ceremonial purposes; doubtless there were many more that went unreported. Perhaps most fascinating, because it was so exasperating to the president, was the appearance of the Russian minister Bodisco, on three different occasions, to proclaim births, deaths, and marriages. In February 1847, for instance, during the critical session of Congress, Bodisco arrived to deliver, "with great solemnity," a letter from Czar Nicholas I, announcing the death of one of his nieces. Polk confided in his diary that "these matters of ceremony are so ridiculous that I could scarcely preserve my gravity." In response to the solemn occasion, the president merely acknowledged to Bodisco that such deaths do occur and then quickly switched to a personal conversation with him. When Bodisco returned in July to proclaim happily the birth of the Czar's grandchild, Polk joked that he regretted that he could not respond with a similar announcement on his part. More than a year later, in November 1848, the Russian minister appeared at the White House with the news of the marriage of one of the czar's sons. Polk remarked in his diary, as he was to do on other similar occasions: "Such ceremonies seem very ridiculous to an American."[1]

Birth announcements from the French, Spanish, and British ministers brought forth from the president private comments, in his diary, of disgust and annoyance. In 1846, the French minister, Alphonse Pageot, arrived twice within about four months to report the births of grandchildren of the French king, Louis Philippe. On the second such occasion, the president, with some hint of sarcasm, congratulated Pageot "on these frequent accessions to the number of the Royal family." In 1847, Polk made a similar remark to the British minister, Richard Pakenham, who, with amazing regularity, arrived to report that Victoria had given birth to yet another child. This prompted the president to observe that there was no likelihood "of a failure in the direct line of a successor to the Throne." Pakenham responded with good humor. In the spring of 1848, the British chargé "called in full Court dress" to report the birth of a princess. This visit elicited from Polk the private opinion that "such ceremonies appear very ridiculous to a plain Republican." One detects ridicule when Polk reported upon the visit of the Spanish minister to offer "the important announcement" of the birth of the queen's niece. Repeatedly the president stressed in his diary that had the precedent not already been established, he would not participate in such ceremonies.[2]

Polk's Jacksonian sensitivities and American arrogance became evident in his dealings with foreign diplomats who addressed him in some language other than English. The new chargé from Sweden, for example, when being presented to Polk, evidently did not know which language to use, for there was an embarrassing period of silence, which was finally broken when he spoke in French to Nicholas Trist, chief clerk in the State Department, who translated for Polk. The president left the occasion uncertain as to whether the chargé had been embarrassed or alarmed. In December 1846, when the envoy from Peru addressed Polk in French, the president did not, of course, understand him, "as I speak only the English language." Polk smugly prided himself, however, on replying in English, without waiting for a translation, because "upon such occasions of ceremony the interchange of civilities is always substantially the same." Secretary Buchanan, who witnessed the ceremony and who understood French, afterwards informed the president that he had "made an appropriate reply." A year later, when the envoy from the Republic of New Granada presented his credentials and spoke in Spanish to the president, Polk did not hesitate to respond in English and was somewhat miffed to discover, in a conversation with the diplomat, that "he speaks English tolerably well."[3]

At least two of the foreign representatives who presented themselves to Polk at the White House had already been known by him in another capacity. In August 1848 a new French minister, named Poussin, arrived in Washington as a representative of the new republic that had been created as a consequence of the revolution earlier that year. On the occasion of the presentation of his credentials to the president, Poussin spoke in English, a fact that Polk carefully noted. Even more remarkable, however, was that the president recalled having met Poussin in Lexington, Virginia, in November 1825, when Polk was on his way to Washington to serve his first term in Congress and Poussin was an assistant to Simon Bernard, the French engineer who worked for several years in the United States. Not to be outdone by this incredible display of memory, Poussin averred that he also remembered having met Polk on that occasion twenty-three years earlier! In January 1849 the envoy Roenne from the new German Empire appeared at the White House to be received officially by the president. Roenne apparently spoke in English, although the fact is not recorded, for he had lived in the United States for many years. Polk reported that he had known Roenne when the latter was the Prussian envoy and Polk was serving in Congress.[4]

About two and a half months prior to Roenne's arrival, Polk had made a special gesture to acknowledge the departure of Baron Gerolt, who had been recalled from Washington as the Prussian envoy. The president staged a private dinner party in honor of Gerolt, the only such event mentioned in the diary, although the diplomatic corps was invited to White House dinners on stated occasions. This banquet was different, however, for it was arranged to compliment and praise Gerolt, "the only Foreign Minister at Washington . . . whose feelings and opinions are with the Democratic party of the U.S." Polk was very pleased with himself for having made this generous overture to the Prussian minister and his wife.[5]

Among other groups and individuals who called upon the president at the White House were Indians. Although the Polk administration, unlike the Jackson presidency, is not recognized for major developments in Indian affairs, it nevertheless dealt repeatedly with grievances and treaty negotiations. In fact, in his fourth annual message to Congress, in December 1848, Polk boasted of eight major Indian treaties, whereby the United States government had acquired more than 18.5 million acres of land—a vast new region for white expansion and settlement. In addition to the continuation of a successful removal policy, vigorously inaugurated by the Jackson administration, the Polk presidency disturbed Indian tribal sovereignty by asserting the administration's right, through the commissioner of Indian Affairs, to supervise the expenditure of Indian funds. Commissioner Medill stipulated, for example, that contracts made by Indian tribes that provided for the payment of goods or money were to be nullified. This was an attempt to allow a better enforcement of trade and intercourse laws, but was attacked by political leaders who were worried about the consequences of weakening the authority of chiefs in the various tribes. The Polk administration also shifted course concerning the education of Indian youths. Whereas it had been the practice to subsidize schooling for Indians in various states, Medill implemented a new policy that prescribed educational opportunities only within the Indian lands and mandated that such training should be principally in manual labor. Congress supported this alteration of earlier policy. By the conclusion of its term, the Polk administration proudly pointed to the sixteen manual-labor schools, with over eight hundred students, and to the eighty-seven boarding and district schools, with nearly three thousand students.[6] Given the impressive education program, no one could justifiably claim that Polk had been neglectful of the future welfare of the Indian tribes.

There was probably more than one irony in Polk's continuing concentration of Indian tribes in the region immediately west of Arkansas, Missouri, and Iowa. For one thing, this policy stirred increasing, rather than decreasing, anxiety among white residents who feared an Indian war, the likelihood of which seemed to be encouraged by the congregating of more and more Indians in a somewhat limited geographical area. A second paradox is that the massing of Indian tribes in the Kansas region set the stage for difficulties in the 1850s, when the pressures for a transcontinental railroad became irresistible. The acquisition of southwestern and northwestern regions by the Polk administration stirred Americans to migrate, but their westward movements were rendered more complicated by the growing presence of Indian tribes. Polk and many members of Congress understandably gave no support to a proposal, put forth in 1848 by Congressman Abraham McIlvaine of Pennsylvania, calling for the creation of a permanent Indian country in the region adjacent to the states.[7]

Regardless of Polk's policies, or because of them, representatives from a number of tribes visited him during his presidency—sometimes as a gesture of friendship and sometimes as a not-too-subtle method of lobbying. Polk recorded several instances of ceremonial visitations by various delegations of Indians, and in the process he revealed something of his attitude toward Indian peoples. In September 1845, for example, the president held three conferences with a delegation from the Six Nations of New York. He listened to their grievances and to their desires to migrate elsewhere. A Tuscarora chief offered gifts of a beaded bag to Mrs. Polk and a beaded pocketbook to the president, both of which had been made by the chief's wife. On the following day the Indians met with Sarah Childress Polk, who presented the chief with a shawl for his wife and a gold pin for himself. Moreover, the president promised them $100 to pay for their expenses in coming to Washington. Polk noted that they had addressed him "as their Great Father, and Mrs. Polk as their Great Mother," and that they seemed to be quite gratified with the discussions and the agreements reached. A Potawatomi delegation arrived in Washington at the end of October and appeared at the president's office, "painted & in full Indian costume," although some "were in citizen's dress." Their visit at the White House attracted a crowd of spectators, who observed the ceremonies and heard the Indians address the president in their native tongue. A second conference with the Potawatomis, almost a month later, revealed the breakdown in communication between them and the commissioners who had been appointed to devise a new treaty with them. Polk urged them to talk once more with the commissioners, so that "the door would be opened again." But difficulties continued, and treaty negotiations dragged on for months.[8]

The Cherokees came to Washington in the spring and summer of 1846. The president first received a delegation in March, at which time the Cherokees delivered papers outlining the problems within that Indian nation. Eventually a new treaty was devised and ratified by the Senate in August, an event that Polk labeled "an important one." He met with the Cherokee delegation a few days after the ratification of the treaty and "congratulated them upon the happy adjustment of the difficulties which had distracted and divided them for more than a dozen years" and "rejoiced to learn that they were returning to their nation to live as brothers and friends." Polk was naturally pleased that the Ross party now seemed willing to accept the original removal treaty of 1835, which had reflected "the wise policy of Gen'l Jackson to remove all the Indian Tribes residing within the States to the West of the Mississippi."[9]

The group of Indians that most fascinated the president was the Comanche and "other bands and tribes of wild Indians from the prairies in the North of Texas," who arrived in July 1846. An important peace treaty had been negotiated in Texas between them and the United States two months earlier but was not finally proclaimed until the spring of 1847. After the ceremonies, which were attended by some forty to fifty chiefs, braves, and women, the Comanches listened to a brief piano concert and then took a tour of the White House. "The large mirrors in the parlours attracted their attention more than anything else. When they saw themselves at full length," reported an observant and bemused president, "they seemed to be greatly delighted." He further confided that when they had arrived in Washington, they were "nearly in a naked state, with little more than a breech clout on them." But by the time they appeared at the White House for the ceremonies, "they were dressed in American costume," although some of them could hardly "be restrained from tearing their clothes off themselves, & especially the squaws." Following their White House tour, the Comanches went out onto the lawn, where the Marine Band was performing, and many of them immediately took off their shoes and "walked barefooted as soon as they got into the grounds." There must be considerable irony in the fact that their chief was named Santa Anna, a name that would haunt Polk during the Mexican War. The chief confessed to Polk that prior to the Washington visit, he had thought that the Comanches could easily defeat any nation in the world, but now, having "found the white men more numerous than the stars," the chief had changed his mind. This prompted Polk to believe that the Comanche sojourn would "no doubt have a fine effect in impressing them with our numbers and power, and may be the means of preserving peace with them." Before departing from Washington, the Comanches made two more visits to the president's office, the second of which was a farewell ceremony. The president gave a silver medal to each of the chiefs "as a token of friendship, with which they seemed to be well pleased." Evidently satisfied, the Comanches left Washington, "promising to keep the peace and be friendly with the U. States."[10] In his dealings with the Comanche Indians, Polk gave more than a hint of his concept of them as a childlike, primitive, and therefore inferior people.

The Winnebagos arrived in late September 1846 to inaugurate discussions about a cession treaty. President Polk apparently enjoyed the opening ceremony with this group, "the largest and finest looking men of any tribe who have visited me." After brief formal speeches from the president and one of the chiefs, a designated representative presented Polk "a pipe with a flat wooden Stem 4 or 5 feet long richly ornamented with beads and feathers & with a silver band around it." Perhaps to the president's utter surprise, "one of the chiefs struck fire with flint and steel and lighted the Pipe." Then, in a scene that is not easy to imagine, the Winnebagos invited the staid, proper Polk to smoke the pipe, which he did; whereupon the pipe was circulated around the room for all of the chiefs and braves to smoke. Evidently recovering from both the smoke and the manual dexterity that was required in order to handle a four- or five-foot pipe stem, the president entreated the Winnebagos "to preserve peace with the White men," and he told them that "as long as they did so I would be their friend & the friend of their people." Concluding by promising a gift for the principal chief, Polk invited the Indians to return to his office for another visit before they left Washington. Accordingly, two weeks later they appeared once more at the White House, preceded by the news that they and the Indian commissioners had reached an agreement on the terms of a cession treaty. Its terms specified that the Winnebagos would move within a year to a tract of 800,000 acres west of the Mississippi River; in return for this, the government agreed to pay $150,000 to the tribe for its ceded lands and $40,000 for release of hunting privileges. At the farewell ceremony the president first stressed the importance of the Winnebagos' "remaining at peace with the U.S." and then, with no intended irony, he presented to the brother of the absent principal chief "a fine double-barrelled gun to take to his brother as a present." As the Winnebagos left the room, "apparently well pleased" and "in a fine humour," Polk apprised them that their agent would be given $500 with which to purchase gifts for them.[11]

Although other Indian tribes made ceremonial visits to the White House, Polk unfortunately did not provide much information about such.[12] The Indian appearances, although some of them were particularly enjoyable, represented functions that distracted the president and deprived him of time for other more pressing matters.

The president was beset, however, with many other ceremonial visitors, usually groups, such as clergymen, school children, Masonic lodges, patriotic fraternities, and the like. These, along with some individuals, appeared with regularity at Polk's office, in addition to the hundreds of visitors who came seeking patronage or the scores of political leaders who came seeking either influence or emoluments or both. Much as was the case with the foreign diplomats, the president did not take kindly to the many interruptions of a ceremonial nature, though it must be admitted that he enjoyed some of them. Insofar as identifiable groups are concerned, Polk saw more clergymen than members of any other category or profession. One such gathering he particularly noted was the visit of Presbyterian ministers in October 1848. Agreeing to their request that there be prayers, the president was impressed with the Rev. Roland Hill, who led the intercessions, because he was a man of eighty years who until recently had kept a personal diary ever since he had begun his ministry. This prompted Polk to regret that he had not begun keeping a diary "at the beginning of my political life. All public men should do so."[13] Certainly, political historians would join in Polk's admonition to all leaders.

In February 1846 a missionary to China paid a visit to the president, in order to introduce him to a young Chinese man who had converted to Christianity. When the brief ceremony had concluded, the Chinese visitor boasted, through his interpreter, that "he had seen the King of this country and would tell it to his countrymen when he got home." Being somewhat annoyed but also amused by this comment, Polk quickly told his guest that "there was no king in this country, but that he had seen a citizen who had been chosen by the people to manage the Government for a limited time." Afterwards the young Chinese man called upon Mrs. Polk, whom he referred to as "the Queen." Obviously, something had been lost in translation.[14] Polk had been in office for eleven months when this ceremony took place, but it is doubtful even at that early date that he perceived of himself only as a manager of the government. Frankly, his democratic sensibilities and sensitivities seemed to have gotten the better of him when he responded to the visitor from China.

John Tyler was the only former president to call upon Polk at the White House. Although in Washington as a member of Congress, John Quincy Adams did not enjoy much favor at the president's mansion. It may be recalled that Polk had attempted to arrange a special dinner invitation for Adams in December 1845 (a topic discussed in chapter 7), but without success. Former president Martin Van Buren never visited Washington during Polk's presidency, although his son, John, did so with some frequency. John Van Buren and Polk did confer upon at least one occasion, but the president's plans to invite John to dinner at the White House were thwarted repeatedly by Sarah Polk, who "countermanded the order." In fact, she confessed that once she had burned the dinner ticket that Polk had instructed his private secretary to send to John Van Buren. She was quite irritated with the younger Van Buren because he had "neglected the courtesies of life" by not calling and paying "his respects to her." In any event, when John Tyler arrived in Washington for a visit in May 1846, an extremely busy month for Polk, he first made a sort of ceremonial courtesy call upon the president, who extended a special dinner invitation to him. Three days later, Tyler joined a small gathering of other dignitaries for a banquet at the White House.[15]

In addition to these sorts of functions that occurred at the president's mansion, there were numerous banquets and receptions to attend. Polk brought most of this upon himself through his democratic concept of the office as requiring public access to him and the White House. Accordingly, on every Tuesday and Friday evening (except when he was ill or otherwise indisposed) the president threw open the doors of the mansion to any and all who might wish to attend the public receptions. If the pressures of business were too great, Polk did not go downstairs for these events, but such times were the exception rather than the rule. He was favorably inclined toward these ceremonial occasions, because they "are very pleasant, and afford me moreover an opportunity to devote the other evenings of the week to business."[16] Unfortunately for him, on Tuesday and Friday evenings he frequently had to combine business with his public receptions. In addition, often on Wednesday evenings there were concerts provided by the Marine Band, some of which the president himself attended at least for a short time. Again the general public was invited. It is simply incomprehensible to the modern-day mind to consider the White House's being extremely accessible to the people; but so it was during much of the nineteenth century. Moreover, it was the locale for many ceremonial banquets that were staged by the president for invited guests, such as congressmen, members of the Supreme Court, foreign diplomats, and others.[17] Held with admirable regularity, these events were usually as nonpartisan as Polk could preside over; in fact, he prided himself on the fact that when politicians were invited, he always endeavored to include Whigs. After all, the president's mansion belonged to them also.

As had been the custom during prior administrations, Polk opened the White House on New Year's Day for a general reception. On each such occasion he stood on his feet for three to four hours, shaking hands and greeting thousands of visitors, whom he once described as "a dense column of human beings of all ages and sexes." As a matter of fact, there were so many people at the 1849 celebration that many left early. More often than not, he noticed particular people (i.e., politicians) who were among the hordes of hundreds. At the 1847 reception, for example, he thought he detected an unusual number of Whigs in attendance; a year later he commented especially upon the presence of Senator Daniel Webster and Congressman William T. Haskell of Tennessee, both of whom were Whig opponents. In 1849, Polk took special cognizance of his Democratic nemesis from Tennessee, Andrew Johnson, who had been "politically if not personally hostile to me during my whole term. He is very vindictive and perverse in his temper and conduct." The most fascinating thing about the New Year's Day reception in 1849, however, was Polk's dissertation on how to shake hands without suffering injury or bad effects. With unusual levity the president revealed to a group of gentlemen at the reception his secrets in the art and science of handshaking, the key point being, as Polk phrased it, to "shake and not be shaken, grip and not be gripped, taking care always to squeeze the hand of his adversary as hard as he squeezed him." The president further amused his listeners by disclosing that when he was approached by a strong man, "I generally took advantage of him by being a little quicker than he was and seizing him by the tip of his fingers, giving him a hearty shake, and thus preventing him from getting a full grip upon me." Amidst the laughter that greeted this extraordinary display of humor from Polk, the president added that although he was being somewhat playful, still "there was much philosophy in" his strategy of handshaking.[18]

January and February usually brought other festivities and other handshaking in which Polk was involved. For some time it had been customary to stage an 8th of January Ball, in commemoration of Jackson's great military victory at New Orleans. According to the information provided in Polk's diary, he attended the 1846 and 1847 events, but he made no mention of the ones in the succeeding two years. The first that he visited as president was almost a faux pas, because the invitation committee did not invite him until the morning of the dance. Because it was a great day of celebration, recorded Polk, he "thought it unnecessary that I should intimate to them that they had been tardy in calling." That night he went to Carusi's Saloon, the site of the ball, for about two hours. The 8th of January Ball in 1847 had some added, unplanned excitement in the form of a fire in one of the rooms at Carusi's. Polk's niece interrupted his enjoyment of the evening by informing him that smoke was pouring from one of the rooms; whereupon the president immediately left, taking Justice John Catron's wife with him in his carriage. After depositing her at Coleman's Hotel, he then rode on to the White House. Polk learned later that the fire had been readily extinguished and that, in fact, some of the revelers had reassembled and continued the festivities "until a late hour."[19]

Likewise there was a tradition to hold a Birthnight Ball in February, to honor the nation's first president. Polk makes no mention of such an event in 1849, but he does refer to them in the previous years, although the 1848 ball was canceled because of the sudden, critical illness of John Quincy Adams. Polk had already decided not to attend, out of respect for Adams. His first Birthnight Ball as president was in 1846; it was marked by a large crowd at Carusi's, among whom were a number of foreign diplomats. It was called to Polk's attention by several persons that neither the vice-president nor any cabinet members were at the ball, a fact that startled the president but which he dismissed on the grounds of inadvertence or oversight. Polk went, as expected, to the 1847 celebrations—one of which was held at Carusi's, with a small attendance, and the other at Jackson Hall, which was "numerously attended." He had been escorted to both by a delegation of congressmen who had called upon him at the White House earlier in the evening.[20]

In December 1847, Mayor William W. Seaton of Washington, and Senator Stephen A. Douglas invited Polk to a special New Year's Eve dinner in honor of Generals John A. Quitman and James Shields. At first, Polk seemed to be pleased with the gesture, then he wondered aloud if any other presidents "had ever attended similar entertainments." After a curious discussion on this topic, all three men concurred that Polk should not accept the banquet invitation; but Douglas and Seaton suggested that the president might send a toast to be offered at the dinner. The next morning, however, Polk informed Douglas that he could not even convey a toast, let alone attend. Authorizing the senator to express Polk's gratification for the invitation, the president declared that "the proprieties of my station & the usage always observed by my predecessors must prevent me from" attending the festivities.[21] One wonders if Polk would have occupied such a strange position if he had been invited to a dinner honoring Gen. Gideon J. Pillow, his personal friend and political ally.

The president managed to dampen the spirits of would-be celebrators on at least two other occasions. In May 1847 he would not authorize the illumination of the federal government's buildings in

Washington to commemorate military victories in Mexico. He forbade this, upon the concurring advice of several cabinet members, because the buildings ''are not fireproof, are very combustible, & contain the most valuable public records of the Government.'' He did, however, permit the White House and the residences of the heads of executive departments to be illuminated. Almost a year later, in April 1848, citizens in Washington were anxious to stage parades and celebrations in honor and support of the revolution that was occurring in France. On the night of the thirteenth, when a torchlight procession was passing in front of the presidential mansion, Polk allowed himself merely to go to the front door and look out. About a week and a half later, yet another parade, accompanied by speeches, was held, which the president was invited to join, ''but believing that it was not appropriate for the President of the U. States to do so, I declined to do so.'' In these instances, Polk may have had more than some quaint notion of propriety to serve as an impediment to his participation in these activities. It should be conceded that on balance, he handled the ceremonial aspects of his office—which also included attending funerals, school commencements, and cornerstone layings—in an admirable manner.[22]

One final aspect of Polk's ceremonial functions needs to be considered. Beginning in 1846 and continuing throughout his term, the president was expected to pose for portraits and daguerreotypes, a requirement that seems to have been more ceremonial than anything else. Over a span of two years, for example, some seven different portraits were done, while there were six different attempts to make daguerreotypes of the president, one of which was not successful.

As if Polk were not already busily engaged with the 1845/46 Congressional session, with diplomatic negotiations over Oregon, and with the approaching war with Mexico, he found it necessary to devote numerous hours of his very valuable time to posing for portraits in 1846. In the third week of January, for instance, the renowned artist George P. A. Healy arrived at the White House to begin a painting of Polk, as requested by Justice John Catron. The president gave Healy seven sittings for this portrait, complaining from time to time that he would never again agree to pose for a painting while Congress was in session. Finally, on 9 February, the artist finished, but the president was not free of Healy. On 26 February, he reappeared at the White House, requesting a two to three hour sitting, so that he could do a copy of the portrait that he had earlier completed. Moreover, about two weeks later, Healy returned to commence a second portrait of the president, this one to be taken to France by the artist. While Healy was working on this new painting, another artist, Savinien E. Debourjal, attempted to make a miniature of Polk. Both men, working simultaneously in March and April, required nine sittings from the president. No wonder that Polk grumbled: "These sittings for artists are becoming very irksome and fatiguing." Finally on 6 April, Healy and Debourjal completed their separate projects, much to the relief of the president, who was becoming increasingly irritated. Sandwiched in between Healy's two separate portrait endeavors, John G. Chapman in mid February was granted at least three sittings by Polk, whose likeness Chapman was doing at the behest of the War Department, which needed it for Indian medals.[23] Suffice it to say that these various artists provided more than ample distraction for Polk during these critical months of 1846.

The president was not troubled again by portrait painters until early 1847. Having vowed never again to allow portrait sittings while Congress was in session, Polk broke this pledge in the middle of January, when an artist by the name of Ellis arrived, upon the request of Ransom H. Gillet, register of the Treasury, to do a likeness of the president on ivory or shell. Busily engaged with the session of Congress, Polk compelled Ellis to work on the cameo while the president was laboring at his desk, for "I had not time to give him a sitting in any other way." After Congress had adjourned, Thomas Sully, who had been commissioned by the Dialectic Society of the University of North Carolina, appeared at the White House to do a portrait of Polk. Beginning on 20 May, Sully hurriedly completed the painting on 25 May, just three days prior to Polk's departure for Chapel Hill.[24]

The final portrait of the president was done by Minter Kellogg in March and April 1848, while Congress was in session. Having painted a portrait of Polk in 1840 while he was governor of Tennessee, Kellogg was ready to capture the president's features on canvas once again. Polk's diary makes only three references to sittings for Kellogg, but it seems likely that he gave the artist more than these. Although the last mention of a sitting was on 8 April, Kellogg was still around late in the month, for he dined with Polk on 22 April. In any event, the portrait was evidently completed expeditiously.[25]

Making a concession to new technological developments, the president agreed to have daguerreotypes of him taken on at least six different occasions. While sitting for portrait artists in 1846, Polk also permitted a Mr. Shank of Cincinnati to take a daguerreotype of him, much as Shank had done for the ladies in the family. The president reported, apparently with some satisfaction, that Shank "took several good likenesses." In mid June, artist Healy arrived to try to take daguerreotypes of the president and his cabinet, who went downstairs to join the ladies, including Dolley Madison, in the parlor for the daguerreotypes. But Healy was unsuccessful in three attempts; such were the perils of the somewhat primitive state of modern technology. A year and a half later, however, Polk sat for a successful daguerreotype, executed by a Mr. Plumbe. The final daguerreotypes were taken in February 1849, about two weeks before Polk gave up the presidency to Taylor. The renowned Mathew B. Brady of New York, evidently without difficulty, took daguerreotypes on three different days—first of Polk himself, then of Polk and also of Buchanan and Mason, and finally, on the third day, of the president and his cabinet. With that, Polk concluded this unusual aspect of his ceremonial responsibilities.[26]

Despite the conviction held by some of Polk's detractors, he did exhibit a human side throughout the years of his presidency. Although this was apparent from time to time in his ceremonial functions and in his dealings with congressmen, cabinet members, and other politicians, it was perhaps most plainly visible in his relationships with friends and members of his family. Polk discovered, as practically all presidents have, that various relatives could not resist the urge to visit the White House and even take up residence there. His diary records the comings and goings of nephews, nieces, cousins, one brother, sisters, one uncle and in-laws, some of whom descended upon the president's mansion at most inopportune times. Not surprisingly, Polk depended heavily upon his wife, Sarah Childress Polk, to manage this aspect of the presidential years. She seemed to relish these opportunities, particularly the prolonged visits by nieces—doubtless to compensate for the lack of children of her own. It would be misleading and indeed incorrect, however, to claim that the president himself remained uninvolved in dealing with his family, as they filled up the guest rooms at the White House. The diary records scores of times when Polk engaged in various activities with family members during their visits to Washington; in fact, he even took some of them on his infrequent vacation trips. One wishes that he had told us more about his family-related involvements; but there is enough of this story to be found in the diary and correspondence to depict a personal dimension of the president.

One of the very first indications that Polk's tenure was going to have a family flavor came when he hired his nephew Joseph Knox Walker to be his private secretary, a post that young Walker held throughout the four years. (One is reminded here of President Jackson, who employed his nephew Andrew Jackson Donelson as his secretary.) At the time Walker assumed the assignment he was twenty-nine years old, the third son of Polk's sister Jane Maria Walker and her husband, James. When one calculates all of the Walker family members who were in and out of Washington at one time or another, there is little question that this branch of the family, more than any other, made its presence felt and known. In any event, J. Knox Walker, as he was called, fulfilled the duties of his job effectively and devotedly throughout four difficult years. Other than domestic servants, Polk evidently had no staff besides Walker. Walker and his wife, Augusta Tabb Walker, lived at the White House, along with their children. As a matter of fact, they added to the population of their uncle's home by giving birth to a daughter in March 1846 and to a son twenty-one months later, in December 1847. By the latter date the Walker family had expanded to four children, one or two of whom accompanied the Polks to church on Sunday from time to time.[27]

Walker seemed to be fond of making trips, and Polk seemed to be fond of mentioning them. After Congress had adjourned in August 1846, for example, Walker took off, by himself, to Tennessee to visit for some five or six weeks. A second outing by Walker, a quick pleasure visit to Annapolis in January 1847, elicited strong criticism from his uncle: ''I was vexed at the occurrence, and think it so thoughtless & inexcusable on his part that I must require an explanation when he returns.'' The president then added an unfavorable evaluation of his nephew, the only one in the diary: ''In truth he is too fond of spending his time in fashionable & light society, and does not give that close & systematic attention to business which is necessary to give himself reputation and high standing in the estimation of the more solid & better part of the community. This I have observed for some months with great regret.''[28] These are not merely the words of lament from a president about one of his aides; they are more than that: indeed, they touch the dimension of the concern of an uncle for his nephew. Apparently the two were able to patch up their differences, because there are no other negative assessments of Walker in the diary.

Mention was made earlier of the prolonged visits by nieces. Johanna Rucker of Murfreesboro, the daughter of Sarah Polk's sister, was the first to have this privilege, which eventually was enjoyed by three other nieces. Miss Rucker arrived in Washington in October 1845 and remained with the Polks at the White House until June 1847, nearly two full years. During the first five months of 1846 she had the company of her cousin Sarah Naomi Walker—J. Knox Walker's sister, a daughter of the president's sister Jane—who stayed at the White House. Johanna Rucker finally departed from Washington in the summer of 1847 to accompany her aunt, Sarah Childress Polk, on a trip to Tennessee. Afterwards, no nieces stayed at the president's mansion for protracted visits until August 1848, when two of them arrived; one was Sarah Polk

Rucker (evidently Johanna's sister); the other was Virginia Hays, daughter of Ophelia Clarissa Polk Hays, the president's sister. These two remained at the White House until the end of the presidential term in March 1849.

Of all the many family members who frequented the White House and who laid claim to at least some of their famous relative's time, none was more a problem and a concern than young Marshall Tate Polk, Jr., son of Polk's late brother. When his uncle became president, the nephew was about fourteen years old and was evidently quite immature. His mother had long since married again, this time to Dr. William C. Tate of Morganton, North Carolina, but this had not diminished Polk's interest in his young nephew. Shortly after Polk became president, Marshall, who had accompanied his uncle to Washington, accepted Polk's invitation to send him to Georgetown College. The teenager declared: "I will go cheerfully and beg that you will forgive the reluctance I have shown in doing that which you thought best for me and I promise that in the future I will exert myself all that I can to advance myself in my studies with as little expence as possible, and as little trouble to you." As the president was to learn repeatedly, Marshall was impressive with promises but disappointing in actual fulfillment of those vows. Undaunted by past or present difficulties with his nephew, however, the president enrolled Marshall in Georgetown College in September 1845 and paid his tuition and expenses; then, two weeks later, Polk rode over to the campus, with Mrs. Polk, to visit Marshall. Upon completion of the term, Marshall left for North Carolina in August 1846 to visit his mother, promising Polk that he would return to Washington in time to commence the new session at Georgetown College.[29]

True to his word, Marshall arrived at the White House in mid September. When the second term ended in the summer of 1847, however, his very unhappy uncle determined to withdraw Marshall from Georgetown College and to place him instead in a different school, located also in Georgetown and run by the Reverends Whittingham and Spencer. Polk's decision was the consequence of Marshall's poor work at Georgetown College. But after a two-month stint at the Whittingham and Spencer school, Marshall was transferred by Polk to a school in Alexandria, run by Benjamin Hallowell. Once enrolled at the Alexandria school, Marshall continued to visit the White House on weekends and during holidays with noticeable regularity, much as he had been accustomed to doing.[30]

During Marshall's absence in the spring of 1848 to visit his mother, who was critically ill, Polk arranged to send his seventeen-year-old nephew to the military academy at West Point, where he would join his cousin Lucius Marshall Walker—and suffer by comparison. Two days after his return to Washington, Marshall was therefore given $90 by his uncle for traveling expenses and also for the purchase of clothing and other articles. Much to the dismay, and possibly embarrassment, of his uncle, Marshall had serious problems at the academy from the moment he entered it until after Polk had left the presidency. Young Marshall's difficulties revolved around poor conduct, for which he accumulated quite a number of demerits, and a lack of commitment to study. Two weeks before Polk died, he wrote again to his nephew to admonish him to do well at the academy.[31] With that, the fascinating but troubling uncle-nephew relationship came to an end.

Polk's humane and generous qualities were not confined solely to family members. For example, DeWitt Clinton Yell, a student at George-town College who was the son of Archibald Yell of Arkansas, a long-time friend of Polk's and a former congressman, was the recipient of compassionate concern in April 1847, when the message came of his father's death on a Mexican battlefield. Distraught over the receipt of this news about Archibald, Polk mourned: "I deeply deplore his loss. He was a brave and a good man, and among the best friends I had on earth, and had been so for 25 years." And then the president pledged that he would help to educate young DeWitt Clinton and would "take great interest in him."[32]

Being faithful to his word, the president immediately sent for Yell, who arrived at the White House, accompanied by his fellow George-town student Marshall T. Polk. Polk described Clinton, as he was called, as being "greatly distressed" at the news of his father's death. Clinton remained with the Polks for two or three days, before returning to college; shortly afterwards the president again invited Yell to the White House, during which visit Polk broached the subject of Yell's future education. Although having assumed Yell's expenses at Georgetown, the president inquired if Clinton would be interested in an appointment to West Point—a subject that Polk was to pursue with determination over a period of months. Eventually, in early 1848, young Yell made the decision not to accept an appointment to West Point, a decision that puzzled and disappointed Polk.[33] No one can claim, however, that the president failed to show the kind of concern and interest in Clinton that is both admirable and slightly amazing.

While the above discussions of the president's involvement with relatives and friends do not exhaust the subject, they do illumine the myriad ways in which he was called upon to be more than the chief executive of the nation. Indeed, he was challenged to be a person of consolation, of encouragement, of support, of hospitality, and of generosity. He accepted these challenges and met them—much as he did with the challenges of the office of the presidency.

Needless to say, handling all of these demands put a severe strain upon Polk in many ways, one of the most obvious of which manifested itself in his various bouts of illness. Indeed, only a few weeks after his inauguration, he was felled by sickness, and then again in June he spent almost a week in his room, battling another round of illness, after which he showed "considerable debility and exhaustion" for some time. Luckily, he had no recurring problems again until some minor complaints in December. The incredible pressures and challenges of the year of 1846 did not affect Polk's health until the end of the congressional session in August. By that time he was "much enfeebled and prostrated," but he scheduled his first vacation trip as a hopeful reprieve from the cares and worries of the year. Unfortunately, he became ill while on vacation, or as he described it, "My stomach was deranged & I felt a soreness & aching in my limbs." Within a couple of days, however, he had recovered and had no further problems.[34]

The following year, 1847, was not so kind to the hard-working president. In February, for example, he suffered from a "violent cold" for about three days, and in April, May, and August he experienced minor ailments. His most serious illness, however, occurred in late September and continued for almost two full weeks. He first suffered from chills and fever on Saturday, 25 September, in response to which he took some "simple medicine" in hopes that he would not need to send for the doctor. On Monday morning he again experienced a severe attack of chills and fever, and before the day had ended, he had been ministered to by two physicians. The following day began thus: "This morning I was under the operation of Medicine & was quite unwell." Doctors visited throughout the day once more, and there was no Tuesday cabinet meeting, a rare situation. The remainder of the week was spent in battling chills and fever, taking medicine, and being confined to bed; as he phrased it, "I continued quietly on my bed during the day." On Saturday, again there was no cabinet meeting, for Polk managed only to sit up for about a half-hour that day. On Monday, 4 October he attempted for the first time to go to his office: "I rose & dressed myself about 10 o'clock, and wrapping myself up walked to the office, but was so feeble that I returned to my chamber in a few minutes." He did not succeed in going to the office again until Friday at the end of the week. Meanwhile, the Tuesday cabinet meeting had been held in Polk's bedroom, and the president had seen various members of the cabinet individually during the week. Finally, on Saturday, the regular cabinet meeting was held in Polk's office for the first time in two weeks. He spent the next day lounging in his chamber until 4 o'clock in the afternoon, when he took a short carriage ride.[35] Unfortunately for Polk, just as he began to recover, Sarah Polk became ill, compelling him then to deal with her serious bout with chills and fever.

Although the president suffered from a severe cold in November, he remained healthy for the rest of 1847 and on through 1848, until the summer months. The summer affliction occurred while Congress was in session, which made the problem even more vexing for Polk. On Tuesday, 6 June the president was stricken with a very bad cold and was forced to lie down on a sofa during the cabinet meeting that day. Dr. Hall came to the White House the next day to check on his famous patient and to prescribe medicine for him. For the next several days, Polk, though obviously ill, continued to conduct as much business as he could possibly handle in his weakened condition. After 12 June there is no further mention in his diary of being sick until 16 June, when he experienced chills and fever and sent for Dr. Hall, who again prescribed medicine. Polk did not resume normal office routines and activities until a week later, on the twenty-third. In the interim, because of recurring chills, he had been largely confined to his chamber, where he frequently received special political leaders and members of the cabinet. Erroneously believing that he had fully recovered, Polk adopted a business-as-usual approach until 29 June: "Before sun-rise this morning I was taken with a violent diarrhea accompanied with severe pain. I was very soon prostrated by it." Dr. Hall arrived shortly thereafter to examine the president and to prescribe medicine. Polk spent that day and the following day in his bedroom, though he managed to conduct some official business. On Saturday, 1 July he summoned up enough strength to go to his office for the regular cabinet meeting, during which he became so "fatigued & exhausted I was compelled to retire to my own chamber." Sunday was spent quietly, except for a brief conference in his office with two congressmen and a carriage ride in the afternoon. On Monday morning the president reported to his office as usual, though he was "still feeble" from his "late attack" and had to retire at the noon hour to his bedroom for a rest, after which he returned briefly to his office. On the next day, "though in feeble health," the president attended the Fourth of July ceremonies at the cornerstone laying for the Washington Monument.[36]

Following the June/July 1848 period of illness, Polk had no further health problems, except for very minor ones. In any event, the years of toil and labor took their toll on Polk, and he left Washington as an old fifty-three-year-old man, whereas he had arrived in town as the youngest man, at the age of forty-nine, ever to have been elected president. The portraits and daguerreotypes unwittingly recorded the aging process that had occurred. It should be noted, however, that at no time did Polk face any serious or life-threatening illnesses. His ailments were certainly minor in comparison to those experienced by his mentor, Andrew Jackson. It is erroneous to conclude that Polk was physically unable to handle the presidency during the latter half of his term.

Behind the man in the White House, whether ill or healthy, was a woman—Sarah Childress Polk. The daughter of a wealthy and prominent family in Murfreesboro, she had been married to Polk twenty-one years when he assumed the presidency. Being a childless couple, like the Jacksons, they lavished attention and affection upon their nieces and nephews, as did the Jacksons. As already indicated, a steady influx of relatives invaded the premises throughout the four years of the administration. Sarah even declined to accompany Polk on his August 1848 vacation trip so that she could entertain various family members who had arrived at the White House. As a matter of fact, entertaining guests was one of her principal responsibilities.

Sarah Polk managed that task impressively. Of course, she had had experience during the fourteen years that she and her husband had lived in Washington while he was a member of Congress and Speaker of the House. A cursory reading of Polk's diary imposes a sense of weariness, if one notes all the references to parties, dinners, evening receptions, and the like. The demands of making arrangements for such gatherings and then making sure that each event went off satisfactorily kept Mrs. Polk busy. Her most controversial decision, made at the outset of the administration, was to ban dancing at the White House. Criticized by some for this break with tradition, Sarah nevertheless remained firm in her conviction that the presidential mansion was no place for dancing, because such would be undignified and disrespectful. Her prohibition of dancing did not deter her from hosting glittering parties and receptions, replete with fine wines and liquors.[37] In order to have appropriate as well as impressive settings for entertainment, her first major undertaking was to refurbish the White House, a task made possible by Congress's generous appropriations. Testimony to her administrative skills and aesthetic good taste was the praise that greeted the completion of the improvements to the furnishings and rooms at the mansion. About three years later, Sarah Polk refused to permit new gaslights to be placed in the main reception room, although they were installed elsewhere throughout the mansion. During the first night that the gaslights were turned on in the White House, they suddenly went out. The guests discovered that the only lighted room was the one that

Sarah had preserved for the elegant candle-lit chandeliers. Thereafter her wise practicality was lauded.[38]

Beginning in 1847, she also assumed the responsibility for remodeling and refurbishing the Felix Grundy house in Nashville, which the Polks had recently purchased. This was to be home for them, upon retirement from the presidency. Taking her duties seriously, Sarah Polk made a special trip to Tennessee in the summer of 1847 to inspect the house and to make decisions about improvements to it. After her return to Washington, she continued her involvement with the Nashville house by ordering materials and furnishings for it. Finally, in November 1848, she went to New York City, partly to escort two nieces but primarily to select furniture for the remodeled house. It was to be shipped, so that it would arrive in Tennessee before the Polks returned there in the following spring.[39]

Long before retirement became a reality, Sarah Polk served repeatedly as a gracious hostess, an efficient administrator, and a supportive spouse at the White House. Numerous comments were made about her attractive personality, her engaging manner, her quiet sensitivity—compliments that continued from the commencement of the presidency down to the very last ceremonies. As Vice-President Dallas observed, even before the inauguration, Sarah was "certainly mistress of herself, and, I suspect, of somebody else also." Later during the presidential term, even a severe critic of Polk's administration, Senator Charles Sumner of Massachusetts, declared that Sarah's "sweetness of manner won me entirely."[40] At one evening reception, a guest startled the crowd by announcing to Sarah Polk: "Madame, I have long wished to see the lady upon whom the Bible pronounces a woe!" He relieved the audible gasp when he added, "Does not the Bible say, 'Woe unto you when all man shall speak well of you?'" She captivated Washington society—congressmen, cabinet members, diplomats, wives, and plain folk—much as she had done years earlier during her residence in the nation's capital. She evidently had the gregarious, charming personality that her husband frequently lacked; in that sense, they made a good, balanced pair. Being mistress of herself, Sarah handled official dinners and parties with equanimity. Neither foreign diplomats nor Supreme Court justices nor congressional leaders caused her apprehension; she easily engaged in conversation with them. Feminist leader she was not, but equal partner with her president-husband she was.

Polk justifiably took pride in Sarah's abilities and accomplishments. He was fully confident that she was an asset to him personally and to his administration. He relished telling the story of Henry Clay's visit to the White House in February 1848. He and Clay, along with Sarah, had a pleasant conversation, at the conclusion of which Clay averred that "he had heard a general approbation expressed of her administration, but that he believed there was some difference of opinion about her husband's administration." In response, Sarah thanked him for his compliment and then added that "if a political opponent of my husband is to succeed him I have always said I prefer you, Mr. Clay, and in that event I shall be most happy to surrender the White House to you." Everyone reacted with "a hearty laugh."[41] On another occasion, Senator Thomas Hart Benton, who had been invited to the White House for a 6 o'clock dinner, became a little anxious when the appointed hour had passed without dinner being served. Benton therefore inquired of Sarah Polk if she had not invited him for a 6 o'clock meal. She quickly retorted, "Colonel Benton, have you not lived in Washington long enough to know that the cooks fix the hour for dinner?" "Madame," the Missouri senator responded, "you have the advantage of me."[42] No wonder that when the Polks hosted a White House dinner for President-elect Zachary Taylor, it was Sarah Polk who was placed at the table between Taylor and Lewis Cass, the defeated rival. That delicate assignment was not too much for her.

The Polks had a warm, caring relationship as husband and wife. Partial evidence is found when Sarah Polk became quite ill in October 1847. This occurred as the president himself had scarcely recovered from a prolonged episode of chills and fever. The diary reveals his concern and care for Sarah; as a matter of fact, on 11 October he spent the better part of the day in her chamber and "assisted the servant maid in waiting upon her." During the cabinet meeting on the following day, he excused himself from the session several times to visit Sarah and to check on her condition. During the next three or four days the president stayed close to her room for periods at a time, so that he could keep watch over her, although she was beginning to show noticeable improvement. On 15 October, Sarah Polk was able to sit up for most of the day, and four days later, apparently sufficiently recovered, she went on a carriage ride with the president, her concerned and dutiful husband.[43]

Needless to say, it was Sarah who ministered to him during his various illnesses. She also worried about his lack of recreation and exercise and tried to entice him to take carriage rides with her, sometimes successfully, sometimes not. When Polk went off to the watering spas in August 1848, she longed for him to return but warned him not to come back until he had fully rested and recovered from his fatigue.[44] This ten-day vacation trip was one of only three times that the Polks were separated during the four years of the presidency. Her trip to New York City, referred to above, was another brief separation. His trip to the northeastern states and hers to Tennessee, both in the summer of 1847, constituted their longest period of being apart. It is worth noting that on all three occasions, they exchanged letters. In fact, the president wrote at least seven letters to Sarah during the prolonged separation in 1847. Their devotion to each other is readily apparent in their letters. It is not asking too much to believe that in the loneliness of the presidency, Polk depended upon Sarah as a source of strength and comfort.

He also depended upon her for assistance with the presidency. Already alluded to are examples of how she administered the social aspects of the administration. But she did more; in fact, one observer noted that "she was always in the parlor with Mr. Polk." Although an exaggeration, the statement nonetheless points to the fact that Sarah Polk discussed matters of state with the president and with other leaders upon occasion. She did not sit in on cabinet meetings, of course; that was unthinkable at the time; but her opinion was evidently sought and given on governmental affairs. Moreover, because Polk was averse to wasting time with newspapers, Sarah read through the most important ones, marked the articles that he should peruse, and stacked them beside his chair in his office.[45] She served therefore as a sort of information officer for the president.

She also functioned as something of a religious model or guide for him. Apparently she calculated that Polk needed the experience of corporate worship—for personal reasons more than political ones. In response therefore to both her persistent encouragement and also to his own inner yearnings, the president became a habitual attender of Sunday church services. Most often he went with her to the First Presbyterian Church, further testimony of her persuasive powers. Without question he compiled a remarkable record of church attendance. Of the 183 Sundays accounted for in the diary, he attended church on 147 of them; translated into percentages, these figures mean that he was in church about 80 percent of the Sundays. In fact, during the very demanding year of 1846, his attendance percentage was 88.5, higher than in either 1847 or 1848. In 1846 he missed only six Sundays during the entire year; bad weather and illness accounted for five of those, and the pressure of public duties accounted for the other one, 7 June. Contrary to widespread belief, he did not miss church on the Sunday that he worked on his war-declaration message. In both 1847 and 1848 most of his absences were directly attributable to illness; but in both years he did permit the duties of his office to prevent his attendance at church. One senses, as the presidential years unfolded, that he yielded more and more to the pressures of the job, and his record of church attendance indicates something of that trend. Still, Polk was an extremely faithful churchgoer; his attendance percentage never dropped below 73 for any given year. Remarkably, furthermore, his infrequent out-of-town trips did not preclude church attendance for him. When he traveled to Chapel Hill, North Carolina, in 1847, for example, he attended Episcopal services in the morning and Presbyterian services in the afternoon of 30 May. A few weeks later, on his important political trip to the northeastern states, he attended church with a vengeance. In New York City on 27 June, for instance, he went to the Episcopal church in the morning, the Presbyterian church in the afternoon, and the Dutch Reformed church in the evening. Then, on 4 July in Portland, Maine, Polk attended the Unitarian church in the morning and the Congregational church in the afternoon,[46] demonstrating not only a notable ecclesiastical ecumenical-mindedness but also a political savoir-faire.

There is no debate that Polk established admirable records for church attendance while serving his presidential term. Trying to assess what his faithful attendance meant to him is much more difficult, however, for the president was not prone to reveal such matters. It appears that for him, church attendance was a duty, an obligation, perhaps even a partly ceremonial function. Because he was usually accompanied by one or more relatives or friends, the Sunday outings to church were also social events. Yet church attendance was more than all of these considerations. Polk himself was not officially a member of any Christian denomination, nor had he ever been. Sarah Childress Polk, on the other hand, was a devoted Presbyterian, although she had formally been one for only about ten years when her husband became president. Polk had grown up under strong and persistent Presbyterian influences, despite his father's anticlericalism and general antagonism toward the church.[47]

One does not have to strain much to discern evidence aplenty of his Calvinist attitudes and approaches; yet he resisted any direct affiliation with the church of Calvin and Knox. Observations about fellow politicians, patronage seekers, generals, and others, which have been referred to in preceding chapters, often reflected Polk's view of humanity. As he confessed in his very first speech to Congress in 1826, "From my earliest infancy I have been taught to believe that from the fall of our first great parent until the present hour, man has been depraved, frail and impure."[48] He certainly had absorbed ample doses of the harsher tenets of Calvinism. Moreover, his stern commitment to discipline and his almost incredible desire for hard work lend further reason to believe that Polk had not escaped the teachings of his youth. Yet, strangely enough, he was attracted to Methodism—a sort of private rebellion against his religious rearing. His interest in the Methodist movement sprang from a camp meeting that he attended in Tennessee while campaigning for reelection to Congress in the early 1830s. Evidently he yearned for the warmth and assurances offered by the evangelistic preacher; perhaps the more democratic appeal of this religious group also elicited his affirmative reaction. Whatever happened then, his quasi-secret admiration for Methodists continued on through his presidential days. To be sure, he attended the First Presbyterian Church in Washington with probably more regularity than most members of that congregation; but he went there mainly to gratify Sarah. As he indicated on his fiftieth birthday, he preferred the Methodist church, an identification that he did not officially make until his deathbed baptism at the hands of the same preacher who had proclaimed spiritual tidings at the camp meeting years earlier.[49]

It is indeed regrettable that Polk did not divulge much about his church experiences except on rare occasions, for his taciturn approach has left subsequent scholars guessing. As has already been indicated, the president almost always attended the First Presbyterian Church, where the Rev. William T. Sprole was the minister. At the end of March 1847, however, Sprole left to become chaplain at the military academy at West Point, whereupon Polk expressed his hope that the church would find a replacement as good as Sprole had been. It took the congregation about nine months to secure a new pastor; in the interim, Polk and others were subjected to a number of visiting ministers. One of them was simply too young to suit the president, whose revealing comment about the preacher was: "His sermon to-day was a fair one for a man of his age." Finally, in January 1848, the Rev. E. Ballentine arrived as the new minister of the church. Polk was initially noncommittal, but at the end of the month he rendered a mixed evaluation of the new cleric: "He is not a great man, but, I would judge, is a pious man and of good education." By the end of that year, however, the president had become more positive in his appraisal of the Reverend Mr. Ballentine; in fact Polk lauded a "very solemn and impressive sermon by the Pastor." On his last Sunday to worship at the church, 4 March 1849, Polk praised the excellent sermon delivered by Ballentine and then was much impressed, if somewhat taken aback, when the minister and leaders of the congregation approached the Polks at the conclusion of the service "with many expressions of their friendship and affectionate Regard." The president confided in his diary: "The congregation to-day seemed to realize that they were about to part with us, and that in all probability we would never worship with them again."[50] There is a rare warmth in Polk's comments here.

241

Sometimes when the president visited other churches, he was inclined to render observations. On his fiftieth birthday, for example, he went to the Foundry Methodist Church and described the sermon as "solemn and forcible," one that aroused reflections within him about his fifty years. Polk even went so far as to record the exact verse of Scripture that constituted the text for the sermon, a practice that he abandoned subsequently. When he attended a Baptist church, he heard a sermon that "enforced the doctrine of predestination more strongly than I had heard it for many years, and perhaps in my life." This is quite a claim from a person who had imbibed Calvinistic teachings all of his life and who had been regularly attending Presbyterian services. In September 1847 the president's old friend from college days and also a resident of Tennessee, Bishop James H. Otey, arrived in Washington for a visit. The bishop and his family dined with the president on Saturday evening, and then, on the following day, Polk attended Trinity Episcopal Church, where he heard Bishop Otey preach "a very eloquent and able sermon." Upon occasion the president went to the Capitol on Sundays to attend religious services there, which were usually conducted by one of the chaplains. Once, however, a visiting minister delivered the sermon. There is no doubt that the president, although distracted by the preacher, listened attentively, for he made a careful but very critical notation about the sermon in his diary: "The subject of the discourse was the Cross of Christ, a noble theme. The minister laboured very much and seemed to be making a very great effort. There was nothing solemn or impressive in the manner or matter of the sermon; and the idea was constantly in my mind that the minister was endeavouring to make a display of eloquence & learning, in which I think he failed."[51] There is more than a hint in this observation that Polk was serious about attending church, that in fact he sought nourishment in the proclamation from the pulpit, and that he was generally a somewhat critical man in the pew.

Polk revealed a good bit, relatively speaking, about himself in various private musings that are scattered throughout the diary. To be sure, much has already been revealed in this chapter and in preceding chapters about some of Polk's private thoughts concerning various people and situations, but there is merit in focusing narrowly upon how he saw himself, both as president and as a person. Sundry examples of these instances provide the final aspect of depicting the man in the White House.

For a person who is generally considered to be methodical and organized, Polk not surprisingly utilized special days of remembrance to permit himself the luxury of writing some private thoughts in his diary.

Naturally, his own birthday was a favorite time for personal reflection. Curiously, his comments on his fiftieth birthday (his first as president) and his fifty-third (his last as president) were remarkably parallel. On both occasions he mused introspectively, more so than at other times during his presidential years. For example, on 2 November 1845 he contemplated the fact that he had lived fifty years and that "before fifty years more would expire, I would be sleeping with the generations which have gone before me. I thought of the vanity of this world's honours, how little they would profit me half a century hence, and that it was time for me to be 'putting my House in Order.'" Three years later, on his birthday, as he neared the completion of his term of office, he returned to the theme of the "vanity & emptiness of worldly honors and worldly enjoyments," reflecting, no doubt, his inability to escape his Calvinist background. Polk concluded his musings on this birthday with both a recognition, that "I have been highly honoured by my fellow-men and have filled the highest station on earth," and with a reminder, that "I will soon go the way of all the earth. I pray God to prepare me to meet the great event."[52]

The president dealt with somewhat less profound thoughts and reflections upon the occasions of his fifty-first and fifty-second birthdays. On the former he merely registered a complaint about the year "of great anxiety and labour" that had just ended. Similarly, in November 1847, he repeated his weariness with the job of being president by expressing the wish that his term were entirely over, "for I am sincerely desirous to have the enjoyment of retirement in private life."[53] He repeated these same thoughts on 3 March 1848, a day which, he noted, signaled the end of his third year as president. He grumbled that the presidency thus far had been "years of incessant labour, anxiety, & responsibility." Slightly more than a year earlier, he had made note of 28 January as being the anniversary of his departure from Columbia for Washington. As he reflected on that, he complained again of the "great labour" and "vast responsibilities," ending with his famous observation: "In truth, though I occupy a very high position, I am the hardest working man in this country." Judging by what is known of his activities and involvements as president, Polk was reasonably accurate in this assessment of himself and his situation. At any rate, it seems entirely justifiable for him to protest about the travail and demands. Perhaps his most memorable self-perception in this regard was made in September 1847, on a day that happened to be Sarah Childress Polk's birthday, although the president made no mention of that happy event. Instead, he again lamented the burdens of the office, saying, "With me it is emphatically true that the Presidency is 'no bed of roses.'"[54]

Evidently keen on marking anniversaries, Polk noted on 13 February 1849 that on that date exactly four years earlier, he had arrived in Washington as president-elect. Although returning to the recurring theme of labor, anxiety, and responsibility once more, he also expressed the quiet excitement of knowing that he was only two or three weeks away from a final reprieve. In a marvelous statement he declared: ''I will soon cease to be a servant and will become a sovereign.'' He anxiously awaited the forthcoming day when ''as a private citizen I will have no one but myself to serve, and will exercise a part of the sovereign power of my country.'' Polk indicated, quite revealingly, that he was sure that he would ''be happier in this condition than in the exalted station I now hold.''[55] In these observations the president exhibited the kind of Jacksonian notions that were frequently articulated but seldom actualized. More important, however, he unveiled the deep weariness that had enveloped him and also the thread of hope to which he had clung for surcease from the vicissitudes of public and private challenges. It is undeniably sad that he was never to enjoy being ''sovereign,'' for death, four months later, deprived him of that new role.

On rare occasions while he was still serving as president, Polk managed to escape from the pressures of office with out-of-town trips. He readily understood the need for rest and relaxation from a personal point of view, although in practice he allowed himself very few opportunities. By the end of the summer of 1846, Polk was nearly at the point of total exhaustion, physically and emotionally, and he therefore planned a brief excursion to Fortress Monroe. Or as he phrased it, ''My long confinement to my office has considerably enfeebled me & rendered some recreation necessary.'' Moreover, he was certain that ''no public interest will, I think, suffer by my absence.'' Two years later, in August 1848, he again penned almost these identical words when he thought of his need for a brief escape from the presidency: ''My long confinement and great labour has exceedingly exhausted me, and I feel the absolute necessity of having some rest.'' In a few days he left Washington for Bedford Springs, Pennsylvania, and Berkeley Springs, Virginia.[56] Curiously, although he made two out-of-town trips in the summer of 1847, he did not express the same sort of compelling desire to have rest and relaxation. It could be argued, of course, that because Congress had been adjourned since March 1847, Polk was not near the point of physical and emotional collapse, as he was in both August 1846 and 1848, after the prolonged sessions of Congress.

Regardless of the particular needs that prompted these jaunts, there seems to be a common thread running through all four of them. For example, during the August 1846 trek to Fortress Monroe, although Polk was ill for two or three days during the vacation, he was much gratified with the respect and attention that he received. Professing to want only a few days of recreation and no ceremonies, parades, or public attention, the president nonetheless concluded his assessment of the trip thus: "I received all the attention I expected and more than I desired." The following summer, during his trip to North Carolina which was a delightful and sentimental vacation, Polk could not refrain from making note of the respect and adulation that he received along the way; he even described the journey from Gaston to Raleigh as "a continued triumphal procession." At the conclusion of his North Carolina trip, the president summarized it with these revealing words: "My reception at the University, and the attentions paid me on the route going and returning, was all that I could have desired it to be." A few weeks later, after returning from a journey through the northeastern states, a politically motivated and politically inspired trip, he wrote in his diary: "My whole tour was an exceedingly gratifying one. My reception was everywhere respectful & cordial." This same motif was repeated once more when Polk traveled in August 1848 to Bedford Springs and Berkeley Springs. On this particular vacation trip, however, there was a brief contretemps over whether the hotel proprietor at Berkeley Springs would provide seats in a carriage to take Polk and his entourage to the railroad depot. For a moment or two the president did not get proper respect and attention; but when some young men offered him the use of their places in the carriage, Polk magnanimously declined by declaring that "during my absence from Washington I had no other or greater privileges than any other citizen, and that I would take care of myself." Luckily for him, he did not have to rely entirely on these Jacksonian concepts, for other persons quickly corrected the situation.[57]

What one detects in all of Polk's accounts of his travels away from the nation's capital is that he very much appreciated the adulation and deference that he received, despite Jacksonian protestations to the contrary. Indeed it seems as though he *needed* the respect and attention of the people; subconsciously or inadvertently he made mention of this in all descriptions of his journeys. For a person and a president who received little praise and sometimes little respect in Washington, it is no wonder that these human needs had to be satisfied somewhere—if not in Washington, why not in Richmond or Norfolk or Gaston or Raleigh or Bedford Springs? By most reckonings, Polk lacked the kind of personal magnetism that almost effortlessly attracts attention, cooperation, and commitment; he therefore hungered for recognition and appreciation, and he rejoiced when crowds, either out in the hinterlands or in other cities, offered such to him.

Whether seeking praise and respect or contemplating the vanity of worldly honors or considering his own mortality, Polk was a complicated figure. His diary and voluminous correspondence, like prisms, refract the rays of his presidential term in variegated colors, depicting not only a driven chief executive who was determined to have his way on expansion issues, diplomatic fronts, economic questions, patronage squabbles, and political infighting, but also a private figure, distracted and absorbed by the trappings of ceremonial functions, by family concerns, and by personal desires and needs. The man in the White House, though cool and aloof at times, calculating and conniving at times, and petty and jealous at times, had redeeming features, many of which are visible in his role as a person who happened also to be president. Prophet without honor in his own country? Perhaps. But also a human being, who had absolutely incredible demands and pressures placed upon him—some of which were of his own making, some not. As one takes a look at some of the realities of how this president functioned day and night, in great matters of state and in less glamorous matters, one should develop a greater appreciation for the manner in which he not only endured but also excelled.

9

★ ★ ★ ★ ★

EPILOGUE:
THE ELECTION AND BEYOND

The retirement from public life and private distractions that Polk evidently sought would not come until after the presidential election had taken place and a successor had been inaugurated. But the election of 1848 was a long time in coming. As Polk was acutely aware, and even overly so, it loomed large throughout his administration. In fact, in his darker moments, he indicted various congressmen and cabinet members and even generals with the charge of being motivated by ambitions and concerns over the forthcoming presidential race. Ironically, more often than not, it was Polk himself who endeavored to make that an issue. Indeed, he did so as soon as he had received word of his nomination by the Baltimore convention in 1844, for apparently trying to win advantage within the party and attempting also to be a thoroughgoing Jacksonian purist, Polk committed himself to serve only one term. As he phrased it, if elected by the people in 1844, he would "enter upon the discharge of the high and solemn duties of the office with the settled purpose of not being a candidate for re-election." He made this pledge ostensibly to give freedom and open choices to the Democratic party four years later.[1] Yet, the one-term vow became something of a curse for Polk, who, instead of ridding himself of the problem of the presidential contest, actually succeeded in making it a viable concern throughout his four years. Even though he extracted a commitment from his cabinet members that they would not seek the presidential nomination as long as they were part of his official family, Polk's one-term pledge more or less opened up electoral maneuvering on the part of the cabinet members, most especially James Buchanan. Hoping for harmony within his administration and particularly within the Democratic party, Polk took the extraordinary stance of a one-term covenant. Almost from the outset, however, it was obvious that few people believed the genuineness of his pledge.

The president had been in office only seven months, for example, when the first public statement appeared speculating that in 1848, Polk would be renominated by the Democrats, after the other contenders had knocked each other out of the race. Shortly after the new year of 1846 had arrived, Polk found himself repeating to various visitors, including Governor Hugh J. Anderson of Maine, Senator William Allen of Ohio, and Richard M. Johnson of Kentucky, his consistent determination not to be a candidate for the Democratic nomination. Assuring Johnson that he occupied a "fixed & unalterable resolution on this subject, from the day I wrote my letter of acceptance of the Baltimore nomination," Polk was exasperated, even at this early date, to be questioned about plans for his political future. Moreover, he coupled the repetition of his original one-term vow with a declaration that he would not assist any persons who sought the nomination. In other words, he intended to hold fast to a hands-off policy concerning 1848.[2]

Polk's diary in 1847 indicates that once again, nagging questions about his aspirations and strategies were confronting him. He was particularly disturbed by the rumors, circulating late in the year, that he intended to promote the nomination of Lewis Cass by the Tennessee party convention, in order to generate confusion among the Democratic contenders and thereby open the way for his own candidacy. Emphatically denying these rumors in a rather pointed exchange with Secretary Buchanan, himself a presidential hopeful, Polk insisted that he had done nothing in Tennessee or elsewhere to foster Cass's candidacy. Surmising that Buchanan was nervous about his own prospects for the national nomination, Polk thought Buchanan was becoming increasingly unreliable as a member of the administration.[3]

Not surprisingly, the election year of 1848 accelerated the comments and concerns about Polk's plans. During the early months of the new session of Congress, a small parade of congressmen marched to the White House to implore the president to reconsider his avowal of a one-term tenure. Moreover, they begged him to cease making public statements about not seeking a second term, lest the Democratic party find itself in such a predicament that it would need to turn to Polk, as the only candidate who could unite the party and restore harmony for the campaign. But the president gave them short shrift and merely renewed his consistent determination to retire at the end of his four years. About two weeks later, presidential aspirant Cass paid a visit to Polk to discuss rumors that were being aired in newspapers and privately, alleging that the president was dissatisfied with Cass, particularly with his work in the Senate. Polk quickly dismissed such stories as being false and reassured Cass that he had made no effort to promote the nomination of any prospective candidate. Professing satisfaction, Cass departed; whereupon the president wrote in his diary that Cass had always been a faithful backer of his administration and should he be nominated, Polk would "support him with great pleasure. There is no other whom I would support with more pleasure."[4] Thankfully, Buchanan did not have access to Polk's diary. In any event, by early April the president had decided to take some steps to head off any real or imagined ground swell in his own behalf. Accordingly, in "a full and confidential conversation" with Postmaster General Cave Johnson, Polk asked him to reprint the letter that Polk had written in June 1844 to the committee of the Democratic National Convention, despite Johnson's argument that Polk would be a stronger candidate than anyone else and that he was the only person who could unify the party. Turning a deaf ear to these ego-boosting sentiments and blandishments, the president revealed that he would probably devise a letter to the forthcoming convention to repeat categorically his intention not to run for president.[5]

In May, prior to the convention at Baltimore, Polk spent time drafting this proposed letter and reading excerpts to sundry political visitors. On the eve of the assembly he finally completed the letter and addressed it to his long-time friend Dr. J. G. M. Ramsey of Knoxville, believing that it should be handled by a delegate from his home state. To practically all who called upon him during the week or so before the Baltimore conclave, the president read his new statement. It therefore could hardly have been news when eventually it was actually presented to the convention itself. As delegates on their way to the Baltimore assembly passed through Washington, they could not resist the impulse to appear at the president's office, often to plead with Polk to permit himself to be a candidate. With his accustomed tenacity, he offered a firm refusal. By giving the letter to Ramsey on 21 May, Polk closed the door once and for all on his political aspirations; he nevertheless continued to receive visitors who either questioned him about his candidacy or else urged his claims to a second term.[6]

The letter, which Ramsey dutifully carried to Baltimore, simply reiterated Polk's pledge, made four years earlier, to serve only one term. In it Polk urged the convention to unite harmoniously behind a candidate who would continue the great principles of the party; he expressed his appreciation for the privilege of serving as president; and he pledged his support to the persons who would be nominated by the convention. Polk need not have worried, for there was little disposition on the part of the conclave to push his renomination and reelection. Instead, there were three active hopefuls: Buchanan, Cass, and Woodbury—all of whom had close connections, willy-nilly, with Polk and his administration. Certainly the president should have been pleased by the party platform that was adopted at Baltimore: among other things, it praised him and his presidency. It is not difficult to imagine that Polk privately pored over and savored these eloquent and effusive claims: "That the confidence of the Democracy of the Union in the principles, capacity, firmness, and integrity of James K. Polk . . . has been signally justified by the strictness of his adherence to sound Democratic doctrines, by the purity of purpose, the energy and ability which have characterized his administration in all our affairs at home and abroad; that we tender to him our cordial congratulations upon the brilliant success which has hitherto crowned his patriotic efforts, and assure him, that at the expiration of his Presidential term, he will carry with him to his retirement the esteem, respect, and admiration of a grateful country."[7] Polk could not have said it better himself.

A majority of the delegates at the Baltimore conclave eventually swung to the side of Lewis Cass, senator from Michigan, expansionist, and secretary of war under Jackson. Learning of the nomination only hours after it occurred, thanks to the telegraphic messages relayed to Washington, Polk summoned Cass to his office at the White House. Cass arrived "in a fine humour," and the two of them had a "pleasant conversation." Unfortunately, Polk did not confide the contents of this enjoyable chat, except to note, revealingly and approvingly, that Cass indicated that he would inform the party of his intention to serve only one term. Five days later, after the convention had concluded and the delegates had dispersed, the president and Cass held another conference, this one not quite as amiable as the earlier one. Arriving with a draft of the letter that was intended for the convention committee, Cass asked Polk to scrutinize it; in the process, Cass got more than he had bargained for. Armed with blue pencil, editor Polk proceeded to recommend changes and deletions and additions throughout the document, probably to the dismay of the proud Cass. "My suggestions seemed to strike him with force," boasted Polk, but Cass shrewdly "did not say what he would do." The president particularly noted, albeit privately, that the nominee had not incorporated a clause, promised a few days before by Cass, that would "endorse and approve the whole course of my administration." When the two men reached that part of the document, Cass merely mentioned that in response to some pressures from fellow congressmen, he had modified that section somewhat. To ease Cass's obvious discomfort and embarrassment, Polk "as a matter of delicacy . . . made no remark upon this part of the letter."[8] In any event, the letter, with modifications and alterations, appeared in the *Washington Union* on 1 June. Polk proudly observed the various changes that had been made in it, believing that he had been responsible for the improvements. Crusty old Thomas Ritchie arrived, however, to chastise the president about some parts of the document, saying to him: "You had not your spectacles on when you read Gen'l Cass's draft of his letter the other day, or you would not have approved the concluding paragraph and some other paragraphs of it." Apparently not taking kindly to the president's functioning as an editor, Ritchie informed Polk of the various alterations that he had had to make in the document.[9] All jealousy of authorship aside, Cass was the party's man, and both Polk and Ritchie pledged their support.

A week later they learned, along with everyone else, that the Whig Convention at Philadelphia had named Zachary Taylor as its standard-bearer. Fresh from wars in Mexico and wars with the Polk administration, Taylor was exceedingly popular, a sort of folk hero in approximately the same mold as William Henry Harrison or even Andrew Jackson. But as historian Holman Hamilton has aptly observed, "To a very great degree, Taylor politically was a child of chance." He could not have been nominated four years earlier for any party's ticket; in 1848, however, he was available. In fact, all political groups and parties courted him, hoping to cash in on his visibility and his lack of previous political involvement, which were deemed assets in 1848. Meanwhile, Henry Clay—the grand old man of the Whig party and a personal friend of Polk's, his rival in 1844—had no possibility for the nomination, advancing years and changing issues having by-passed him. In truth, there was really no serious candidate other than Taylor, once he made a commitment to the Whig, rather than the Democratic, party. He attracted such an unusual mixture of followers and supporters within the party, however, that no one could be sure of who controlled the Whigs. Indicative of the party's uncertainty about itself, although not about its candidate, it adopted no platform at the Philadelphia conclave. As historian David Potter has noted: "While the Democrats had adopted a platform whose meaning no one could be sure about, the Whigs found a way to be evasive without equivocation: they adopted no platform at all." Smelling the chance for victory, however, northern Whigs and southern Whigs, antislavery Whigs and proslavery Whigs, united behind this southern slaveholder, a professional soldier who had never held any civil office and who had never voted in any presidential election.[10] "Old Rough and Ready" furnished the rough-hewn personality that image makers dream of; it was as though Whigs had discovered 1840 again.

Even stranger things happened in 1848, however. Barnburner Democrats, who had long been at odds with the Polk administration, got involved in a squabble with their New York rivals, the Hunker Democrats, at the Baltimore convention. This resulted in their walking out of the convention in protest and, by so doing, tapping widespread reservoirs of discontent. These Barnburners, whose titular leader was Martin Van Buren, a man who had nursed and cultivated bruised feelings and antagonisms toward Polk for four years, gravitated quickly to the notion that they should offer up a presidential candidate of their own. Accordingly, they convened in late June at Utica, New York, for just such a purpose. After a moment or two of quixotic flirtation with the possibility of supporting Taylor for the nomination, the convention delegates coalesced around Van Buren as the overwhelming preference. Professing no desire whatsoever to be a candidate for any public office, Van Buren certainly did not appear to be seeking this latest accolade; but he definitely was sympathetic to the goals and hopes affirmed by the Barnburners. Without much difficulty, therefore, these renegade Democrats chose Van Buren as their nominee. Upon learning of this turn of events, Polk castigated the Barnburners and especially Van Buren, whose course he labeled as "selfish, unpatriotic, and wholly inexcusable." The president genuinely feared the stirring up of the slavery question by such a political group.[11]

Months earlier, the Liberty party, embracing its customary stance in opposition to the extension of slavery, held a nominating convention at which it chose John P. Hale to head its ticket. Waiting almost two months before actually accepting this nomination, Senator Hale was the quintessential reluctant candidate. Doubtless he sensed the political turmoil that was brewing and wondered if the Liberty party would remain a viable answer or option to it. In any event, after the Barnburner convention at Utica, sentiment quickly spread across the Northeast and the Northwest for a larger movement that would encompass a wide spectrum of dissenters and protesters. From such notions developed the call for a great convention at Buffalo in August.[12]

"A motley horde of political nonconformists" assembled there for a conclave that was part religious revival, part political convention, and part pep rally. The three distinctive groups who gathered in Buffalo were Barnburner Democrats, Liberty-party followers, and Conscience Whigs, those Whigs who were not able to throw principles to the wind in order to back a southern slaveholder from Louisiana. Although just about every conceivable attitude or notion was represented, the most prevalent bond was the antislavery commitment. This heterogeneous multitude had to wrestle with political infighting and ideological preferences, to be sure; yet harmonious unity was remarkably evident whenever the slavery question was addressed. The disparate groups rallied around this as they confronted the sensitive matter of selecting the nominees. Eventually the Barnburners prevailed, as they successfully pushed Van Buren's nomination, while Conscience Whigs won by gaining the vice-presidential selection for Charles Francis Adams. It was an odd ticket by most reckonings: Van Buren, who had been Jackson's right-hand man for years, linked with Adams, the son of John Quincy Adams, a man who was anathema to most Democrats. As one historian has phrased it, "The tail and head of the Free Soil ticket seemed to compose an incongruous duality." Nevertheless, the delegates at Buffalo had succeeded in picking two recognizable figures, thereby increasing voter appeal in November. The old Liberty-party people got their reward when the platform was written and adopted, as the new party pledged itself to the battle cry of "Free Soil, Free Speech, Free Labor, and Free Men." The three important elements that had united to create the Free Soil party at Buffalo thus left the convention generally satisfied with the recognition and emoluments that each had received there. Even before they had departed the exhilarating environs of their bold new ventures, however, the anxious Polk had learned about their decisions. Needless to say, news from the Buffalo conclave dismayed the president, much as that from the Utica convention had done; in Calvinistic language he declared, "Mr. Van Buren is the most fallen man I have ever known."[13]

Regardless of what fate Polk assigned to his foe Van Buren, the candidates and their parties waged a vigorous campaign across the nation. In several respects it was reminiscent of the 1840 "Log Cabin and Hard Cider" ballyhoo.[14] Some scholars have claimed that the Free Soil convention at Buffalo was the highlight of the campaign, for it gave a new and penetrating focus to American politics and elevated the concerns of the people.[15] There is no doubt that the Free Soilers contributed an ideological hue to the electioneering, but outside of certain specified regions of the country, few voters noticed. Instead, it was almost politics as usual, at least insofar as Democrats and Whigs were concerned. Polk remained true to his pronouncements about a hands-off position, for he evidently did nothing in the campaign, except to remove some Barnburner Democrats from federal appointments (a topic discussed in chapter 6) and to write letters. Perhaps he harbored latent hostility toward Cass or toward the party, which prompted Polk to be uninvolved; or perhaps he subconsciously wanted a second try at the presidency after all. Doubtless he did not believe that protocol or political etiquette would permit him the luxury of engaging in a campaign in behalf of his successor. Besides, Polk was still the president in 1848, beset by numerous official problems and demands and by many private distractions as well; he simply did not possess the time and energy to throw himself into a political canvass. We cannot know for certain, however, why Polk remained above the battle throughout the summer and fall months. It must have demanded unusual restraint on his part not to campaign publicly against two of his most persistent and troublesome nemeses, Van Buren and Taylor. But restrain himself he did; Cass had to go it alone.

Not entirely alone, however, for he, like Taylor and Van Buren, was assisted by a host of enthusiastic supporters in all corners of the nation. For Cass, as well as for Van Buren, however, such loyalty and backing were insufficient, as election day would reveal. For the first time in United States history, voters throughout the country went to the polls on the same day to render their verdicts. In November, nearly 2.9 million trooped to the polls, of whom the victorious Taylor attracted 47 percent, Cass slightly over 42 percent, and Van Buren a distant third, with only 10 percent. Although he captured nearly 300,000 votes in 1848 (or five times the vote for the Liberty party in 1844), Van Buren failed to carry a single state, even though he outpolled his Democratic rival in Vermont, Massachusetts, and New York. Taylor carried the traditional Whig states in the North and won upset victories in the very important states of New York and Pennsylvania, which were traditionally Democratic. In the South he ran remarkably strong, carrying the normal Whig states and also taking Georgia and Louisiana away from the Democratic column. The most favorable interpretation of Cass's electoral results is that he maintained the Democratic hold on the West, even to the extent of capturing Ohio from the Whigs. Generally speaking, however, he ran behind Polk's popular vote in 1844. The most significant story that emerges from the election returns is that, strange to say, voters remained fiercely committed to the party that they had always supported. Despite the candidacies and events of 1848, there was very little shifting among the nation's voters, who had long been known for their tenacity and constancy. Moreover, there seems to have been little question that Taylor's military achievements stood him in good stead both in the North and in the South; Cass was no match, and Van Buren did not even try to compete on this score.[16] Hence the antislavery question, while visible and vocal in 1848, had little noticeable impact upon the outcome of the election, which is not to minimize Van Buren's strong third-party popular vote or the eventual importance of this issue.

Amidst the rejoicing that Whigs expressed, the discouraged Polk sat in the White House, gloomily receiving the news of Taylor's victory. There is a strong suspicion, however—recalling, for example, his arguments in behalf of accepting Trist's treaty in early 1848—that the president had anticipated the Whig success; he was a shrewd enough political observer that he could not have been caught off guard by the outcome. He nonetheless deeply regretted Taylor's election, because, in his estimation, the general was "wholly unqualified for the station," being "without political information and without experience in civil life." Moreover, since Taylor had "no opinions or judgment of his own upon any one public subject, foreign or domestic, he will be compelled to rely upon the designing men of the Federal party who will cluster around him." Polk bitterly speculated that his old foe would attempt to reverse "the whole policy of my administration, and to substitute the Federal policy in its stead."[17] The ironic twist that Taylor's victory offered, after all of the confrontations between him and Polk, was not lost on the president. It was a difficult pill to swallow, to be sure; but Polk quickly lost himself in the routines of preparing his annual message, the convening of Congress, as well as personal matters. A professional politician for all of his adult life, Polk knew that the better part of wisdom was to accept the voters' verdict, however distasteful, and go on with the duties and responsibilities of office.

Polk therefore did not concern himself further with the transfer of power until early in 1849. The president caustically noted that Taylor's letter of resignation as major general stipulated that the effective date should be 31 January, an indication that Taylor "seems resolved to hold on to the office as long as possible." No longer a general, Taylor arrived in Washington on 23 February, about a week and a half before Inauguration Day. Three days later, he called upon Polk at the White House; it was a historic occasion for a number of reasons, not the least of which was that these two men, despite their long years of public service and their feuds during the war, had never met and evidently had little concept of what the other one looked like. True to his best ceremonial form, Polk "received Gen'l Taylor with courtesy and cordiality" and then invited him to dinner on 1 March. Afterwards, the president instructed his private secretary, J. Knox Walker, to issue dinner tickets for the proposed Thursday banquet.[18]

The festivities of that evening were elaborate and pleasant. About forty persons assembled at the White House for the gala event. The guest list was most impressive: General Taylor was there, as was his vice-president, Millard Fillmore; they were joined by the defeated candidate, Lewis Cass, by various senators, representatives, and cabinet members, and by editor Ritchie. Vice-President Dallas was unable to attend at the last moment, however, because the Senate was still in session, a fact that did not prevent several senators from partaking of the Thursday-evening dinner. Dallas's wife attended, however, as did Sarah Childress Polk and two of the president's nieces, Virginia Hays and Sarah Polk Rucker. Sarah Polk had the sensitive assignment of being seated between Taylor and Cass at the dinner table; but she no doubt handled this duty with her usual grace and charm. At any rate, Polk praised the evening's activities for its food "finely gotten up in Julian's (the French cook) best style" and for the astonishing fact that "not the slightest allusion was made to any political subject." What is equally remarkable, for a room full of prominent politicians of both parties, everyone "seemed to enjoy themselves."[19] Once again, Polk had demonstrated that he knew how to be a gracious host and a considerate chief executive.

Two days later the president prepared to vacate both the residential and the office sections of the White House. On that Saturday, his cabinet members appeared before him to offer their resignations to Polk, who of course accepted them. In what may be one of the most cogent and illuminating lines in his entire diary, Polk proudly wrote: "I disposed of all the business on my table down to the minutest detail and at the close of the day left a clean table for my successor." While doubtless an accurate statement of what the office actually looked like, it fails of course to take cognizance that Polk was leaving the great unfinished business of slavery in the West for Zachary Taylor to confront. Nevertheless, at sunset on 3 March, Polk looked around the office for the last time, closed the door, and went, with Sarah Polk and the two nieces, to the hotel where they were to stay for the next two days. Afterwards he departed for the Capitol, to be ready to deal with last-minute legislation passed by Congress; both there and at his hotel suite he continued, until about 6:30 in the morning of the fourth, to sign legislation, make appointments, and in other ways complete the duties of his office.[20] A few hours later he went to the First Presbyterian Church for the last time. Near the close of the day, Polk commented once again upon the sense of relief that he felt now that he was surrendering the job of president and also the sense of anticipation of better things for himself. "I am sure I shall be a happier man in my retirement than I have been during the four years I have filled the highest office in the gift of my countrymen."[21] Unfortunately for him, the remaining days of his life were so numbered that he would not be permitted to find much of the happiness that had eluded him for so long.

For the moment, however, there was the happy occasion of the inauguration, although one assumes that Polk would have been more joyful if Cass, rather than Taylor, had been taking the oath of office that day. In any event, on 5 March, Polk rode with Taylor from the hotel to the Capitol, and while in the carriage, some conversation took place about the future of California and Oregon, a topic that was undeniably close to Polk's heart. Taylor reputedly stated the view that both California and Oregon should form independent governments, because they were too distantly located from the rest of the nation. Although alarmed by such comments, Polk, feeling the constraints of the ceremonial occasion, kept a civil tongue. Arrival at the Capitol cut short these embarrassing moments. But a very critical and somewhat arrogant Polk could find nothing to laud about Taylor's Inaugural Address: "He read it in a very low voice and very badly as to his pronunciation and manner." Nevertheless, once the speech had ended and the oath of office had been administered, Polk shook hands with the new president while expressing words of good cheer: "I hope, Sir, the country may be prosperous under your administration." Afterwards the two men rode together down Pennsylvania Avenue to the hotel where Polk was staying; arriving there, Polk took leave of President Taylor and retired to his quarters, though not before he had formed a final distinct and negative impression of the new president: "Gen'l Taylor is, I have no doubt, a well meaning old man. He is, however, uneducated, exceedingly ignorant of public affairs, and, I should judge, of very ordinary capacity. He will be in the hands of others, and must rely wholly upon his Cabinet to administer the Government."[22] Not an altogether fair appraisal, it represents nonetheless what one would have expected of Polk, who had been quarreling with Taylor since the early beginnings of the Mexican War. Although somewhat bitter about being succeeded by Taylor, Polk was also genuinely concerned about the future of the nation and probably would have voiced something of that apprehension regardless of who his successor was.

The primary item on Polk's agenda, however, was his departure from Washington and a return to Tennessee, which he had not visited for four years. Arrangements had already been made for an elaborate journey by boat and train, which would provide ample time and occasion for ceremonial activities all along the way. Polk could have elected to take the shortest route back to Tennessee, but he did not, evidently wanting to savor the final moments of public adulation and respect.

Polk, his wife, their nieces, and several friends left by train on the morning of 6 March, heading south toward home. The trip, initially characterized by ceremonies and festivities, was an enjoyable, even exciting, one; but after the first two weeks, the journey began to take on a nightmarish quality as Polk worried about his personal health and then, in fact, became quite ill. By train the former president and his entourage, on the first day, went through Fredericksburg, Richmond, and Petersburg, making a brief stop at each of them, en route to Wilmington, North Carolina. After arriving there and remaining over-night, the Polk party went by boat to Charleston and thence to Savannah.[23] Departing from the latter city by train, they traveled overland to Macon and eventually to Columbus, the last part of this trek, however, being taken in horse-drawn carriages. After spending a day and night at Columbus, Georgia, the Polk group went by carriage to Opelika, Alabama, where they boarded a train for Montgomery. Upon arriving in the capital city, where they were feted, Polk began to worry about his health and therefore consulted a physician. On Sunday, 18 March he and his traveling companions journeyed by boat down the Alabama River toward Mobile, where they were greeted with ceremo-nies and celebrations. At Mobile, Polk consulted with the famous Dr. Josiah Nott, who gave him medicine to take in case of an attack of cholera.[24] Traveling only by steamboat after departing from Montgom-ery, the Polk party left Mobile for New Orleans, where they arrived on the twenty-first.

From this point on, the trip, which Polk had described as "thus far a triumphal march," began to change in complexion and nature. While in New Orleans, however, he was still able to focus enough upon the festivities so that he enjoyed most of them and, in fact, yielded to pressures from local leaders that he not hasten from their city. Already being squeamish about his health, Polk was subjected to a remarkable breakfast in New Orleans, all the dishes of which "were prepared in the French style of cooking, and to one unaccustomed to it it was difficult to tell of what they were composed." Worried about all the unfamiliar food and wines that were spread out on the tables before him, Polk merely "took a cup of coffee and something on my plate to save appearances, but was careful to eat none of it." Instead, he quietly asked a waiter to bring him some corn bread and broiled ham, and astonishingly enough, the hotel restaurant was able to produce such mundane foods for the former president. Confronted by a "sumptuous and magnificent Din-ner" the next evening, Polk evidently managed to deal with it success-fully, for there is no mention of hurried whispers to waiters for bland victuals.[25] Afterwards, he departed from New Orleans to ascend the Mississippi River.

After a brief visit into Baton Rouge, Polk, who was becoming more and more fearful of cholera, refused to go ashore at any other stops along the river, although he did receive some visitors aboard ship. By the time the boat docked briefly at Vicksburg, the former president was suffering more noticeably from "a derangement of stomach & bowels." While stopped at this port city, Polk learned that Henry Clay had gone up the river and Sam Houston had gone down the river that same afternoon. When Clay's boat had approached Vicksburg, a gun salute had been fired, for it was believed that Polk was also on board. Upon learning of that mistake, Clay remarked, "I hope, gentlemen, I am not stealing Mr. Polk's thunder."[26] This provides the only note of levity appearing in the account of the trip during the last two weeks of the journey. When Polk's boat reached Memphis, Tennessee, he was met by two of his nephews, Samuel P. Walker and Samuel P. Caldwell, both of whom were residents of that city. They, along with others, implored Polk to leave the boat for a visit in town; and he reluctantly agreed to go ashore to touch Tennessee soil for the first time since he had left the state in January 1845.[27]

After departing from Memphis, however, the former president began to suffer greatly: "My bowels were affected and the shaking of the Boat had become inconvenient to me." He therefore summoned a physician to his boat when it landed at Paducah, Kentucky. Assuring Polk that he did not have cholera, the doctor nevertheless agreed to accompany him up river to Smithland, Kentucky, where Polk abandoned ship for the greater comforts of a hotel room. A second medical opinion concurred with the first, but Polk was bedridden in Smithland for four days, his longest stay at any town along his route. His physical and emotional spirits lifted on 31 March, however, when his brother-in-law, Dr. William R. Rucker, arrived at Smithland to retrieve his daughter but also to check on the ailing former president.[28] On the next day, Polk determined to take the boat to Nashville; accompanied by Dr. Rucker, the entourage encountered another of Polk's brothers-in-law, Dr. John B. Hays, a few miles downstream from Nashville. Like Rucker, Hays came aboard to check on his daughter and also to examine Polk. Finally, on 2 April, Polk and his party reached Nashville, where an immense crowd awaited him at the docks. The cheering and friendly faces emboldened Polk enough so that he could participate in brief ceremonies.[29] He was home now, after twenty-eight grueling days of travel, marred by personal illness; and it was good, exceedingly good, to be home. Sovereign now, no longer servant, Polk was anxious to adjust quickly to his new role as a former president, seeking that fugitive happiness to which he sometimes referred.

For the next two and one-half months, Polk visited with family and friends, superintended construction work at Polk Place, his increasingly elegant Nashville home, and arranged his papers and books. With the burdens of the presidency lifted from his shoulders, he seemed to gain a new lease on life, but not for long. The temporary rejuvenation that he experienced was deceiving, for the years had taken such a toll that he was highly susceptible to any disease or illness that frequented his environment. Suddenly, in June, he was stricken for the last time; lingering for several days, he was attended by a group of physicians, but to no avail. Knowing that the end of his days was at hand, Polk sought formal admission into the Christian church, through the mode of baptism, a rite that was performed by the Rev. John B. McFerrin of the McKendree Methodist Church. Ironically, Polk's mother had arrived from Columbia with her minister in the hope of persuading her son to accept baptism and admission into the Presbyterian church.[30] But Polk, on his deathbed, elected to affiliate with the group that he had long admired, albeit from a distance. With that accomplished, the former president sank to the edge of death and then yielded to the final search for happiness on 15 June.

It was over—first the presidency, three months earlier, and now life itself. Maligned, misunderstood, and burdened with incredible duties and responsibilities, Polk nevertheless had stayed on course as an expansionist, a low-tariff man, and a reformer of the banking system. His achievements, great as they were, suffered, however, from the taint of the war with Mexico—and continue to suffer from that tarnishing remembrance. The territorial accomplishments also unleashed the slavery controversy, a dispute that eventually would rend the garments of Unionism. Polk, in the judgment of many persons both then and now, shares in that tragedy in a very direct way. To be sure, he did not comprehend how expansionism, a great unifying force for the nation, as he saw it, could tear it apart. Despite his faults and liabilities as president, however, the record shows that he was a highly effective chief executive, if not a dynamic leader. Denied the gift of personal popularity, Polk nonetheless achieved remarkable things in spite of this unfortunate deprivation. Nevertheless, greatness, like beauty, is in the eye of the beholder; and many observers have thus far refrained from bestowing the encomium of greatness upon this eleventh president.

Let it be noted, however, that Polk's passing from the presidency and from life itself brought an end to an important chapter in American life. The decade of the 1840s, for example, had been noted for the maturation of the national two-party system. Whigs and Democrats had competed for the presidency with startling fervor and dedication and with virtual equality or parity, though disturbing signs were already apparent in the election of 1848. The fragmentation of the two-party system occurred quickly, so that shortly after the 1852 presidential election, the national Whig party disappeared, to be replaced by the Republican party and the American party. Although Polk's Democratic party endured throughout the 1850s, it was beset with strife and conflict, which culminated eventually in the dramatic split in 1860. The questions that brought about the collapse of the traditional two-party system during the 1850s were not the old arguments over economic policies; instead, they were the new quarrels over slavery and the West.

The economic issues that Congress and the presidency had fought over early in the 1840s—the national bank and the tariff—were resolved by the Polk administration. With the passage of the Independent Treasury, for instance, the matter of the banking system in relationship to the federal government was settled, not to be disturbed again until the Civil War years. The Polk presidency also offered a new tariff in 1846, one that substantially modified the tariff that had been enacted by the previous Whig administration and one that endured almost to the eve of the Civil War. On the hoary question of whether internal improvements should be underwitten by the federal government, Polk proved to be a formidable opponent, as he succeeded in blocking such measures. In sum, the Polk administration took care of the traditional economic issues, thereby eliminating them from the agenda of the 1850s.

Virtually everyone remembers Polk and his expansionist successes. He produced a new map of the United States, which fulfilled a continent-wide vision that dated back at least to the days of a young secretary of state named John Quincy Adams. There would be no significant territorial acquisitions after the Polk years, however, until a half-century later, when the nation ventured beyond the continent to fulfill new imperial aspirations.

The waves of nationalism, which were so evident in the Jackson years and in the Polk years, concealed a dangerous undertow of sectionalism. After Polk's departure, the territorial expansionism that he had promoted gave a new surge to sectionalism. Indeed, this situation was becoming increasingly apparent during his presidency, but it became pronounced and menacing in the 1850s. The antislavery reformers of the 1830s and 1840s, for example, turned their attention to slavery in the West after expansionism had opened up that region. Their activities, which were linked with those of northern political leaders, stirred vehement reactions from the South. The clashing rhetoric and tactics on both sides produced treacherous tides of sectional division that engulfed national unity.

Fortunately for Polk, death spared him from the transformations of the 1850s. He would not have understood them, and he would not have approved of them. Paradoxically, his presidency pointed the nation to a challenging future, but Polk himself belonged to an earlier period. Indeed, one senses that he was continually looking backward to an almost idyllic Old Mecklenburg. He was, in truth, a symbol for an age. But it was an age that seemed to vanish once the decade of the 1850s had begun.

NOTES

Preface

1. I am relying here and elsewhere in my Preface upon the observations made by Charles A. McCoy in his book *Polk and the Presidency* (Austin: University of Texas Press, 1960), chaps. 1 and 8; see also Norman A. Graebner, "James Polk," in *America's Ten Greatest Presidents,* ed. Morton Borden (Chicago: Rand McNally & Co., 1961), p. 115. In his provocative new study, Robert H. Wiebe observes in passing that presidential authority during the nineteenth century had been seriously eroded and that Polk's forceful leadership represented a fluke of personality (*The Opening of American Society: From the Adoption of the Constitution to the Eve of Disunion* [New York: Alfred A. Knopf, 1984], p. 250).

2. Robert W. Johannsen, *To the Halls of the Montezumas: The Mexican War in the American Imagination* (New York: Oxford University Press, 1985), p. 15.

3. Graebner, "James Polk," p. 134.

4. Ibid., pp. 116–18, 122.

Chapter 1
The Emergence of Polk

1. See Glyndon Van Deusen, *The Jacksonian Era, 1828–1848* (New York: Harper & Row, 1959), chap. 1. The famous French visitor Alexis de Tocqueville called Americans a "restless people."

2. The statistics in this and the ensuing paragraphs are gleaned from *Statistical History of the United States from Colonial Times to the Present* (Stamford, Conn., 1965).

3. The prepresidential biographical summary is based upon Charles G. Sellers, *James K. Polk: Jacksonian, 1795–1843* (Princeton, N.J.: Princeton University Press, 1957); see also the account in Frank B. Williams, Jr., *Tennessee's Presidents* (Knoxville: University of Tennessee Press, 1981).

4. Sellers, *James K. Polk: Jacksonian*, p. 92.

5. It has been widely reported that Polk underwent an operation for gallstones at the hands of surgeon Dr. Ephraim McDowell in about 1812. But a recent article builds a persuasive argument against the notion of gallstone surgery and in support of surgery for urinary bladder stones. Moreover, the author, Dr. Robert W. Ikard, speculates that Polk's surgery may have left him impotent (''Surgical Operation on James K. Polk by Ephraim McDowell or the Search for Polk's Gallstone,'' *Tennessee Historical Quarterly* 43 [1984]: 121–31). There is no proof of this claim; the only plausible allegation, it seems to me, is that perhaps the surgery rendered Polk sterile.

6. For a discussion and analysis of Polk's three gubernatorial campaigns see Sellers, *James K. Polk: Jacksonian*, chaps. 11, 13, and 14; and also Paul H. Bergeron, *Antebellum Politics in Tennessee* (Lexington: University Press of Kentucky, 1982), chaps. 3 and 4.

7. Sellers, *James K. Polk: Jacksonian*, p. 440.

8. My recounting of the struggle over the party nominations, the campaign, and the election relies heavily and principally upon Charles G. Sellers, *James K. Polk: Continentalist, 1843–1846* (Princeton, N.J.: Princeton University Press, 1966), chaps. 1–4; Sellers, ''Election of 1844,'' in *History of American Presidential Elections, 1789–1968*, ed. Arthur M. Schlesinger, Jr., 4 vols. (New York: Chelsea House, 1971), 1:747–861; and Eugene I. McCormac, *James K. Polk: A Political Biography* (Berkeley: University of California Press, 1922), chaps. 12 and 13. I have also borrowed from William J. Cooper, Jr., *The South and the Politics of Slavery, 1828–1856* (Baton Rouge: Louisiana State University Press, 1978), pp. 189–219.

9. Exerting a positive impact upon Polk's chances in New York was the fact that Silas Wright carried that state in the gubernatorial election that immediately preceded the presidential one. Reluctantly abandoning his seat in the United States Senate, Wright yielded to intense pressure from New York Democrats to seek the governor's chair. With regard to the fifteen states that went for Polk, it should be noted that he did not win either a majority or a plurality of the popular vote in South Carolina, for it did not permit the popular selection of electors. Instead, the legislature chose the presidential electors.

10. The boisterous campaign of 1840 had persuaded 2.4 million voters to participate, a figure that represented slightly over 80 percent of the eligible voters. The quieter campaign in 1844 attracted an impressive 2.7 million voters, or about 79 percent of the nation's eligible voters.

CHAPTER 2
THE PRESIDENT'S MEN: THE CABINET

1. Polk to Johnson, 21 Dec. 1844, as quoted by Eugene I. McCormac in *James K. Polk: A Political Biography* (Berkeley: University of California Press, 1922), p. 287, and by Charles G. Sellers in *James K. Polk: Continentalist, 1843–1846* (Princeton, N.J.: Princeton University Press, 1966), pp. 164–65.

2. My account of the selection of the cabinet is heavily dependent upon the version found in McCormac, *James K. Polk*, pp. 284–99, and in Sellers, *James K. Polk, Continentalist*, pp. 162ff.

3. See, especially, Sellers, *James K. Polk: Continentalist*, pp. 165–66, 180–81; McCormac, *James K. Polk*, pp. 287–90.

4. McCormac, *James K. Polk*, pp. 292–94; Sellers, *James K. Polk: Continentalist*, pp. 194–95.

5. Philip S. Klein, *President James Buchanan: A Biography* (University Park: Pennsylvania State University Press, 1962), p. 163; John M. Belohlavek, *George Mifflin Dallas: Jacksonian Patrician* (University Park: Pennsylvania State University Press, 1977), pp. 100–101; Norman A. Graebner, "James K. Polk: A Study in Federal Patronage," *Mississippi Valley Historical Review* 38 (1951/52): 617–18; Sellers, *James K. Polk: Continentalist*, pp. 193–94.

6. McCormac, *James K. Polk*, p. 291; Sellers, *James K. Polk: Continentalist*, p. 178; Henry Barrett Learned, "The Sequence of Appointments to Polk's Original Cabinet: A Study in Chronology, 1844–1845," *American Historical Review* 30 (1924/25): 78; Donald B. Cole, *Martin Van Buren and the American Political System* (Princeton, N.J.: Princeton University Press, 1984), p. 400; John Niven, *Martin Van Buren: The Romantic Age of American Politics* (New York: Oxford University Press, 1983), pp. 549–50.

7. Sellers, *James K. Polk: Continentalist*, pp. 179–80, 184–86; Cole, *Martin Van Buren*, p. 400; Niven, *Martin Van Buren*, pp. 550–51, 553–54.

8. Sellers, *James K. Polk: Continentalist*, pp. 196, 198–200; McCormac, *James K. Polk*, pp. 291–92, 294–96, 298; Niven, *Martin Van Buren*, pp. 555, 559; Cole, *Martin Van Buren*, p. 402.

9. Ivor D. Spencer, *The Victor and the Spoils: A Life of William L. Marcy* (Providence, R.I.: Brown University Press, 1959), pp. 130–31, 133–35; Charles A. McCoy, *Polk and the Presidency* (Austin: University of Texas Press, 1960), pp. 61–62; Sellers, *James K. Polk: Continentalist*, pp. 176–77, 197–98, 200–201, 204; Learned, "Sequence of Appointments," pp. 79–81; Niven, *Martin Van Buren*, pp. 553, 555, 558, 560–61. Niven concludes that Polk probably preferred Marcy over Butler, because Marcy was safer on the Texas question and was less under the influence of Van Buren (see ibid., p. 562).

10. James P. Shenton, *Robert John Walker: A Politician from Jackson to Lincoln* (New York: Columbia University Press, 1961), pp. 58–59, 60–62, 66–67; Belohlavek, *George Mifflin Dallas*, pp. 100–102; Graebner, "James K. Polk," p. 618; Learned, "Sequence of Appointments," pp. 78–79; Sellers, *James K. Polk: Continentalist*, pp. 195–96, 203.

11. McCormac, *James K. Polk*, p. 298; Sellers, *James K. Polk: Continentalist*, pp. 196, 203; Learned, "Sequence of Appointments," p. 82. A year later, Polk explained that he had chosen Mason because "he was my College associate and personal friend" (see James K. Polk, *The Diary of James K. Polk during His Presidency, 1845 to 1849*, ed. Milo M. Quaife, 4 vols. [Chicago: A. C. McClurg & Co., 1910], 1:370).

12. Russel B. Nye, *George Bancroft: Brahmin Rebel* (New York: Alfred A. Knopf, 1944), pp. 134-35; M. A. DeWolfe Howe, *The Life and Letters of George Bancroft*, 2 vols. (New York: Charles Scribner's Sons, 1908), 1:262-63; Bancroft to Polk, 4 Mar. 1845, James K. Polk Papers, Library of Congress.

13. Dorothy Ganfield Fowler, *The Cabinet Politician: The Postmasters General, 1829-1909* (New York: Columbia University Press, 1943), pp. 58-60; Clement L. Grant, "The Public Career of Cave Johnson" (Ph.D. diss., Vanderbilt University, 1951), pp. 194, 196; Sellers, *James K. Polk: Continentalist*, pp. 183-84, 195.

14. Brian G. J. Walton, "James K. Polk and the Democratic Party in the Aftermath of the Wilmot Proviso" (Ph.D. diss., Vanderbilt University, 1968), pp. 158-59. Donald B. Cole concludes that in selecting his cabinet, Polk played "a careful, clever game, but in the end his decision to ignore Van Buren split the party" (see *Martin Van Buren*, p. 404).

15. Polk, *Diary*, 2:60-61, 62, 65, 66, 121-23, 125, 143; Nye, *George Bancroft*, p. 159. It should be noted that two other names were mentioned as possible appointees to the English post before Bancroft was selected. Robert J. Walker, secretary of the Treasury, expressed an interest to Buchanan, which was conveyed to Polk (on 27 May 1846), who was favorably disposed; then, on 10 July, Polk conferred with both Marcy and Senator Dix about naming the latter to the English post (see *Diary*, 1:432, 2:19).

16. Polk, *Diary*, 2:102, 138, 159-60, 167, 191, 193; Philip Greely Clifford, *Nathan Clifford, Democrat (1803-1881)* (New York: G. P. Putnam's Sons, 1922), pp. 139, 143, 149.

17. Polk, *Diary*, 2:274-75; McCoy, *Polk and the Presidency*, p. 65. Ten days after the Clifford-Polk interview, Clifford wrote to his wife: "I have had many anxious hours but begin to feel more at home." That day the Senate had unanimously confirmed Clifford's nomination, a fact that doubtless cheered him (see Clifford, *Nathan Clifford*, p. 151).

18. Polk, *Diary*, 3:372-73, 375, 378-85, 389-93; McCormac, *James K. Polk*, p. 548.

19. Polk, *Diary*, 3:431, 468; Polk to Vroom, 30 May 1848 (incorrectly classified by Library of Congress as 25 May letter), Polk Papers. It is worth noting that Toucey had paid a special visit to Polk on 20 May 1848, at which time Toucey shrewdly expressed his preference that Polk should seek a second term as president (see Polk, *Diary*, 3:455).

20. Vroom to Polk, 5 June 1848; Polk to Toucey, June 8, 1848; and Toucey to Polk, 12 June 1848—all in Polk Papers; Polk, *Diary*, 3:491.

21. Polk, *Diary*, 3:333, 353-55, 359-60; Klein, *President James Buchanan*, p. 190.

22. Polk, *Diary*, 2:399–405, 4:210–11.

23. Walton, "James K. Polk and the Party," pp. 137–40, 143; McCoy, *Polk and the Presidency*, pp. 63–64.

24. Walton, "James K. Polk and the Party," pp. 160–61, 163.

25. Ibid., p. 166; McCoy, *Polk and the Presidency*, pp. 62–63; Shenton, *Robert John Walker*, p. 92; Polk, *Diary*, 2:166–67, 171, 174, 179, 186, 191, 192, 194–95, 3:18, 95–96, 131, 139, 142, 143. Polk, increasingly worried over developments regarding Mexico, called Buchanan to return from his vacation in the summer of 1845 (see Klein, *President James Buchanan*, p. 184).

26. See table 16 in Walton, "James K. Polk and the Party," pp. 168–69. Walton has counted 364 cabinet meetings, whereas Learned has found a total of 392 meetings reported in the president's diary (see Henry Barrett Learned, "Cabinet Meetings under President Polk," *Annual Report of the American Historical Association for the Year 1914*, vol. 1, p. 236). Apparently not until the Lincoln-Johnson years did a cabinet convene more often than did Polk's cabinet (see ibid., p. 232). Leonard D. White seems to be completely off target in his observations that "attendance of department heads was irregular" at the cabinet meetings and that little business was transacted at some of the cabinet sessions. The latter claim allows room for debate, except that White seems to place emphasis upon those very rare meetings of the cabinet when Polk recorded little about them (see *The Jacksonians: A Study in Administrative History, 1829–1861* [New York: Macmillan Co., 1954], p. 93).

27. Walton, "James K. Polk and the Party," pp. 167, 170, 172, and table 17, on p. 171.

28. Ibid., pp. 173, 175, 177–78, and table 18, on p. 174.

29. Ibid., pp. 182, 184–86, 187, and table 20, on pp. 179–80.

30. Ibid., pp. 188, 191, 198, 200, 202, 203, 207, and table 22, on p. 189, tables 23–27, on pp. 192–96, table 28, on p. 197; Klein, *President James Buchanan*, pp. 179, 181, 189, 190, 192; see also Shenton, *Robert John Walker*, pp. 103–4.

31. Polk, *Diary*, 1:48–49, 73, 85, 124; McCoy, *Polk and the Presidency*, p. 75; Sellers, *James K. Polk: Continentalist*, pp. 328–29. For a reference to Marcy's report in 1845 see Spencer, *Victor and the Spoils*, p. 145.

32. Polk, *Diary*, 1:48, 73, 84–85, 96, 101–2, 123–24; McCormac, *James K. Polk*, pp. 665–66; Sellers, *James K. Polk: Continentalist*, pp. 325–28. This December rumor was reminiscent of one a few months earlier, which had alleged that Walker had authored Polk's famous tariff letter to Kane in the presidential campaign (see Shenton, *Robert John Walker*, p. 53).

33. Polk, *Diary*, 1:73, 85, 89, 95–96, 99–100, 102. Polk's annual message was his "principal instrument of legislative initiative" and was therefore worthy of elaborate attention and energy (see Sellers, *James K. Polk: Continentalist*, p. 325).

34. Polk, *Diary*, 2:209–10, 253–54, 259–60, 265–66. Under apparent pressure to get the annual message off to Congress, Polk convened the cabinet for its regular meeting on 5 December and then for a special meeting on Sunday, 6 December for the purpose of making a final review of the document. Budget requests, especially those by the Navy and War departments, received a full

hearing from the cabinet on 7 November. The extraordinarily high estimates that were offered by Secretary Marcy elicited considerable debate and comment, particularly from Secretary Buchanan (see Polk, *Diary*, 2:219–21; and Spencer, *Victor and the Spoils*, pp. 159–60).

35. Polk, *Diary*, 3:178–79, 212–13, 215–16, 218–19, 221–22, 229, 231–32, 241–42.

36. Ibid., pp. 216–17, 220, 225–27, 228–30, 232–33, 234–35, 238–39.

37. Ibid., 4:165–66, 174–76, 180–81, 189–91, 195–96. These transactions present an excellent example of Polk's acting as a director of the budget (see McCoy, *Polk and the Presidency*, p. 74).

38. Polk, *Diary*, 4:182–83, 197–98, 201–3, 204–5, 206–9, 210, 212–14, 216–18, 222; see Learned, "Cabinet Meetings," p. 238.

39. McCoy, *Polk and the Presidency*, p. 140; Polk, *Diary*, 3:24.

40. Polk, *Diary*, 3:97–99. McCoy interprets, as one of Polk's purposes in this incident, the desire to humiliate "the haughty Buchanan in front of the other Cabinet members" and thereby remind them "that Polk was the master" (see *Polk and the Presidency*, pp. 72–73).

41. Polk, *Diary*, 4:116, 120, 130–31; McCoy, *Polk and the Presidency*, pp. 69, 70.

42. With regard to Cave Johnson's social contact with the president, Fowler exaggerates, while Grant seems to underestimate it (see Fowler, *Cabinet Politician*, pp. 60–61, and Grant, "Public Career of Cave Johnson," p. 243).

43. Polk, *Diary*, 1:164, 2:455. It is very important to note that beginning in late 1847 and continuing until the end of the Polk administration, Secretary Buchanan hosted numerous private dinners but apparently never invited the president (see Klein, *President James Buchanan*, pp. 203–4). In his diary, Polk made reference to a Buchanan party of 23 January 1846; oddly, it occurred on the same night that the president himself hosted a party for the number of congressmen. It is not clear whether or not Polk was invited; Polk reported that his private secretary and nephew J. Knox Walker attended but that Mrs. Polk declined to attend. The next morning, Walker gave Polk a report on the gossip at the Buchanan party (see Polk, *Diary*, 1:189).

44. Polk, *Diary*, 1:349–50, 2:84.

45. Ibid., 1:96, 3:222, 178.

46. Actually, Buchanan suffered from a nervous tic in his leg and a polyp in his nose, the latter requiring surgery. Strangely enough, Polk never mentioned any ailments experienced by his secretary of state and consequently never visited him. From Buchanan's own letters, it is apparent that he was physically exhausted from his labors during the Polk administration (see Klein, *President James Buchanan*, pp. 192–93).

47. Examples of Polk's visitations to his cabinet members are readily available in the *Diary*, passim. For a reference to Marcy's illness in August 1847 see Spencer, *Victor and the Spoils*, p. 166.

48. Polk, *Diary*, 4:349–51, 354–55. One should be reminded that when Polk and Taylor met on 26 February 1849, it was the first time they had ever done so.

CHAPTER 3
PRELUDE TO EXPANSIONISM: TEXAS

1. Thomas R. Hietala, *Manifest Design: Anxious Aggrandizement in Late Jacksonian America* (Ithaca, N.Y.: Cornell University Press, 1985), p. 54.

2. Ibid., pp. 26–32, 35; David M. Pletcher, *The Diplomacy of Annexation: Texas, Oregon, and the Mexican War* (Columbia: University of Missouri Press, 1973), pp. 120–21, 140; Frederick Merk, *Slavery and the Annexation of Texas* (New York: Alfred A. Knopf, 1972), pp. 9–10.

3. Hietala, *Manifest Design*, pp. 66–69; Pletcher, *Diplomacy*, pp. 114, 140.

4. Merk, *Slavery*, pp. 12–16, 162–63, 19, 24, 26–27, 33–43; Hietala, *Manifest Design*, pp. 16–20, 22–24, 44–45; Pletcher, *Diplomacy*, pp. 119, 121, 123, 129, 133, 135.

5. Hietala, *Manifest Design*, pp. 37–38, 40; Merk, *Slavery*, pp. 44–82; Pletcher, *Diplomacy*, pp. 135–36, 142–45, 147–49.

6. Pletcher, *Diplomacy*, pp. 180, 177; Frederick Merk, *The Monroe Doctrine and American Expansionism, 1843–1849* (New York: Alfred A. Knopf, 1966), p. 30.

7. Pletcher, *Diplomacy*, pp. 177, 186–89, 207.

8. Ibid., pp. 178, 179; Merk, *Slavery*, pp. 121–26, 138–39; Charles G. Sellers, *James K. Polk: Continentalist, 1843–1846* (Princeton, N.J.: Princeton University Press, 1966), p. 168; Eugene I. McCormac, *James K. Polk: A Political Biography* (Berkeley: University of California Press, 1922), p. 310.

9. Sellers, *James K. Polk: Continentalist*, pp. 172–73; Pletcher, *Diplomacy*, pp. 180–81; Merk, *Slavery*, pp. 152–53. Milton Brown, the framer of the successful House resolution, later asserted that neither he nor a number of other supporters would ever have endorsed the proposal had they been aware at the time that the United States would subsequently make a claim for the disputed region in Texas between the Nueces and the Rio Grande (see Merk, *Monroe Doctrine*, p. 142 n).

10. Sellers, *James K. Polk: Continentalist*, pp. 186–88, 171, 189, 205–6, 208; Pletcher, *Diplomacy*, pp. 181, 182; Merk, *Slavery*, pp. 154–60.

11. Sellers, *James K. Polk: Continentalist*, pp. 208, 215–16; Pletcher, *Diplomacy*, p. 183.

12. James K. Polk, *The Diary of James K. Polk during His Presidency, 1845 to 1849*, ed. Milo M. Quaife, 4 vols. (Chicago: A. C. McClurg & Co., 1910), 4:38–47, 49, 51–52; Sellers, *James K. Polk: Continentalist*, p. 219; Hietala, *Manifest Design*, p. 220.

13. Sellers, *James K. Polk: Continentalist*, pp. 205, 206, 207, 215, 216, 218–19, 220; McCormac, *James K. Polk*, pp. 314–15, 316–17; Pletcher, *Diplomacy*, pp. 182–83.

14. Sellers, *James K. Polk: Continentalist*, pp. 217, 220–21; Pletcher, *Diplomacy*, p. 184.

15. Polk to Donelson, 7 Mar. 1845, in McCormac, *James K. Polk*, p. 353; Sellers, *James K. Polk: Continentalist*, pp. 221, 218; Pletcher, *Diplomacy*, p. 191.

16. Sellers, *James K. Polk: Continentalist*, pp. 221–23; Pletcher, *Diplomacy*, pp. 194, 196; Merk, *Monroe Doctrine*, p. 35.

17. Bancroft to Stockton, 22 Apr. 1845, in Glenn W. Price, *Origins of the War with Mexico: The Polk-Stockton Intrigue* (Austin: University of Texas Press, 1967), pp. 48, 77.

18. Ibid., pp. 110, 112, 122–23, 125–26, 149; Sellers, *James K. Polk: Continentalist*, pp. 224, 225–26; Pletcher, *Diplomacy*, pp. 197, 198, 199, 200, 269; Merk, *Monroe Doctrine*, p. 151.

19. Pletcher, *Diplomacy*, pp. 192, 194, 195; McCormac, *James K. Polk*, pp. 356, 357; Sellers, *James K. Polk: Continentalist*, p. 225.

20. Pletcher, *Diplomacy*, pp. 185, 190–93, 195, 196, 201; McCormac, *James K. Polk*, p. 360; Merk, *Monroe Doctrine*, pp. 33–34.

21. Sellers, *James K. Polk: Continentalist*, pp. 230, 231, 259; Pletcher, *Diplomacy*, pp. 202–3, 254, 258–59, 274. One of the first acts of the Polk administration in regard to relations with Mexico was to recall Wilson Shannon, the United States minister in Mexico City; in effect he was replaced by secret agent Parrott.

22. McCormac, *James K. Polk*, pp. 358–59, 361; Sellers, *James K. Polk: Continentalist*, p. 226; Pletcher, *Diplomacy*, pp. 196–97.

23. McCormac, *James K. Polk*, p. 362; Pletcher, *Diplomacy*, pp. 254–55; Sellers, *James K. Polk: Continentalist*, p. 227.

24. Sellers, *James K. Polk: Continentalist*, pp. 227–30; Pletcher, *Diplomacy*, pp. 255–56; McCormac, *James K. Polk*, pp. 366–67.

25. Sellers, *James K. Polk: Continentalist*, pp. 260–62; Pletcher, *Diplomacy*, pp. 259–61, 270, 271, 273.

26. McCormac, *James K. Polk*, pp. 363, 371–72; Pletcher, *Diplomacy*, pp. 200–201; Sellers, *James K. Polk: Continentalist*, pp. 226–27, 229.

27. Pletcher, *Diplomacy*, pp. 204, 205.

CHAPTER 4
POLK AND THE WINNING OF THE SOUTHWEST

1. See such studies as Albert K. Weinberg, *Manifest Destiny: A Study of Nationalist Expansionism in American History* (Baltimore, Md.: Johns Hopkins Press, 1935); Frederick Merk, *Manifest Destiny and Mission in American History: A Reinterpretation* (New York: Alfred A. Knopf, 1963), chap. 2; and Norman A. Graebner, ed., *Manifest Destiny* (Indianapolis, Ind.: Bobbs-Merrill, 1968). Merk argues that Manifest Destiny was not a true reflection of American ideals and sentiments. Instead, a more accurate expression would be *mission*, a loftier set of principles that sought to restrict aggressive expansionism.

2. Graebner, *Manifest Destiny*, p. lxviii; Merk, *Manifest Destiny*, pp. 35–39, 50–51; see also the observations about the penny press that are made by Robert W. Johannsen in *To the Halls of the Montezumas: The Mexican War in the American Imagination* (New York: Oxford University Press, 1985), pp. 16ff.

3. Norman A. Graebner, *Empire on the Pacific: A Study in American Continental Expansion* (New York: Ronald Press Co., 1955).

4. Thomas R. Hietala, *Manifest Design: Anxious Aggrandizement in Late Jacksonian America* (Ithaca, N.Y.: Cornell University Press, 1985), pp. 71–73, 83–84, 86, 88–89, 93.

5. Ibid., pp. 96–97, 104, 108, 109, 111, 113, 116.

6. Ibid., chap. 5, especially pp. 137, 158, 164, 170.

7. Cf. Graebner, *Manifest Destiny*, pp. xix–xxi; Hietala, *Manifest Design*, pp. 173, 177, 185, 191, 193–94, 196, 261; and Johannsen, *To the Halls of the Montezumas*, chap. 10. Hietala employs the label "exceptionalism."

8. In his study of expansionism during the 1840s, Hietala argues that there was a deliberate strategy on the part of Democratic leaders, including President Polk, to force territorial aggrandizement. In essence, there was a "manifest design" (see *Manifest Design*, passim).

9. Philip S. Klein, *President James Buchanan: A Biography* (University Park: Pennsylvania State University Press, 1962), pp. 183–84; Charles A. McCoy, *Polk and the Presidency* (Austin: University of Texas Press, 1960), p. 95; David M. Pletcher, *The Diplomacy of Annexation: Texas, Oregon, and the Mexican War* (Columbia: University of Missouri Press, 1973), pp. 275–76; Eugene I. McCormac, *James K. Polk: A Political Biography* (Berkeley: University of California Press, 1922), pp. 383–84.

10. James K. Polk, *The Diary of James K. Polk during His Presidency, 1845 to 1849*, ed. Milo M. Quaife, 4 vols. (Chicago: A. C. McClurg & Co., 1910), 1:33–36; Charles G. Sellers, *James K. Polk: Continentalist, 1843–1846* (Princeton, N.J.: Princeton University Press, 1966), pp. 263–64, 266; Pletcher, *Diplomacy*, pp. 276–77; McCormac, *James K. Polk*, pp. 384–85.

11. Polk, *Diary*, 1:91–94; Pletcher, *Diplomacy*, pp. 287, 289–90; McCormac, *James K. Polk*, pp. 389–92.

12. Pletcher, *Diplomacy*, pp. 352–56, 359, 361; McCormac, *James K. Polk*, pp. 394–95.

13. Pletcher, *Diplomacy*, pp. 361, 364–65; McCormac, *James K. Polk*, pp. 395–96.

14. Polk, *Diary*, 1:227–30, 233–34, 238; Pletcher, *Diplomacy*, pp. 366–68; Klein, *President James Buchanan*, p. 186; McCormac, *James K. Polk*, pp. 396–400.

15. Polk, *Diary*, 1:282, 287; Pletcher, *Diplomacy*, pp. 368–69, 371; McCormac, *James K. Polk*, p. 401.

16. Polk, *Diary*, 1:319, 322; Pletcher, *Diplomacy*, p. 379; McCormac, *James K. Polk*, pp. 403–5.

17. Sellers, *James K. Polk: Continentalist*, p. 231.

18. Pletcher, *Diplomacy*, pp. 280–83, 421, 286; Frederick Merk, *The Monroe Doctrine and American Expansionism, 1843–1849* (New York: Alfred A. Knopf, 1966), pp. 111–12.

19. Pletcher, *Diplomacy*, pp. 284–85, 291, 429–30.

20. McCormac, *James K. Polk*, pp. 423–27; Pletcher, *Diplomacy*, pp. 426–27, 430–33; Merk, *Monroe Doctrine*, pp. 118, 131.

21. Pletcher, *Diplomacy*, pp. 433–37; Otis A. Singletary, *The Mexican War* (Chicago: University of Chicago Press, 1960), pp. 64–66.

22. For a brief summary of developments—e.g., revolt by Californians, Kearny's arrival in California and his actions, and American victories in January 1847—see Singletary, *Mexican War*, pp. 66–69.

23. Pletcher, *Diplomacy*, pp. 364, 373–75; McCormac, *James K. Polk*, pp. 409–11.

24. Polk, *Diary*, 1:305–17; Pletcher, *Diplomacy*, pp. 378–80; McCormac, *James K. Polk*, pp. 402–3.

25. Polk, *Diary*, 1:319, 322, 325–28, 337–38, 354.

26. Ibid., pp. 354, 363, 382, 384–85; McCormac, *James K. Polk*, pp. 405–7; Pletcher, *Diplomacy*, pp. 380–83.

27. Polk, *Diary*, 1:386–90; Pletcher, *Diplomacy*, pp. 376–77, 384–85.

28. Polk, *Diary*, 1:390–95; Pletcher, *Diplomacy*, pp. 386–89; John H. Schroeder, *Mr. Polk's War: American Opposition and Dissent, 1846–1848* (Madison: University of Wisconsin Press, 1973), pp. 16–18, 23–24; McCormac, *James K. Polk*, pp. 415–16.

29. Pletcher, *Diplomacy*, pp. 390–91; Johannsen, *To the Halls of the Montezumas*, p. 8; Schroeder, *Mr. Polk's War*, pp. 33–34.

30. Quoted in Pletcher, *Diplomacy*, p. 456.

31. Polk, *Diary*, 1:395–96, 400–401, 413–18; Ivor D. Spencer, *The Victor and the Spoils: A Life of William L. Marcy* (Providence, R.I.: Brown University Press, 1959), pp. 153, 155–56; Pletcher, *Diplomacy*, pp. 396–99; McCormac, *James K. Polk*, pp. 418–19.

32. Polk, *Diary*, 1:419–21, 424; McCormac, *James K. Polk*, pp. 419–20.

33. Polk, *Diary*, 1:425–26, 428.

34. Ibid., pp. 400–401, 403–4; Johannsen, *To the Halls of the Montezumas*, pp. 30, 39–41. Much enthusiasm greeted the call for volunteers as young men throughout the nation rushed to sign up for military duty (see Johannsen, pp. 25–28). Johannsen also notes another advantage of relying upon volunteers: "It was a civilian war from the outset, clothed with all the romance of a conflict that touched the popular imagination" (ibid., p. 25).

35. Polk, *Diary*, 1:403–4, 407–8.

36. Ibid., pp. 437–40, 443–44, 450–51, 473; Pletcher, *Diplomacy*, p. 422; McCormac, *James K. Polk*, pp. 421–22.

37. Pletcher, *Diplomacy*, pp. 398, 400, 422, 461.

38. Polk, *Diary*, 1:408–11; McCormac, *James K. Polk*, p. 421.

39. Polk, *Diary*, 1:396–400; McCormac, *James K. Polk*, pp. 416–18; Pletcher, *Diplomacy*, pp. 397–98.

40. Pletcher, *Diplomacy*, pp. 397–98, 527; McCormac, *James K. Polk*, p. 423; Polk, *Diary*, 1:495–97.

41. Pletcher, *Diplomacy*, pp. 445–46; Polk, *Diary*, 3:290–92; Anna Kasten Nelson, "The Secret Diplomacy of James K. Polk during the Mexican War, 1846–1847" (Ph.D. diss., George Washington University, 1972), pp. 50, 56–76.

For information about the visit of William Linn Brown to Havana prior to Mackenzie's trip see Nelson, "Secret Diplomacy," pp. 46–48.

42. Polk, *Diary*, 2:50–51; Pletcher, *Diplomacy*, pp. 448, 461–63.

43. Polk, *Diary*, 2:144–51, 154, 156–58; Pletcher, *Diplomacy*, p. 467; McCormac, *James K. Polk*, pp. 446–47. In September 1846 the United States rejected a British offer to mediate the grievances between Mexico and the United States (see Pletcher, *Diplomacy*, p. 453).

44. Polk, *Diary*, 2:56–60, 66, 70, 76–77; James D. Richardson, comp., *A Compilation of the Messages and Papers of the Presidents, 1789–1902*, 10 vols. (Washington, D.C.: Bureau of National Literature and Art, 1903), 4:456 (hereafter cited as *Messages of the Presidents*); Schroeder, *Mr. Polk's War*, pp. 43–44.

45. Polk, *Diary*, 2:70–73, 75–76; Schroeder, *Mr. Polk's War*, pp. 45–47.

46. Polk, *Diary*, 2:77–78.

47. Schroeder, *Mr. Polk's War*, pp. 53–54, 73–75, 78, 82, 87, 145, 150, 153–55.

48. Ibid., p. 132; Ernest McPherson Lander, Jr., *Reluctant Imperialists: Calhoun, the South Carolinians, and the Mexican War* (Baton Rouge: Louisiana State University Press, 1980), pp. 77, 79.

49. Polk, *Diary*, 2:160–61; Lander, *Reluctant Imperialists*, pp. 59, 61–63.

50. Polk, *Diary*, 2:282–84, 292–93; Lander, *Reluctant Imperialists*, pp. 62–65.

51. Polk, *Diary*, 2:371–72, 457–59; Lander, *Reluctant Imperialists*, pp. 65–69, 71–72; Schroeder, *Mr. Polk's War*, pp. 68–69. Hietala argues that as Calhoun's racism increased, his support of imperialism waned. Calhoun wanted only the territory that whites could occupy and dominate (see *Manifest Design*, p. 118).

52. Lander, *Reluctant Imperialists*, pp. 158–60, 162, 166, 168.

53. Schroeder, *Mr. Polk's War*, pp. 41, 55, 125, 157.

54. Pletcher, *Diplomacy*, pp. 458–59; Schroeder, *Mr. Polk's War*, pp. 35–36, 38–39, 92, 94–95, 97–98, 101, 104–5, 107–8, 112.

55. Schroeder, *Mr. Polk's War*, pp. 58, 106, 162.

56. Polk, *Diary*, 2:181–86; Pletcher, *Diplomacy*, pp. 464–65.

57. Polk, *Diary*, 2:179–80, 195–200, 203–6; Pletcher, *Diplomacy*, pp. 468, 471; McCormac, *James K. Polk*, pp. 448–49, 451–52.

58. Polk, *Diary*, 2:221–22, 225–29, 231–32, 236–37; Pletcher, *Diplomacy*, pp. 471–72.

59. Polk, *Diary*, 2:234–43; Spencer, *Victor and the Spoils*, p. 161; McCormac, *James K. Polk*, pp. 453–55.

60. Polk, *Diary*, 2:244–48; Spencer, *Victor and the Spoils*, pp. 160–61; Pletcher, *Diplomacy*, pp. 472–73; Singletary, *Mexican War*, pp. 111, 120.

61. Polk, *Diary*, 2:327–28; Pletcher, *Diplomacy*, p. 473.

62. Polk, *Diary*, 2:270–73, 275–77, 282–83, 286, 293–95, 297, 301–4, 310, 334; Pletcher, *Diplomacy*, pp. 474–75, 482–83; Spencer, *Victor and the Spoils*, p. 162; McCormac, *James K. Polk*, pp. 463–64.

63. Nelson, "Secret Diplomacy," pp. 121–28; Pletcher, *Diplomacy*, pp. 476–77.

64. Nelson, "Secret Diplomacy," pp. 128–29, 132–36; Pletcher, *Diplomacy*, pp. 492–93; Polk, *Diary*, 2:476–77.

65. Nelson, "Secret Diplomacy," p. 133; Polk, *Diary,* 3:22.

66. Polk, *Diary,* 2:323, 325–27, 331–33; McCormac, *James K. Polk,* pp. 465–66; Pletcher, *Diplomacy,* pp. 477–78; Nelson, "Secret Diplomacy," pp. 174–75, 182–84.

67. Polk, *Diary,* 2:333, 335–39, 341–42; Pletcher, *Diplomacy,* pp. 478–80; Nelson, "Secret Diplomacy," pp. 185–88.

68. Polk, *Diary,* 2:432–33; Pletcher, *Diplomacy,* pp. 481–82.

69. Polk, *Diary,* 2:465–69; Pletcher, *Diplomacy,* pp. 499–500; Nelson, "Secret Diplomacy," pp. 205, 207–9.

70. Polk, *Diary,* 2:471–75, 477–78; Pletcher, *Diplomacy,* pp. 500–501; Nelson, "Secret Diplomacy," pp. 210–13.

71. Polk, *Diary,* 2:478–81.

72. Pletcher, *Diplomacy,* p. 504.

73. Ibid., pp. 504–7; McCormac, *James K. Polk,* pp. 493–509; Singletary, *Mexican War,* pp. 122–24; Polk, *Diary,* 3:57–59, 61–63, 76–79, 82–86, 89–93. Secretary Marcy, proving himself to be an astute judge of both Scott and Trist, confided to a friend: "Both Trist and Scott [are] interminable writers—when they begin they never know when to stop—when they have said enough and what is worse—when they have said too much" (to Wetmore, 26 Sept. 1847, quoted in Nelson, "Secret Diplomacy," p. 235).

74. Pletcher, *Diplomacy,* pp. 508–11, 516–17; McCormac, *James K. Polk,* pp. 510–17; Nelson, "Secret Diplomacy," pp. 237–41.

75. Polk, *Diary,* 3:163–65, 168; Pletcher, *Diplomacy,* p. 528.

76. Polk, *Diary,* 3:170–72, 185–87, 189–90; Pletcher, *Diplomacy,* pp. 521, 528–29; McCormac, *James K. Polk,* pp. 518–19.

77. Polk, *Diary,* 3:189–90, 195–97, 199–201; Pletcher, *Diplomacy,* pp. 529–30, 552–53. Polk's annual message of December 1847 outlined his position concerning California and New Mexico (see Richardson, *Messages of the Presidents,* 4:540–42).

78. Polk, *Diary,* 3:275–77, 280, 283; Pletcher, *Diplomacy,* pp. 538–40; McCormac, *James K. Polk,* pp. 522–25, 531–32.

79. Polk, *Diary,* 3:286, 300–301, 310–17, 324; Pletcher, *Diplomacy,* pp. 540–49; McCormac, *James K. Polk,* pp. 525–27, 532–34.

80. Polk, *Diary,* 3:329–30.

81. Ibid., pp. 345–52; Pletcher, *Diplomacy,* pp. 558–60; Spencer, *Victor and the Spoils,* pp. 172–73; McCoy, *Polk and the Presidency,* pp. 103–4; McCormac, *James K. Polk,* pp. 538–41.

82. Polk, *Diary,* 3:359–72; Pletcher, *Diplomacy,* pp. 561–63.

83. Polk, *Diary,* 3:372–73, 375, 378–83, 389–92.

84. Ibid., pp. 385–86, 396–98, 399–402, 404–12, 414.

85. Pletcher, *Diplomacy,* pp. 551, 553, 556–57, 560–61; Hietala, *Manifest Design,* pp. 158–65; see also Merk, *Manifest Destiny,* pp. 116ff., 191–201.

86. Spencer, *Victor and the Spoils,* pp. 168–71; McCoy, *Polk and the Presidency,* pp. 132–33; Pletcher, *Diplomacy,* pp. 557, 565; Nelson, "Secret Diplomacy," pp. 256–58.

87. Polk, *Diary*, 3:430, 433–34, 436–38, 443; Merk, *Monroe Doctrine*, pp. 206–9, 231; Pletcher, *Diplomacy*, pp. 568–69; Hietala, *Manifest Design*, p. 247; McCoy, *Polk and the Presidency*, pp. 109–10.

88. Polk, *Diary*, 3:444–45; Merk, *Monroe Doctrine*, pp. 209–14, 217–23, 226–29; Hietala, *Manifest Design*, pp. 247–48; Pletcher, *Diplomacy*, pp. 570–71.

89. Polk, *Diary*, 3:446; Merk, *Monroe Doctrine*, pp. 252–54, 257–59; Pletcher, *Diplomacy*, pp. 572–73.

90. Polk, *Diary*, 3:469, 475–81.

91. Ibid., pp. 482–83, 485–86.

92. Ibid., pp. 486–88.

93. Ibid., pp. 492–94, 499–500; Merk, *Monroe Doctrine*, pp. 259–64; Pletcher, *Diplomacy*, p. 573.

94. The quotation is from Polk's fourth annual message to Congress, in December 1848 (see Richardson, *Messages of the Presidents*, 4:632).

95. In this paragraph I am drawing from Professor Robert Johannsen's most impressive book *To the Halls of the Montezumas* (cited earlier).

CHAPTER 5
POLK AND THE WINNING OF THE NORTHWEST

1. See Thomas R. Hietala, *Manifest Design: Anxious Aggrandizement in Late Jacksonian America* (Ithaca, N.Y.: Cornell University Press, 1985), pp. 71–78, 178–80.

2. For a comprehensive discussion of the background of Oregon and of the various aspects of the Oregon problem see Frederick Merk, *The Oregon Question: Essays in Anglo-American Diplomacy and Politics* (Cambridge, Mass.: Belknap Press of Harvard University Press, 1967).

3. David M. Pletcher, *The Diplomacy of Annexation: Texas, Oregon, and the Mexican War* (Columbia: University of Missouri Press, 1973), pp. 215, 218–20; Charles G. Sellers, *James K. Polk: Continentalist, 1843–1846* (Princeton, N.J.: Princeton University Press, 1966), pp. 240–42; Eugene I. McCormac, *James K. Polk: A Political Biography* (Berkeley: University of California Press, 1922), p. 562.

4. Pletcher, *Diplomacy*, p. 223; Frederick Merk, *The Monroe Doctrine and American Expansionism, 1843–1849* (New York: Alfred A. Knopf, 1966), pp. 72–73.

5. Sellers, *James K. Polk: Continentalist*, pp. 235, 243, 244; Pletcher, *Diplomacy*, pp. 236–37.

6. Pletcher, *Diplomacy*, pp. 239–41; Sellers, *James K. Polk: Continentalist*, pp. 236–38.

7. Pletcher, *Diplomacy*, pp. 241–42; Sellers, *James K. Polk: Continentalist*, p. 245.

8. Pletcher, *Diplomacy*, pp. 242–43, 246–47; Sellers, *James K. Polk: Continentalist*, pp. 246, 248.

9. McCormac, *James K. Polk*, p. 567; John A. Munroe, *Louis McLane: Federalist and Jacksonian* (New Brunswick, N.J.: Rutgers University Press, 1973), pp. 517–19; Pletcher, *Diplomacy*, p. 247; Sellers, *James K. Polk: Continentalist*, p. 248.

10. Pletcher, *Diplomacy*, p. 248; McCormac, *James K. Polk*, pp. 568–69; Sellers, *James K. Polk: Continentalist*, pp. 248–49.

11. Pletcher, *Diplomacy*, p. 248; McCormac, *James K. Polk*, pp. 570–71; Sellers, *James K. Polk: Continentalist*, pp. 250, 251; Munroe, *Louis McLane*, pp. 520–21.

12. Philip S. Klein, *President James Buchanan: A Biography* (University Park: Pennsylvania State University Press, 1962), pp. 179–80; McCormac, *James K. Polk*, pp. 571–74; Pletcher, *Diplomacy*, pp. 249, 272; Sellers, *James K. Polk: Continentalist*, pp. 252–54.

13. Munroe, *Louis McLane*, pp. 520–21; Sellers, *James K. Polk: Continentalist*, pp. 254–55; Pletcher, *Diplomacy*, pp. 250–51, 296–97; Klein, *President James Buchanan*, p. 180.

14. Pletcher, *Diplomacy*, pp. 252–53; Sellers, *James K. Polk: Continentalist*, p. 254.

15. Pletcher, *Diplomacy*, pp. 298–300; Sellers, *James K. Polk: Continentalist*, pp. 255–57; James K. Polk, *The Diary of James K. Polk during His Presidency, 1845 to 1849*, ed. Milo M. Quaife, 4 vols. (Chicago: A. C. McClurg & Co., 1910), 1:62–67, 73–83; Munroe, *Louis McLane*, pp. 521–22; McCormac, *James K. Polk*, pp. 574–76.

16. Polk, *Diary*, 1:68–72; Merk, *Monroe Doctrine*, p. 67; McCormac, *James K. Polk*, pp. 576–77; Pletcher, *Diplomacy*, pp. 300–302.

17. Pletcher, *Diplomacy*, pp. 301, 303; Sellers, *James K. Polk: Continentalist*, pp. 258, 373.

18. Pletcher, *Diplomacy*, pp. 306–8, 310, 311; Merk, *Oregon Question*, p. 368; McCormac, *James K. Polk*, pp. 579–81; Merk, *Monroe Doctrine*, p. 78; Sellers, *James K. Polk: Continentalist*, p. 376; Polk, *Diary*, 1:109–12, 115–16.

19. Polk, *Diary*, 1:117–23; Pletcher, *Diplomacy*, p. 318; Klein, *President James Buchanan*, p. 181.

20. Sellers, *James K. Polk: Continentalist*, p. 377; McCormac, *James K. Polk*, p. 582; Pletcher, *Diplomacy*, pp. 321–22; Polk, *Diary*, 1:133–36.

21. Polk, *Diary*, 1:139–42, 147; Pletcher, *Diplomacy*, p. 327; Sellers, *James K. Polk: Continentalist*, p. 360.

22. Polk, *Diary*, 1:147–49, 151; Pletcher, *Diplomacy*, pp. 322–24; Sellers, *James K. Polk: Continentalist*, pp. 377–78; McCormac, *James K. Polk*, pp. 582–83; Merk, *Oregon Question*, p. 220. In contrast to Sellers, Frederick Merk believes that Polk's strategy of rejecting arbitration was a good one, especially in light of strong sentiment in the nation against arbitration (see *Oregon Question*, p. 232).

23. Polk, *Diary*, 1:131–32; Pletcher, *Diplomacy*, pp. 319, 321, 335–36; Sellers, *James K. Polk: Continentalist*, pp. 363–64, 365, 372.

24. Sellers, *James K. Polk: Continentalist*, pp. 366–67; Pletcher, *Diplomacy*, p. 328; Polk, *Diary*, 1:153–56, 158–62.

25. Pletcher, *Diplomacy*, pp. 318, 319–20; Sellers, *James K. Polk: Continentalist*, pp. 362–63; Merk, *Monroe Doctrine*, p. 95; McCormac, *James K. Polk*, pp. 585–86. For an able discussion of the Congressional leaders among the expansionists see Merk, *Oregon Question*, pp. 371–78.

26. Sellers, *James K. Polk: Continentalist*, pp. 363–69, 386, 387; Pletcher, *Diplomacy*, pp. 329, 332; Merk, *Monroe Doctrine*, p. 93; McCormac, *James K. Polk*, p. 592; Merk, *Oregon Question*, p. 228.

27. Pletcher, *Diplomacy*, pp. 316, 324, 325, 330–31; Merk, *Oregon Question*, pp. 301–2, 304; Sellers, *James K. Polk: Continentalist*, pp. 378–79, 380; Klein, *President James Buchanan*, pp. 180–81; Munroe, *Louis McLane*, pp. 524–25.

28. Sellers, *James K. Polk: Continentalist*, p. 381; Pletcher, *Diplomacy*, pp. 325, 326, 344, 345, 346, 347; Klein, *President James Buchanan*, p. 182; Polk, *Diary*, 1:241–46.

29. Pletcher, *Diplomacy*, pp. 339, 340, 350, 351; Munroe, *Louis McLane*, p. 526; Sellers, *James K. Polk: Continentalist*, p. 383.

30. Merk, *Monroe Doctrine*, p. 94; Sellers, *James K. Polk: Continentalist*, pp. 385–86, 388; Pletcher, *Diplomacy*, pp. 327–29.

31. Polk, *Diary*, 1:246–47, 249–52; Pletcher, *Diplomacy*, pp. 332–33, 344–45, 348–49; Sellers, *James K. Polk: Continentalist*, pp. 388–90, 394; Merk, *Oregon Question*, p. 380.

32. Pletcher, *Diplomacy*, pp. 347–48; Merk, *Oregon Question*, pp. 381–83; Sellers, *James K. Polk: Continentalist*, pp. 391, 392; Polk, *Diary*, 1:262–65, 267–81.

33. Sellers, *James K. Polk: Continentalist*, pp. 390, 393; Pletcher, *Diplomacy*, pp. 348, 349; Polk, *Diary*, 1:284–87.

34. Merk, *Monroe Doctrine*, pp. 102–3; Sellers, *James K. Polk: Continentalist*, pp. 396–97; McCormac, *James K. Polk*, pp. 599–600; Pletcher, *Diplomacy*, p. 350.

35. Munroe, *Louis McLane*, pp. 532–33; Pletcher, *Diplomacy*, pp. 402, 405–8; Sellers, *James K. Polk: Continentalist*, pp. 405–6, 410.

36. Polk, *Diary*, 1:444–45, 447–49, 451–55; Pletcher, *Diplomacy*, pp. 411–12; McCormac, *James K. Polk*, pp. 606–8; Sellers, *James K. Polk: Continentalist*, p. 411; Klein, *President James Buchanan*, p. 183.

37. Polk, *Diary*, 1:456–62; Pletcher, *Diplomacy*, pp. 412–13; Sellers, *James K. Polk: Continentalist*, p. 411; McCormac, *James K. Polk*, pp. 608–9; Merk, *Oregon Question*, pp. 389–90.

38. Polk, *Diary*, 1:462–63, 465–67; Pletcher, *Diplomacy*, p. 413; James D. Richardson, comp., *A Compilation of the Messages and Papers of the Presidents, 1789–1902*, 10 vols. (Washington, D.C.: Bureau of National Literature and Art, 1903), 4:449–50.

39. Polk, *Diary*, 1:468, 470–73, 475–79; Sellers, *James K. Polk: Continentalist*, pp. 412–13; Pletcher, *Diplomacy*, pp. 413–15.

40. Sellers, *James K. Polk: Continentalist*, pp. 413–14; Merk, *Oregon Question*, pp. 391–93; Hietala, *Manifest Design*, pp. 236–37.

41. Hietala, *Manifest Design*, pp. 230–31.

42. Ibid., pp. 238–39.

CHAPTER 6

PATRONAGE AND THE PRESIDENT

1. James K. Polk, *The Diary of James K. Polk during His Presidency, 1845 to 1849*, ed. Milo M. Quaife, 4 vols. (Chicago: A. C. McClurg & Co., 1910), 2:329–30, 3:419, 2:278.

2. Charles G. Sellers, *James K. Polk: Continentalist, 1843–1846* (Princeton, N.J.: Princeton University Press, 1966), p. 267; Eugene I. McCormac, *James K. Polk: A Political Biography* (Berkeley: University of California Press, 1922), pp. 322–23.

3. Leonard D. White, *The Jacksonians: A Study in Administrative History, 1829–1861* (New York: Macmillan Co., 1954), pp. 106, 362.

4. Polk, *Diary*, 3:162; Philip S. Klein, *President James Buchanan: A Biography* (University Park: Pennsylvania State University Press, 1962), p. 166; Kermit L. Hall, *The Politics of Justice: Lower Federal Judicial Selection and the Second Party System, 1829–61* (Lincoln: University of Nebraska Press, 1979), p. 61.

5. Sellers, *James K. Polk: Continentalist*, pp. 268–69; Norman A. Graebner, "James K. Polk: A Study in Federal Patronage," *Mississippi Valley Historical Review* 38 (1951/52): 622; White, *Jacksonians*, p. 311.

6. Graebner, "James K. Polk," pp. 615, 629; Polk, *Diary*, 1:261, 2:113.

7. Polk, *Diary*, 1:255, 2:85, 4:122, 161, 198.

8. Ibid., 2:178, 382, 4:246, 240.

9. Ibid., 2:361, 3:386, 4:50, 274–75, 2:8–10, 3:183, 1:372. In 1847, Sarah M. H. Maury published a book in which she described Polk as "habitually grave and thoughtful," a man who smiled but never laughed (cited by Thomas R. Hietala in *Manifest Design: Anxious Aggrandizement in Late Jacksonian America* [Ithaca, N.Y.: Cornell University Press, 1985], p. 249n).

10. Polk, *Diary*, 1:412, 2:379–80, 382–83.

11. Ibid., 3:331, 4:274, 275; Charles A. McCoy, *Polk and the Presidency* (Austin: University of Texas Press, 1960), p. 193; McCormac, *James K. Polk*, p. 348.

12. Sellers, *James K. Polk: Continentalist*, p. 269; Graebner, "James K. Polk," pp. 625–26; McCoy, *Polk and the Presidency*, pp. 198–99.

13. White, *Jacksonians*, pp. 113–14; McCoy, *Polk and the Presidency*, pp. 199–200; Polk, *Diary*, 1:466–67, 491, 2:329.

14. McCoy, *Polk and the Presidency*, pp. 203, 222; Graebner, "James K. Polk," pp. 614–15; Polk, *Diary*, 1:446–47, 2:20, 278, 314, 3:249, 490, 4:193–94, 275.

15. McCoy, *Polk and the Presidency*, p. 201; Sellers, *James K. Polk: Continentalist*, pp. 296–97; White, *Jacksonians*, pp. 112, 115; Hall, *Politics of Justice*, p. 61.

16. Sellers, *James K. Polk: Continentalist*, pp. 455–56; Graebner, "James K. Polk," p. 628; White, *Jacksonians*, p. 114; Polk, *Diary*, 1:466, 497–98, 486, 490, 2:24–25.

17. Polk, *Diary*, 4:8, 239–40, 369–70.

18. Ibid., 2:445, 3:13–14, 202–4; White, *Jacksonians*, pp. 111–12; Graebner, "James K. Polk," p. 629.

19. Polk, *Diary*, 1:372, 4:134–35, 188, 318–19, 333.

20. Ibid., 2:296, 381, 382–83, 3:343, 4:244–45, 2:426; McCoy, *Polk and the Presidency*, p. 202; Graebner, "James K. Polk," pp. 630, 631; White, *Jacksonians*, p. 115; Sellers, *James K. Polk: Continentalist*, p. 297.

21. Polk, *Diary*, 2:310–13.

22. Ibid., 4:28–30; White, *Jacksonians*, pp. 121–22.

23. Polk, *Diary*, 1:127–28, 132, 239–40, 329; James P. Shenton, *Robert John Walker: A Politician from Jackson to Lincoln* (New York, 1961), pp. 67–68; McCoy, *Polk and the Presidency*, pp. 168–69.

24. Graebner, "James K. Polk," p. 624; Sellers, *James K. Polk: Continentalist*, pp. 356, 447–48.

25. Polk, *Diary*, 2:35–41, 4:265. On the day after his tense interview with the president in July 1846, Johnson wrote a letter to his Greeneville friend Blackston McDannel, in which he strongly criticized Polk's patronage in Tennessee and elsewhere, saying, "Take Polk's appointments all and all and they are the most *damnable* set that were ever made by any president since the government was organized" (see Johnson to McDannel, 22 July 1846, in LeRoy P. Graf and Ralph W. Haskins, eds., *The Papers of Andrew Johnson*, 7 vols. to date (Knoxville: University of Tennessee Press, 1967–   ), 1:331–32.

26. Dorothy Ganfield Fowler, *The Cabinet Politician: The Postmasters General, 1829–1909* (New York: Columbia University Press, 1943), pp. 61–62; McCoy, *Polk and the Presidency*, pp. 192–93.

27. Fowler, *Cabinet Politician*, pp. 62–64; McCoy, *Polk and the Presidency*, p. 196.

28. Fowler, *Cabinet Politician*, p. 63; Polk, *Diary*, 1:45; Ronald N. Satz, *American Indian Policy in the Jacksonian Era* (Lincoln: University of Nebraska Press, 1975), pp. 162–64.

29. Klein, *President James Buchanan*, pp. 165, 169; Polk, *Diary*, 1:87–89; Ivor D. Spencer, *The Victor and the Spoils: A Life of William L. Marcy* (Providence, R.I.: Brown University Press, 1959), pp. 140–41; Polk, *Diary*, 2:380, 381, 383–84, 390–91, 392, 395, 457.

30. Russel B. Nye, *George Bancroft: Brahmin Rebel* (New York: Alfred A. Knopf, 1944), pp. 134, 149; White, *Jacksonians*, p. 358; Sellers, *James K. Polk: Continentalist*, p. 296.

31. Shenton, *Robert John Walker*, pp. 73, 67–68; McCoy, *Polk and the Presidency*, pp. 168–69, 194–95; Polk, *Diary*, 1:15–16, 345–46.

32. Polk, *Diary*, 1:37, 3:478, 480, 4:5–7, 8–9.

33. The terms Hunker and Barnburner gained currency among New York Democrats in the mid 1840s. Generally speaking, the former was a conservative faction in the party, whereas the latter was a radical segment. Van Buren and Silas Wright were the preeminent leaders of the Barnburner wing of the state party. For a full treatment of the warring New York factions see the old but reliable study by Herbert D. A. Donovan, *The Barnburners: A Study of the Internal Movements in the Political History of New York State and of the Resulting Changes in Political Affiliation, 1830–1852* (New York: New York University Press, 1925).

34. Sellers, *James K. Polk: Continentalist*, pp. 292, 202, 284–85; Donald B. Cole, *Martin Van Buren and the American Political System* (Princeton, N.J.: Princeton University Press, 1984), p. 404; John Niven, *Martin Van Buren: The Romantic Age of American Politics* (New York: Oxford University Press, 1983), pp. 561–64. When Samuel J. Tilden visited Polk to remind him of his earlier pledge, made first to Van Buren's son, that Wright and Van Buren could control New York patronage, the president bristled and denied having made such a commitment. He resented the pressure that the Barnburners were placing upon him. Thereafter, according to Niven, Polk lost all credibility with the Barnburners (see *Martin Van Buren*, pp. 564–65).

35. Polk, *Diary*, 1:103–4; Niven, *Martin Van Buren*, pp. 572–73.

36. Polk, *Diary*, 2:218, 3:441; Graebner, "James K. Polk," p. 627. For a discussion of the defeat of Wright see Donovan, *Barnburners*, chap. 8.

37. Sellers, *James K. Polk: Continentalist*, pp. 286–87, 288–89; White, *Jacksonians*, p. 176; Shenton, *Robert John Walker*, pp. 72–73; Niven, *Martin Van Buren*, p. 564.

38. Sellers, *James K. Polk: Continentalist*, pp. 289–90; Graebner, "James K. Polk," pp. 624–25; Niven, *Martin Van Buren*, p. 564; Jerome Mushkat, *Tammany: The Evolution of a Political Machine, 1789–1865* (Syracuse, N.Y.: Syracuse University Press, 1971), pp. 223–26.

39. Polk, *Diary*, 2:19, 60–61, 62, 66.

40. Ibid., 2:79, 279, 405; Fowler, *Cabinet Politician*, p. 65.

41. Polk, *Diary*, 2:399–401.

42. Ibid., 2:401–5; Graebner, "James K. Polk," p. 627; McCoy, *Polk and the Presidency*, p. 197; McCormac, *James K. Polk*, p. 470.

43. Polk, *Diary*, 4:9–12, 36–37; Donovan, *Barnburners*, pp. 107–8.

44. Polk, *Diary*, 4:57–58, 83–85.

45. Ibid., 4:93–94, 106–8; McCoy, *Polk and the Presidency*, pp. 106–7. Organized in New York City by John McKeon and others, the so-called Irish directory sought to raise money to send to Ireland to support the patriots there in making their demands against Britain.

46. Polk, *Diary*, 4:110–15; McCoy, *Polk and the Presidency*, p. 198.

47. There was little agreement in New York during the 1840s and subsequently among historians about which side was favored with patronage by Polk. The president was thoroughly exasperated by the charges and countercharges directed at him by both the Barnburner and the Hunker groups. He certainly made valiant attempts to reward both groups, but the presence of Marcy in the cabinet doomed his efforts. Had the Barnburners accepted all the positions offered to them by Polk, however, they certainly would have held quite a respectable share of the major federal posts in New York (see Cole, *Martin Van Buren*, p. 404; Niven, *Martin Van Buren*, pp. 565, 571; Graebner, "James K. Polk," pp. 626–27).

48. Sellers, *James K. Polk: Continentalist*, pp. 292–93, 480; Charles McCool Snyder, *The Jacksonian Heritage: Pennsylvania Politics, 1833–1848* (Harrisburg: Pennsylvania Historical and Museum Commission, 1958), pp. 187, 191; John M.

Belohlavek, *George Mifflin Dallas: Jacksonian Patrician* (University Park: Pennsylvania State University Press, 1977), pp. 104, 105, 107; Hall, *Politics of Justice,* p. 70; Klein, *President James Buchanan,* pp. 167–68; Graebner, "James K. Polk," pp. 628, 629. Senator Daniel Sturgeon seems to have played an inconsequential role in Pennsylvania patronage matters.

49. Polk, *Diary,* 2:260–61. Shunk remained in office as governor, having been successful in his reelection bid in late 1847 (see Snyder, *Jacksonian Heritage,* p. 203).

50. Polk, *Diary,* 2:18, 63–64, 74, 3:4–6.

51. Ibid., 2:207–8, 290, 3:6–8.

52. Ibid., 2:405–6, 459–61, 3:8. Polk's selection of Rush may be seen as a belated reward to Dallas for the president's unwillingness in 1845 to give Rush the collectorship at Philadelphia (see Polk to Dallas, 23 Aug. 1845, and Dallas to Polk, 3 Sept. 1845, both in Polk Papers; and Belohlavek, *George Mifflin Dallas,* p. 105).

53. Polk, *Diary,* 2:460–61, 488–90, 491. Rush visited Polk on 5 May, read Polk's new version, and approved it (see ibid., 3:12–13).

54. Ibid., 3:182–83, 303–4, 339–40.

55. Sellers, *James K. Polk: Continentalist,* pp. 293–95; Belohlavek, *George Mifflin Dallas,* p. 105; Klein, *President James Buchanan,* p. 171; Polk, *Diary,* 1:136.

56. Sellers, *James K. Polk: Continentalist,* pp. 351, 354; Lee F. Crippen, *Simon Cameron: Ante-Bellum Years* (Oxford, Ohio: Mississippi Valley Press, 1942), pp. 81, 82–83; Polk, *Diary,* 1:218–21, 264–65.

57. Polk, *Diary,* 1:426–27, 429–30, 432–34, 435–36, 437; Crippen, *Simon Cameron,* p. 82; McCoy, *Polk and the Presidency,* pp. 166–67; Sellers, *James K. Polk: Continentalist,* p. 354; Snyder, *Jacksonian Heritage,* pp. 192–93. The Elred mentioned here is probably Judge Nathaniel B. Elred (Warren County, Pa.), who was an active candidate in early 1845 for the United States Senate seat to which David Sturgeon was elected.

58. Polk, *Diary,* 1:468–69, 485–87, 488–90; Sellers, *James K. Polk: Continentalist,* pp. 354–55; Crippen, *Simon Cameron,* p. 82; McCoy, *Polk and the Presidency,* pp. 167–68. For Horn's own version of his interview with Cameron, see Horn to Polk, 14 June 1846, Polk Papers. Horn reported his unhappiness with the Cameron meeting.

59. Polk, *Diary,* 3:208–10. The Buchanan-Dallas rivalry reached a climax in 1848, when both sought the presidential nomination from the Democratic party in Pennsylvania. Buchanan received his state's endorsement but did not, of course, win the national nomination (see Joseph G. Rayback, *Free Soil: The Election of 1848* [Lexington: University Press of Kentucky, 1970], pp. 131–35; Snyder, *Jacksonian Heritage,* pp. 212–13).

60. Klein, *President James Buchanan,* p. 169; Belohlavek, *George Mifflin Dallas,* p. 109; Sellers, *James K. Polk: Continentalist,* pp. 297, 298; Polk, *Diary,* 1:39, 45–47, 97–99.

61. Polk, *Diary,* 1:137–39, 143–46; Klein, *President James Buchanan,* p. 170; Sellers, *James K. Polk: Continentalist,* pp. 351–52; Belohlavek, *George Mifflin*

Dallas, pp. 106, 109–10; McCoy, *Polk and the Presidency*, pp. 52–53. The controversy over the Court appointment seems to have enhanced Dallas's standing in the administration, at least temporarily (see Dallas to Rush, 4 Dec. 1845, as cited in Belohlavek, *George Mifflin Dallas*, p. 110).

62. Polk, *Diary*, 1:183–90, 194–97, 198–201; Crippen, *Simon Cameron*, pp. 79–81; Klein, *President James Buchanan*, pp. 170, 171; Sellers, *James K. Polk: Continentalist*, pp. 352–53, 354.

63. Polk, *Diary*, 1:215–18, 234–35.

64. Ibid., 1:464–65, 492, 2:1–2, 4–6, 21–24, 60–61, 63; Klein, *President James Buchanan*, pp. 172, 173–74.

65. Polk, *Diary*, 1:453–64; Snyder, *Jacksonian Heritage*, p. 206; Hall, *Politics of Justice*, pp. 71–73; see also Wm. J. Leiper to Polk, 9 and 10 June 1846; Francis R. Shunk to Polk, 9 June 1846; Daniel Sturgeon to Polk, 9 June 1846; and David Wilmot to Polk, 9 June 1846—all in Polk Papers. Governor Shunk did indeed name Read to the attorney general's post, thus filling Kane's vacancy; but Read resigned after five months in office (see Snyder, *Jacksonian Heritage*, pp. 198–99).

66. Hall, *Politics of Justice*, pp. 62, 73, 77, 165.

67. Ibid., pp. 63–64.

68. Ibid., pp. 64–66. For discussion of judicial appointments in Florida, Texas, and the Oregon Territory see ibid., pp. 66–70, 74–76; and Polk, *Diary*, 1:382–84.

69. Graebner, "James K. Polk," p. 613; Hall, *Politics of Justice*, p. 61. During his four years, Polk filled hundreds of positions in the federal bureaucracy; the exact number of appointments is not easy to determine.

70. Hietala contends that Polk never reconciled himself to the realities that he must reward loyal congressmen; White has a different view, as do I (Hietala, *Manifest Design*, p. 223; White, *Jacksonians*, pp. 112, 115).

71. Hietala, *Manifest Design*, p. 224.

CHAPTER 7

THE PRESIDENT, THE PRESS, AND THE CONGRESS

1. Richard A. Bland, "Politics, Propaganda, and the Public Printing: The Administration Organs, 1829–1849" (Ph.D. diss., University of Kentucky, 1975), p. 214; James E. Pollard, *The Presidents and the Press* (New York: Macmillan Co., 1947), p. 229; John Tebbel and Sarah Miles Watts, *The Press and the Presidency: From George Washington to Ronald Reagan* (New York: Oxford University Press, 1985), p. 120. For a discussion of Polk's journalistic involvement during the 1830s see Paul H. Bergeron, "James K. Polk and the Jacksonian Press in Tennessee," *Tennessee Historical Quarterly* 41 (1982): 257–77.

2. Bland, "Politics," pp. 128–29; Eugene I. McCormac, *James K. Polk: A Political Biography* (Berkeley: University of California Press, 1922), pp. 300–301; Culver H. Smith, *The Press, Politics, and Patronage: The American Government's Use of Newspapers, 1789–1875* (Athens: University of Georgia Press, 1977), pp.

163-64; Elbert B. Smith, *Francis Preston Blair* (New York: Free Press, 1980), p. 163.

3. Bland, "Politics," pp. 131, 132, 133, 135-36; Charles Henry Ambler, *Thomas Ritchie: A Study in Virginia Politics* (Richmond, Va.: Bell Book & Stationery Co., 1913), p. 246; Smith, *The Press,* pp. 164-65; McCormac, *James K. Polk,* pp. 302-3; Charles G. Sellers, *James K. Polk: Continentalist, 1843-1846* (Princeton, N.J.: Princeton University Press, 1966), pp. 274-75; Pollard, *Presidents and the Press,* pp. 233-35.

4. Bland, "Politics," pp. 133-34, 135; Ambler, *Thomas Ritchie,* pp. 247, 251-52; Smith, *The Press,* pp. 165-66; Sellers, *James K. Polk: Continentalist,* p. 277; McCormac, *James K. Polk,* pp. 304-6.

5. Sellers, *James K. Polk: Continentalist,* pp. 277-78; Bland, "Politics," pp. 139-41; Smith, *The Press,* pp. 164-67; Ambler, *Thomas Ritchie,* p. 253; McCormac, *James K. Polk,* pp. 332-33; Tebbel and Watts, *The Press and the Presidency,* pp. 117-18.

6. Bland, "Politics," pp. 141-44; Sellers, *James K. Polk: Continentalist,* pp. 278-79; Smith, *Francis Preston Blair,* p. 165; Smith, *The Press,* pp. 167-68; Ambler, *Thomas Ritchie,* pp. 252-53; James P. Shenton, *Robert John Walker: A Politician from Jackson to Lincoln* (New York: Columbia University Press, 1961), pp. 71-72; Lee F. Crippen, *Simon Cameron: Ante-Bellum Years* (Oxford, Ohio: Mississippi Valley Press, 1942), p. 64-67; Thomas R. Hietala, *Manifest Design: Anxious Aggrandizement in Late Jacksonian America* (Ithaca, N.Y.: Cornell University Press, 1985), p. 225.

7. Bland, "Politics," pp. 145, 163; Sellers, *James K. Polk: Continentalist,* p. 280.

8. Bland, "Politics," pp. 144-45, 146; Smith, *The Press,* pp. 168-69.

9. Bland, "Politics," pp. 146-47, 148-49, 151, 152, 164, 214-15; Pollard, *Presidents and the Press,* pp. 241-42.

10. Charles A. McCoy, *Polk and the Presidency* (Austin: University of Texas Press, 1960), p. 188; Bland, "Politics," pp. 159-61; Sellers, *James K. Polk: Continentalist,* p. 451; James K. Polk, *The Diary of James K. Polk during His Presidency, 1845 to 1849,* ed. Milo M. Quaife, 4 vols. (Chicago: A. C. McClurg & Co., 1910), 1:43-44.

11. Bland, "Politics," pp. 152-54; Polk, *Diary,* 1:350-53; Pollard, *Presidents and the Press,* pp. 243-44.

12. Bland, "Politics," pp. 154-56; Sellers, *James K. Polk: Continentalist,* p. 450; Polk, *Diary,* 1:356-59, 361-63, 365-66; Hietala, *Manifest Design,* p. 229.

13. Bland, "Politics," pp. 158-59; Polk, *Diary,* 2:136-37, 139, 170-71, 172-73.

14. Bland, "Politics," pp. 186-87; Brian G. J. Walton, "James K. Polk and the Democratic Party in the Aftermath of the Wilmot Proviso" (Ph.D. diss., Vanderbilt University, 1968), pp. 60-63.

15. Bland, "Politics," pp. 177-80, 181, 182, 183-84; McCoy, *Polk and the Presidency,* p. 190; Ambler, *Thomas Ritchie,* pp. 266-68; Polk, *Diary,* 2:371-73,

375-79; Hietala, *Manifest Design*, pp. 240-41; Pollard, *Presidents and the Press*, pp. 246-47; Tebbel and Watts, *The Press and the Presidency*, pp. 124-25.

16. Polk, *Diary*, 4:214, 215; McCoy, *Polk and the Presidency*, p. 189; Bland, "Politics," pp. 149-50.

17. Polk, *Diary*, 1:126-27, 2:478-80, 483-84.

18. Ibid., 2:482-86; Pollard, *Presidents and the Press*, pp. 248-49; Tebbel and Watts, *The Press and the Presidency*, p. 127.

19. Polk, *Diary*, 2:486-87.

20. Ibid., 3:333-34, 353-56.

21. Ibid., 3:396-414; Pollard, *Presidents and the Press*, pp. 250-51; Tebbel and Watts, *The Press and the Presidency*, pp. 128-29. A few months later, Polk was again bothered by John Nugent, who followed the president in August during his vacation trip to Bedford Springs, Pennsylvania. When Polk learned of the reporter's presence in the vicinity, he sarcastically commented: "He has, no doubt, followed me to the Springs to see what new slander he can invent for his employers to be published in the *Herald*." The president, taking precautions not to speak to Nugent or to converse with anyone in Nugent's presence, labeled the reporter "an unprincipled scoundrel." (see *Diary*, 4:95-96).

22. Hietala, *Manifest Design*, p. 224; Pollard, *Presidents and the Press*, pp. 147, 181.

23. Sellers, *James K. Polk: Continentalist*, pp. 446-48.

24. Ibid., pp. 324-25, 310; McCoy, *Polk and the Presidency*, p. 145.

25. Walton, "James K. Polk and the Party," pp. 209, 211-13.

26. Ibid., pp. 214, 220-21, 224, 230-31, 232, 233-34, 235-36, 243-44, 245-46, 247-48, 249-50.

27. See Hietala, *Manifest Design*, pp. 101-2, 107-8, 116. My discussion of the tariff, the Independent Treasury, and internal improvements borrows from my article "President Polk and Economic Legislation," *Presidential Studies Quarterly* 15 (1985): 782-95.

28. Edward Stanwood, *American Tariff Controversies in the Nineteenth Century*, 2 vols. (1903; reprint, New York: Russell & Russell, 1967), 2:29; F. W. Taussig, *The Tariff History of the United States*, 8th ed. (New York: G. P. Putnam's Sons, 1931), pp. 113-14.

29. James D. Richardson, comp., *A Compilation of the Messages and Papers of the Presidents, 1789-1902*, 10 vols. (Washington, D.C.: Bureau of National Literature and Art, 1903), 4:378-79; Sellers, *James K. Polk: Continentalist*, p. 451; Stanwood, *American Tariff Controversies*, pp. 44-60.

30. Richardson, *Messages of the Presidents*, 4:403-6; Stanwood, *American Tariff Controversies*, pp. 41-44; McCormac, *James K. Polk*, pp. 666-67.

31. Sellers, *James K. Polk: Continentalist*, pp. 451-52; Stanwood, *American Tariff Controversies*, p. 70n.

32. Taussig, *Tariff History*, pp. 114, 145, 156; Stanwood, *American Tariff Controversies*, pp. 70-71, 73-75; Sellers, *James K. Polk: Continentalist*, pp. 452-53. The 1842 tariff was such an elaborate and complex measure, primarily protective

in nature, that there is little ground for comparison with the 1846 bill (see Stanwood, *American Tariff Controversies*, pp. 28–30).

33. Polk, *Diary*, 1:421–22; Sellers, *James K. Polk: Continentalist*, pp. 453–54; McCoy, *Polk and the Presidency*, pp. 181–82.

34. Sellers, *James K. Polk: Continentalist*, pp. 452–57; Polk, *Diary*, 2:10–11; Joel H. Silbey, *The Shrine of Party: Congressional Voting Behavior, 1841–1852* (Pittsburgh, Pa.: University of Pittsburgh Press, 1967), p. 71.

35. Sellers, *James K. Polk: Continentalist*, p. 458; Polk, *Diary*, 2:25–27.

36. Sellers, *James K. Polk: Continentalist*, pp. 460, 462–63, 464; McCoy, *Polk and the Presidency*, pp. 151–52; Polk, *Diary*, 2:26, 29–30, 32–33, 35, 43–45, 48–49.

37. Sellers, *James K. Polk: Continentalist*, pp. 464–67; McCoy, *Polk and the Presidency*, p. 152; Polk, *Diary*, 2:25, 47–49, 50, 51–52.

38. Polk, *Diary*, 2:27–28, 49, 53–54, 55.

39. Silbey, *Shrine of Party*, pp. 72–73; John M. Belohlavek, *George Mifflin Dallas: Jacksonian Patrician* (University Park: Pennsylvania State University Press, 1977), pp. 113–15, 117.

40. Richardson, *Messages of the Presidents*, 4:406–8; Sellers, *James K. Polk: Continentalist*, pp. 209, 344–45; McCormac, *James K. Polk*, pp. 667, 668. For a very able discussion of Van Buren's efforts to establish an Independent Treasury see James C. Curtis, *The Fox at Bay: Martin Van Buren and the Presidency, 1837–1841* (Lexington: University Press of Kentucky, 1970), pp. 75–151, and Major L. Wilson, *The Presidency of Martin Van Buren* (Lawrence: University Press of Kansas, 1984), chaps. 4–7.

41. McCormac, *James K. Polk*, pp. 669–70; Sellers, *James K. Polk: Continentalist*, p. 469.

42. Polk, *Diary*, 1:368–71, 377; McCormac, *James K. Polk*, pp. 671–72; Sellers, *James K. Polk: Continentalist*, pp. 469–71. The warehouse bill permitted importers to store imported goods in government warehouses for as long as three years. It passed the Senate on 15 July and the House on 1 August.

43. Sellers, *James K. Polk: Continentalist*, pp. 346, 452–53; Polk, *Diary*, 1:288–89; Silbey, *Shrine of Party*, pp. 68–70.

44. Silbey, *Shrine of Party*, pp. 75–76. The figures given by Silbey apply to both sessions of the Twenty-ninth Congress.

45. Sellers, *James K. Polk: Continentalist*, pp. 472–73; Silbey, *Shrine of Party*, pp. 75–76. Again Silbey's data are drawn from both sessions of the Twenty-ninth Congress, not just from the first session (1845/46).

46. Polk, *Diary*, 2:47, 51, 54, 56, 58–59, 61, 62–63.

47. Richardson, *Messages of the Presidents*, 4:461, 462, 463, 464, 465; Sellers, *James K. Polk: Continentalist*, p. 473.

48. Polk, *Diary*, 2:64–66.

49. Ibid., 2:171–72.

50. Silbey, *Shrine of Party*, p. 84; Richardson, *Messages of the Presidents*, 4:610–11; Polk, *Diary*, 2:398.

51. Polk, *Diary*, 3:116, 166, 169, 179, 244, 247–49.

52. Richardson, *Messages of the Presidents*, 4:612, 613, 615–17, 618–21, 623–25, 626.

53. Polk, *Diary*, 3:250.

54. Ibid., 4:35–36, 50, 52–53, 60–61, 64, 65, 66.

55. Ibid., 4:128–29, 140, 144–45, 157–58, 167–68, 363–64.

56. Richardson, *Messages of the Presidents*, 4:457–58; McCormac, *James K. Polk*, pp. 616–17; Sellers, *James K. Polk: Continentalist*, p. 479.

57. Sellers, *James K. Polk: Continentalist*, pp. 479—81.

58. Ibid., pp. 481—83; Polk, *Diary*, 2:75—76.

59. David Potter, *The Impending Crisis, 1848—1861* (New York: Harper & Row, 1976), p. 66; Walton, "James K. Polk and the Party," pp. 64—65.

60. Sellers, *James K. Polk: Continentalist*, p. 479.

61. Richardson, *Messages of the Presidents*, 4:504; McCormac, *James K. Polk*, pp. 621, 625; Potter, *Impending Crisis*, pp. 65–66.

62. Polk, *Diary*, 2:288–90, 308–9, 335; McCormac, *James K. Polk*, p. 628; McCoy, *Polk and the Presidency*, p. 156; Potter, *Impending Crisis*, pp. 64, 69.

63. Potter, *Impending Crisis*, pp. 69–71; Walton, "James K. Polk and the Party," pp. 58–59, 83–84.

64. Richardson, *Messages of the Presidents*, 4:558–59; McCormac, *James K. Polk*, pp. 629–30, 631, 632–33; Potter, *Impending Crisis*, p. 72; Polk, *Diary*, 3:501–2.

65. Richardson, *Messages of the Presidents*, 4:584; Potter, *Impending Crisis*, p. 72; McCormac, *James K. Polk*, p. 633.

66. McCormac, *James K. Polk*, pp. 634–37; Potter, *Impending Crisis*, pp. 72–74; Polk, *Diary*, 3:501–5; 4:17–18, 19–22, 23–24.

67. Potter, *Impending Crisis*, pp. 74–75; McCormac, *James K. Polk*, pp. 637–39; Polk, *Diary*, 4:33–35, 61–62; Bland, "Politics," pp. 161–62.

68. Polk, *Diary*, 4:67–76; McCormac, *James K. Polk*, pp. 640–42; Richardson, *Messages of the Presidents*, 4:607, 608; Potter, *Impending Crisis*, p. 76. Silbey's roll-call voting data for both the Twenty-ninth and the Thirtieth Congresses show that the national legislature divided along sectional, rather than partisan, lines in the votes taken on slavery-extension issues. He has found, for example, that in the House of the Thirtieth Congress, 83.3 percent of the northern representatives were antislavery, while 100 percent of the southern representatives were proslavery. There were some slight differences in the Senate, with 68 percent of the northern senators being antislavery (32 percent were moderate) and 80 percent of the southern senators being proslavery (20 percent were moderate); see *Shrine of Party*, pp. 89–93.

69. Polk, *Diary*, 4:67; Potter, *Impending Crisis*, pp. 68, 78–80; Sellers, *James K. Polk: Continentalist*, pp. 480–81. In a typical comment, Polk wrote that the slavery question "is a mere political question on which demagogues & ambitious politicians hope to promote their own prospects for political promotion" (*Diary*, 4:251).

70. Richardson, *Messages of the Presidents*, 4:542; McCormac, *James K. Polk*, pp. 644–45; Polk, *Diary*, 4:135–37, 140–43, 146–47; McCoy, *Polk and the Presidency*, pp. 159–60.

71. Richardson, *Messages of the Presidents,* 4:636, 638–42; McCormac, *James K. Polk,* pp. 645–47; McCoy, *Polk and the Presidency,* pp. 160–61.

72. McCormac, *James K. Polk,* pp. 647–48, 649; Polk, *Diary,* 4:231–33, 235–37, 254–55, 257–58.

73. Polk, *Diary,* 4:249–51, 252–53, 280–85, 285–88, 289–91; McCormac, *James K. Polk,* pp. 648–50; McCoy, *Polk and the Presidency,* pp. 163–64.

74. McCormac, *James K. Polk,* p. 650; Polk, *Diary,* 4:296–97.

75. Polk, *Diary,* 4:297–300; McCormac, *James K. Polk,* pp. 650–51.

76. McCormac, *James K. Polk,* pp. 651–52, 653; Polk, *Diary,* 4:312–13.

77. McCormac, *James K. Polk,* pp. 653–54; Polk, *Diary,* 4:364–69.

78. Polk, *Diary,* 3:381–82, 2:349–50, 3:488–89; McCoy, *Polk and the Presidency,* pp. 180–81.

79. Polk, *Diary,* 1:13, 115–16, 2:115–16, 288.

80. Ibid., 1:128–31, 2:493; McCoy, *Polk and the Presidency,* p. 57.

81. Polk, *Diary,* 3:258–60, 264–65, 284–85.

82. Ibid., 2:322–24, 3:257–58, 417–18, 2:123, 130–31, 133–34; McCoy, *Polk and the Presidency,* p. 54.

83. Polk, *Diary,* 3:356, 362–63, 2:296–98, 299.

84. Ibid., 3:259, 443–44, 2:134; McCoy, *Polk and the Presidency,* pp. 56–57. Hietala emphasizes Polk's failings in the matter of warm social contacts (see *Manifest Design,* pp. 248–49).

85. See, e.g., Polk, *Diary,* 2:440, 444.

CHAPTER 8

THE MAN IN THE WHITE HOUSE

1. James K. Polk, *The Diary of James K. Polk during His Presidency, 1845 to 1849,* ed. Milo M. Quaife, 4 vols. (Chicago: A. C. McClurg & Co., 1910), 2:374, 3:87, 4:201.

2. Ibid., 1:236–37, 374–75, 3:87, 456–57, 4:211–12.

3. Ibid., 2:103, 285, 3:243.

4. Ibid., 4:53–54, 310.

5. Ibid., 4:179–80. Polk surmised that the new French minister, Poussin, might have similar pro-Democratic-party leanings.

6. James D. Richardson, comp., *A Compilation of the Messages and Papers of the Presidents, 1789–1902,* 10 vols. (Washington, D.C.: Bureau of National Literature and Art, 1903), 4:65; Ronald N. Satz, *American Indian Policy in the Jacksonian Era* (Lincoln: University of Nebraska Press, 1975), pp. 232–36, 271; see also Thomas R. Hietala, *Manifest Design: Anxious Aggrandizement in Late Jacksonian America* (Ithaca, N.Y.: Cornell University Press, 1985), pp. 144–52, for a discussion of the connection between expansionism and Indian policies.

7. Satz, *American Indian Policy,* pp. 278, 234–35.

8. Polk, *Diary,* 1:20–23, 25–26, 83, 100–101. The Potawatomi cession and removal treaty was finally negotiated in June 1846. By its provisions the bands of

Potawatomi ceded their lands to the government in return for a payment of $850,000 and a promise of a new tract of land on the Kansas River. For the treaties during the Polk administration see Charles J. Kappler, comp. and ed., *Indian Affairs: Laws and Treaties*, 5 vols. (reprint, New York: AMS Press, 1971), 2:552–82.

9. Polk, *Diary*, 1:301–2, 2:80–82. For a brief discussion and interpretation of the 1846 Cherokee treaty see John R. Finger, *The Eastern Band of Cherokees, 1819–1900* (Knoxville: University of Tennessee Press, 1984), pp. 46–47.

10. Polk, *Diary*, 2:3–4, 29, 46.

11. Ibid., 2:162–63, 169, 178, 186–87. Years later, Sarah Childress Polk gave to the Tennessee Historical Society the pipe that had been given to President Polk by the Winnebagos in 1846 (see Anson Nelson and Fanny Nelson, *Memorials of Sarah Childress Polk* [New York: Anson D. F. Randolph & Co., 1892], p. 166). The Menominees visited Polk in February 1849 and offered him a pipe, but the president did not record whether he puffed on it or not (see *Diary*, 4:317). They had already, in October 1848, signed a treaty negotiated in Wisconsin, by which they ceded their lands and agreed to a 600,000 acre tract located near the Winnebagos. The treaty was ratified in January, just prior to their arrival in Washington.

12. See, e.g., Polk, *Diary*, 2:499, 3:409, 472, 4:16, 296. At the end of Polk's term, the newly created Interior Department took charge of the Indian Office.

13. Ibid., 4:163–64.

14. Ibid., 1:237–38.

15. Ibid., 1:128–31, 4:245–46, 1:430–31, 440.

16. Ibid., 1:293–94.

17. Claims that Polk dreaded social events and failed to sense their importance seem off the mark (see Hietala, *Manifest Design*, pp. 248–49).

18. Polk, *Diary*, 1:150, 2:299–300, 3:272–73, 4:263–65.

19. Ibid., 1:157–58, 2:317–18.

20. Ibid., 3:351–52, 1:243–44, 2:389.

21. Ibid., 3:267–69.

22. Ibid., 3:18–19, 425, 432. As later years would reveal, the most significant cornerstone laying that Polk participated in was the May 1847 ceremonies for the new Smithsonian Institution. The previous August, after many years of difficulty and controversy, Congress had finally accepted the Smithson grant. In September 1846 the president had met with the Smithsonian Regents in an effort to select the site for the construction of the first building. Agreement upon the site was required of the president, as well as his cabinet, but a lack of unanimity within the administration delayed the process. Eventually, in December, Polk was able to persuade his cabinet to endorse a site located between Twelfth and Fourteenth streets, his own original preference. Construction began in the spring of 1847, and shortly before his presidential term ended, Polk and his wife inspected the progress that was being made on the project (see ibid., 2:120, 124–25, 264–65, 272–73, 3:1–2, 4:308). See also George B. Goode, ed., *The Smithsonian Institution, 1846–1896: The History of Its First Half Century* (Washing-

ton, D.C.: City of Washington, 1897), pp. 26, 28–31, 53–54, 61, 62, 248–49, 250–51, 254–55; Paul H. Oehser, *The Smithsonian Institution* (New York: Praeger Publishers, 1970), pp. 19, 21–22, 24; Webster P. True, *The Smithsonian Institution* (New York: Smithsonian Institution Series, Inc., 1929), pp. 246–47, 250, 251.

23. Polk, *Diary,* 1:182, 183, 193, 204, 207, 211, 214, 222, 225, 227, 253, 284, 290, 292, 303, 305, 315, 316–17, 318–19. Although Polk rendered the French miniaturist's name as Debousier, the artist was undoubtedly Savinien E. Dubourjal, a long-time friend and fellow traveler of Healy's.

24. Ibid., 2:324–25, 330, 3:32–34.

25. Ibid., 3:396, 420, 431.

26. Ibid., 1:255, 473–74, 3:298, 4:334, 335, 337. The daguerreotypist Plumbe who is referred to was probably John Plumbe, who had a gallery on Pennsylvania Avenue in Washington.

27. Ibid., 1:290, 3:244. Like Walker, Andrew J. Donelson and his family had lived at the White House during Jackson's presidency.

28. Ibid., 2:345–46.

29. Marshall T. Polk to James K. Polk, 21 June 1845, James K. Polk Papers; Polk, *Diary,* 1:26, 2:62; Marshall's stepfather, Dr. William C. Tate, visited the Polks and presumably Marshall in October 1845 (see ibid., 1:77).

30. Ibid., 2:140–41, 143, 3:115, 187.

31. Receipt, 7 June 1848, Polk Papers; Polk, *Diary,* 3:481–82; Polk to Marshall T. Polk, 25 May 1849, Letterbook copy, Polk Papers. Had he lived, doubtless President Polk would have been greatly pleased to learn that his nephew finally graduated from West Point in July 1852, ranking twenty-third in his class of forty-three cadets. Many years later, however, this same Marshall Polk, while state treasurer of Tennessee, left Nashville under mysterious conditions after a serious discrepancy in state funds was unearthed. Arrested in Texas, apparently on his way to Mexico, Polk was returned to Tennessee to stand trial. Eventually he was imprisoned for his financial misbehavior and died in prison in 1884.

32. Polk, *Diary,* 2:451–52.

33. Polk to William Moore, 29 Apr. 1847 and 3 Apr. 1848, Letterbook copies, Polk Papers.

34. Charles G. Sellers, *James K. Polk: Continentalist, 1843–1846* (Princeton, N.J.: Princeton University Press, 1966), p. 304; Polk, *Diary,* 2:74, 94.

35. Polk, *Diary,* 2:374, 376, 3:181–88.

36. Ibid., 3:483–84, 488–89, 492, 494, 497–98, 506–8, 4:1.

37. Nelson and Nelson, *Memorials,* p. 92; Sellers, *James K. Polk: Continentalist,* pp. 307–8. Several sources incorrectly claim that all alcohol was banned from the White House.

38. Sellers, *James K. Polk: Continentalist,* pp. 306–7; Nelson and Nelson, *Memorials,* p. 118; Esther Singleton, *The Story of the White House,* 2 vols. (New York: McClure Co., 1907), 1:303–4.

39. Nelson and Nelson, *Memorials,* pp. 109–10; Polk, *Diary,* 3:70, 4:186, 203.

40. The Dallas and Sumner quotations are found in Sellers, *James K. Polk: Continentalist*, pp. 193, 308. The other is found in Nelson and Nelson, *Memorials*, p. 113, and in Laura C. Holloway, *The Ladies of the White House*, 2 vols. (New York: Funk & Wagnalls, 1886), 2:148–49.

41. Polk, *Diary*, 3:325–26. A slightly different version of this incident appears in Nelson and Nelson, *Memorials*, pp. 113–15.

42. Nelson and Nelson, *Memorials*, p. 112.

43. Polk, *Diary*, 3:187–91, 193–95.

44. See the two letters from Sarah Childress Polk, reprinted in Nelson and Nelson, *Memorials*, pp. 116–17.

45. Ibid., p. 94. One source makes the unsubstantiated claim that Sarah Polk was actually hired as one of Polk's official secretaries and that she handled his official papers and reminded him of appointments (see Jane McConnell and Burt McConnell, *First Ladies: From Martha Washington to Mamie Eisenhower* (New York: Thomas Y. Crowell Co., 1953), pp. 125–26.

46. Polk, *Diary*, 3:42, 71, 72.

47. See Earl I. West, "Religion in the Life of James K. Polk," *Tennessee Historical Quarterly* 26 (1967): 357–71.

48. Quoted ibid., p. 365; also in Charles G. Sellers, *James K. Polk: Jacksonian, 1795–1843* (Princeton, N.J.: Princeton University Press, 1957), pp. 106–7.

49. Polk, *Diary*, 1:86.

50. Ibid., 2:443–44, 455, 3:99–100, 295, 321, 4:372–73.

51. Ibid., 1:86, 3:27–28, 178, 4:280.

52. Ibid., 1:86, 4:177.

53. Ibid., 2:216, 3:210.

54. Ibid., 3:371, 2:360, 3:162.

55. Ibid., 4:330–31.

56. Ibid., 2:87, 4:78, 85.

57. Ibid., 2:91, 93, 99, 3:38–39, 41, 50, 73, 4:100–101.

CHAPTER 9
EPILOGUE: THE ELECTION AND BEYOND

1. Polk to Democratic Committee, 12 June 1844, in Charles G. Sellers, "Election of 1844," in *History of American Presidential Elections, 1789–1968*, ed. Arthur M. Schlesinger, Jr., 4 vols. (New York: Chelsea House, 1971), 1:854.

2. Joseph G. Rayback, *Free Soil: The Election of 1848* (Lexington: University Press of Kentucky, 1970), p. 143; James K. Polk, *The Diary of James K. Polk during His Presidency, 1845 to 1849*, ed. Milo M. Quaife, 4 vols. (Chicago: A. C. McClurg & Co., 1910), 1:248–49, 266, 280, 402–3.

3. Polk, *Diary*, 2:328, 3:254–57.

4. Ibid., 3:319–21, 333–35.

5. Ibid., 3:421–22.

6. Ibid., 3:448–49, 451–53, 454, 455–56, 457, 458–59, 461, 463.

7. James K. Polk to J. G. M. Ramsey, 20 May 1848, Letterbook copy, James K. Polk Papers; this letter is conveniently reprinted in Charles A. McCoy, *Polk and the Presidency* (Austin: University of Texas Press, 1960), pp. 208–12; the Democratic party's platform appears in Holman Hamilton, "Election of 1848," in *History of American Presidential Elections*, 2:900. For more on the Democratic convention see Rayback, *Free Soil*, pp. 187–92.

8. Polk, *Diary*, 3:462–63, 470–72.

9. Ibid., 3:474.

10. Ibid., 3:488; Hamilton, "Elections of 1848," pp. 866–67; David Potter, *The Impending Crisis, 1848–1861* (New York: Harper & Row, 1976), p. 81; Rayback, *Free Soil*, pp. 194–200.

11. Polk, *Diary*, 3:502; Rayback, *Free Soil*, pp. 206–10; Frederick J. Blue, *The Free Soilers: Third Party Politics, 1848–54* (Urbana: University of Illinois Press, 1973), pp. 55–58; Richard H. Sewell, *Ballots for Freedom: Antislavery Politics in the United States, 1837–1860* (New York: Oxford University Press, 1976), pp. 148–49.

12. Rayback, *Free Soil*, pp. 110–12; Blue, *Free Soilers*, pp. 11–14.

13. Rayback, *Free Soil*, pp. 218–30; Blue, *Free Soilers*, pp. 70–80; Sewell, *Ballots for Freedom*, pp. 156–61; Hamilton, "Election of 1848," p. 871; Polk, *Diary*, 4:65, 67.

14. For a summary of electioneering see Hamilton, "Election of 1848," pp. 872–92.

15. Rayback, *Free Soil*, p. 230.

16. Ibid., pp. 278–92.

17. Polk, *Diary*, 4:184.

18. Ibid., 4:266, 349, 352–53.

19. Ibid., 4:358–59.

20. Ibid., 4:362–63.

21. Ibid., 4:372–73. Because the fourth of March fell on a Sunday, the inauguration ceremonies were postponed until the fifth.

22. Ibid., 4:374–76.

23. For an elaboration upon the ceremonies and activities at Wilmington and Charleston see ibid., 4:379–84; *Wilmington Chronicle*, 8 Mar. 1849; *The Commercial* (Wilmington), 6 and 8 Mar. 1849; *Charleston Mercury*, 1, 2, 5, 8, 9, 10, and 12 Mar. 1849.

24. Polk, *Diary*, 4:400.

25. Ibid., 4:401–5.

26. Ibid., 4:408–9.

27. Ibid., 4:410–11. Between Vicksburg and Memphis three persons had died of cholera on board Polk's ship. Moreover, one man had died in the vicinity of Baton Rouge, and yet another passenger had died on the boat while en route from Montgomery to Mobile. Thus Polk had more than ample reason to be fearful of contracting cholera.

28. Ibid., 4:412–14.

29. Ibid., 4:414–16.

30. Eugene I. McCormac, *James K. Polk: A Political Biography* (Berkeley: University of California Press, 1922), p. 721; Anson Nelson and Fanny Nelson, *Memorials of Sarah Childress Polk* (New York: Anson D. F. Randolph & Co., 1892), pp. 145–51.

BIBLIOGRAPHICAL ESSAY

Because of various constraints, I shall resist the temptation to provide a comprehensive bibliography of the topics that surround James K. Polk and his presidential administration. Therefore the following is a selective list of works that seem to be particularly pertinent.

Two bibliographical aids of somewhat limited value, largely because of their respective publication dates, are Don E. Fehrenbacher, comp., *Manifest Destiny and the Coming of the Civil War, 1840–1861* (New York: Appleton-Century-Crofts, 1970); and Ramón Eduardo Ruiz, ed., *The Mexican War: Was It Manifest Destiny?* (Hinsdale, Ill.: Dryden Press, 1963). These two works lead one invariably to many of the major studies available on the 1840s.

Likewise helpful are two general surveys of the Jacksonian period, in which the Polk presidency is firmly rooted. Both are volumes in the New American Nation Series; they are Glyndon G. Van Deusen, *The Jacksonian Era, 1828–1848* (New York: Harper & Row, 1959); and David M. Potter, *The Impending Crisis, 1848–1861* (New York: Harper & Row, 1976). Obviously, given their chronological coverage, neither work devotes a great deal of attention to the Polk administration; nevertheless, they enable a reader to put the Polk presidential years in a larger framework. The Van Deusen book is colored by a Whiggish hue; whereas Potter's magisterial work has no obvious flaws.

Because in writing this study of Polk's presidency it was not my purpose to investigate collections of primary materials, there is little to say about such in this brief essay. Naturally, the James K. Polk Papers in the Library of Congress are indispensable to any comprehensive, definitive study of the man and his career. I have consulted that collection only sparingly, however. It is hoped that the volumes of the *Correspondence of James K. Polk* will soon reach and cover the presidency; when they do, they will be absolutely essential. I have depended heavily upon the published version of Polk's presidential diary, edited by Milo M. Quaife, *The Diary of James K. Polk during His Presidency, 1845 to 1849,* 4 vols. (Chicago: A. C. McClurg & Co., 1910). Despite the dangers that lurk in such sources, this diary is truly remarkable, for both the information and the insights that it provides. The very recently edited and published journal of Polk's tour of northeastern states casts new light upon a previously little-known but politically significant presidential activity (see Wayne Cutler, ed., *North for Union: John Appleton's Journal of a Tour to New England Made by President Polk in June and July 1847* [Nashville, Tenn: Vanderbilt University Press, 1986]). Tantalizing because of its "inside" information about the president, his wife, and his administration is the old *Memorials of Sarah Childress Polk,* by Anson Nelson and Fanny Nelson (New York: Anson D. F. Randolph & Co., 1892). Finally, in a more official way, of much assistance is James D. Richardson, comp., *A Compilation of the Messages and Papers of the Presidents, 1789–1902,* 10 vols. (Washington, D.C.: Bureau of National Literature and Arts, 1903). Polk's administrative documents display his philosophical and ideological bent from time to time and also reveal his literary eloquence upon occasion.

The first two published biographies of Polk qualify by some reckonings as primary materials, primarily because they both appeared in the year after Polk's death. Lucien B. Chase, a Tennessee congressman during Polk's presidency, authored *History of the Polk Administration* (New York: G. P. Putnam, 1850). Overall a laudatory account, it treats the major developments and events of the presidential years. John S. Jenkins, a prolific writer, also produced a biography in that same year. Curiously, there are two versions of it; one carries the title *The Life of James Knox Polk, Late President of the United States* and was published in Auburn, New York, by James M. Alden. The other is entitled *James Knox Polk and a History of His Administration* and was published in Auburn and Buffalo by John E. Beardsley. Identical books from start to finish, they contain much prepresidential coverage. The Jenkins study, which was dedicated to William L. Marcy, praises Polk and his accomplishments.

Evidently forgotten by authors and scholars after the publication of the 1850 books, Polk was the subject of no major biography until more than seventy years later. In 1922 Eugene I. McCormac published his *James K. Polk: A Political Biography* (Berkeley: University of California Press). Based upon impressive research, McCormac's study seeks to give Polk due recognition for his achievements as president. Polk had to wait for more than a century after his death, however, before a truly worthy biography would appear. In 1957 Professor Charles G. Sellers launched the first of a promised three-volume biography; entitled, *James K. Polk: Jacksonian, 1795–1843* (Princeton, N.J.: Princeton University Press), this study provides a comprehensive treatment and analysis of Polk's prepresidential life and career. Nine years later, in 1966, Sellers produced the next installment of the trilogy: *James K. Polk: Continentalist, 1843–1846* (Princeton, N.J.: Princeton University Press). As the dates in the title suggest, the author begins by getting Polk nominated and elected and concludes by abandoning him at the termination of the noteworthy congressional session that ended in August 1846. In this second volume there are hints that Sellers felt some disenchantment with Polk; if true, that helps to explain why twenty years have elapsed and still there is no third volume to complete the biography. All scholars regret that Professor Sellers has not yet produced the final part of his definitive study.

Of course, other works exist that shed light and understanding upon Polk and his career. One such work is a study of his presidential administration, *Polk and the Presidency* (Austin: University of Texas Press), published in 1960 and authored by Charles A. McCoy. Using the lens of a political scientist, McCoy focuses upon a topical analysis of how the Polk administration functioned. In this same connection one should also consult Leonard D. White, *The Jacksonians: A Study in Administrative History, 1829–1861* (New York: Macmillan Co., 1954).

Polk's official family—his vice-president and his cabinet—have prompted several biographical or administrative treatments. A very able study of the vice-president is *George Mifflin Dallas: Jacksonian Patrician* (University Park: Pennsylvania State University Press, 1977), by John M. Belohlavek. A helpful overview of the Post Office and its leaders is found in Dorothy Ganfield Fowler's *The Cabinet Politician: The Postmasters General, 1829–1909* (New York: Columbia University Press, 1943). The major study of Polk's postmaster general is Clement L. Grant's "The Public Career of Cave Johnson" (Ph.D. diss., Vanderbilt University, 1951). The best biography of Polk's controversial secretary of state is by Philip S. Klein, *President James Buchanan: A Biography* (University Park: Pennsylvania State University Press, 1962). The influential secretary of the Treasury has been studied by James P. Shenton in his *Robert John Walker: A Politician from Jackson to Lincoln* (New York: Columbia University Press, 1961). Polk's reliable but pedestrian secretary of war is portrayed by Ivor D. Spencer in *The Victor and the Spoils: A Life of William L. Marcy* (Providence, R.I.: Brown University Press, 1959). Because of his fame as an intellectual and a historian, George Bancroft, who served Polk as secretary of the navy and as a diplomat, has been accorded several biographies. The most recent is by Lilian Handlin, *George Bancroft: The Intellectual as Democrat* (New York: Harper & Row, 1984); it contains very little, however, about Bancroft's career as a servant of the Polk administration. Slightly more is found in the earlier biography by Russel B. Nye, *George Bancroft: Brahmin Rebel* (New York: Alfred A. Knopf, 1944). The man who served as attorney general during the second half of Polk's presidency is treated in Philip Greely Clifford, *Nathan Clifford, Democrat (1803–1881)* (New York: G. P. Putnam's Sons, 1922). Isaac Toucey, who replaced Clifford in 1848, has not been the subject of a published biography. The only person to serve in two different positions in Polk's cabinet and to be a holdover from the Tyler administration is John Y. Mason, who still lacks a published scholarly biography. Although its title is somewhat misleading, new and important information about Polk's cabinet is available in Brian G. J. Walton, "James K. Polk and the Democratic Party in the Aftermath of the Wilmot Proviso" (Ph.D. diss., Vanderbilt University, 1968).

As I have attempted to show in my study of the presidency, Polk's relationship with the press was a vital one. This theme is explored in a very able study by Richard A. Bland, "Politics, Propaganda, and the Public Printing: The Administration Organs, 1829–1849" (Ph.D. diss., University of Kentucky, 1975). Important material is likewise found in Culver H. Smith, *The Press, Politics, and Patronage: The American Government's Use of Newspapers, 1789–1875* (Athens: University of Georgia Press, 1977). Two biographies lend further enlightenment about press relationships; they are Elbert B. Smith's *Francis Preston Blair* (New York: Free Press, 1980), and Charles Henry Ambler's *Thomas Ritchie: A Study in Virginia Politics* (Richmond, Va.: Bell Book & Stationery Co., 1913). Two broader studies that attempt, with a small measure of success, to view the Polk experience in conjunction with other presidents are James E. Pollard, *The Presidents and the Press* (New York: Macmillan Co., 1947), and the very recent book by John Tebbel and Sarah Miles Watts, *The Press and the Presidency: From George Washington to Ronald Reagan* (New York: Oxford University Press, 1985).

The topics of expansionism and diplomacy have spawned numerous studies involving the Polk presidency. The notion of Manifest Destiny, for example, has been examined and discussed in several works. The classic study of this topic is Albert K. Weinberg's *Manifest Destiny: A Study of Nationalist Expansionism in American History* (Baltimore, Md.: Johns Hopkins Press, 1935). Nearly thirty years later it was challenged by Frederick Merk in his book *Manifest Destiny and Mission in American History: A Reinterpretation* (New York: Alfred A. Knopf, 1963). Shortly thereafter, Merk offered a companion volume, *The Monroe Doctrine and American Expansionism, 1843–1849* (New York: Alfred A. Knopf, 1966). Merk argues that Manifest Destiny was something of an aberration in the American experience and that actually the notion of "mission" reflected the more legitimate and nobler American concerns. The most significant and controversial recent book is Thomas R. Hietala's *Manifest Design: Anxious Aggrandizement in Late Jacksonian America* (Ithaca, N.Y.: Cornell University Press, 1985). Colored by a strong anti-Polk and anti-Democratic bias, Hietala's study contends that territorial expansionism was a deliberate strategy or plot and that Manifest Destiny was a sort of euphemism that masked the greedy impulses of the expansionists.

Among the more important works on Texas annexation and related concerns are the following classic studies: William C. Binkley, *The Expansionist Movement in Texas, 1836–1850* (Berkeley: University of California Press, 1925), and Justin H. Smith, *The Annexation of Texas* (New York: Baker & Taylor, 1911). An updated account is found in Frederick Merk, *Slavery and the Annexation of Texas* (New York: Alfred A. Knopf, 1972). Another of Merk's books, *The Monroe Doctrine and American Expansionism*, cited above, is also informative. The strongest anti-Polk interpretation of the 1845 dealings in Texas is presented by Glenn W. Price in his *Origins of the War with Mexico: The Polk-Stockton Intrigue* (Austin: University of Texas Press, 1967). The most balanced and most convincing account is presented by David M. Pletcher in his impressive study *The Diplomacy of Annexation: Texas, Oregon, and the Mexican War* (Columbia: University of Missouri Press, 1973), upon which I have relied heavily.

Southwestern expansionism in general and the Mexican War in particular have not lacked for scholarly attention. Here one thinks again of such works as Merk's *The Monroe Doctrine and American Expansionism* and the important emphasis upon Pacific ports made by Norman A. Graebner in his *Empire on the Pacific: A Study in American Continental Expansion* (New York: Ronald Press Co., 1955). Matters of diplomacy are comprehensively and carefully treated in Pletcher's *Diplomacy of Annexation*. Concerning certain aspects of that diplomacy, one should consult Anna Kasten Nelson, ''The Secret Diplomacy of James K. Polk during the Mexican War, 1846–1847'' (Ph.D. diss., George Washington University, 1972).

The Mexican War itself has been examined in several important works. The classic study is Justin H. Smith, *The War with Mexico*, 2 vols. (New York: Macmillan, 1919), an exhaustive treatment with a decided pro-American slant. The most recent comprehensive study of the military aspects is K. Jack Bauer, *The Mexican War, 1846–1848* (New York: Macmillan, 1974). Seymour V. Connor and Odie B. Faulk, in *North America Divided: The Mexican War, 1846–1848* (New York: Oxford University Press, 1971), offer an imposing bibliography of nearly one hundred pages. The military side of the war experience is told quite engagingly, although briefly, by Otis A. Singletary in *The Mexican War* (Chicago: University of Chicago Press, 1960). Other works that emphasize particular aspects of the war years include John D. P. Fuller, *The Movement for the Acquisition of All Mexico, 1846–1848* (Baltimore, Md.: Johns Hopkins Press, 1936), and Ernest McPherson Lander, Jr., *Reluctant Imperialists: Calhoun, the South Carolinians, and the Mexican War* (Baton Rouge: Louisiana State University Press, 1980). In a book that is openly hostile to Polk, John H. Schroeder explores domestic disagreement over the war effort (see *Mr. Polk's War: American Opposition and Dissent, 1846–1848* [Madison: University of Wisconsin Press, 1973]). Robert W. Johannsen's recent scholarly tour de force is entitled *To the Halls of the Montezumas: The Mexican War in the American Imagination* (New York: Oxford University Press, 1985). His analysis of social-cultural ramifications of the war experience is not only path breaking; it is also a magisterial accomplishment. The Mexican War will never be thought of in the same way again.

Curiously, the acquisition of the Pacific Northwest has not excited the interest of scholars as much as the Southwest has. Again Pletcher's *Diplomacy of Annexation* is indispensable. Also influential is Frederick Merk's, *The Oregon Question: Essays in Anglo-American Diplomacy and Politics* (Cambridge, Mass.: Belknap Press of Harvard University Press, 1967). The second volume of the Polk biography by Sellers, *James K. Polk: Continentalist*, is most impressive on the political and diplomatic resolution of the Oregon controversy. From the trans-Atlantic perspective, further light is shed by the biography of the United States minister to Great Britain, *Louis McLane: Federalist and Jacksonian* (New Brunswick, N.J.: Rutgers University Press, 1973), by John A. Munroe.

Closely linked with the diplomatic and shooting wars of the Polk presidency were the political wars. Insight and information are provided, in a quantitative format, upon relationships with Congress by two admirable studies: Thomas B.

Alexander, *Sectional Stress and Party Strength: A Study of Roll-Call Voting Patterns in the United States House of Representatives, 1836–1860* (Nashville, Tenn.: Vanderbilt University Press, 1967), and Joel H. Silbey, *The Shrine of Party: Congressional Voting Behavior, 1841–1852* (Pittsburgh, Pa.: University of Pittsburgh Press, 1967). Alexander's impressive work emphasizes the importance of sectionalism, whereas Silbey's emphasizes party loyalties. Further exploration of the connections between Congress and the president is found in the McCormac and Sellers biographies and in McCoy's study, *Polk and the Presidency.*

The critical problem of patronage has not been addressed directly except in a few places, such as in the article by Norman A. Graebner, "James K. Polk: A Study in Federal Patronage," *Mississippi Valley Historical Review* 38 (1951/52): 613–32. Of course the topic is examined in both the McCormac and the Sellers biographies and briefly in McCoy's administrative study. Material concerning patronage during the Polk years is also provided in Kermit L. Hall, *The Politics of Justice: Lower Federal Judicial Selection and the Second Party System, 1829–61* (Lincoln: University of Nebraska Press, 1979). Unquestionably, the best source for an investigation of Polk's patronage is the *Diary*, where the topic is referred to almost constantly. Because the president had major problems with both New York and Pennsylvania, there are other specific works that add information. Enhancing one's grasp of the New York situation, for instance, are such works as the biography of William L. Marcy, cited above, and the old study by Herbert D. A. Donovan, *The Barnburners* (New York: New York University Press, 1925). Two new biographies of Van Buren also render assistance; they are John Niven, *Martin Van Buren: The Romantic Age of American Politics* (New York: Oxford University Press, 1983); and Donald B. Cole, *Martin Van Buren and the American Political System* (Princeton, N.J.: Princeton University Press, 1984). With regard to the Keystone State, the biographies of Buchanan and Dallas, both cited earlier, are essential, as is the biography *Simon Cameron: Ante-Bellum Years* (Oxford, Ohio: Mississippi Valley Press, 1942), by Lee F. Crippen. Also important is Charles McCool Snyder, *The Jacksonian Heritage: Pennsylvania Politics, 1833–1848* (Harrisburg: Pennsylvania Historical and Museum Commission, 1958).

Conflict between the president and Congress over economic issues has been treated in several works, although not as extensively as it should be. Again, matters of tariff, internal improvements, and the Independent Treasury are discussed and analyzed in the Sellers and McCormac biographies and in McCoy's work. Additionally, attention is paid to the 1846 tariff in the old traditional studies: Edward Stanwood, *American Tariff Controversies in the Nineteenth Century*, 2 vols. (New York, 1903; reprint, New York: Russell & Russell, 1967); and F. W. Taussig, *The Tariff History of the United States*, 8th ed. (New York: G. P. Putnam's Sons, 1931). To place economic issues in a broader context, one should consult George Rogers Taylor, *The Transportation Revolution, 1815–1860* (New York: Holt, Rinehart & Winston, 1951), and Paul W. Gates, *The Farmer's Age; Agriculture, 1815–1860* (New York: Holt, Rinehart & Winston, 1960).

The politics of presidential elections is best understood by examining, first, Richard P. McCormick's seminal study *The Second American Party System: Party Formation in the Jacksonian Era* (Chapel Hill: University of North Carolina Press, 1966). Although McCormick concludes his analysis with the 1840 contest, the points he makes about the emergence of presidential campaigns are significant for placing the 1844 and 1848 elections into the framework of the competitive, evenly balanced two-party system. McCormick ventures briefly into the 1840s in his newer study, *The Presidential Game: The Origins of American Presidential Politics* (New York: Oxford University Press, 1982). Also quite instructive, from a regional viewpoint, is William J. Cooper, Jr., *The South and the Politics of Slavery, 1828–1856* (Baton Rouge: Louisiana State University Press, 1978), although its emphasis upon the single issue of slavery seems strained. The best account of the 1844 election is offered by Charles G. Sellers in two different places: *James K. Polk: Continentalist*, chapters 1–4, and in his essay, "Election of 1844," in *History of American Presidential Elections, 1789–1968*, edited by Arthur M. Schlesinger, Jr., 4 vols. (New York: Chelsea House, 1971), 1:747–861. Other studies that relate to this significant contest are James C. N. Paul, *Rift in the Democracy* (Philadelphia: University of Pennsylvania Press, 1951), and Oscar D. Lambert, *Presidential Politics in the United States, 1841–1844* (Durham, N.C.: Duke University Press, 1936).

The defeat of the Democratic party and the successful election of Zachary Taylor in 1848 have been studied by several scholars. In addition to the Cooper book, mentioned above, one may examine with profit the study by Chaplain W. Morrison, *Democratic Politics and Sectionalism: The Wilmot Proviso Controversy* (Chapel Hill, N.C.: University of North Carolina Press, 1967). Holman Hamilton has written an extensive essay, "Election of 1848," in *History of American Presidential Elections*, 2:865–918. The most comprehensive and illuminating work on the election is Joseph G. Rayback, *Free Soil: The Election of 1848* (Lexington: University Press of Kentucky, 1970). Focusing upon the antislavery element in the 1848 presidential contest, as well as other elections, are two monographs: Frederick J. Blue, *The Free Soilers: Third Party Politics, 1848–54* (Urbana: University of Illinois Press, 1973), and Richard H. Sewell, *Ballots for Freedom: Antislavery Politics in the United States, 1837–1860* (New York: Oxford University Press, 1976). One should also consult the latest biography of Taylor for scrutiny of his career as a Mexican War general, presidential candidate, and then the nation's president (see K. Jack Bauer, *Zachary Taylor: Soldier, Planter, Statesman of the Old Southwest* [Baton Rouge: Louisiana State University Press, 1985]). Two other studies of particular value for the late 1840s and beyond are David Potter, *The Impending Crisis*, referred to earlier, and Michael F. Holt, *The Political Crisis of the 1850s* (New York: John Wiley & Sons, 1978).

INDEX